Dark Web Pattern Recognition and Crime Analysis Using Machine Intelligence

Romil Rawat
Shri Vaishnav Vidyapeeth Vishwavidyalaya, India

Shrikant Telang
Shri Vaishnav Vidyapeeth Vishwavidyalaya, India

P. William
Sanjivani College of Engineering, Savitribai Phule Pune University, India

Upinder Kaur
Akal University, Talwandi Sabo, India

Om Kumar C.U.
School of Computer Science and Engineering (SCOPE), Vellore Institute of Technology, India

A volume in the Advances in Digital Crime, Forensics, and Cyber Terrorism (ADCFCT) Book Series

Published in the United States of America by
    IGI Global
    Information Science Reference (an imprint of IGI Global)
    701 E. Chocolate Avenue
    Hershey PA, USA 17033
    Tel: 717-533-8845
    Fax: 717-533-8661
    E-mail: cust@igi-global.com
    Web site: http://www.igi-global.com

Library of Congress Cataloging-in-Publication Data

Names: Rawat, Romil, 1986- editor.
Title: Dark Web pattern recognition and crime analysis using machine
  intelligence / Romil Rawat, Shrikant Telang, P. William, Upinder Kaur
and Om Kumar C.U., editors.
Description: Hershey, PA : Information Science Reference, [2022] | Includes
  bibliographical references and index. | Summary: "The reference book
  will show the depth of Darkweb Environment by highlighting the Attackers
  techniques, crawling of hidden contents, Intrusion detection using
  advance algorithms, TOR Network structure, Memex search engine indexing
  of anonymous contents at Online Social Network, and more"-- Provided by
  publisher.
Identifiers: LCCN 2021059244 (print) | LCCN 2021059245 (ebook) | ISBN
  9781668439425 (hardcover) | ISBN 9781668439432 (paperback) | ISBN
  9781668439449 (ebook)
Subjects: LCSH: Computer crimes. | Computer crimes--Investigation. | Dark
  Web.
Classification: LCC HV6773 .D374 2022 (print) | LCC HV6773 (ebook) | DDC
  364.16/8--dc23/eng/20220103
LC record available at https://lccn.loc.gov/2021059244
LC ebook record available at https://lccn.loc.gov/2021059245

This book is published in the IGI Global book series Advances in Digital Crime, Forensics, and Cyber Terrorism (ADCFCT) (ISSN: 2327-0381; eISSN: 2327-0373)

British Cataloguing in Publication Data
A Cataloguing in Publication record for this book is available from the British Library.

All work contributed to this book is new, previously-unpublished material. The views expressed in this book are those of the authors, but not necessarily of the publisher.

For electronic access to this publication, please contact: eresources@igi-global.com.

Advances in Digital Crime, Forensics, and Cyber Terrorism (ADCFCT) Book Series

Bryan Christiansen
Global Research Society, LLC, USA
Agnieszka Piekarz
Independent Researcher, Poland

ISSN:2327-0381
EISSN:2327-0373

MISSION

The digital revolution has allowed for greater global connectivity and has improved the way we share and present information. With this new ease of communication and access also come many new challenges and threats as cyber crime and digital perpetrators are constantly developing new ways to attack systems and gain access to private information.

The **Advances in Digital Crime, Forensics, and Cyber Terrorism (ADCFCT) Book Series** seeks to publish the latest research in diverse fields pertaining to crime, warfare, terrorism and forensics in the digital sphere. By advancing research available in these fields, the **ADCFCT** aims to present researchers, academicians, and students with the most current available knowledge and assist security and law enforcement professionals with a better understanding of the current tools, applications, and methodologies being implemented and discussed in the field.

COVERAGE

- Information Warfare
- Identity Theft
- Data Protection
- Database Forensics
- Mobile Device Forensics
- Hacking
- Crime Scene Imaging
- Telecommunications Fraud
- Encryption
- Cryptography

IGI Global is currently accepting manuscripts for publication within this series. To submit a proposal for a volume in this series, please contact our Acquisition Editors at Acquisitions@igi-global.com or visit: http://www.igi-global.com/publish/.

Titles in this Series

For a list of additional titles in this series, please visit: www.igi-global.com/book-series/advances-digital-crime-forensics-cyber/73676

Media and Terrorism in the 21st Century
Elnur Ismayil (Istanbul Medeniyet University, Turkey) and Ebru Karadogan Ismayil (Uskudar University, Trkey)
Information Science Reference • © 2022 • 299pp • H/C (ISBN: 9781799897552) • US $195.00

World Politics and the Challenges for International Security
Nika Chitadze (International Black Sea University, Georgia)
Information Science Reference • © 2022 • 427pp • H/C (ISBN: 9781799895862) • US $195.00

Technologies to Advance Automation in Forensic Science and Criminal Investigation
Chung-Hao Chen (Old Dominion University, USA) Wen-Chao Yang (National Central Police University, Taiwan) and Lijian Chen (Henan University, China)
Information Science Reference • © 2022 • 289pp • H/C (ISBN: 9781799883869) • US $225.00

Intelligence and Law Enforcement in the 21st Century
Eugene de Silva (Virginia Research Institute, USA) and Asanga Abeyagoonesekera (Parliament of Sri Lanka, Sri Lanka)
Information Science Reference • © 2021 • 253pp • H/C (ISBN: 9781799879046) • US $225.00

Social Engineering and Information Warfare Operations Emerging Research and Opportunities
Rhonda L. Johnson (Upper Iowa University, USA)
Information Science Reference • © 2021 • 150pp • H/C (ISBN: 9781799842705) • US $145.00

Evaluating Emerging Threats and New Research Opportunities in Digital Crime and Forensics
Rhonda Johnson (Upper Iowa University, USA)
Information Science Reference • © 2021 • 350pp • H/C (ISBN: 9781799822288) • US $195.00

Confluence of AI, Machine, and Deep Learning in Cyber Forensics
Sanjay Misra (Covenant University, Nigeria) Chamundeswari Arumugam (Sri Sivasubramaniya Nadar College of Engineering, India) Suresh Jaganathan (Sri Sivasubramaniya Nadar College of Engineering, India) and Saraswathi S. (Sri Sivasubramaniya Nadar College of Engineering, India)
Information Science Reference • © 2021 • 248pp • H/C (ISBN: 9781799849001) • US $225.00

Cyber Security Auditing, Assurance, and Awareness Through CSAM and CATRAM
Regner Sabillon (Universitat Oberta de Catalunya, Spain)
Information Science Reference • © 2021 • 260pp • H/C (ISBN: 9781799841623) • US $195.00

701 East Chocolate Avenue, Hershey, PA 17033, USA
Tel: 717-533-8845 x100 • Fax: 717-533-8661
E-Mail: cust@igi-global.com • www.igi-global.com

Table of Contents

Section 4
Online Social Network Applications for Suspicious Pattern Recognition

Detailed Table of Contents

Section 1
Threat Detection and Content Analysis

To enable digital cities and provide autonomous driving experiences, intelligent transportation systems (ITS) are deployed. This technique imparts vigorous features because of the quick mobility of nodes. Real-time data security and privacy are the most important and underappreciated preconditions in vehicular communication. The functionality of a wireless network should be dispersed over several automobiles/ infrastructure, such as processing capability in fog, edge, and cloud servers, to reduce latency and increase service quality (QoS). In the past, several mathematical methods have been utilized to tackle optimality problems. This chapter analyzes multi-access edge and fog computing techniques for the security and privacy of a 6G-driven vehicular communication network in the internet-of-everything (IoE) Industry 5.0. It also includes a summary of 6G research directions as well as a number of potential 6G communication applications along with dark web crimes.

The previous work adopts an evolving methodology in neural system. The chapter is a new darknet transactions summary. It is a system administration structure for real-time automating of the wicked intention discovery method. It uses a weight agnostic fuzzy interface construction. It is an efficient and reliable computational rational forensics device for web exchange examination, the exposure of malware transactions, and decoded business testimony in real-time. The suggestion is an automatic searching neural-net structure that can execute different duties, such as recognizing zero-day crimes. By automating the spiteful purpose disclosure means from the darknet, the answer reduces the abilities and training wall. It stops many institutions from adequately preserving their most hazardous asset. The system uses two types of datasets – training and prediction sets. The errors are detected using back propagation. The recommendation detects the attacks earlies by 6.85% and 13% of resources compared to the previous work.

Chapter 3

Sonam Mehta, Devi Ahilya Vishwavidyalaya, India
Pragya Shukla, Devi Ahilya Vishwavidyalaya, India

This chapter proposes a scheme for the identification of copy-move forgery by inducing adaptive over-segmentation and matching of feature points with the help of discrete cosine transform (DCT). Copy-move forging is an image tampering technique that involves concealing undesired things or recreating desirable elements within the same image to create modified tampered images. Traditional methods added a large number of false matches. To conquer this problem, a new algorithm is proposed to incorporate an adaptive threshold method. So, the block feature matching mechanism is used, and the matching feature blocks classify the feature points using patch matching and Hough transform. Forged regions are detected with the help of the newly proposed algorithm. The results of the proposed method show that it can substantially reduce the number of false matches that lead to improvements in both performance and computational costs. This demonstrates the suggested algorithm's resistance against a variety of known attacks. Comparative results are presented for a better evaluation.

Section 2
Cyber Terrorism: The Emerging Challenges

Chapter 4

Ravindrababu Jaladanki, P. V. P. Siddhartha Institute of Technology, India
Syed Imran Patel, Bahrain Training Institute, Higher Education Council, Ministry of Education, Bahrain
Imran Khan, Bahrain Training Institute, Higher Education Council, Ministry of Education, Bahrain
Karim Ishtiaque Ahmed Mohammed, Bahrain Training Institute, Higher Education Council, Ministry of Education, Bahrain
Thenmozhi M., Vellore Institute of Technology, India
Arun Kumar Tripathi, KIET Group of Institutions, India

Cyber-physical systems (CPSs), which are more susceptible to a range of cyber-attacks, play an increasingly crucial role in power system security today. Digital communication has become a global phenomenon in the last decade. Sadly, cyber terrorism is on the rise, and abusers are able to hide behind the anonymity of the internet. A hybrid model for detecting instances of cyber terrorism in Twitter datasets was proposed in this study after a survey of prominent classification algorithms. Logistic regression, linear support vector classifier, and naive bayes are the methods utilised for evaluation. Four metrics were used to evaluate the performance of the classifiers in experiments: precision, F1, accuracy, and recall. The findings show how well each of the algorithms worked, along with the metrics that went along with them. Linear support vector classifier (SVC) was the least effective, while hybrid model (EM) was the most successful.

Chapter 5

Vinod Mahor, IES College of Technology, Bhopal, India

Sadhna Bijrothiya, Maulana Azad National Institute of Technology, Bhopal, India

Rakesh Kumar Bhujade, Government Polytechnic, Daman, India

Jasvant Mandloi, Government Polytechnic, Daman, India

Harshita Mandloi, Shri Vaishnav Vidyapeeth Vishwavidyalaya, India

Stuti Asthana, UT Administration of Dadra and Nagar Haveli and Daman and Diu, India

Everyone uses the world wide web for their everyday tasks. The WWW is divided into several side by sides, deep-net, and black net. It is dangerous to use the world wide web to obtain the deep or secret-net. In this chapter, the dawdler structure will be used for a faster and safer search. Various types of data will be gathered during the search process and kept in the data. The data categorization procedure will be used to determine the webpage's side by side. The fuzzy k-nearest neighbor approach is used in the arrangement procedure. The fuzzy k-nearest neighbor approach categories the results of the dawdling structure stored in the data. Data will be generated in the form of webpage addresses, page information, and other data by the dawdling structure. the fuzzy k-nearest neighbor arrangement result will result in web side by side data. In this chapter, to focus on many dataset tests, there is as much as 30% of the online surface net, 25% deep-net, 24.5% charter, and 30% secret web.

Chapter 6

Danish Nisarahmed Tamboli, NBN Sinhgad School of Engineering, India

Shailesh Pramod Bendale, NBN Sinhgad School of Engineering, India

Propaganda has existed for ages, and the internet is merely its newest medium of communication to be misused to promote falsehoods, misinformation, and disinformation. Over time, it has been a successful strategy that nation-states, organizations, and individuals have employed to affect and alter public opinion. Modern propagandists are fast to take advantage of novel communication channels and are eager to use its relative insecurities. Databases and personal devices have been hacked and have also disseminated misinformation more swiftly and extensively via social media outlets and news platforms. This sophisticated strategy is described as cyber propaganda. This has further given rise to anarchists that have developed platforms such as "Assassination Market," where a person or a group of people with similar ideologies can now buy murder.

Section 3
Machine Intelligence for Crime Organization and Analysis

Chapter 7

Shruthi J., BMS Institute of Technology and Management, India

Sumathi M. S., BMS Institute of Technology and Management, India

Bharathi R., BMS Institute of Technology and Management, India

Vidya R. Pai, BMS Institute of Technology and Management, India

Companies must foresee most critical security threats to keep one step ahead of attackers. Because attackers always refine their techniques to avoid detection and because attackers are persistently imaginative, network traffic analysis solutions have evolved providing organizations with a feasible path forward. Maintaining network visibility has gotten more challenging and time demanding as DevOps, cloud computing, and IoT (internet of things) gain popularity. Network traffic analysis can incorporate its core functionalities to detect malicious intent. The authors developed a unique darknet traffic analysis and network management solution to automate the malicious intent detection process. This strong computational intelligence forensics tool decodes network traffic, viral traffic, and encrypted communication. WANNs, a weight-independent neural network design, can detect zero-day threats. With a sophisticated solution, many businesses can protect their most valuable assets from malicious intent detection on the dark web.

Chapter 8

Sanjaya Kumar Sarangi, Utkal University, India
Muniraju Naidu Vadlamudi, Institute of Aeronautical Engineering, India
Balram G, Anurag University, India
C. Sasidhar Sarma, Annamacharya Institute of Technology and Science, India
D. Saidulu, Guru Nanak Institutions Technical Campus (Autonomous), India
Sakthidasan Sankaran K., Hindustan Institute of Technology and Science, India

The dark web is a virtually untraceable hidden layer of the internet that is frequently used to store and access secret data. However, a number of situations have been documented in which this platform has been used to covertly undertake illicit and unlawful operations. Traditional crime-solving procedures are inadequate to meet the demands of the current crime environment. Machine learning can be used to detect criminal patterns. Past crime records, social media sentiment analysis, meteorological data, and other sources of data can be used to feed this machine learning technique. Using machine learning, there are five phases to predicting crime. These are data gathering, data classification, pattern recognition, event prediction, and visualization. Using crime prediction technologies, law enforcement agencies can make better use of their limited resources. In this chapter, the authors show the importance of learning the principles of various policies on the dark web and cyber crimes, guiding new researchers through cutting-edge methodologies.

Chapter 9

Sumit Dhariwal, Manipal University Jaipur, India
Avani Sharma, Manipal University Jaipur, India
Biswa Mohan Shaoo, Manipal University Jaipur, India

Data mining has been used to present difficulties in this chapter in order to reduce crime. Crime is a major issue for which we must pay a high price in a variety of ways. Here, the authors look at how machine-learning techniques may be used in an image processing method to aid in the detection of and speed up the investigative process by identifying criminal tendencies. The authors look at the supervised approaches, as well as some enhancements, to help in the identification of criminal trends. They tested their approaches with real-world crime data from a police department, and they were satisfied with the results. They also employed clustering approaches to improve the prediction accuracy of criminal record categorization. They also utilized a clustering approach to assist classify crime records and improve prediction accuracy. They created a weighting system for the characteristics below. The machine-learning framework works with geospatial crime plotting and helps detectives and other law enforcement professionals increase their efficiency. It may also be used to combat terrorism and ensure national security.

Chapter 10

Amit Kumar Mishra, Amity School of Engineering and Technology, Amity University, India
Vikram Rajpoot, Madhav Institute of Technology and Science, India
Ramakant Bhardwaj, Amity University, India
Pankaj Kumar Mishra, Amity School of Engineering and Technology, Amity University, India
Pushpendra Dwivedi, iNurture Education Solution Pvt. Ltd., India

Global terrorist activities increase with the evolution of various social media sites such as Facebook, Twitter, etc. Various organizations use a wide scope of network capabilities of social media to broadcast their information, propaganda, as well communicate their strategic objectives. So, by analyzing such growing terrorist activity over online social media using mining and analysis, various valuable insights can be predicted. This chapter approaches an effective way of analyzing such activities by identifying nearest nodes in the network. The terrorist network mining algorithm has assisted by successfully achieving terrorist activities and their behavior on nodes of social network using centrality algorithm. The algorithm works in two phases: 1) fuzzification of data to measure centrality between nodes in the network and 2) applying genetic approach for the optimization of data and to increase the searching capability for appropriate cluster centers.

Chapter 11

Ranjana Sikarwar, Amity University, India
Harish Kumar Shakya, Amity University, India
Rahul Bharadwaaj, Indian Institute of Information Technology, Bhopal, India

Data mining (DM) and machine learning techniques have been used to identify specific patterns and similarities in existing cybercrimes to predict the cyberattacks. Since dealing with big data is a complex task as it requires computationally accurate and efficient techniques, difficulty arises in the analysis of irregular activities on cyberworld. DM techniques offer predictive solutions against cybercrimes and modus operandi. DM methods include classification, association, and clustering while different methods related to machine learning are supervised, semi-supervised, and unsupervised. AI can serve as a smart tool for criminal usage for carrying out malicious activities either by enhancing or changing the existing threats or posing new threats altogether. The expansion of existing threats such as drug trafficking improve frequency of smuggling activities by turning to unmanned underwater vehicles. Also using cheap quadcopter and facial recognition software together could increase the terrorist attacks on civilians.

Chapter 12

Sonali Gupta, J. C. Bose University of Science and Technology, India

WWW is a repository of hyperlinked data sources that contains heterogeneous data in the form of text, audio, video, and metadata. Search engines play an important role in searching information from these data sources. They offer the users an interface to retrieve the data from these resources. The search engines gather, analyze, organize, and handle the data available in these data sources and return thousands of results in the form of web pages. Often the returned web pages include a mixture of relevant and irrelevant information. To return more significant and relevant response pages, a mechanism to rank the returned pages is desirable. Page ranking algorithms play an important role in ranking web pages so that the user could get the relevant result according to the user query. The proposed technique is used to rank the hidden web pages based on the meta information of the pages downloaded by crawler and the calculated value for the chosen parameters.

Chapter 13

Shadab Pasha Khan, Oriental Institute of Science and Technology, India
M. A. Rizvi, National Institute of Technical Teachers Training and Research Institute, India
Rehan Khan, Oriental Institute of Science and Technology, India

The future is all about machines or devices. Smart devices are strong enough to create a network, establish connections among nodes, and exchange data as and when required. Internet and IoT are two sides of the same coin responsible for ubiquitous connectivity (24x7x365). The modern digital society depends upon IoT in the future to come, which would inherently invite various threats and new challenges due to its diversity. The entire internet is divided into multiple levels (i.e., surface web, deep web, and dark web), which is further explored in terms of providing anonymity. Non-electronic devices can also be connected which then forms the internet of everything (IoE). Security is often ignored by many manufacturers due to the rise in demand which leads to privacy issues. Over the period of time due to IIoT, Industry 4.0, new threats and high-profile IoT-driven cyber-attacks have been identified. For IoT security, we must switch to ML and DL methodologies to identify and resolve new threats and vulnerabilities.

Section 4
Online Social Network Applications for Suspicious Pattern Recognition

Chapter 14

Vinod Mahor, IES College of Technology, Bhopal, India
Sujit Kumar Badodia, Shri Vaishnav Vidyapeeth Vishwavidyalaya, India
Anil Kumar, School of Computing and IT, Manipal University Jaipur, India
Sadhna Bijrothiya, Maulana Azad National Institute of Technology, Bhopal, India
Ankit Temurnikar, IES College of Technology, Bhopal, India

The need for more comfortable and humane living spaces has accelerated the development of smart homes. Many extremely intelligent houses are part of the internet of things. It operates with the dark web and ensures the privacy of incognito relays and massive data to properly manage customer requests. This increased demand gives rise to a great deal of concern regarding scalability, efficiency, and safety for a smart home system. Detailed data or the lowest levels that can be in a target set are granular data. In this chapter, the authors present the combination of integrating block-chain technology, dark web, and cloud computing in an effective manner. Blockchain technology is decentralized because it can serve processing services. To ensure the safety of the smart home network, the model employs multivariate correlation analysis and the detection of correlations between traffic functions. The performance of the architecture was evaluated with various performance parameters, and blockchain was found to be an effective security solution for future networks on the internet.

The COVID-19 virus has affected every country on the globe; India is amongst the most with over 3.39 billion people who have been infected, and computer use has expanded since. As cybercrime (breaching, spoofing, DDOS assault, and phishing) is one of the most serious problems facing society today, it's crucial to understand what causes such attacks. Although many methods have been proposed to detect cybercrime, criminological theory of crime is one of them. But the most successful method for detecting these malicious activities is machine learning. This is because most of the cyberattacks have some common characteristics which can be identified by machine learning methods. In this context, an approach has been made in the chapter to review machine learning methods to understand the traits of cyber-criminals and crime committed on the dark web along with suitable methods to tackle them.

Chapter 16

The dark web has been in existence since about the emergence of the internet. There is still a wealth of material indexed on the web that is freely available to anyone with internet connection, regardless of region. There is even more information and data that is concealed and needs specific rights to access. Tor is well-known and extensively used anonymity software that is built on the Tor network and provides secrecy over the vulnerable web. The personal data defense is generally beneficial. This chapter provides a brief summary of established methods to gain access to this section of the web as well as examples of its talents being abused.

Preface

The technological advancement using Machine Learning, Artificial Intelligence and Intelligent Hardware based design created cyber warfare among security agencies and cyber criminals (terrorist organizations) to create web shield and protection against tracking, Cyber attack methods are progressively modern, and obstructing the attack is increasingly troublesome, regardless of whether a sort of counter measure or another is taken. All together for a fruitful treatment of the present circumstance, it is vital to have a forecast of cyber attacks, proper safety measures, and viable use of cyber intelligence that empowers these activities. Malevolent hackers share different sorts of data through specific networks, for example, the dark web, showing that a lot of intelligence exists in cyberspace. This paper centers around gatherings on the dark web and proposes a way to deal with extricate discussions which incorporate significant data or intelligence from colossal measures of gatherings and recognize qualities of every gathering utilizing procedures, for example, AI, regular language handling, etc. This methodology will permit us to get a handle on the arising dangers in cyberspace and take suitable measures against malignant exercises. A great many people think about IoT, in any event to the degree of the need to screen and control the hundreds and thousands of individual sensors and gadgets that go to make up a Machine Learning based system. The vast majority will have additionally known about ransomware. The outcomes could be unmistakably more focused on and centered attacks, put together not with respect to the fundamental cycle of breaking into a system with one malware endeavor and dispatching an attack. Rather it will be founded on embeddings untold quantities of Bots into systems to notice the exercises and recognize the feeble focuses and on the whole choose where and when to attack. Dark Web is perhaps the most testing and untraceable mediums embraced by the cyber lawbreakers, terrorists, and state-supported government agents to satisfy their unlawful thought processes. Cyber-violations occurring inside the Dark Web are indistinguishable this present reality wrongdoings. Nonetheless, the sheer size, unusual ecosystem and namelessness gave by the Dark Web administrations are the basic showdowns to follow the lawbreakers. To find the likely arrangements towards cyber-violations assessing the cruising Dark Web wrongdoing dangers is an essential advance.

The Dark Web project is a drawn out logical examination program that plans to contemplate and comprehend the worldwide psychological warfare (Jihadist) wonders through a computational, data-driven methodology. The Online gatherings, including web destinations, discussions, talk rooms, online journals, informal communication locales, recordings, virtual world, and so forth We have created different multilingual data mining, text mining, and web mining procedures to perform connect examination, content investigation, web measurements (specialized refinement) examination, notion investigation, origin investigation, and video investigation in our exploration. The methodologies and strategies created in this venture add to propelling the field of Intelligence and Security Informatics. Such advances will assist related partners with performing illegal intimidation explore and encourage global security and harmony.

This monograph plans to give a representation of the Dark Web scene, recommend a systematic, computational way to deal with understanding the issues, and outline with chosen strategies, techniques. It will carry helpful information to researchers, security experts, counterterrorism specialists, and strategy producers. The monograph can likewise fill in as a source of perspective material or reading material in alumni level courses identified with data security, data strategy, data affirmation, data systems, psychological warfare, and public arrangement.

Dark Web Pattern Recognition and Crime Analysis Using Machine Intelligence is organized into four distinct sections that provide comprehensive coverage of important topics. The sections are:

1. Threat Detection and Content Analysis
2. Cyber Terrorism: The Emerging Challenges.
3. Machine Intelligence for Crime Organization and Analysis
4. Online Social Network applications for Suspicious Pattern Recognition

The following paragraphs provide a summary of what to expect from this research reference

Section 1, "Threat Detection and Content Analysis," serves as a foundation for the approaches defined for malicious threat detection and analysis by addressing models and techniques used to analyze vulnerable details.

Introducing the book is "Darknet Traffic Analysis and Network Management for Malicious Intent Detection by Neural Network Frameworks" by Siddhartha Choubey, Abha Choubey, and Apurv Verma. Malicious contents of dark web identification strategy is presented using Machine Learning approach. Section 1 concludes and leads into the following portion of the book with dark web environment analysis given in the chapter "Minimum Prediction Error at an Early Stage in Darknet Analysis" by Ambika N.

Section 2, "Cyber Terrorism: The Emerging Challenges," presents in-depth coverage of the conceptual design and architecture of cyber terrorism and global illicit activities.

Opening the section is "Machine Learning Models in Detecting Cyber Crimes and Cyber Terrorism in India" by Ravindrababu Jaladanki, Syed Imran Patel, Imran Khan, Karim Ishtiaque Ahmed Mohammed, Thenmozhi M., and Arun Kumar Tripathi. Through Models for Crime detection, this section lays excellent groundwork for later sections that will get into present and future applications for Cyber Terrorism Threats. The section concludes with an excellent work by Danish Nisarahmed Tamboli, and Shailesh Pramod Bendale, "Crowdfunded Assassinations and Propaganda by Dark Web Cyber Criminals."

Section 3, "Machine Intelligence for Crime Organization and Analysis," presents extensive coverage of the Machine Learning and Artificial Intelligence techniques for crime analysis.

The first chapter, "Neural Net Architecture Strategy Identifying Zero-Day Attacks in Dark Web," by Shruthi J., Sumathi M. S., Bharathi R., and Vidya R. Pai, lays a framework for the types of works that can be found in this section. The section concludes with "Internet of Things Security Challenges and Concern for Cyber Vulnerability."

Section 4, "Online Social Network Applications for Suspicious Pattern Recognition," presents coverage of Cyber crime case studies and reviews approaches for modeling and triggering criminal's events.

The section begins with "Cyber Security for Secured Smart Home Applications Using Internet of Things, Dark Web, and Blockchain Technology in the Future." Chapters in this section will look into dark web crime cases and offer alternatives to crucial questions on the subject of Dark Web Threats. The section concludes with "Dark Web for the Spread of Illegal Activities Using Tor."

OBJECTIVES, IMPACT, AND VALUE

The upcoming book will show the depth of Dark web Environment by highlighting the Attackers techniques, crawling of hidden contents, Intrusion detection using advance algorithms, TOR Network structure, Memex search engine indexing of anonymous contents at Online Social Network, IoT Platform, and Intelligent applications activities, Artificial Intelligence and Machine Learning framework and many more.

The cyber criminals and Terrorist activities are more dangerously activating and fluctuating at dark web platform due to anonymous behaviors for the purpose of information stealing, Fake post circulating, International illicit movement promotions, Illegal activities trafficking by keeping distance and hiding from law enforcement agencies.

The purpose of the book to show and present the shortcomings faced by researchers and practitioners due to unavailability of data about dark web, and quality contents for analysis and further research.

The organizations, academia, security agencies and security practitioners will get the benefit of information presented in the book because it has covered the most influential topics of interest, which is not found in any book summaries.

The current researchers are working on dark web crime analysis and publishing research articles in conferences, even the government is also supporting for hidden combating the crime threat.

Romil Rawat
Shri Vaishnav Vidyapeeth Vishwavidyalaya, India

Shirkant Telang
Shri Vaishnav Vidyapeeth Vishwavidyalaya, India

P. William
Sanjivani College of Engineering, Savitribai Phule Pune University, India

Upinder Kaur
Akal University, Talwandi Sabo, India

Om Kumar C. U.
School of Computer Science and Engineering (SCOPE),
Vellore Institute of Technology, India

Section 1
Threat Detection and Content Analysis

Chapter 1

Multi–Access Edge and Fog Computing Technique Analysis for Security and Privacy of 6G–Driven Vehicular Communication Network in Industry 5.0 Internet

Priya Kohli
Graphic Era University (Deemed), India

Sachin Sharma
Graphic Era University (Deemed), India

Priya Matta
Graphic Era University (Deemed), India

ABSTRACT

To enable digital cities and provide autonomous driving experiences, intelligent transportation systems (ITS) are deployed. This technique imparts vigorous features because of the quick mobility of nodes. Real-time data security and privacy are the most important and underappreciated preconditions in vehicular communication. The functionality of a wireless network should be dispersed over several automobiles/ infrastructure, such as processing capability in fog, edge, and cloud servers, to reduce latency and increase service quality (QoS). In the past, several mathematical methods have been utilized to tackle optimality problems. This chapter analyzes multi-access edge and fog computing techniques for the security and privacy of a 6G-driven vehicular communication network in the internet-of-everything (IoE) Industry 5.0. It also includes a summary of 6G research directions as well as a number of potential 6G communication applications along with dark web crimes.

DOI: 10.4018/978-1-6684-3942-5.ch001

INTRODUCTION

The advanced and latest crime phenomenon occured in the criminal law enforcement is the use of dark web for crimes. The offence of deploying the Dark web is a that threatens the society should be penalized by the criminal law. Using wireless connection and various gadgets to execute any crimes is the fundamental sign that this type of crime is different from other types of crime.

Sixth-generation (6G) communication networks have recently been deployed and have integrated a variety of technologies, including sensitive sensors, automated vehicles, mesmeric multi-media, and Dark web of Things (IoT) technologies. Many transmission nodes and endpoints are required for such sophisticated approaches. Furthermore, these technologies face a number of hurdles, including scarcity in any connected network and numerous challenges relating to each node privacy and security. The main idea behind implementing a 6G network is to merge the physical and digital worlds in all aspects. Furthermore, the coming epoch will be defined by automation. Almost all computations will be performed on the system rather than over the network. As a result, the intelligent network must be synchronised across all nodes.

Maintaining reliable connection between numerous wireless components mounted on a vehicle or along a nearby road. Additionally, offering technical assistance for a variety of new apps and approaches that are appropriate for an automated environment in 2030 and beyond. However, the most significant challenges in adopting a 6G network environment are the processing of information in bulk, the management of bulky information, and the implementation of large amounts of data.

Intelligence Edge Computing (IEC) is an advancement of existing cloud computing techniques that enables easy access to a variety of users. IEC is a technology specified by the European Telecommunications Standards Institute (ETSI) that may make wireless connections and connect to various cloud resources. Industry Specification Group (ISG) used IEC in addition to ETSI to improve the storage and processing speed at the network's edge. In addition, IEC provides mobile vehicles with portability and wireless connection, allowing them to send and receive vital messages at any time and in any area. Email, fax, file transfer, and other types of messages can be sent over a wireless network. Bluetooth, cellular networks, satellite communication systems, and other networks are utilised to convey these messages in a dynamic environment. IEC technology is designed to reduce bandwidth, reaction time, and implementation costs, among other things.

As the effectiveness of a network improves, the network's complexities grow. 6G gigantic network IoT faces numerous issues which which are discussed in Figure 1.

To overcome all of the abovementioned obstacles, the massive IoT will have to rely on a variety of clever learning techniques as well as the precise use of Fog and Edge computing devices located near the vehicle. By offloading computations from the cloud machine and performing them on the edge computing device, fog computing and edge computing devices reduce computation latency. To boost network efficiency, fog devices will intelligently combine idle/spare resources from all available devices. Fog devices, edge devices, and other available devices' computational resources will be critical in addressing the demands of highly demanding future applications. Devices can offload tasks and cache data to fog nodes by establishing multiple fog nodes at various locations. When compared to the centralised computing supplied by the cloud, one of the key advantages of fog computing is the decentralised computing service. Moreover, improved latency is achieved as data and tasks are accessed and analyzed near to the end devices. Fog computing also improves the usage of frequency spectrum and enhances the network

Figure 1. 6G Challenges

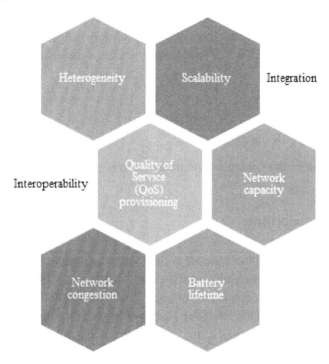

capacity. It also has positive impact on application reliability as computation and storage capabilities are strengthened by the placement of fog nodes.

Motivation and Contributions

This survey focuses on reviewing the main techniques (Multi Access Edge & Fog computing) for security and privacy of 6G vehicular communication. Many of the previous works focused on different aspects of IEC in 5G and 6G. The expectations of Multi Access Edge and Fog computing in 6G are high as they provide a promising transformative platform (an enhanced effective end-user experience) and spreading in new fields such as IoT, new services and models, rapidly exceeding gigabits speeds, and enhancement in network performance with better reliability. Networks and services in 6G technology are expected to deliver enormous economic benefits because they rely on successful IEC mobile edge and Fog communication. However, due to the emerging service models which most often use a large number of terminal devices, the increased computing and data needs may overshadow the computing and storage infrastructure.

Organization

The outline of the remaining chapter is: Section II comprises of the proposed and surveys of computing techniques. Section III includes an overview of Edge and Fog computing in Vehicular communication, specifically their advantages while deploying and various challenges faced), while Section IV includes an introduction of Industry 5.0 Dark web-of-Everything(IoE) and various applications. In Section V, an introduction to 6G computing techniques is dicussed, whereas Section VI includes an analysis of Fog and Multi Access Edge computing techniques for 6G vehicular communication. Furthermore, Section VII comparative analysis of Fog and Multi Access Edge computing is done and in Section VIII research direction to 6G communication is discussed. Finally, Section IX concludes the chapter and discuss future work.

LITERATURE REVIEW

In this section, related work of 6G vehicular communication is presented using multi access edge and fog computing.

Multi Access Edge Computing

(Chuan Sun et al.,2021) investigated the issue of cooperative computation offloading for MEC in 6G mobile networks. They have proposed a Multi Access Edge Computing (MEC) architecture that supports the cooperation of edge-cloud and the cooperation of edge-edge. The optimization problem of the cooperative computation offloading has been modeled as a Markov decision process. (Tiago Koketsu Rodrigues et at.,2021) proposed a mathematical model of the total service delay of a Cybertwin-based multiaccess edge computing system that includes user mobility, migration of virtual servers, multiple physical servers at different network tiers, fronthaul and backhaul communication, processing, and content request/caching. (Tiago Koketsu Rodrigues et at.,2021) proposed a heuristic algorithm for determining the best server for each user in a multiple mobile users, multiple servers, multi-tiered scenario. Their algorithm considers the time needed for transmitting and processing tasks when minimizing the total service delay as well as the time needed for service setup and migration of data between servers. (Dajun Zhang et al.,2021) proposed a novel framework for blockchain-based, hierarchical multi-access edge computing for the future VANET ecosystem (BMEC-FV). In the underlying VANET environment. This trust model ensure the security of the communication link between vehicles. Multiple MEC servers calculate the trust between vehicles through computing offloading. Meanwhile, the blockchain system plays an important role to manage the entire BMEC-FV architecture. This framework optimize the throughput and the quality of services (QoS) for MEC users in the lower layer of the system architecture. (Zhuofan Liao et al.,2020) proposed a Distributed-Two-Stage Offloading (DTSO) strategy to give trade-off solutions. In the first stage, by introducing the queuing theory and considering channel interference, a combinatorial optimization problem is formulated to calculate the offloading probability of each station. In the second stage, the original problem is converted to a non-linear optimization problem, which is solved by a designed Sequential Quadratic Programming (SQP) algorithm. To make an adjustable trade-off between the latency and energy requirement among heterogeneous applications, an elasticity parameter is specially designed in DTSO. Simulation results show that, compared to the latest works, DTSO can effectively reduce latency and energy consumption and achieve a balance between them based on application preferences. (Kelkar et al.,2021) presents the NVIDIA hyper-converged platform which supports 5G/6G network connectivity along with Mobile Edge Computing (MEC). They discussed 3 uses-cases that points out the existing NVIDIA AI/ML development framework aong with Aerial. Aerial seeds the research ecosystem with a first-class out-of-the-box (OOB) experience with a standards compliant 5G NR PHY. Researchers can run the supplied 3GPP compliant test vectors, and perform over-the-air experiments, using standard servers equipped with a GPU-based PCIe card. (Xian Liu et al.,2021) worked on the core concept of stemmed from the wait-and-see model in stochastic programming and indicates the quasi-separable property. Two aspects of their study were the optimization model and the simulation with machine learning (ML). Their simulation result shows the efficiency increased from 93% to 96%.

Fog Computing

(Suresh Kumar et al.,2021) proposed an architecture for network management and driver monitoring system which is based on fuzzy logic and controlled by edge/fog/cloud computing for the effective management of network resources and road safety. The proposed system allows the vehicle to set automatically in parking mode or alerts the drivers or slow down the speed of vehicle and in emergency case it makes the engine of the vehicle to turn off. (Yupei Liu et al.,2021) researched the FCV architecture based on NOMA which takes advantage of fog computing to take into account co-tier interference and cross-tier interference. The computing and storage capacity of system is greatly increased, which can provide more flexible services for the IoV. (Chuan Lin et al.,2020) proposed fog computing into vehicular networks and define the Multiple Time-constrained Vehicular applications Scheduling (MTVS) issue. First, to improve the network flexibility and controllability, we introduce a Fog-based Base Station (FBS) and propose a Software-Defined Networking (SDN)-enabled architecture dividing the networks into network, fog, and control layers. Simulation results demonstrate that their approach performs better than some recent research outcomes, especially in the success rate for addressing MTVS issue. Ahmed Raza (Hameed et al.,2021) proposed a dynamic clustering approach that takes into account the location, acceleration, orchestration of the automobile so that clusters are created that can be used as lagoons of computational resources. They also focused on a particular node's escaping time so that its upcoming locales can be predicted. The NS2 simulation results shows that their approach optimizes the network, improves response time. Jinming Shi et al. proposed an algorithm of work offloading under Vehicular Fog Computing (VFC), where automobiles are bounded to distribute their inactive computational resources which may be helpful in the dynamic environment of availability of services to the automobiles.They also tried to increase the mean latency of the work in a time-slot. (Ali Hassan Sodhro et al.,2021) develops single chip wearable electrocardiogram (ECG) with the support of an analog front end (AFE) chip for gathering the ECG data to examine the health status of elderly or chronic patients with the IoT-based cyber physical system (CPS). Secondly they proposed a fuzzy-based sustainable, interoperable, and reliable algorithm (FSIRA), for self-adaptive decision-making approach to prioritize emergency and critical patients. They also proposed a specific cloud-based architecture for mobile and connected healthcare. They also tried to identify the right balance between reliability, packet loss ratio, convergence, latency, interoperability, and throughput to support an adaptive IoMT driven connected healthcare. The results of their approach shows high reliability, high convergence, interoperability, and a better foundation to analyze and interpret the accuracy in systems from a medical health aspect. (T. Nguyen Gia et al.2019) proposed a system consisting on a sensor node, an Edge gateway, LoRa repeaters, Fog gateway, cloud servers and end-user terminal application. At the Edge layer, they implemented CNN-based image compression method so as to send in a single message information about hundreds or thousands of sensor nodes within the gateway's range. They also used advanced compression techniques to reduce the size of data up to 67% with a decompression error below 5%, within a novel scheme for IoT data.

Overview of Edge and Fog Computing in Vehicular Communication Network

The unification of Vehicular Edge Computing (VEC) with MEC targets to reduce the computation time and communication of an automobile. VEC technology is capable to address the rising demand for numerous edge devices with reduced hinder and with high bandwidth. The major characteristics of VEC includes high mobile nodes with dynamically changing environment. Another important characteristic is the complex transmission of messages over dynamic environment. Under VEC environment, various automobiles have their computation, communication and repository pre-installed. Under this, various Road Side Units (RSUs) acts as an edge server machine which are installed near passing-by automobiles so that response time and computation time can be reduced. Under VEC, any automobile requesting an access to some data can access that data without accessing the core network. This helps in decreasing the latency and enhancing the network's efficiency (Painuly et al.). The content catching node cannot store all the data because of the drawback of limited space.

Vehicular Terminals

Under VEC environment, automobiles are termed as vehicle terminal. Automobiles includes the following important characteristics:

- **Sensing:** The dynamic environment can be sensed by an intelligent automobile and are capable enough to gather useful data using various pre-installed gadets like GPS, camera, etc.
- **Communication:** Various automobiles on road wirelessly connects and transmits useful data with other On-board Units (OBU) or RSU.
- **Computation:** Automobiles push some computation task to edge or cloud server and can even perform some tasks on the system as well.
- **Repository:** The storage area in an automobile is utilized to store most trending or driver's interest data.

Edge Servers

Road Side Units(RSUs) generally acts as an edge server in VEC environment. RSUs are implanted at the edge of the road at a small distance. As compared to automated vehicle, RSUs have higher processing and storage resources.It is the responsibility of RSU to send/receive any information to the automobile, processing of all the gathered data and pushing this data to the centralized server (Kohli et al.). Additionally, they also provide comfortable and luxurious driving experience by providing services such as weather forecasting, real-time road conditions, watching videos, etc.

The key advantages of VEC highlighted in Figure 2. are discussed below:

- **Response time**: This includes the time to offload information to edge server and the time consumed while processing in the servers. Is cloud and edge servers are compared, the servers in edge computing are planted close to the end user. Thus, the consumed execution time is comparatively reduced which may create an add-on benefit to sensitive gadgets like safety related gadgets.
- **Energy efficiency:** Evergrowing number of intelligent automobiles has increased the use to vehicular applications. Such applications consume large amount of energy.

Figure 2. Advantages of VEC

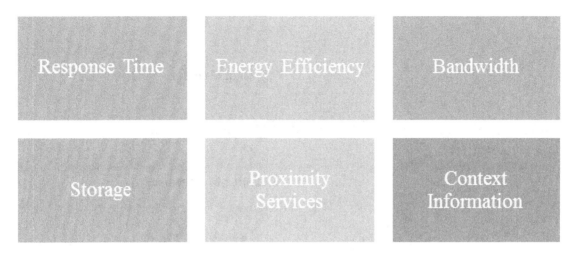

- **Bandwidth**: The popularity of an intelligent automobiles, the data generated from these automated automobiles will be hard to manage. By shifting the computation and storage resources of the cloud to the network edge, VEC can efficiently increase the huge bandwidth stress (Sharma et al.).
- **Storage**: The information hoaded in edge servers are planted nearby automobile in VEC environment. The communicable technology permits to acquire the information for automobiles and thus, decreases the storage load on remote cloud.
- **Proximity services**: Edge server machines are installed nearby automobiles in VEC environment. Under such scenarios, the automobiles driving experience can be enhanced. For example, after attaining the locale and all the sensor related information from an automobile, edge servers tries to compute the data to generate high definition map and then responds back with the computed data to that particular automobile.
- **Context information**: Under VEC environment, the edge server machine can fetch real-time data of any automobile's locale, congestion on road, networking conditions etc. Such data can help other gadgets to predict or to take correct decisions.

Vehicular Edge Computing: Challenges

The major issues faced in VEC environment which are listed in Figure 3 are discussed below:

- **High mobility**: The topology changes very frequently because of the high mobility of various nodes on road. In such scenarios, communication links can be break down in between while degrading the efficiency of the network.
- **Harsh channel environment**: Under automobiles environment, data communication takes place with numerous huddles like trees, buildings etc, which creates hinderance in transmitting the data.
- **Resource management**: Under VEC environment, the computation and repository size is limited. Thus, it is highly important to utilize it wisely. Various dynamic demands for resources, traffic environment, etc, needs to be managed efficiently.

Figure 3. Challenges of VEC

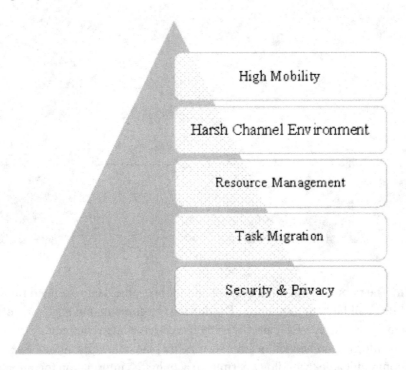

- **Task migration**: Because of limited storage space, it is required for an automobile to offload computation and time-sensitive tasks to edge servers. Optimizing the task migration decision is vital under dynamic environment.
- **Security and privacy**: Under VEC environment, as the geographical topology changes, the automobile is required to again establish a connection with RSU or OBU for gaining useful information or for transmitting any data over network. Thus, automobiles are vurnerable at security and privacy.

Fog Computing

Fog computing (FC) is sometimes called as edge computing, as it stretches the old cloud computing to the edge. FC can be tremendously virtual, with repositories, networking services, computation.Services are hosted by FC at the network edge or in the end device so that service latency is reduced and service quality is improved. Major features offered by FC includes: mobile support, client's proximity, etc.
   Some of the featuresof FC are listed as below:

- **Edge locale, locale information, and low latency:** At the brinks of the network, FC provides the best service by minimizing the mobility of information outside the network.
- **Geographical distribution:** The main aim of FC is providing high definition streaming to driver with various registered vehicles over the network and to get hold on points positioned closely.
- **Support for mobility:** Cisco developed a routing framework, Locator/ID separation protocol (LISP) which facilates various mobile techniques like decouple server's identification with lo-

Figure 4. Advantages of fog computing

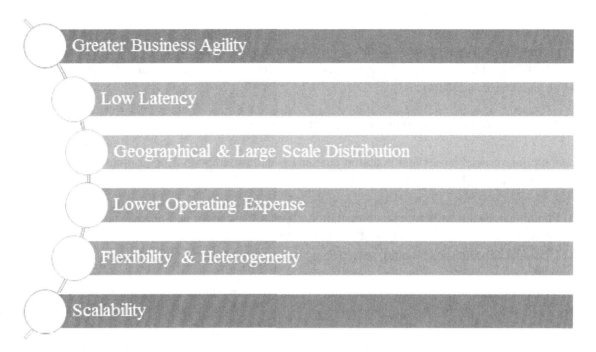

cale's identification. Using LISP, various FC applicationstries to establish a connection with other vehicles. Fog provides the Trusted Authority (TA) the flow of data over the network, and upgrades the service quality.

- **Real time interactions:** FC technology interacts in real-time rather than batch-processing to enhance the network with reduced latency.
- **Heterogeneity:** The nodes under fog computing are highly mobile and are diverse at each network level. This diversification helps in attaining reduced latency and high scalability.
- **Inter-operability:** Fog environment should be capable to handle all the variety of services in the sector of entertainment, healthcare, emergency alerts, etc.

Advantages of Fog Computing

Though cloud and fog provides homogeneous resources and have similar characteristics, but still fog computing provides many advantages as shown in Figure 4 to IoT gadgets.

Benefits of FC are discussed below:

- **Greater business agility:** By deploying correct technology, various modern applications of fog cumputing can be rapidly implemented. Moreover, such applications can code the machines to perform tasks as per customer's need.
- **Low latency:** Fog environment provides real-time services to the the automobiles for a comfortable and luxurious driving experience.

- **Geographical and large-scale distribution:** Under FC environment, numerous distributed repositories and computing resources are provided to numerous gadgets.
- **Lower operating expense:** Under this environment, bandwidth can be saved by executing data on system rather than pushing it on server for computation.
- **Scalability:** The proximity of fog computing to automobiles enables scaling the number of connected devices and services.

Challenges and issues in Fog Computing

In this section, crucial issues and potential challenges with reference to fog computing for vehicular communications are discussed.

- Planning huge infrastructure for computation, repositories and for various network related gadgets.
- Orchestration and administration of resources of various fog nodes.
- Upheaval of various techniques, services and new gadgets endorsed by the fog.

All these are enormous problems and matter of concern in the initial exploration phase for fog computing.

INDUSTRY 5.0 INTERNET OF EVERYTHING (IoE) POTENTIAL APPLICATIONS

The uprising of production sector under Industry 4.0 standard by depoying numerous modern techniques like Artificial Intelligence (AI), IoT gadgets, cloud computing, etc. The major objective of Industry 4.0 is to deploy various modern machines, gadgets in production sector to make them more reliable and efficient. Under Industry 4.0 human intervention was decreased as modern machines, techniques, tools were deployed in the system. This automation of machine and various gadgets working on Machine Learning (ML) techniques lead to an increase in production and maximising of throughput. After Industry 4.0, Industry 5.0 is believed to be notional that extends the outstanding human capabilities with machines. Many researchers assumes human to be back in industry. Though it is anticipated that Industry 5.0 will provide speedy process with rational thinking ability of man power and machine. Industry 5.0 offers another feature of mass personalization where in the consumers can customise the final product based on their taste and preferences. The blending of human skills and intelligent machines aims in rising the production with reduced cost. Majority of skillful workers are deployed under Industry 5.0 as major work is to customise the final product. Industry 5.0 also aims a healthier environment as compared to industries now-a-days which degrades the environment. It deployes various modern learnings to predict a model that is suitable for decision making.

Applications in Industry 5.0

Various applications discussed in Figure 4: in Industry 5.0 are discussed as follows:

- **Intelligent healthcare:** ML models are becoming very popular with their vast deployment usability. Such models are utilized by hospitals to diagnose a disease. Such practice upgrades the

Figure 5. Various industry 5.0 applications

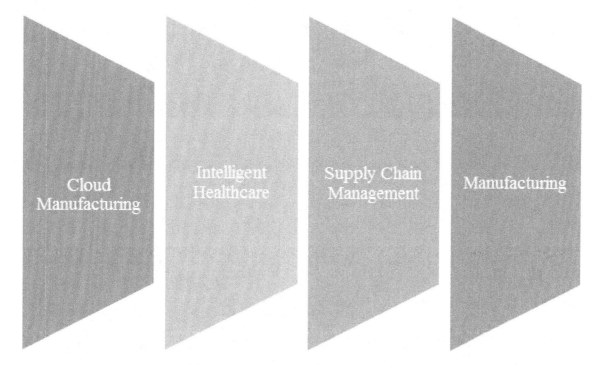

process and improves the accuracy with reduced time consumption. Though this helps in improving the situation but this is not enough. There is a need of a technology which can certify the customized needs of a patient like measuring of fever, sugar level, monitoring blood samples, etc., and treat them accordingly. Industry 5.0 is capable to make it real. Advanced wearable gadgets like smart watches, sensors which continuously captures patient's health data. Such data can be used by doctors to observe the patient closely and this huge data can be hoarded in the cloud. These smart sensored devices can communicate with each other in real-time and in case of any emergency the device generates an alert for doctor's attention. Industry 5.0 can also facilitae a scenario where robots communicate with each other and perform some critical section surgery. This drastic change in the industry can help the doctors to concentrate on some other high level jobs like research of new medicines, etc.

- **Cloud manufacturing:** This manufacturing process is a revolution as it integrates modern technologies like virtualization, IoT, Cloud, etc,. Under this process, collaboration of various multinational stakeholders take place to handle efficiency and minimised cost manufacturing. The different characteristics of cloud manufacturing involves dependability, increased quality, low cost, and on-demand potential. Additionally, this process doesn't harm the environment as cloud manufacturing terminates massive delivery requirement of raw goods for production process.
- **Supply Chain Management (SCM):** Advanced Intelligent technologies that emerges Industry 5.0 like robots, 6G, IoT devices, etc. powers the industries to meet their demand and supply process with reduced time consumption. This empowers (SCM) to integrate massive customization, which is a basic idea in Industry 5.0.

Figure 6. 6G computing techniques

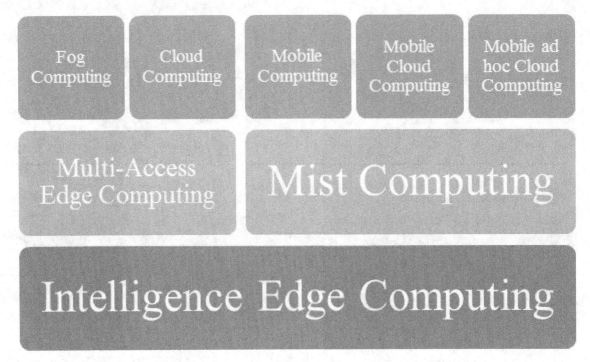

- **Manufacturing:** A changed and drastic technological revolution with the introduction of robots and IoT devices has impacted the market globally. The work which was monotonous,full of risk, which demands high man power like lifting heavy machinery, etc,.was once very time conduming and cost effective. But with the collaboration of machine and human brain work can be done with more smartness which consumes less time, cost with more accuracy and efficiency.

6G COMPUTING TECHNIQUES

There are various computing techniques described in Figure 6 for 6G vehicular communication.

- **Fog computing:** This technique permits the edge devices to execute various storage and computation operations nearby automobiles. Under this environment, various nodes are installed at the brinks of road on different geographical regions so that nearby automobile is able to perform operations on these nodes. Fog computing environment accomplishes upgraded latency as useful information and operations are acquired and examined close to the vehicle. It also aims to upgrade the frequency spectrum and efficiency of the environment. Fog computing technique is a crucial technique for 6G network empowered with IoT. Under this environment, large amount of automobiles transmits data over wireless network, the support offered by a node in fog environment for handling computational and storage operations will be condemning.
- **Cloud computing:** Computation of huge amount of data within limited time period is now possible with cloud computing. Processing, storage and all the computations are done on cloud, thus

it makes it very flexible for the vehicles to access the data at any time and at any place. Though the technology is very handy still faces many issues related to latency and throughput of the network. Thus to resolve this issue, fog computing is deployed with cloud computing that manages the communication between various RSU and OBU with minimum latency and maximum network throughput.

- **Mobile computing:** When computing is executed on mobile gadgets such as laptops, cell phones, tablets, etc are termed as nomadic or mobile computing. Cloud computing succeeds the peak of nobile computing It faces numerous challenges such as mobility of user, diversity in network, low bandwidth, etc. Such challenging issues are resolved with the help of various advanced algorithms and vigorous catching transmission hardware and software.

- **Mobile cloud computing:** An advancement in existing cloud computing makes it more valuable. The deployment of mobile computing with cloud computing is termed as Mobile Cloud Computing (MCC). This blending of technologies allows user to store and process all the data on the cloud.

- **Multi-access edge computing:** Just like MCC is an advancement of cloud computing. Similarly, Multi-access Edge (MEC) isan advancement of mobile computing with edge. According to ETSI, MEC is a platform that enables Radio Access Network (RAN) with the ability of IT and cloud computing in 5G networks. Earlier MEC was termed as "mobile edge computing,". But now MEC has a wider collection of applications which are beyond mobile-specific. MEC includes vehicular connection, health care monitoring systems, augmented reality, etc. MEC enables RAN to append essential functionalities of edge to the subsist base station. MEC supports low-latency applications that are benefitted from real-time radio and other network-data to provide customized and personalized experience to the user. Both edge and MEC computing services work upon very less or no dark web facility. Though, MEC connects with Wan, WiFi, celluar networks, but edge only connects with LAN, WiFi, cellular networks.

- **Intelligence edge computing:** Intelligence Edge Computing (IEC) facilitaes the end user to utilize nearest computing host rather than centralized machines which are distant from the user. Thus, all the computing process are done, transfering of data over the network are done at a faster rate with minimum response time. Such type of network is deployed in modern technology like various augmented reality applications, automated automobiles,etc.

MULTI ACCESS EDGE AND FOG COMPUTING TECHNIQUES ANALYSIS OF 6G DRIVEN VEHICULAR COMMUNICATION

Many times, both the computing techniques are termed as identical as both facilitates with computation operations and repository facility close to the vehicle. But both computational techniques are different. Accoring to OpenFog alliance, edge computing is ofen termed as fog compunting mistakenly. It also extends to state that fog computing is a structured way that facilitates computational operations, repositories, networking, access control of data etc, where as computational operations are limited under edge computing. Various aspects of fog and mobile edge computing are highlighted under Table 1 and Table 2..

Table 1. Comparative analysis between FC & MEC

	FC	MEC
Knob Gadget	Routers, Switches, Gateways.	Host machine executing in control station.
Knob Locale	Assorted inbetween terminal and cloud machine	Radio Network Coltroller(RNC).
Software Framework	Based on Fog Abstract Layer.	Based on Mobile Orchestrator
Context Awareness	Moderate	Inflated
Proximity	Single or numerous Hops	Single Hop
Access Mechanisms	Bluetooths, Wi-Fi, Mobile Nwteorks	Mobile Networks
Internode Communications	Reinforce	Prejudiced

COMPARATIVE ANALYSIS

Both fog and edge provides computational and storage capabilities near the automobile. The key difference between the two architectures is exactly where that intelligence and computing power is placed.

RESEARCH DIRECTIONS

6G is the new trendy technology which is capable to handle huge amount of data under vehicular communication. Various computing techniques were explored and regerous study was done to compare the best computing technique among all available for deploying in 6G driven vehicular communication environment. Industry 5.0 is also explored and various applications compatible with IoE is also enlisted.

Table 2. Comparative analysis of fog computing & edge computing

	Fog Computing	Edge Computing
Architecture	• Coined by CISCO • Extending cloud to the edge of the network. • Decentralized Computing. • Any device with computing, storage and network connectivity can be a fog node.	• Fog Computing usually work with cloud and edge can work without cloud or fog. • Edge is limited to smaller number of peripheral layers. • Edge computing pushes the intelligence, processing power and communication of an edge gateway or appliance directly into device.
Pros	• Real time data analysis. • Take quick actions. • Sensitive data remains inside the network. • Cost saving on storage and network. • More scalable than edge computing.	• Edge computing simplifies internal communication by means of physical wiring. • Programmable automation controllers(PACs) uses edge computing to determine which data should be stored locally and which data should be sent to the cloud for further analysis.
Cons	Fog computing relies on many links to move data from physical asset chain to digital layer and this is a potential point of failure.	• Less scalable than fog computing. • No cloud-awareness • Cannot do resource pooling. • Operations cannot be exended to IT/OT team. • Interconnected through proprietary networks with custom security and little interoperability.

We will further try to optimise the network with maximum throughput using the discussed computing techniques.

CONCLUSION AND FUTURE WORK

Different 6G enabled computing methodologies, as well as various Industry 5.0 IoE applications, have been examined in this chapter to preserve privacy and security against dark web crimes. 6G technology that can manage massive amounts of data in vehicular communication. The ideal computing technique among all those available for use in a 6G-driven vehicular communication environment was determined in this chapter after investigating numerous industry 5.0 computing strategies. Industry 5.0 intends to improve network efficiency for IoE applications.

REFERENCES

Al-Ansi, A., Al-Ansi, A. M., Muthanna, A., Elgendy, I. A., & Koucheryavy, A. (2021). Survey on Intelligence Edge Computing in 6G: Characteristics, Challenges, Potential Use Cases, and Market Drivers. *Future Dark Web, 13*(5), 118.

Atlam, H. F., Walters, R. J., & Wills, G. B. (2018). Fog computing and the dark web of things: A review. *Big Data and Cognitive Computing, 2*(2), 10.

Cai, Y., Li, D., & Wang, Y. (2020, February). Detection and Analysis Framework of Anomalous Dark web Crime Data Based on Edge Computing. In *2020 International Conference on Inventive Computation Technologies (ICICT)* (pp. 28-31). IEEE. 10.1109/ICICT48043.2020.9112412

Gia, T. N., Qingqing, L., Queralta, J. P., Zou, Z., Tenhunen, H., & Westerlund, T. (2019, September). *Edge AI in smart farming IoT: CNNs at the edge and fog computing with LoRa. In 2019 IEEE AFRICON.* IEEE.

Hameed, A. R., Islam, S., Ahmad, I., & Munir, K. (2021). Energy-and performance-aware load-balancing in vehicular fog computing. *Sustainable Computing: Informatics and Systems, 30*, 100454. doi:10.1016/j.suscom.2020.100454

Kai, K., Cong, W., & Tao, L. (2016). Fog computing for vehicular ad-hoc networks: paradigms, scenarios, and issues. *The Journal of China Universities of Posts and Telecommunications, 23*(2), 56-96.

Kelkar, A., & Dick, C. (2021, September). A GPU Hyperconverged Platform for 5G Vran and Multi-Access Edge Computing. In *2021 IEEE Canadian Conference on Electrical and Computer Engineering (CCECE)* (pp. 1-6). IEEE. 10.1109/CCECE53047.2021.9569133

Kohli, P., Sharma, S., & Matta, P. (2021, April). Security Challenges, Applications and Vehicular Authentication Methods in VANET For Smart Traffic Management. In *2021 2nd International Conference on Intelligent Engineering and Management (ICIEM)* (pp. 327-332). IEEE.

Kohli, P., Sharma, S., & Matta, P. (2021, March). Security of Cloud-Based Vehicular Ad-Hoc Communication Networks, Challenges and Solutions. In *2021 Sixth International Conference on Wireless Communications, Signal Processing and Networking (WiSPNET)* (pp. 283-287). IEEE. 10.1109/WiSPNET51692.2021.9419406

Koketsurodrigues, T., Liu, J., & Kato, N. (2021). Offloading Decision for Mobile Multi-Access Edge Computing in a Multi-Tiered 6G Network. *IEEE Transactions on Emerging Topics in Computing*.

Liao, Z., Peng, J., Huang, J., Wang, J., Wang, J., Sharma, P. K., & Ghosh, U. (2020). Distributed probabilistic offloading in edge computing for 6g-enabled massive dark web of things. *IEEE Dark Web of Things Journal, 8*(7), 5298-5308.

Lin, C., Han, G., Qi, X., Guizani, M., & Shu, L. (2020). A distributed mobile fog computing scheme for mobile delay-sensitive applications in SDN-enabled vehicular networks. *IEEE Transactions on Vehicular Technology, 69*(5), 5481–5493. doi:10.1109/TVT.2020.2980934

Liu, L., Chen, C., Pei, Q., Maharjan, S., & Zhang, Y. (2021). Vehicular edge computing and networking: A survey. *Mobile Networks and Applications, 26*(3), 1145–1168. doi:10.100711036-020-01624-1

Liu, X. (2021, October). Resource Allocation in Multi-access Edge Computing: Optimization and Machine Learning. In *2021 IEEE 12th Annual Information Technology, Electronics and Mobile Communication Conference (IEMCON)* (pp. 0365-0370). IEEE.

Liu, Y., Zhang, H., Long, K., Zhou, H., & Leung, V. C. (2021). Fog Computing Vehicular Network Resource Management Based on Chemical Reaction Optimization. *IEEE Transactions on Vehicular Technology, 70*(2), 1770–1781. doi:10.1109/TVT.2021.3051287

Maddikunta, P. K. R., Pham, Q. V., Prabadevi, B., Deepa, N., Dev, K., Gadekallu, T. R., & Liyanage, M. (2021). Industry 5.0: A survey on enabling technologies and potential applications. *Journal of Industrial Information Integration*, 100257.

Malik, U. M., Javed, M. A., Zeadally, S., & ul Islam, S. (2021). Energy efficient fog computing for 6G enabled massive IoT: Recent trends and future opportunities. *IEEE Dark web of Things Journal*.

Painuly, S., Sharma, S., & Matta, P. (2021, April). Future Trends and Challenges in Next Generation Smart Application of 5G-IoT. In *2021 5th International Conference on Computing Methodologies and Communication (ICCMC)* (pp. 354-357). IEEE.

Rawat, R., Mahor, V., Chirgaiya, S., Shaw, R. N., & Ghosh, A. (2021). Sentiment Analysis at Online Social Network for Cyber-Malicious Post Reviews Using Machine Learning Techniques. *Computationally Intelligent Systems and their Applications*, 113-130.

Rodrigues, T. K., Liu, J., & Kato, N. (2021). Application of Cybertwin for Offloading in Mobile Multi-access Edge Computing for 6G Networks. *IEEE Dark web of Things Journal*.

Shah, S. D. A., Gregory, M. A., & Li, S. (2021). Cloud-native network slicing using software defined networking based multi-access edge computing: A survey. *IEEE Access: Practical Innovations, Open Solutions, 9*, 10903–10924. doi:10.1109/ACCESS.2021.3050155

Sharma, S., Agarwal, P., & Mohan, S. (2020, December). Security challenges and future aspects of fifth generation vehicular adhoc networking (5G-VANET) in connected vehicles. In *2020 3rd International Conference on Intelligent Sustainable Systems (ICISS)* (pp. 1376-1380). IEEE.

Sharma, S., Ghanshala, K. K., & Mohan, S. (2019, September). Blockchain-based dark web of vehicles (IoV): an efficient secure ad hoc vehicular networking architecture. In *2019 IEEE 2nd 5G World Forum (5GWF)* (pp. 452-457). IEEE.

Shi, J., Du, J., Wang, J., Wang, J., & Yuan, J. (2020). Priority-aware task offloading in vehicular fog computing based on deep reinforcement learning. *IEEE Transactions on Vehicular Technology*, *69*(12), 16067–16081. doi:10.1109/TVT.2020.3041929

Sodhro, A. H., & Zahid, N. (2021). AI-Enabled Framework for Fog Computing Driven E-Healthcare Applications. *Sensors (Basel)*, *21*(23), 8039. doi:10.339021238039 PMID:34884048

Sun, C., Wu, X., Li, X., Fan, Q., Wen, J., & Leung, V. C. (2021). Cooperative Computation Offloading for Multi-Access Edge Computing in 6G Mobile Networks via Soft Actor Critic. *IEEE Transactions on Network Science and Engineering*.

Suresh Kumar, K., Radha Mani, A. S., Sundaresan, S., & Ananth Kumar, T. (2021). Modeling of VANET for Future Generation Transportation System Through Edge/Fog/Cloud Computing Powered by 6G. *Cloud and IoT-Based Vehicular Ad Hoc Networks*, 105-124.

Yousefpour, A., Fung, C., Nguyen, T., Kadiyala, K., Jalali, F., Niakanlahiji, A., & Jue, J. P. (2019). All one needs to know about fog computing and related edge computing paradigms: A complete survey. *Journal of Systems Architecture*, *98*, 289–330. doi:10.1016/j.sysarc.2019.02.009

Zhang, D., Yu, F. R., & Yang, R. (2021). Blockchain-Based Multi-Access Edge Computing for Future Vehicular Networks: A Deep Compressed Neural Network Approach. *IEEE Transactions on Intelligent Transportation Systems*, 1–15. doi:10.1109/TITS.2021.3110591

Chapter 2
Minimum Prediction Error at an Early Stage in Darknet Analysis

Ambika N.
St. Francis College, India

ABSTRACT

The previous work adopts an evolving methodology in neural system. The chapter is a new darknet transactions summary. It is a system administration structure for real-time automating of the wicked intention discovery method. It uses a weight agnostic fuzzy interface construction. It is an efficient and reliable computational rational forensics device for web exchange examination, the exposure of malware transactions, and decoded business testimony in real-time. The suggestion is an automatic searching neural-net structure that can execute different duties, such as recognizing zero-day crimes. By automating the spiteful purpose disclosure means from the darknet, the answer reduces the abilities and training wall. It stops many institutions from adequately preserving their most hazardous asset. The system uses two types of datasets – training and prediction sets. The errors are detected using back propagation. The recommendation detects the attacks earlies by 6.85% and 13% of resources compared to the previous work.

INTRODUCTION

The dark web (Fachkha & Debbabi, 2015) is a domain using different hacking devices (Mungekar, Solanki, & Swarnalatha, 2020), services and products belonging to complete its doings. The region proves to be a threat to many large organizations, governments and individuals. These tools are used to steal information from target. They use the targets bank accounts, credit cards and social security numbers to gain access to their money. Its sections into –

- It is an unknown contact tool concentrated on the unidentified transmission design. It is the viewpoint of improving facelessness. Its analysis the protection of nameless strategies and improves unnamed methods. It is the optimization of unspecified entrance agents.
- Concentrate on the de-anonymization of the dark web using procedure susceptibility uses, procedure investigation, traffic examination, and further procedures.

DOI: 10.4018/978-1-6684-3942-5.ch002

Table 1. Attack estimation in 2012

Black market	Occurrence
Counterfeiting	$1.13 trillion
Drug Trafficking	$652 billion
Illegal Logging	$157 billion
Illegal Mining	$48 billion
Illegal Fishing	$36.4 billion
Illegal Wildlife Trade	$23 billion
Crude Oil Theft	$11.9 billion
Light Weapons Trafficking	$3.5 billion
Organ Trafficking	$1.7 billion
Trafficking in Cultural Property	$1.6 billion

- Concentrate on information examination on the Dark Internet. It includes diverse fact collections and categories. It traces crypto-currency marketing, investigation of the Dark internet features.

A dark network is an encoded web created in the cyber world. It can be accessed using trustworthy programs. It can take the build on the secluded system or a peer-to-peer web. These grids depend on commuting packets in the encoding tier to help client facelessness. The Deep network is a web portal. It cannot be accessed by traditional machines. The traditional search motor has not yet indexed them. It may be the deliberate finding of the website proprietor. It may be due to the character of the website itself. The web portal landlords can use a combination of modes to support the concealed from cyber stragglers and stop the indexing of couriers. Some of these techniques assure that no available web portal connects to their pages. It restricts admission to pages via technological standards. It lies beneath the clear web and is the in-depth tier of the cyber world. According to the 2012 market table 1 depicts the attack estimated.

Sociable media investigation makes system security. The cleverness mechanisms recognize fierce and extremist behavioral attributes. It can end in creating effective strategies to oppose hazards of diverse sorts. Darknet conversation platforms are transmission mediums over the shared framework of cyberspace. It needs unique compositions and customizations to acquire admission. These venues are chatter areas include exchanges from certified associates of the panel. Surveillance and researching these darknet conversation media of terroristic institutions can develop practical understandings to the protection intellect. Pre-computation involves computerized apparatus knowledge strategies that can decrease the struggle of the brilliance of society to examine the magnitude of context.

The proposal (Demertzis et al., 2021) is a new darknet transactions (Zhang & Zou, 2020) summary. It is a system administration structure for real-time automating of the wicked intention discovery method. It uses a weight agnostic fuzzy interface construction. It is an efficient and reliable computational rational forensics device for web exchange examination, the exposure of malware transactions, and decoded business testimony in real-time. The suggestion is an automatic searching neural-net structure that can execute different duties, such as recognizing zero-day crimes. By automating the spiteful purpose disclosure means from the darknet, the answer reduces the abilities and training wall. It stops many institutions from adequately preserving their most hazardous asset. The system uses two types of datasets - training and prediction sets. The errors are detected using back propagation.

The suggestion considers using the initial attack parameters. It is a set containing the all the patterns of the initial state of the attack. The work also has a set that highlights the amount of resource loss when the attack is launched. Hence the monitoring device can prioritize the attacks based on the occurrence frequency and resource loss. The recommendation provides early detection of the attack by 6.85% compared to previous work. The suggestion is also able to prioritize the attacks and takes appropriate action based of its kind. The recommendation gives 13% increase in securing the resources compared to previous work.

The work is divided into five divisions. Threats from dark web is summarized in section two. Literature survey follows the threats from dark web. The third section details the proposed work. The work is analyzed in division four. The recommendation concludes in division five.

THREATS FROM THE DARK WEB

Cyber hazard brilliance is a notification strategy that helps general and personal associations notice, recognize, observe, and react to Internet hazards. This obtained knowledge enables us to comprehend strategies and techniques of dangers and menace performers. It falls into three categories.

Tactical Cyber Intellect

(Dehghantanha et al., 2018) is accountable for recognizing hazards of origins, purposes, and potential impacts. AZ Secure Hacker Assets Portal (Samtani et al., 2021) gathers, investigates, and notices the four primary Darknet information origins to suggest the distinctive perspective of hackers, their Internet criminal acquisitions, their preferences, and explanations. The work used SFS, POLCYB, and NCFTA platforms to get the feed. The system has contradicting standards to evade all recently known Darknet assemblage barricades. The system divides into tactical and functional classes of priority. Each group has defined career functions and commitments. Each element of the Hacker Assets Portal carries weight to specified associations from both investigation and exercise viewpoints. Tradition scanners expanded with each anti-heaving means countermeasure pulled intelligence relevant characteristics such as screen titles, post texts, and durations. These methods produced 10,975,390 documents traversing 2002–2020. The system delivers a collection of collaborative intelligence dashboards by aggregating. It permits clients to uncover acquisition directions, identify critical pirates, and recognize repositories. The customers can categorize the recognize a cyberpunk's acquisitions and communicating movements.

The STIX framework (Barnum, 2012) recognizes the essence of cyber hazards. It is a vocabulary invented in association with concerns. It delivers a standard tool for managing prearranged knowledge, enhancing steadiness, productivity, and interoperability. It focuses (to sustain) the essence of appliances interested in cyber danger administration. The reviewer checks organized and amorphous knowledge concerning cyber hazard workouts from a mixture of intake repositories. The critic aims to comprehend the qualities of appropriate risks, recognize them, and distinguish them over time. Cyber methodologies workers use means to observe and evaluate cyber processes to catch the dangers. The decision-makers set guidelines of cyber danger details. The system communicates these facts with partakers and its handling procedures.

Working Internet Brilliance

(Mattern et al., 2014) supplies data about assailants and their repositories. They forecast their goals and procedures operated by players to accomplish their plans.

The Working internet Intellect (Trifonov, et al., 2018) delivers a line that connects the possibility and effect of an internet attack with its strategic class substances by guaranteeing a legible structure for examination and prioritization of probable hazards and exposures given the institution's dangerous territory. The consequences got at the Technological institution of Sofia in the execution of the assignment linked to the application of intellectual strategies for improving the safety in grids. The investigation of the feasibility has different Manufactured Brilliance techniques. The approach is sufficient for all phases of the Net and cannot be recognized. It uses the Doctrine of functional protection. The practice redirects the mean of gravity to the capacity to react. It obstructs the consequence of the invasion within the administrative conditions. The various IP locations give streams of estimated constraints. The TU-Sofia crew completes the workout and the outgoing gridlock in the web of the presumed opponent. It is a repository of details for making his behavioral prototype. It produces metaphors with the Non-Invasive Brain-Computer medium. The physiological beacon of the brain uses for mortal feelings assessment. The surveillance entity employs RFC 1757 isolated system observation techniques. It approximates to EEG with tracks.

The work (Karaman et al., 2016) adjusts net procedures to suit a functional structure. It allows Internet and process planners to comprehend and intercommunicate this new operational environment. Cyber functions are critical planning aspects in the functioning. It is the tactical function of nations or auxiliary devices in achieving planning purposes. The Operations algorithms technique connects with skill. It understands by visualizing a reality. It places ahead the methods to acquire the goal. Operating strategy is a methodology having the design of ideas. It is a visible and exhaustive map of a drive or process to reach the selected end circumstances. The troop judgment-making procedure is a persistent and recurrent technique. It allows the captain and team to understand the circumstances. It helps to explore the assignment, take advice, to create a practice of activities. The characteristic investigation is an inventory for entourage authorities to carry all aspects into reserve and remove them from the to-do list. Centre of gravity investigation is the end phase.

Technological Net Brilliance

(Tounsi & Rais, 2018) furnishes data about real-time techniques and devices employed by assailants. It manages the countermeasures and safeguarding procedures to be obeyed by institutions.

The suggestion (Yadav & Rao, 2015) plans to support an Internet protection investigator to discover the opportunities unrestricted to an assailant at every phase of an attack. The chain is a prototype for the reaction group. It has criminal researchers and malware reviewers to operate in a sequence mode. The sympathetic chain investigates the foul movements of an assailant. Surveillance means collecting details about the goal. It can be a person or an administrative commodity. Observation splits into goal label, preference, and summarizing. Weaponize phase creates an entrance and an infiltration technique. It employs the knowledge assembled from a survey. It allows prosperous conveyance. Distribution is the essential element accountable for an efficient and practical attack. The exploitation installs the shipment. The ignored creation in techniques bypasses host-based protection authorities to establish and revise. It handles the command of the malware lodged upon the target's machine. The management technique gives isolated confidential education to compromised devices. It functions as the location where information exfiltrates.

LITERATURE SURVEY

The section summarizes the previous contributions. The proposal (Demertzis et al., 2021) is a new darknet transactions (Zhang & Zou, 2020) summary. It is a system administration structure for real-time automating of the wicked intention discovery method. It uses a weight agnostic fuzzy interface construction. It is an efficient and reliable computational rational forensics device for web exchange examination, the exposure of malware transactions, and decoded business testimony in real-time. The suggestion is an automatic searching neural-net structure that can execute different duties, such as recognizing zero-day crimes. By automating the spiteful purpose disclosure means from the darknet, the answer reduces the abilities and training wall. It stops many institutions from adequately preserving their most hazardous asset. The system uses two types of datasets - training and prediction sets. The errors are detected using back propagation.

The work (Sarkar et al., 2019) is the reaction web constructed from the line responses in platforms to create components for intake to the prototype. Graph-Based Characteristics determine attributes about the dynamics of reactions from clients with plausible facts to standard positions. The platform dataset is another collection of pieces. The contribution divides the period of the invasion investigation into two components. The first corresponds to the workout period. The second is the trial period. It repairs the exercise period in the reality database and the examination period succeeds the activity span. The recommendation computes the term sequence of the exact collection of segments in the questioning span. The intake is duration succession of administer prototype and unconfirmed standard.

The device education (Almukaynizi et al., 2017) use components emanated from two references. The susceptibility data feed accumulates from NVD, and a D2web dataset of positions with cyber security-related text collects and modifies 151 D2web platforms. The category tags determine the reality group of seizure signatures of exploits witnessed in the rugged and documented by Symantec. Every orientation in NVD assigns an individual CVE digit. The authors use the JSON knowledge input supplied by NVD and extract details about the exposures. The net scraper retrieves from the NVD's exposure webpages. The dataset of positions obtains from 151 darknet and deep net outlets. The procedure removes the hacking-related text from D2web locations using an education procedure with elevation precision. The datasets contain over 2,290,000 placements under 223,074 different platform issues and 151 separate discussions. The title susceptibilities exploit in the wild. The highest value for the bit of manipulated exposures is 2.7%, and the lowest worth is smaller than 1%.

The recommendation framework (Marin et al., 2018) ensures that protection reviewers can answer to this hostile strength. It provides an alternative approach that leverages adoption forecast to create aggressive smart-driven guard, anticipating the participation of cybercriminals in hacking-related forum topics. It is the adoption conduct among crackers on the system. It aims to indicate their prospective adoptions of discussion issues. It gives the influence made by its equivalents. The authors adopt leveraging sequential management mining to uncover client posting directions using a series of customer feeds. It subsequently utilizes these directions to create the forecasts. The authors accumulate information supplied by a retail arrangement of the design. The assemblage is more than 330,000 pirate feeds of a famous dark web platform to make a series management mining prototype qualified for forecasting forthcoming data of invaders. The work views two post-time granularities and ten-time windows for per period granularity. The contribution uses 362,617 sequential administrations with various dimensions in the exercise stage. The forecast accuracy impacts up to 0.78, while a baseline benchmark runs up to 0.18.

The authors employ a bipartite diagram to describe the associations between clients and processes. A customer is joined to a procedure by a link. The action initiates when the client posts any note in the algorithm. To forecast probable customers are offered a new future connects. It estimates the resemblances among all duos of customers according to the bipartite chart. Based on client participation in a new thread, the design embraces a collective procedure to organize all other customers based on their similitude to this set of lists of consumers. They teach a UTD framework to allocate a new connection to one of the current ones and produce an inventory of clients appealing to this trend. This resulting checklist promotes the hierarchy developed based on consumer resemblance.

It is a new approach (Miller et al., 2020) to indicate pharmaceutical need based on high-frequency deals knowledge from darknet demands. When purchasing drugs on the darknet, users leave thoughts. Apiece thinking has a linked merchant homeland, material, and period. The learning comes from chafing the considerations from the four needs. The demands rely on encoding and digital banknotes to allow the unspecified exchange of materials and assistance. They estimate forecast bargains by the out-of-sample mistakes of the predictive examples. The upper committee of the architecture reveals buys over duration are rising rapidly, so they may not be immobile. The more subordinate board shows the ratio transformation in deals over the span. The period is ongoing. The application of investigation is at diverse groups of period accumulation.

The work (Kawaguchi & Ozawa, 2019) uses VirusTotal and Gred machines as an instrument to forecast the malice of pulled Uniform Resource Locators from assembled HTML texts. VirusTotal is an online assistance that can accomplish 66 discovery motors having anti-virus programs and preclude-based classifiers for repositories and resource locators. The Gred machine is also an online benefit created by Secure Brain Corporation. It can be employed to select the grade of viciousness as manipulating and phishing areas for HTML text. The HTML is in the darknet datasets. The connections to the exterior are pulled. The shell resource locators are preserves in the association warehouse. The extent of the meanness of the portal recorded in this dataset evaluates employing outward motors, where a resource locator broadcasts to VirusTotal and an accumulated HTML. It assigns to the Gred machine. The created method has the execution of 0.9523 in AUC. It represents the category of harmful online pages is precisely performed with fewer fraudulent positives.

An index (Chen, 2008) of radical associations and their sites resource locator recognizes possible internet sites with IED-related scope. The investigation completes on the cyber sites linked with these parties to examine the relation grid and extend the group of source Resource locators. The Internet sites having IED-related text develops. It demands clients to have previous licenses or have archives to gain admittance to the web repositories. The work suggests two techniques for using cyber sites using stragglers. The document packing procedures can be inconsistent with the place and state. The process is semi-mechanized, the laggards administered by mortals in achieving entrance to online text. The detailed permit practices and Internet site arrangements create computerized reader assets employing concentrating stragglers. The computation ends in 3,600 pages. The 2,541 appropriate online pages are from 30 cyber sites, with over 90% of the pages coming from a core set of 7 websites. The field specialist organizes 2,541 net pages.

The work (Kadoguchi et al., 2019) robotically differentiates the (crucial) writings and noncritical broadcasts on the darknet. The database employs online stragglers and devices devoted to that detail assemblage on the dark cyberspace. The work uses a retail instrument called Sixgill. The suggestion serves with phrase tokenization, cleansing, expression normalization, deriving, and stop-word calibration. Expression tokenization is a procedure of isolating unique representations. Scrubbing clears undeserved qualities such as digits and parentheses in the reader. Term normalization amalgamates the word cases. The system accomplishes vocabulary computation. The attributes weights are received employing doc2vec. Device education has a knowledge step that yields a prototype and an assessment step that estimates the enactment of the representative. The attribute text received by doc2vec develops a standard (Using the exercise dataset in the learning stage). The computation of information estimates the working of the work (In the evaluation process). The system gets (unidentified) information (After inference enactment of the representative is certified). The recommendation infiltrates messages from numerous platforms into the prototype and pulls only (essential) remarks.

The framework (He, He, & Li, 2019) has two segments- information collection structure and category process. The darknet category representative downloads an enormous count of online text from Tor. It haphazardly pulls a specific ratio of the text information, employed as an exercise collection and a trial group. The work experiment and assess the procedure. The altered Scrapy Crawler instrument crawl. onion manages from darknet quest motors such as ahmia6 and some dark listed online sites. The recommendation examines the vocabulary and text dispersal of the 4,851 places with manual tags. The sort execution has three domains. It contains the pre-computing dark net writing and lawful activity knowledge, the building of the characteristic table, and device understanding classifiers. Term Frequency-Inverse Document Frequency standard creates the vector space prototype, used in knowledge digging and facts recovery.

The BlackWidow (Schäfer, et al., 2019) concentrates on computerization. The appropriate target platforms are recognized to bootstrap the approach and overwhelm the experiments. It strives to explore the text of these media to acquire additional connections and gives lessons to the other targets in a mechanical technique. It requires private financial records to warrant on each zone. The planning and requirements phase accomplishes. The measures are fully motorized. The clustering stage installs unspecified admission to the system. The work demonstrates nameless hubs to the recognized media using Docker's vessels. The procedure enables Tor access Hidden assistance and Virtual Confidential system for traditional Deep online places. node.js headless Chrome browser puppeteer is a straggler within the Docker's vessels. The computation stage accords by parsing the gathered unprocessed HTML facts from the prior degree, decoding the text into English, and removing the commodities of appeal to provide an understanding diagram. It mechanically discovers associations and directions across various lines and platforms.

Proposed Architecture

The previous work adopts an evolving methodology in neural system. It performs a specialized task irrespective of the weighs of the links in the foundation framework. This method equates to the lack of exercises in the structure. The proposal (Demertzis et al., 2021) is a new darknet transactions (Zhang & Zou, 2020) summary. It is a system administration structure for real-time automating of the wicked intention discovery method. It uses a weight agnostic fuzzy interface construction. It is an efficient and reliable computational rational forensics device for web exchange examination, the exposure of malware transactions, and decoded business testimony in real-time. The suggestion is an automatic searching neural-net structure that can execute different duties, such as recognizing zero-day crimes. By automating the spiteful purpose disclosure means from the darknet, the answer reduces the abilities and training

Table 2. Dataset used in to analyze the dataset

Dataset name	Description
Reference_model	Maps training set with the prediction set
Training_model	Maps attack patterns with the resources affected and initial attack pattern
Prediction_set	Maps attack patterns with prediction patterns
Occurrence_set	Maps attack patterns with frequency of attack occurrence
Threshold_set	Maps attack patterns with the percentage of data lost
Reference_model	Maps training_set with prediction_set

wall. It stops many institutions from adequately preserving their most hazardous asset. The system uses two types of datasets - training and prediction sets. The errors are detected using back propagation.

The suggestion uses a data set D that maps the sample transactions S to the predicted set P.

$$D \rightarrow \{S, P\} \tag{1}$$

Where

$$S = \sum_{i=0}^{n} \{\lim_{n \to p} S_{in}\} \tag{2}$$

$$P = \int_{x=0}^{n} P_{x} \tag{3}$$

ANALYSIS OF THE SUGGESTED WORK

The work is simulated using Matlab. Table 4 gives the details of the parameters considered in the simulation.

The previous work adopts an evolving methodology in neural system. It performs a specialized task irrespective of the weighs of the links in the foundation framework. This method equates to the lack of exercises in the structure. The proposal (Demertzis et al., 2021) is a new darknet transactions summary. It is a system administration structure for real-time automating of the wicked intention discovery method. It uses a weight agnostic fuzzy interface construction. It is an efficient and reliable computational rational forensics device for web exchange examination, the exposure of malware transactions, and decoded business testimony in real-time. The suggestion is an automatic searching neural-net structure that can execute different duties, such as recognizing zero-day crimes. By automating the spiteful purpose disclosure means from the darknet, the answer reduces the abilities and training wall. It stops many institutions from adequately preserving their most hazardous asset. The system uses two types of datasets - training and prediction sets. The errors are detected using back propagation.

Table 3. Algorithm used to create the dataset evaluate patterns at the earlier stage

#For a sequence of instances, evaluate the attack patterns
For i, sequence in enumerates(dataset):
#Training set is the model that encompasses the attack patterns with the resources affected and initial attack pattern
Training_set= create_model(attack_patterns, resources_affected,initial_patterns)
#prediction set contains the prediction patterns mapped to the attack patterns
Prediction_set= create_model(prediction_patterns, attack_patterns)
#create an attack pattern occurrence duration
Occurrence_set=create_model(attack_patterns, frequency_occurrence)
#create a threshold model that encompasses the attacks occurring beyond the threshold. It maps the attack patterns to the percentage of data/resource loss
Threshold_set=create_model(attack_patterns, percentage_datalost)
#reference model is a set mapping training set with the prediction set
Reference_model=create_model(training_set, prediction_set)

The suggestion considers using the initial attack parameters. It is a set containing the all the patterns of the initial state of the attack. The work also has a set that highlights the amount of resource loss when the attack is launched. Hence the monitoring device can prioritize the attacks based on the occurrence frequency and resource loss. The recommendation provides early detection of the attack by 6.85% compared to previous work. Figure 1 represents the same.

The suggestion is also able to prioritize the attacks and takes appropriate action based of its kind. The recommendation gives 13% increase in securing the resources compared to previous work. Figure 2 depicts the same.

Table 4. Description of the simulated results

Parameters used	Description
Reference_model	25 MB
Training_model	12 MB
Prediction_set	7 MB
Occurrence_set	3 MB
Threshold_set	3.5 MB
Reference_model	2.66 MB
Number of attacks considered	10
Number of devices considered	10
Number of attackers	2
Simulated time	60 ms

Figure 1. Depiction of early detection of the attacks

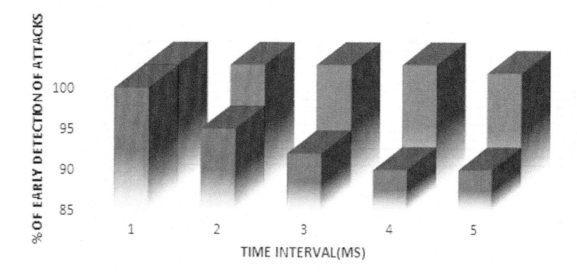

■ (Demertzis, Tsiknas, Takezis, & Iliadis, 2021)　　■ proposed work

CONCLUSION

The previous work adopts an evolving methodology in neural system. It performs a specialized task irrespective of the weighs of the links in the foundation framework. This method equates to the lack of exercises in the structure. The proposal is a new darknet transactions summary. It is a system administration structure for real-time automating of the wicked intention discovery method. It uses a weight agnostic fuzzy interface construction. It is an efficient and reliable computational rational forensics device for web exchange examination, the exposure of malware transactions, and decoded business testimony in real-time. The suggestion is an automatic searching neural-net structure that can execute different duties, such as recognizing zero-day crimes. By automating the spiteful purpose disclosure means from the darknet, the answer reduces the abilities and training wall. It stops many institutions from adequately preserving their most hazardous asset. The system uses two types of datasets - training and prediction sets. The errors are detected using back propagation.

The suggestion work considers mapping the initial stages of attack and the resources damaged due to the attack. It detects the attacks early by 6.85% and 13% of resources are secured compared to the previous work.

Figure 2. Representation of securing the resources based on priority

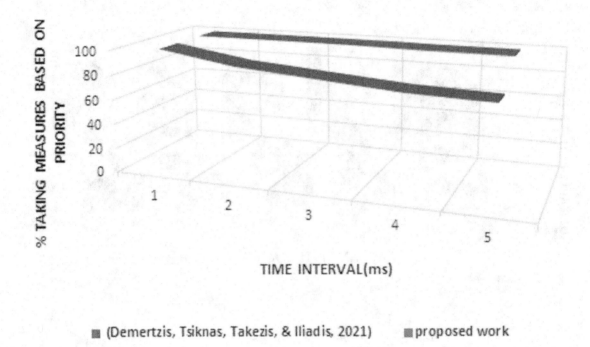

REFERENCES

Almukaynizi, M., Grimm, A., Nunes, E., Shakarian, J., & Shakarian, P. (2017). Predicting cyber threats through hacker social networks in darkweb and deepweb forums. In *Proceedings of the 2017 International Conference of The Computational Social Science Society of the Americas* (pp. 1-7). ACM. 10.1145/3145574.3145590

Ambika, N. (2020). Improved Methodology to Detect Advanced Persistent Threat Attacks. In Quantum Cryptography and the Future of Cyber Security (pp. 184-202). IGI Global.

Ambika, N. (2021). An Improved Solution to Tackle Cyber Attacks. In *Advanced Controllers for Smart Cities* (pp. 15–23). Springer.

Barnum, S. (2012). Standardizing cyber threat intelligence information with the structured threat information expression (stix). *Mitre Corporation*, *11*, 1–22.

Chen, H. (2008). IEDs in the Dark Web: Genre classification of improvised explosive device web pages. In *IEEE International Conference on Intelligence and Security Informatics* (pp. 94-97). IEEE. 10.1109/ISI.2008.4565036

Dehghantanha, A., Conti, M., & Dargahi, T. (2018). *Cyber threat intelligence*. Springer International Publishing. doi:10.1007/978-3-319-73951-9

Demertzis, K., Tsiknas, K., Takezis, D. S., & Iliadis, L. (2021). Darknet traffic big-data analysis and network management for real-time automating of the malicious intent detection process by a weight agnostic neural networks framework. *Electronics (Basel)*, *10*(7), 1–25. doi:10.3390/electronics10070781

Fachkha, C., & Debbabi, M. (2015). Darknet as a source of cyber intelligence: Survey, taxonomy, and characterization. *IEEE Communications Surveys and Tutorials*, *18*(2), 1197–1227. doi:10.1109/COMST.2015.2497690

He, S., He, Y., & Li, M. (2019). Classification of illegal activities on the dark web. In *2nd International Conference on Information Science and Systems* (pp. 73-78). ACM. 10.1145/3322645.3322691

Kadoguchi, M., Hayashi, S., Hashimoto, M., & Otsuka, A. (2019). Exploring the dark web for cyber threat intelligence using machine leaning. In *IEEE International Conference on Intelligence and Security Informatics (ISI)* (pp. 200-202). IEEE. 10.1109/ISI.2019.8823360

Karaman, M., Catalkaya, H., Gerehan, A. Z., & Goztepe, K. (2016). Cyber operation planning and operational design. *Cyber-Security and Digital Forensics*, 21.

Kawaguchi, Y., & Ozawa, S. (2019). Exploring and identifying malicious sites in dark web using machine learning. In *International Conference on Neural Information Processing* (pp. 319-327). Springer. 10.1007/978-3-030-36718-3_27

Marin, E., Almukaynizi, M., Nunes, E., Shakarian, J., & Shakarian, P. (2018). *Predicting hacker adoption on darkweb forums using sequential rule mining. In Intl Conf on Parallel & Distributed Processing with Applications, Ubiquitous Computing & Communications, Big Data & Cloud Computing, Social Computing & Networking, Sustainable Computing & Communications (ISPA/IUCC/BDCloud/Social-Com/SustainCom)*. IEEE.

Mattern, T., Felker, J., Borum, R., & Bamford, G. (2014). Operational levels of cyber intelligence. *International Journal of Intelligence and CounterIntelligence*, *27*(4), 702–719. doi:10.1080/08850607.2014.924811

Miller, S., El-Bahrawy, A., Dittus, M., Graham, M., & Wright, J. (2020). Predicting Drug Demand with Wikipedia Views: Evidence from Darknet Markets. In *Proceedings of the web conference* (pp. 2669-2675). ACM. 10.1145/3366423.3380022

Mungekar, A., Solanki, Y., & Swarnalatha, R. (2020). Augmentation of a SCADA based firewall against foreign hacking devices. *Iranian Journal of Electrical and Computer Engineering*, *10*(2), 1359–1366. doi:10.11591/ijece.v10i2.pp1359-1366

Samtani, S., Li, W., Benjamin, V., & Chen, H. (2021). Informing Cyber Threat Intelligence through Dark Web Situational Awareness: The AZSecure Hacker Assets Portal. *Digital Threats: Research and Practice*, *2*(4), 1–10. doi:10.1145/3450972

Sarkar, S., Almukaynizi, M., Shakarian, J., & Shakarian, P. (2019). Mining user interaction patterns in the darkweb to predict enterprise cyber incidents. *Social Network Analysis and Mining*, *9*(1), 1–28. doi:10.100713278-019-0603-9

Schäfer, M., Fuchs, M., Strohmeier, M., Engel, M., Liechti, M., & Lenders, V. (2019). BlackWidow: Monitoring the dark web for cyber security information. *11th International Conference on Cyber Conflict (CyCon)*, 1-21. 10.23919/CYCON.2019.8756845

Tounsi, W., & Rais, H. (2018). A survey on technical threat intelligence in the age of sophisticated cyber attacks. *Computers & Security, 72*, 212–233. doi:10.1016/j.cose.2017.09.001

Trifonov, R., Manolov, S., Yoshinov, R., Tsochev, G., Nedev, S., & Pavlova, G. (2018). Operational Cyber Threat Intelligence supported by Artificial Intelligence methods. *International Conference on Information Technologies (InfoTech-2018)*, 20-21.

Yadav, T., & Rao, A. M. (2015). Technical aspects of cyber kill chain. In *International Symposium on Security in Computing and Communication* (pp. 438-452). Springer. 10.1007/978-3-319-22915-7_40

Zhang, H., & Zou, F. (2020). A Survey of the Dark Web and Dark Market Research. In *IEEE 6th International Conference on Computer and Communications (ICCC)* (pp. 1694-1705). IEEE.

Chapter 3
An Efficient Technique for Passive Image Forgery Detection Using Computational Intelligence

Sonam Mehta
Devi Ahilya Vishwavidyalaya, India

Pragya Shukla
Devi Ahilya Vishwavidyalaya, India

ABSTRACT

This chapter proposes a scheme for the identification of copy-move forgery by inducing adaptive over-segmentation and matching of feature points with the help of discrete cosine transform (DCT). Copy-move forging is an image tampering technique that involves concealing undesired things or recreating desirable elements within the same image to create modified tampered images. Traditional methods added a large number of false matches. To conquer this problem, a new algorithm is proposed to incorporate an adaptive threshold method. So, the block feature matching mechanism is used, and the matching feature blocks classify the feature points using patch matching and Hough transform. Forged regions are detected with the help of the newly proposed algorithm. The results of the proposed method show that it can substantially reduce the number of false matches that lead to improvements in both performance and computational costs. This demonstrates the suggested algorithm's resistance against a variety of known attacks. Comparative results are presented for a better evaluation.

INTRODUCTION

Powerful tools for digital image processing like Photoshop, which creates digital forgeries from one or more than one images, is fairly simple. Digital image forgery becoming increasingly easy to execute due to the development of computer technology and image processing software. Digital images, however,

DOI: 10.4018/978-1-6684-3942-5.ch003

are the common source of knowledge, and so genuine digital pictures are becoming a crucial problem (Qureshi and Deriche, 2014). Forged images need to be detected to restrict spreading of malicious images through dark web. Crime under dark web needs to be investigated to prevent illegal activities and trouble. There are onion websites which could make use of tampered images. In recent years, researchers have started to concentrate on the digital image manipulation problem. Digital images plays important role in intelligent systems,civil services, judgments, healthcare, sports, education, defense work etc. For security purpose, tampered images needs to be detected. Of the current forms of image interference, copy move forgeries or image splicing are typical manipulations of a digital image, i.e. pasting one or more copied section of a picture to certain sections of the same picture or to another image (Sharma and Nandi, 2014). In copy move forgery, the parts of image are copied from the file and pasted in the same source file. The noise variable, color characteristic and other essential properties are consistent with the rest of the file (Agarwal and Verma, 2019). In past years, many image forgery detection methods were proposed to detect copy-move forgeries. The detection of copy moving forgery techniques can be categorized into two types: feature key point-based algorithms and block-based algorithms. Block-based detection techniques split the input images into blocks of image. Then, by finding similarity between image pixel blocks or transforming coefficients, the manipulated region can be identified. Key point-based forgery detection approaches were introduced where image main points are identified and balanced over the whole picture to avoid any image transformations thus detecting identical areas (Chauhan et al., 2016).

Below figures shows a glimpse of copy-move based forgery. The original image is displayed in Figure 1, while its fake counterpart is shown in Figure 2 where the branch of the tree is copied and placed at the left part of the image. In this work, we have suggested a novel forgery identification scheme. This scheme utilizes an adaptive over-segmentation technique, feature extraction and feature matching mechanism. We have proposed an algorithm based upon block forgery method. The features are extricated as block features from individual image sub block rather than using traditional key point-based method. The key point based method extracts features out of the whole image. Block features are then balanced to find the identified forged pixels, which could suggest the potential forged areas. We have proposed an efficient algorithm, to identify forged areas in an image.

Related Work

The majority of approaches utilized in copy-move image forgery detection are split into categories like: block methods and key point methods (Yadav and Dongre, 2017). The input image is segmented into normal or fixed-size blocks, which are overlapped and then found (Thakur et al., 2016). Further-more, there are differences in how such methods are implemented, such as the process approach utilized to characterize the blocks. The image is separated into blocks, and forgery is detected using the Scale Invariant Feature Transform. The Euclid distance between the blocks is then calculated to find the matching area in the image (Kurien et al., 2019). The copy-move method of forgery detection, which uses quantized Discrete Cosine Transform (DCT) coefficients to ensure that picture blocks are mirrored, is a superior block detection methodology.

In (Elaskily et al., 2020), authors proposed automated copy-move falsification focused on a profound approach to learning. A deep Copy-Move Forgery Detection (CMFD) network of copy movements is particularly planned. CNN is designed to acquire hierarchical representations of features from the reference images used to distinguish distorted and initial pictures. To reduce the data, they used Global Average Pooling (GAP) layer in CNN layers, authors used 2D filters for processing of input image in

Figure 1. Original image

varying layers for feature generation. In (Agarwal and Verma, 2019), authors proposed work in which image is partitioned using SLIC clustering method. VGGNet have been applied for feature extraction to construct depth of pixel of image. Then ADM technique, a patch matching method, is employed for detection of the fake image.

In (Wang et al., 2020), authors worked on the approach in which they extracted key points by employing the FALoG filter and matched keypoints using Rg2NN algorithm. Candidate clustering was used to eliminate false matches. In [24], Yang et al. used copy-move falsification detection techniques (CMFD) to extract picture keypoints utilizing an adaptive uniform distribution threshold and binary robust invariant scalable key-points descriptor. For finding forged regions, they employed mean residual normalized intensity correlation. A hybrid method was introduced in which extracted keypoints are compared to detect a copy move fault in a picture in (Mangat et al., 2020). The proposed method is divided into two

Figure 2. Fake image

stages: first, the keypoints are replaced by utilizing SIFT, and then the blocks are retrieved using kernel PCA. In the second stage, the keypoints are contrasted by utilizing the SVM help vector. In (Kurien et al., 2019), authors analyzed comparison between copy-move forgery detection methods - using Scale Invariant Feature Transform (SIFT) and Discrete Cosine Transform (DCT). In terms of accuracy and precision, the Keypoint based method by utilizing SIFT was the most useful.

Work based upon passive forensic method by usingthe locality preserving projection (LPP) for copy move forgery in the same image (CAO et al., 2015). To perform detection, they calculated similarity matrix which shows adjacent relation between original and tampered image by reducing small block dimension. Convolutional Neural Network (CNN) based approach to detect of fake images was done (Maher et al., 2020). The algorithm used is based upon feature matching along with deep learning. Trigonometric transform in 1D and 2D and Discrete Wavelet Transform (DWT) is performed on the input images. Implementation of feature extraction is done using sequential pairs of convolution and pooling.

Comparison between different image forgery techniques was presented (Yadav and Dongre, 2017). They presented different approaches of copy-move forgery detection methods like block and key point based techniques. Discrete Cosine Transform (DCT) based algorithm uses DCT coefficients which is a strong mechanism to work on images since it decreases difficulty of similarity and cost of calculation work is also reduced.

Discrete Cosine Transform (DCT) was used to detect tampered images. DCT coefficients are used to represent each block (Maind et al., 2014). They introduced new parameters to remove the false matches and applied morphological operations to give the final output. This technique is based upon Principal Component Analysis (PCA) that is applicable on small blocks. Inspite of various research in image forgery detection techniques, there is no technique developed which could detect all kinds of forger- ies. Also, it has been noticed that some techniques gave much better accuracy but their computational complexity is very high.

In (Kang and Cheng, 2010), authors came out with an improved DCT-based method which uses improved Singular value decomposition technique. For matching blocks of the image, they used cor- relation coefficients. It makes the algorithm more effective and fewer features to represent each block in image. PCA feature extraction has been applied to the image blocks, but is the first to extend a key component analysis to a limited fixed scale of the image blocks in order to obtain a reduced dimensional representation. The comparative study of various forgery detection techniques is shown in the Table 1.

CATEGORIZATION OF IMAGE FORGERY TECHNIQUES

Active Approach

Watermarking and digital signatures are the active approaches of image forgery (Yadav and Dongre, 2017). Watermarking deliberately manipulates the identity of the owner (source) by inserting a specific pattern or copyright information. It hides the crucial information in the image like id or any logo of the company etc. Two primary requirements for active image authentication are sensitivity and robustness. Digital signature is a mathematical process which verifies the authenticity of the document by inducing a digital code.

Table 1. Comparative study of other existing methods

Methods	Objective(s)	Limitation/Features	Authors
SURF feature extraction and SVM	Copy move forgery detection	Forgery detection with video images is yet to be done using object recognition.	(Dhivya et al.,2020)
LoG filter and Rg2NN algorithm	Copy move forgery detection	Does not differentiate between source and target parts of forged image.	(Wang et al.,2019)
SURF and RANSAC	Copy move forgery detection	Computational complexity is high.	(Yang et al.,2019)
SIFT, SURF, DCT	Copy move forgery detection	Comparative study	(Yadav and Dongre,2017)
Trignometric transforms and CNN	Copy move forgery detection	Improved accuracy but high computational complexity	(Al_Azrak et al.,2019_
Capsule-Forensics-Noise	Image and Video forgery detection	Cannot detect adversarial machine attacks	(Nguyen et al., 2019)
Locality preserving Projection	Copy move forgery detection	Longer detection time	(Cao et al.,2015)
Block based and Key point based	Copy move forgery attack detection	Comparison of various forgery techniques	(Kaur and Kumar, 2015)

Figure 3. Categories of image forgery techniques

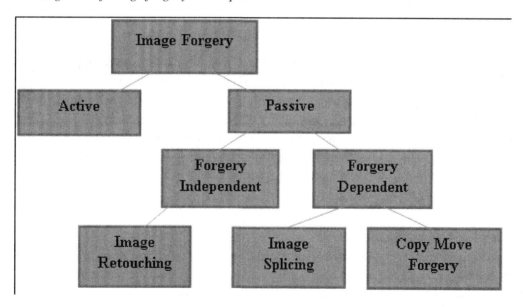

Passive Approach

While various standard approaches are available that can accurately identify forgery, there is no specific approach that will manage all such situations. Passive Approach is a process in which image itself is analyzed with no prior information. In passive approach, internal features of the image are extracted to detect forgery. Tampered image is detected based upon some inconsistency in the image.

Figure 4. Example of image splicing

Categories of Passive Approach

Image Splicing

Image splicing is a process of forgery in which image is cropped and multiple images are merged to create a combined final image (Tanzeela et al., 2013). This procedure is more effective when producing manipulated pictures. A variety of sharp transformations can be added in a spliced image. Sources involve the usage of manipulated photos in a variety of notorious news stories or social media posts. Photo splicing is done in subsequent post-processing methods such as the smoothing of pixel borders.

Image Retouching

Photo retouching incorporates or eliminates something from the photograph to improve the picture's functionality. It may enhance or reduces the image features which alter the image appearance. Certain defects of the image may also be improved through image retouching. This method is common to esthetic, industrial consumers and degrades the quality of the product (Tanzeela et al., 2013). Typically, it is famous in news or fake meaasages photo editors, where they seek to render the subject more appealing by improving those attributes. Image Retouching is known to be less dangerous relative to other forgery techniques. Removing blemishes from a product picture will be a brilliant illustration of the retouching process (Birajdar and Mankar, 2013).

Copy Move Forgery

Copy Move Forgery is a forgery dependent detection technique in which some part of an image is copied. Then this copied part is pasted to other part of the image i.e. copy, transfer and paste a similar area of file. The identical area represents the same picture area so the image characteristics remains the same (Qureshi and Deriche, 2014).

Feature extraction is achieved by employing image processing methods, evaluating the pixel size, and measuring texture and hash values in the image.

PROPOSED METHODOLOGY

We proposed an efficient algorithm that can achieve great performance with low computational complexity. This algorithm is proposed to detect tampered or forged image and it outperforms the existing techniques.

Figure 5. Example of image retouching

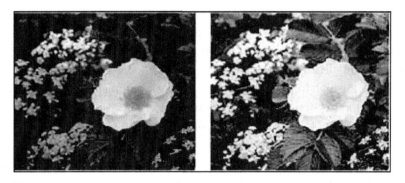

Figure 6. Example of copy move forgery

The framework is shown in the Figure 7. Blocks of images are used for the study of falsification in this process. Images are separated into different sections instead of continuously evaluating the whole picture.

Figure 7. Proposed framework for fake image detection

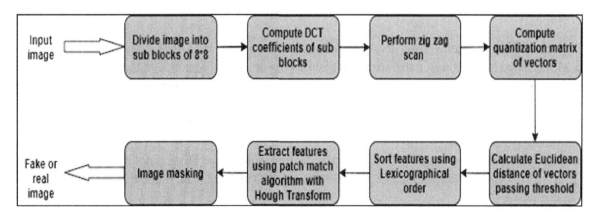

Following steps describe the proposed algorithm which has been adapted to detect fake images:

1. Preprocessing: Choose input image and divide it into 8 (8x8) blocks because it makes it possible to detect forgeries in smaller areas (16 blocks can also be preferred to reduce noise).
2. Adaptive Over-thresholding with DCT: We applied Adaptive Over-thresholding with Discrete Cosine Transform (DCT) onto the blocks of an image. Then corresponding coefficients of DCT in the image are computed. The blocks are then represented with fewer coefficients.
3. Scanning: Remove the high frequency region by zigzag scanning to the result of DCT. The purpose of this is to obtain the low-frequency part in the image.
4. Feature Extraction: We obtain a vector of 1x64 after zigzag scanning, taking the first 16 (lower frequency part) elements of this vector, we do not deal with the rest. This part is divided into a quantization matrix or a determined constant (such as 16). Vector is calculated with the determined number of neighboring vectors. The vectors representing each block are ordered one after the other and we get a matrix, the size of this matrix is "16xblocknumber."

Thus, we have made similar vectors close to each other, and in order not to lose which vector represents which block, we have added the starting coordinates of the blocks to the end of the 1x16 vectors V to make them 1x16, V is denoted as:

$$V = [S1, S2, \ldots\ldots\ldots S16] \tag{1}$$

Where S1, S2,.... are the vectors of the corresponding pixels in the image.

5. 5. Feature Matching & Filtering: After that Euclidean distance is calculated as it works faster in evaluation. Vectors that pass the similarity (Euclid) threshold are also passed through the distance threshold filter. Threshold is applied to filter out bad patch matches which helps in effective performance. Let coordinates of block pairs of image are (u1, v1) and (u2, v2). The Euclidean distance is calculated as:

$$d = ((u1-v2)^2 + (u1-v2)^2)^{1/2} \tag{2}$$

Lexicographical order is used to sort similar features of the image part. After that patch match algorithm along with Hough transform is applied for resorting the features of the image obtained by lexicographical ordering. Hough transform finds matches which are based upon low level geometric features such as edges and curves and patch matching works faster comparatively. Collinear points in the image generate curves through Hough transform. In patch matching, the fine patch matches are found through random sampling.

Shift vectors whose frequency is higher than the threshold, those block pairs are marked as forged region. Let coordinates of block pairs of image are (u1, v1) and (u2, v2), their shift vector (SV) is determined as:

$$SV = (SV1, SV2) = (u1-v2, u1-v2) \tag{3}$$

So, If the distance between the two blocks is not large enough, it is eliminated.

Subsequently, two offset images are generated as an outcome which is stored in the form of matrices of same sizes. The offset images indicate the copied and pasted parts of the forged image.

6.   Post processing: In final phase, masking of image is done for binary evaluation. Black part shows background of the image and white part shows forged regions in the image.

Result Analysis

We have performed the investigations to calculate the results of the suggested method as compared to the state-of-the-art models. The dataset taken for this proposed work for fake image detection is used from MICC-F220 dataset (Yang et al., 2019) and random image dataset comprising of pictures taken from web sources. MICC-F220 dataset contains 220 images out of which 110 are real images and 110 are tampered images. And 200 image sets were taken from database of random web images. Images are of different types like historical, text, nature, sceneries, object based, etc. Proposed algorithm works on the input image irrespective of its characteristics like size and dimension. Any image could be likely as input to the algorithm for its fake detection because algorithm can detect forgery in any given image. Choosing the right value for threshold plays an important role in copy move forgery detection since it reduces the matched vectors and the blocks whose shift vectors are computed. Our method provides great flexibility in the choice of the threshold parameter depending upon the pixel values of the input image.

The tests have been done on a machine having Intel core i5 8th generation processor, GPU driver is of 4 GB, 64 bits processor, RAM size is 8 GB, Windows 10 is used as Operating System. The newly proposed algorithm's code is written in python language by Python 3.5.

Following parameters have been used for checking the performance of newly proposed algorithm:

$$\text{Precision} = \frac{\text{TP} + \text{FP}}{\text{TP}} \tag{4}$$

$$Accuracy = \frac{\text{TP} + \text{TN}}{\left(\text{TP} + \text{FP} + \text{TN} + \text{FN}\right)} \tag{5}$$

$$\text{Recall} = \frac{\text{TP}}{\text{TP} + \text{FN}} \tag{6}$$

Where,
TP (number of True Positive): Forged Image have been detected as tampered
TN (number of True Negative): Original Image is detected as original
FP (number of False Positive): Original image is recognized as fake
FN (number of False Negative): Forged image is recognized as original

Figure 8. Original image

$$\text{F1 Score} = 2 * \frac{\text{Precision*Recall}}{\text{Precision} + \text{Recall}} \qquad (7)$$

Precision shows how the measured values are near among all the values while accuracy shows how the experimental results are more near to an exact value. F1 score gives test of the accuracy of the algorithm. In Figure 8, original image is shown and fake image is shown in Figure 9 where a small squared part from the same image have been copied and pasted at right area of the shown image.

Figure 9. Fake image

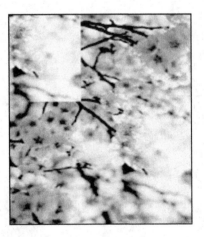

Comparison of different existing models with the proposed technique is given in Table 2. The proposed algorithm gives precision of maximum 0.96. While precision value of SVM was 0.86. Similarly, improved accuracy has been achieved with our approach which is 0.95. Also, F1 score of proposed algorithm is 0.95 which is much better than F1 scores of Support Vector Machine (SVM) and other existing methods as shown in the Table 2. The ground truth i.e. the detected forged area of this image is shown in Figure

Figure 10. Ground Truth: shown copy and paste area of detected forged image

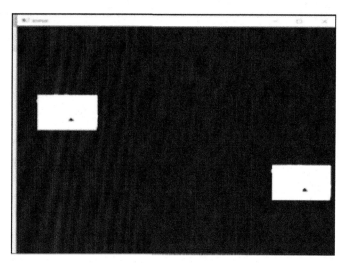

Table 2. Comparison between existing and proposed methods

Method	Precision	Recall	F1 Score	Accuracy
Proposed Method	0.96	0.94	0.92	0.95
SVM (**Dhivya et al., 2020**)	0.86	0.81	0.83	0.82
SIFT (**Kurien et al., 2019**)	0.95	0.61	0.74	0.74
SVM with KPCA (**Mangat et al., 2016**)	0.81	0.70	0.84	0.70
Neural Network (**Mangat et al., 2016**)	0.60	0.65	0.63	0.60

10. White part shows regions which are copied and then pasted in the same image. In this way, copy move forgery has been detected efficiently through the proposed algorithm.

Comparison between existing methods and proposed method in respect of accuracy,precion, recall and F1 score:

Figure 11. Comparison of precision

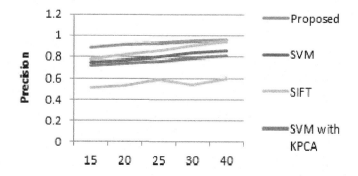

Figure 12. Comparison of recall

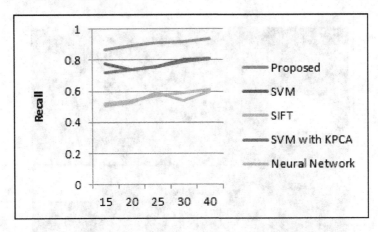

Figure 13. Comparison of F1 score

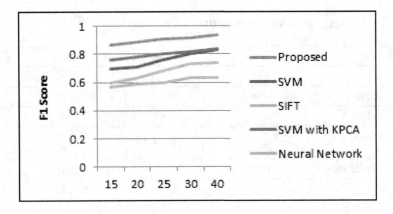

Figure 14. Comparison of accuracy

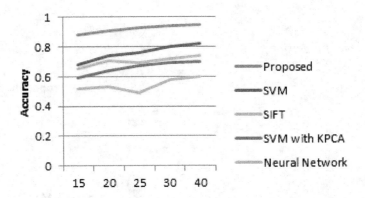

CONCLUSION

We have suggested a new identification algorithm for copy move forgery with adaptive over-segmentation and matching mechanism. The block based feature matching mechanism is suggested, in which the matching feature blocks are used to classify the feature points. In addition, we suggested an algorithm for the detection of the forged regions. The outcome of proposed method is analyzed based upon the investigations done on the image datasets. Results show that algorithm detects fake images more accurately with lesser number of false matches. Also forged detected areas of image are displayed to show the copy-move forgery. Future work could lead to improvement by reducing more number of false matches that have been encountered. Moreover, experiments may be conducted on more challenging image datasets to further enhance the performance of suggested algorithm since proposed model gives less accurate results for very small copied parts of the image sometimes.

REFERENCES

Agarwal,, R., & Verma,, O. P. (2019). An efficient method for image forgery detection based on trigonometric transforms and deep learning. *Multimedia Tools and Applications*.

Birajdar, G., & Mankar, V. (2013). Digital image forgery detection using passive techniques: A survey. *Digital Investigation*, *10*(3), 226–245. doi:10.1016/j.diin.2013.04.007

Cao, G., Chen, Y., Zong, G., & Chen, Y. (n.d.). Detection Of Copy-Move Forgery in Digital Image Using Locality Preserving Projections. *8th International Congress On Image And Signal Processing (Cisp)*. 10.1109/CISP.2015.7407949

Dhivya, S., Sangeetha, J., & Sudhakar, B. (2020). Copy-move forgery detection using SURF feature extraction and SVM supervised learning technique. *Soft Computing*, *24*(19), 14429–14440. doi:10.100700500-020-04795-x

Elaskily, M., Aslan, H., Elshakankiry, O., Faragallah, O., El-Samie, F., & Dessouky, M. (2020). A novel deep learning framework for copy-move forgery detection in images. *Multimedia Tools and Applications*, *79*(27-28), 19167–19192. Advance online publication. doi:10.100711042-020-08751-7

Fridrich, J. (1999). Methods for Tamper Detection in Digital Images. *Proc. of ACM Workshop on Multimedia and Security*, 19–23.

Gonzalez, R., & Woods, R. (n.d.). *Digital Image Processing* (2nd ed.). Addison-Wesley.

Kang, L., & Cheng, X. (2010). Copy-Move Forgery Detection in Digital Image. In *3rd International Congress on Image and Signal Processing*. IEEE Computer Society. 10.1109/CISP.2010.5648249

Kaur, G., & Kumar, M. (2015, September). Study of Various Copy Move Forgery Attack Detection In Digital Images. *International Journal Of Research In Computer Applications And Robotics*, *3*(9), 30–34. doi:10.5120/21082-3764

Kaur, M., & Sharma, R. (2013). Optimization of Copy Move Forgery Detection Technique. *International Journal of Advanced Research in Computer Science and Software Engineering*, *3*(4).

Kurien, N. A., Danya, S., Ninan, D., Raju, C. H., & David, J. Accurate and Efficient Copy-Move Forgery Detection. *9th International Conference on Advances in Computing and Communication (ICACC).* , (2019).10.1109/ICACC48162.2019.8986157

Maher, F., Azrak, A., Sedik, A., Dessowky, M., Ghada, M., Banby, E., Khalaf, A., Elkorany, A., Fathi, E., & Samie, E. An efficient method for image forgery detection based on trigonometric transforms and deep learning. *Multimedia Tools and Applications.* Advance online publication. doi:10.100711042-019-08162-3,2020

Mahor, V., Rawat, R., Telang, S., Garg, B., Mukhopadhyay, D., & Palimkar, P. (2021, September). Machine Learning based Detection of Cyber Crime Hub Analysis using Twitter Data. In *2021 IEEE 4th International Conference on Computing, Power and Communication Technologies (GUCON)* (pp. 1-5). IEEE. 10.1109/GUCON50781.2021.9573736

Maind, R., Khade, A., & Chitre, D. (2014). Image Copy Move Forgery Detection Using Block Representing Method. *International Journal Of Soft Computing And Engineering, 4*(2).

Mangat, S. S., & Kaur, H. (2016). Improved copy-move forgery detection in image by feature extraction with KPCA and adaptive method. *2nd International Conference on Next Generation Computing Technologies (NGCT).* 10.1109/NGCT.2016.7877501

Nguyen, H. H., Yamagishi, J., & Echizen, I. (2019). Capsule-Forensics: Using Capsule Networks To Detect Forged Images And Videos. *IEEE International Conference on Acoustics, Speech and Signal Processing (ICASSP).* 10.1109/ICASSP.2019.8682602

Qiao, M., Sung, A., Liu, Q., & Ribeiro, B. (2011). A novel approach for detection of copy-move forgery. *Fifth International Conference on ADVCOMP (Advanced Engineering Computing and Applications in Sciences.*

Qureshi, A., & Deriche, M. (2014). *A review on copy move image forgery detection techniques.* IEEE SSD International Multi-Conference on Systems, Signals and Devices. doi:10.1109/SSD.2014.6808907

Rajawat, A. S., Rawat, R., Barhanpurkar, K., Shaw, R. N., & Ghosh, A. (2021). Vulnerability Analysis at Industrial Internet of Things Platform on Dark Web Network Using Computational Intelligence. *Computationally Intelligent Systems and their Applications*, 39-51.

Rawat, R., Mahor, V., Chirgaiya, S., & Rathore, A. S. (2021). Applications of Social Network Analysis to Managing the Investigation of Suspicious Activities in Social Media Platforms. In *Advances in Cybersecurity Management* (pp. 315–335). Springer. doi:10.1007/978-3-030-71381-2_15

Sharma, B., & Nandi, G. (2014). A Study on Digital Image Forgery Detection. *International Journal of Advanced Research in Computer Science and Software Engineering, 4*(11).

Thakur, S., Kaur, R., Chadha, R., & Kaur, J. (2016). A Review Paper on Image Forgery Detection in Image Processing. *IOSR Journal of Computer Engineering, 18*(4), 86-89.

Tanzeela, Q., Hayat, K., Khan, S. U., & Madani, S. (2013). Survey on blind image forgery detection. *IET Image Processing.*

Wang, X. Y., Wang, C., Wang, L., Jiao, L. X., Yang, H. Y., & Niu. (2020). A fast and high accurate image copy-move forgery detection approach. Multidimensional Systems and Signal Processing. Advance online publication. doi:10.1007/s11045-019-00688-x

Wu, Y., Abd-Almageed, W., & Natarajan, P. (2018). Detecting copy-move image forgery with source/target localization. *Proceedings of the European Conference on Computer Vision (ECCV)*, 168–184. 10.1007/978-3-030-01231-1_11

Yadav, J., & Dongre, N. (2017). Analysis of Copy-Move Forgery Detection in Digital Image. *International Journal of Engineering Development and Research*, 5(1).

Yang, H. Y., Qi, S. R., Niu, Y., & Wang, X. Y. (2019). Copy-move forgery detection based on adaptive keypoints extraction and matching. *Multimedia Tools and Applications*, 78(24), 34585–34612. Advance online publication. doi:10.100711042-019-08169-w

Section 2
Cyber Terrorism: The Emerging Challenges

Chapter 4
Machine Learning Models in Detecting Cyber Crimes and Cyber Terrorism in India

Ravindrababu Jaladanki

P. V. P. Siddhartha Institute of Technology, India

Syed Imran Patel

Bahrain Training Institute, Higher Education Council, Ministry of Education, Bahrain

Imran Khan

Bahrain Training Institute, Higher Education Council, Ministry of Education, Bahrain

Karim Ishtiaque Ahmed Mohammed

Bahrain Training Institute, Higher Education Council, Ministry of Education, Bahrain

Thenmozhi M.

Vellore Institute of Technology, India

Arun Kumar Tripathi

iD https://orcid.org/0000-0001-5138-2190

KIET Group of Institutions, India

ABSTRACT

Cyber-physical systems (CPSs), which are more susceptible to a range of cyber-attacks, play an increasingly crucial role in power system security today. Digital communication has become a global phenomenon in the last decade. Sadly, cyber terrorism is on the rise, and abusers are able to hide behind the anonymity of the internet. A hybrid model for detecting instances of cyber terrorism in Twitter datasets was proposed in this study after a survey of prominent classification algorithms. Logistic regression, linear support vector classifier, and naive bayes are the methods utilised for evaluation. Four metrics were used to evaluate the performance of the classifiers in experiments: precision, F1, accuracy, and recall. The findings show how well each of the algorithms worked, along with the metrics that went along with them. Linear support vector classifier (SVC) was the least effective, while hybrid model (EM) was the most successful.

INTRODUCTION

Electronic networks and computer technologies are weaponized in cyber terrorism. There must be a

DOI: 10.4018/978-1-6684-3942-5.ch004

terrorist component in order to designate an attack on the Internet as cyber terrorism. There is no comprehensive definition of cyber terrorism, which means that law enforcement, criminal administration, and academicians will be unable to stop the growing threat of cyber terrorism if they don't have a clear understanding of what it is. Technicality, or whether it should be regarded as criminal or technological, is the most challenging part of deciphering cyber terrorism. Barry Collin developed the term 'cyber terrorism' in the late 1980s by combining the two linguistic aspects of cyberspace and terrorism into one word. Barry Collin originated the term "cyber terrorism" in 1997 (Al-Khater, 2020). A cyber-terrorist attack, according to him, is the result of "cybernetics" meeting "terrorism."

Many notable researchers and organisations have attempted to define and explain what cyber terrorism is, despite the lack of a universally recognised workable explanation. Cyber terrorism has been defined in a variety of ways, including the ones listed below: The National Infrastructure Protection Center (NIPC) defines cyber-terrorism as an act of criminal violence, death, and devastation committed via computers with the intention of influencing government policy (Rawat et al., 2021).

Attacks on Internet businesses can be classified as either cybercrime or cyber terrorism, depending on whether the purpose is purely economic or ideological. A cyber terrorism attack can only be perpetrated by people, groups, or organisations that are unaffiliated with one another (Sivakumar, 2021). International law regulates and punishes all forms of state-sponsored cyber warfare.

When it comes to "cyber terrorism," Pollitt defines it as "the premeditated political-motivated attack on information systems, computer programmes, and data that result in harm to non-combatant targets by subnational groups or clandestine operations."

A growing number of people are aware that cyber terrorists are capable of inflicting great harm on the world because of the ever-increasing reliance of modern civilizations on computers and the Internet (Rawat et al., 2021). At the point where the physical and virtual worlds merge, cyber terrorists strike key information infrastructures using ones and zeros. Criminology theory has rarely been used in research on cyber terrorists; instead, academics and government agencies have focused on providing atheoretical descriptions of the problem in the past (Rawat et al., 2011). Cyber terrorists are not a well-known group, nor are cyber terror attacks common or easy to recognise. This presents a significant challenge for academics. Even more difficult to distinguish between cyber terrorism, cybercrime, military-political cyberattacks and international information security is to identify the motivations that separate these concepts (Amir, 2020). Without motivation, it is impossible to legally separate these concepts because one cannot qualify what is happening as a criminal or terrorist act. If the motivations aren't explicitly stated in the applied legal definition, actions of cyber terror may be wrongly categorised (and maybe prosecuted) as cybercrimes.

Cyber Terrorism Attack Types

Cyber terrorists use a variety of methods to carry out cyber terrorism attacks. "Simple unstructured," "advance-structured," and "complex-coordinated" are the three types of cyber terrorism that can be studied at the Naval Postgraduate School in Monterey, California.

- **Simple-Unstructured:** The ability to use third-party tools to perform rudimentary hacks on specific systems (Alkesh Bharati, 2018). Target analysis, command and control, and learning capacity are all lacking in this form of organisation.

- **Advanced-Structured:** Attacks on various systems or networks, as well as the capacity to alter or construct fundamental hacking tools, is required (Foroutan, 2017). In addition to basic target analysis and command and control skills, the organization's capacity to learn is low.
- **Complex-Coordinated:** Coordination of attacks against integrated and heterogeneous defences that can cause massive disruptions. An advanced hacking tool is at the disposal of terrorists. They're also quite good at analysing targets and running commands (Hassen Mohammed Alsafi, 2019). They also have a great deal of experience in the field of organisational learning.

Figure 1. Types of cyberterrorism

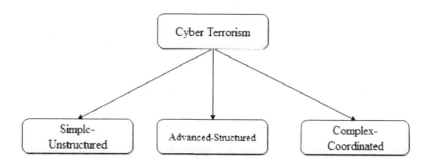

Dark Web

The word "black web" has a sinister ring to it, and for good reason. Websites that aren't accessible through standard online browsing are found in a section of the internet known as the "dark web." In order to find these hidden sites, you must use browsers and search engines that are specifically intended to do so (Rawat et al., 2021).

It's called the "dark web" because it's hidden from search engines like Google. Use of specialised browsers such as the Tor Browser is required to access the black web. When compared to ordinary web-sites, the dark web offers significantly greater levels of privacy and anonymity (Rawat et al., 2021). The term "dark web" refers to unindexed, encrypted content on the internet. To access the black web, users must use specialised browsers such as Tor Browser. When searching the dark web, you'll find sites that use non-public internet data, such as bank account and email passwords, and databases. Users of the dark web are able to protect their anonymity and express themselves without fear of repercussion. Illicit and unethical behaviours are also related with it.

RELATED WORK

Examples of cybercrime include crimes committed using computers or communication tools, as well as crimes committed because of the widespread use of computers. For example, child pornography and cyberstalking are common forms of cybercrime as arc identity theft and other forms of cyber laundering as well as credit card fraud and cyber terrorism (Rawat et al., 2021). For the most part, they result in a breach of personal privacy or security or in harm to public or government property. This paper, therefore, focuses on cybercrime detection and prevention methods in great detail. First, it examines the many types of cybercrime and explains the dangers they pose to computer systems' privacy and security. Then, it explains how cybercriminals could go about perpetrating these crimes against individuals, organisations, and even entire societies. It also examines the current methods for detecting and preventing cybercrime. It objectively assesses the strengths and weaknesses of each technique and critically evaluates its weaknesses (Rawat et al., 2021). Finally, it makes suggestions for the creation of a cybercrime detection model that is more effective than the already used strategies at spotting criminal activity.

Increasing crime rates and the number of criminals have sparked a great deal of anxiety about security, thus the major goal of police authorities is to prevent and identify crime before it occurs. In order to combat crime, modern technologies such as closed-circuit television (CCTV) are commonly installed in both private and public spaces; however these systems require human oversight in order to be effective. It's difficult for a human to keep track of multiple monitors at once. It causes a lot of mistakes. For this reason, P. Sivakumar et al came up with a Deep Learning Algorithm-based Real-Time Crime Detection Technique that watches live video feeds and notifies a nearby Cybercrime Admin when a crime is taking place at the given time and location (Rawat et al., 2021). YOLO is the object-detection algorithm we use in this paper. At 45 frames per second, our architecture can process images in real time.

The modern world is completely reliant on the internet for just about everything. With each passing day, the use of cyberspace is increasing. Everyone in the world is using the Internet more and more each day. As a result, cyber dangers and cybercrimes are becoming more prevalent. The criminal action carried out over the Internet is referred to as 'cyber danger'. The methods used by cybercriminals to circumvent security measures are evolving all the time. To identify zero-day and sophisticated assaults, conventional methods are ineffective. The detection and combat of cybercrime and cyber threats have so far necessitated the development of numerous machine learning approaches. This work by Shaukat et al., 2020 aims to examine some of the most often used machine learning algorithms for detecting some of the most dangerous cyber threats. Deep belief networks, decision trees, and support vector machines are the three main machine learning approaches they study (SVMs). The effectiveness of several machine learning algorithms in detecting spam, intrusions, and viruses was evaluated using widely used and benchmark datasets.

Effective cybercrime intervention necessitates an understanding of the many steps involved. Creating these supply networks, on the other hand, necessitates lengthy, labour-intensive manual labour. The supply chains of cybercrime forums may be efficiently extracted using a method based on machine learning and graph analysis that Bhalerao et al, 2020 have proposed. Over the baselines of 11 percent and 5 percent, our supply chain recognition system can discover 33 percent and 42 percent relevant chains in prominent English and Russian forums, respectively. Understanding and weakening the criminal activity of these forums can be aided by an examination of supply chains. For example, our supply chains reveal the relevance of cash out and money laundering strategies to the functioning of these forums.

Cybercrime is a term used to describe an aggressive, purposeful conduct carried out through internet communication. Many aggressive cyber-attacks like phishing and scamming have increased in recent years due to the lack of awareness about technical improvements. Under-reporting of cybercrimes is a key hindrance to prompt and efficient treatment of cybercrimes, and this can have serious implications. ' For the sake of keeping up with the latest developments in cybercrime, it is necessary to establish robust systems that can quickly and accurately report on new risks (Mahor et al., 2021) An information retrieval model must be developed in order to extract different types of cybersecurity news from diverse web sources. It is the goal of this research by N. Amir et al project to develop a detection model for cyber crimes detailed in news stories and blogs. In addition, a unique source verification model is proposed to examine multiple authenticity parameters and give weightages to these parameters in order to determine the legitimacy of news collected via news articles/blogs.

The following table 1 gives the summary of some studies to detect the cybercrime techniques

MATERIALS AND METHODS

Collection of Data

The data used in this study was gathered from open data sources on Twitter and used in this investigation. To make the data's context as consistent as feasible, we only collected tweets that were related to each other. 4,30,000 tweets were gathered for three different datasets. Since Twitter uses the API as its primary data source, the repository can only display information that is free to the public and adheres to Twitter's principles on fair use and privacy protections.

Included in the datasets are:

- There were tweets relating to the Mumbai terror attack on November 26th.
- From 2015 to 2018, the total number of tweets mentioning and discussing
- Tweets from an alleged ISIS member during the Indian elections of 2019

A tweet's metadata, including the user's name and location, is stored in the databases.

The following details are contained inside this report: in order to identify each tweet's author, the tweet's author's unique identifier (user id) and unique name (user name) are required (Rawat et al., 2021). Screen name – a user-assigned moniker; this moniker need not be unique. When data was collected, it counted how many status updates were posted by a user, how many of those status updates were liked, and how many followers the user had on twitter at that point in time. Location specified by the user is an option. When a tweet is retweeted, the original tweet's whole text, including the user description, time zone, and the user's time zone, as well as any additional information the original tweet may have included, is included in the retweet. a tweet's retweeted status text is its text content (Rawat et al., 2021). An optional tweet can be added to the quoted status to express one's thoughts on the original tweet. When quoting a tweet's status, use the quoted status text as the source. Tweet body hash tags – verified hash tags used in the content of the tweet, regardless of if the author is verified or not – Users who were "referenced" in the tweet by their usernames, such as those who retweeted it or retweeted it themselves, will be notified of the tweet.

Dataset Annotation

As a random sample of the cleaned dataset, nine thousand tweets were selected at random and manually classified as either cyber- or non-cyber terrorism. Three people, who are well-versed in the jargon, slang, and colloquialisms of the Twitter sphere assisted in the human coding of the tweets (Rawat et al., 2021). A Civil Engineering grad, a Veterinary Medicine grad, and a Master's student in Computer

Table 1. Summary of some studies to detect the cybercrime techniques

Author Name	Methodology	Detection Technique	Limitations of the study	Advantages of Our Proposed Technique
Sahoo et al.,	Cooperative vulnerability factor	Examining DC-MG measurements under assault	If the accuracy rate is to be compared to that of other FDIA detection systems, accuracy criteria indicators such as the misfire rate (MR), the false alarm rate (FAR), the hit rate (HR), and the correct reject rate (CRR) are not taken into account.	In the proposed research, both voltage and current measurements are examined. A comparison is made between the criterion indexes for accuracy rate and the other FDIA detection methods. The method employs a free-form approach.
Manandhar et al.,	Kalman filter	FDIAs can be detected in smart grids by employing the mathematical method.	According to the accuracy criterion indexes of the detection methods for the FDIA, the MR, FAR, HR, and CRR are not taken into consideration and are not compared to other detection methods. No consideration is given to the DC system;	The system's mathematical model is not necessary for this job. DC-MG has been compared to various FDIA detection systems in terms of criteria indices of the accuracy rate.
Ozay et al.,	Deep learning	Analyzing FDIA features using historical data and using the recorded properties to identify and diagnose the FDIA	An index of the accuracy rates such the mean, standard deviation, standard error, or correlation coefficient (CRR) is not taken into account for detecting FDIA. No consideration is given to the DC system;	The adaptive learning of hidden characteristics is accomplished through the use of WT and SVD to extract features for use as input in deep learning and deep base models.
Chaojun et al.,	Kullback–Leibler	The ability to distinguish between various types of attacks. Some state variables pose a diagnostic challenge for the detection of FDIAs.	By relying on old data, it is unable to detect even a modest amount of FDIA in the system. An index of the accuracy rates such the mean, standard deviation, standard error, or correlation coefficient (CRR) is not taken into account for detecting FDIA.	Because it relies on signal properties rather than the state variable to detect FDIAs, this research is independent of it. Indexes based on a variety of factors are analysed and compared.
Rawat et al,	Cosine matching and chi-square detection techniques were used.	We found that Chi-square could not identify any of the investigated FDIAs.	MR, FAR, HR, and CRR aren't taken into account while looking for FDIAs, and neither are the other FDIA detection methods when comparing accuracy criteria indexes; neither is the DC system.	FDIAs in smart MG can be detected by this paper; A comparison is made between the criterion indexes for accuracy rate and the other FDIA detection methods.
Peng, J et al	Discordant Element Approach	If existing DC-MG measurements are attacked,	For FDIA detection, the criteria indices of the accuracy rate, such as MR, FAR, HR, and CRR, are not taken into account; and the attack on voltage sensors is not taken into account.	In the proposed research, both voltage and current measurements are examined. A comparison is made between the criterion indexes for accuracy rate and the other FDIA detection methods.

Science round out the team. They were given an overview of the current definitions of cyber terrorism in literature, as well as an understanding of the context in which the tweets were made.

Metrics Used for Evaluation

Measures and metrics were generated. In addition to the boxplot characteristics and the f-measure, these metrics include the following: false positive (FP), true positive (TP), false negative (FN), and f-measure

PROPOSED HYBRID MODEL FOR DETECTING CYBER TERRORISM

Linear SVC, Multinomial NB, and Logistic Regression are the three estimators that make up the Hybrid model. Figure 1 shows the design of the system. First, the data is gathered and then manually annotated. Text is standardised, links and stop words are removed, and the data is sanitised. Individual classifiers are then used to build their own models by separating the data into training and testing sets. Counting is used to vectorize the dataset. All of the models that make up the hybrid are put together by conducting a majority vote on their results.

Using a combination of different machine learning classifiers and models, the proposed hybrid model aims to outperform the individual models. Predictions are made for each of the different classifiers after they are trained on the dataset. As a result, the final prediction is the sum of all of the individual guesses.

Stacking, voting, bagging, and boosting are just a few of the techniques available for making a final forecast (Rawat et al., 2021). The final prediction in this paper is based on the results of a poll. Predicted class labels are used to implement voting here so that the majority rule can be applied. Multinomial NB, Linear SVC, and Logistic Regression are some of the ensemble's component estimators.

- **Linear Support Vector Classifier:** Using the "best fit" hyperplane, this classifier breaks or divides the data into groups. In order to see what the classifier predicts, it is fed a set of feature properties. The Support Vector Machine (SVM) algorithm is used to create this classifier. The linear kernel is employed.

- **Logistic Regression Classifier:** Useful machine learning classifiers like these are common. Many times, they are utilised in binary classifications that produce a single numerical value, such as 0 or 1. Using the logistic function, also referred to as the sigmoid function, an algorithm's predicted label probabilities can be calculated. This function assesses the degree to which the dataset's independent variables are linked to the dependent variable. A forecast is then made based on the binary values of the data. It is possible to take any real-valued number and place it between 0 and 1, but never exactly between those two points. This is the sigmoid function.
- **Naive Bayes:** Naive Bayes Classifiers can be used to forecast the likelihood of an event occurring based on the evidence in the data. A multinomial Nave Bayes algorithm classifier was employed for features that describe discrete frequency counts, such those in the dataset. Why? Because such qualities benefit most from the use of it.
- **Hybrid Algorithm:** The hybrid algorithm is a combination of above three algorithms. This algorithm gives better results compared to individual classifier.

Proposed Algorithm
Step 1.   Collect the data from tweet accounts
Step 2.   As a random sample of the cleaned dataset, nine thousand tweets were selected at random and manually classified as either cyber- or non-cyber terrorism
Step 3.   Standardise the text
Step 4.   Links and stop words are removed, and the data is sanitised.
Step 5.   The dataset is vectorized by counting,
Step 6.   Apply the individual classifiers to dividing the data into training and test sets.

Figure 2. Proposed hybrid model

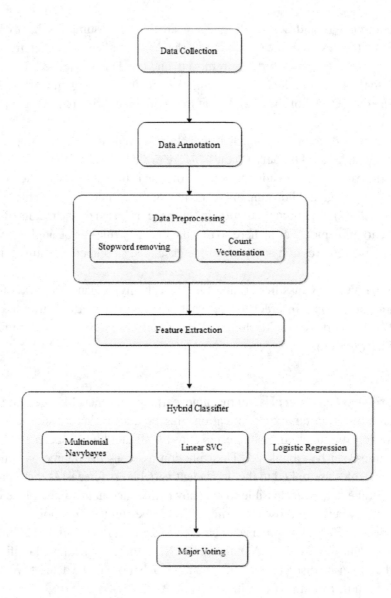

Step 7.   Apply trained data to hybrid classifier to detect the results

RESULTS

Here for results we are using 3 datasets which are mentioned in above that are of total 9000 samples in which 6500 are the trained data and 2500 are the tested data after random selection.

Using three datasets, all classifiers were tested against each other in order to see how well they performed in terms of the metrics of interest. The outcomes are shown in tables 3–5. Images 3-5 show linear graphs depicting the scores against their classifiers.

Table 2. Data Count after random selection

Data type	Data Count
Trained Data	6500
Tested Data	2500

Table 3. Results for dataset1

Classifier	Accuracy	Precision	Recall	F1 Score
Multinomial NB	0.777	0.691	0.761	0.721
Linear SVC	0.581	0.692	0.561	0.609
Logistic Regression	0.825	0.67	0.829	0.728
Hybrid Modelling	0.861	0.701	0.865	0.731

From the above table we can say that the accuracy of logistic regression is high compared to remaining individual classifiers. The precision value is high for Linear SVC; Logistic Regression is high for Recall and again for F1 score. Compared to the all three individual classifiers the hybrid model is got highest value of all metrics for dataset1.

Figure 3. Graphical representation of results for dataset1

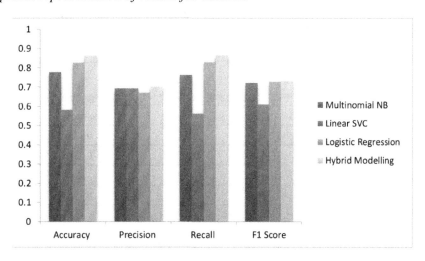

The table 4 represents the metric values for different classifiers

From the above table we can say that the accuracy of logistic regression is high compared to remaining individual classifiers. The precision value is high for Linear SVC; Logistic Regression is high for Recall and again for F1 score. Compared to the all three individual classifiers the hybrid model is got highest value of all metrics for dataset2.

Table 4. Results for dataset2

Classifier	Accuracy	Precision	Recall	F1 Score
Linear SVC	0.39	0.611	0.362	0.451
Logistic Regression	0.743	0.555	0.743	0.534
Multinomial NB	0.301	0.531	0.258	0.346
Hybrid Modelling	0.778	0.621	0.843	0.632

Figure 4. Graphical representation of results for dataset 2

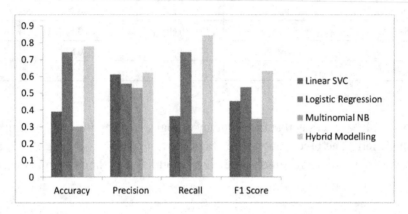

Table 4 gives the evaluation values of dataset3 for different machine learning algorithms and proposed algorithm.

Table 5. Results for dataset3

Classifier	Accuracy	Precision	Recall	F1 Score
Logistic Regression	0.961	0.914	0.953	0.933
Linear SVC	0.842	0.926	0.838	0.878
Multinomial NB	0.5671	0.926	0.55	0.69
Hybrid Modelling	0.982	0.961	0.961	0.954

From the above table we can say that the accuracy of logistic regression is high compared to remaining individual classifiers. The precision value is high for Linear SVC and Multinomial Navie bayes; Logistic Regression is high for Recall and again for F1 score. Compared to the all three individual classifiers the hybrid model is got highest value of all metrics for dataset3.

Figure 5. Graphical representation of results for dataset 3

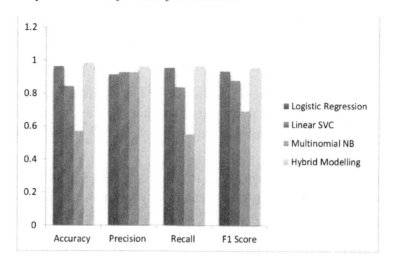

CONCLUSION

Cyber terrorism is garnering a lot of attention today because of the increasing quantity of media coverage and many institutions, particularly those from the public and business sectors are focusing on the problem. For them, it's vital to enhance public awareness of the dangers of cyber terrorism so that we can better protect ourselves and our loved ones. To detect cyber terrorism in social media networks (Twitter), machine learning methodologies were used, and the algorithms' effectiveness was verified and confirmed. According to our results, the suggested Ensemble model surpassed each of its individual subclassifiers. In the dataset provided on Twitter, users' ages and genders are not included, which is a weakness in this technique. It is also limited to English-language tweets and data. A number of the difficulties encountered while experimenting will be addressed moving forward, including the translation of tweet content into other languages and the resolution of other issues. The usage of deep learning techniques is something that will be prioritised in the future.

REFERENCES

Aghajani, G., & Ghadimi, N. (2018). Multi-objective energy management in a micro-grid. *Energy Reports*, *4*, 218–225. doi:10.1016/j.egyr.2017.10.002

Alhakami, W., ALharbi, A., Bourouis, S., Alroobaea, R., & Bouguila, N. (2019). Network anomaly intrusion detection using a nonparametric bayesian approach and feature selection. *IEEE Access, 7*, 52181–52190.

Bharati & Sarvanaguru. (2018). Crime Prediction and Analysis Using Machine Learning. *International Research Journal of Engineering and Technology*, *5*(9), 1037–1042.

Al-Shaer, E. S., Wei, J., Hamlen, K. W., & Wang, C. (2019). *Autonomous Cyber Deception: Reasoning, Adaptive Planning, and Evaluation of Honey Things*. Springer. doi:10.1007/978-3-030-02110-8

Chaojun, G., Jirutitijaroen, P., & Motani, M. (2015). Detecting false data injection attacks in ac state estimation. *IEEE Transactions on Smart Grid*, 6(5), 2476–2483. doi:10.1109/TSG.2015.2388545

Berman, D. S., Buczak, A. L., Chavis, J., & Corbett, C. L. (2019). A Survey of Deep Learning Methods for Cyber Security. *Information (Basel)*, 10(122), 1–35. doi:10.3390/info10040122

Dehghani, M., Khooban, M. H., Niknam, T., & Rafiei, S. M. R. (2016). Time-varying sliding mode control strategy for multibus low-voltage microgrids with parallel connected renewable power sources in islanding mode. *Journal of Energy Engineering*, 142(4), 05016002. doi:10.1061/(ASCE)EY.1943-7897.0000344

Dehghani, M., Khooban, M. H., & Niknam, T. (2016). Fast fault detection and classification based on a combination of wavelet singular entropy theory and fuzzy logic in distribution lines in the presence of distributed generations. *International Journal of Electrical Power & Energy Systems*, 78, 455–462. doi:10.1016/j.ijepes.2015.11.048

Ding, D., Han, Q.-L., Xiang, Y., Ge, X., & Zhang, X.-M. (2018). A survey on security control and attack detection for industrial cyber-physical systems. *Neurocomputing*, 275, 1674–1683. doi:10.1016/j.neucom.2017.10.009

Esmalifalak, M., Liu, L., Nguyen, N., Zheng, R., & Han, Z. (2014). Detecting stealthy false data injection using machine learning in smart grid. *IEEE Systems Journal*, 11(3), 1644–1652. doi:10.1109/JSYST.2014.2341597

Foroutan, S. A., & Salmasi, F. R. (2017). Detection of false data injection attacks against state estimation in smart grids based on a mixture Gaussian distribution learning method. IET Cyber-Phys. *Syst. Theory Appl.*, 2(4), 161–171. doi:10.1049/iet-cps.2017.0013

Giraldo, J., Urbina, D., Cardenas, A., Valente, J., Faisal, M., Ruths, J., Tippenhauer, N. O., Sandberg, H., & Candell, R. (2018). A survey of physics-based attack detection in cyber-physical systems. *ACM Computing Surveys*, 51(4), 1–36. doi:10.1145/3203245 PMID:31092968

Habibi, M. R., & Baghaee, H. R. (2020). Detection of false data injection cyber-attacks in DC microgrids based on recurrent neural networks. *IEEE Journal of Emerging and Selected Topics in Power Electronics*.

Alsafi, Abduallah, & Pathan. (2019). IDPS: An Integrated Intrusion Handling Model for Cloud. *Networking and International Architecture*.

He, Y., Mendis, G. J., & Wei, J. (2017). Real-time detection of false data injection attacks in smart grid: A deep learning-based intelligent mechanism. *IEEE Transactions on Smart Grid*, 8(5), 2505–2516. doi:10.1109/TSG.2017.2703842

Shaukat, K., Luo, S., Chen, S., & Liu, D. (2020). Cyber Threat Detection Using Machine Learning Techniques: A Performance Evaluation Perspective. *2020 International Conference on Cyber Warfare and Security (ICCWS)*, 1-6. 10.1109/ICCWS48432.2020.9292388

Khraisat, A., Gondal, I., & Vamplew, P. (2019). An anomaly intrusion detection system using C5 decision tree classifier. In *Trends and applications in knowledge discovery and data mining* (pp. 149–155). Springer.

Lakshmanaprabu, Shankar, Ilayaraja, Nasir, & Chilamkurti. (2019). Random forest for big data classification in the internet of things using optimal features. *International Journal of Machine Learning and Cybernetics, 10*, 2609 - 2618.

Manandhar, K., Cao, X., Hu, F., & Liu, Y. (2014). Detection of faults and attacks including false data injection attack in smart grid using Kalman filter. *IEEE Transactions on Control of Network Systems, 1*(4), 370–379. doi:10.1109/TCNS.2014.2357531

Ferraro, Giordani, & Serafini. (2019). fclust: An R Package for Fuzzy Clustering. *The R Journal, 11*(1), 1 - 5.

Rodriguez, M. Z. (2019). *Clustering algorithms: A comparative approach.* PLOS.

Abu Saleh, M. (2019). Crime Data Analysis in Python using K Means clustering. *International Journal for Research in Applied Science and Engineering Technology, 7*(4), 151–155. doi:10.22214/ijraset.2019.4027

Mehrdad, S., Mousavian, S., Madraki, G., & Dvorkin, Y. (2018). Cyber-physical resilience of electrical power systems against malicious attacks: A review. *Curr. Sustain. Renew. Energy Rep., 5*(1), 14–22. doi:10.100740518-018-0094-8

Mohammadi-Ivatloo, B., Shiroei, M., & Parniani, M. (2011). Online small signal stability analysis of multi-machine systems based on synchronized phasor measurements. *Electric Power Systems Research, 81*(10), 1887–1896. doi:10.1016/j.epsr.2011.05.014

Amir, N., Latif, R., Shafqat, N., & Latif, S. (2020). Crowdsourcing Cybercrimes through Online Resources. *2020 13th International Conference on Developments in eSystems Engineering (DeSE),* 158-163. 10.1109/DeSE51703.2020.9450747

Ozay, M., Esnaola, I., Vural, F. T. Y., Kulkarni, S. R., & Poor, H. V. (2015). Machine learning methods for attack detection in the smart grid. *IEEE Transactions on Neural Networks and Learning Systems, 27*(8), 1773–1786. doi:10.1109/TNNLS.2015.2404803 PMID:25807571

Sivakumar, R. R., & K. S. (2021). Real Time Crime Detection Using Deep Learning Algorithm. *2021 International Conference on System, Computation, Automation and Networking (ICSCAN),* 1-5. 10.1109/ICSCAN53069.2021.9526393

Rawat, D. B., & Bajracharya, C. (2015). Detection of false data injection attacks in smart grid communication systems. *IEEE Signal Processing Letters, 22*(10), 1652–1656. doi:10.1109/LSP.2015.2421935

Rajawat, A. S., Rawat, R., Mahor, V., Shaw, R. N., & Ghosh, A. (2021). Suspicious Big Text Data Analysis for Prediction—On Darkweb User Activity Using Computational Intelligence Model. In *Innovations in Electrical and Electronic Engineering* (pp. 735–751). Springer. doi:10.1007/978-981-16-0749-3_58

Rawat, R., Mahor, V., Chirgaiya, S., Shaw, R. N., & Ghosh, A. (2021). Sentiment Analysis at Online Social Network for Cyber-Malicious Post Reviews Using Machine Learning Techniques. *Computationally Intelligent Systems and their Applications*, 113-130.

Rawat, R., Mahor, V., Chirgaiya, S., Shaw, R. N., & Ghosh, A. (2021). Analysis of Darknet Traffic for Criminal Activities Detection Using TF-IDF and Light Gradient Boosted Machine Learning Algorithm. In *Innovations in Electrical and Electronic Engineering* (pp. 671–681). Springer. doi:10.1007/978-981-16-0749-3_53

Rajawat, A. S., Rawat, R., Barhanpurkar, K., Shaw, R. N., & Ghosh, A. (2021). Vulnerability Analysis at Industrial Internet of Things Platform on Dark Web Network Using Computational Intelligence. *Computationally Intelligent Systems and their Applications*, 39-51.

Rajawat, A. S., Rawat, R., Barhanpurkar, K., Shaw, R. N., & Ghosh, A. (2021). Blockchain-Based Model for Expanding IoT Device Data Security. *Advances in Applications of Data-Driven Computing*, 61.

Rawat, R., Dangi, C. S., & Patil, J. (2011). Safe Guard Anomalies against SQL Injection Attacks. *International Journal of Computers and Applications*, 22(2), 11–14. doi:10.5120/2558-3511

Rajawat, A. S., Rawat, R., Shaw, R. N., & Ghosh, A. (2021). Cyber Physical System Fraud Analysis by Mobile Robot. In *Machine Learning for Robotics Applications* (pp. 47–61). Springer. doi:10.1007/978-981-16-0598-7_4

Rawat, R., Rajawat, A. S., Mahor, V., Shaw, R. N., & Ghosh, A. (2021). Dark Web—Onion Hidden Service Discovery and Crawling for Profiling Morphing, Unstructured Crime and Vulnerabilities Prediction. In *Innovations in Electrical and Electronic Engineering* (pp. 717–734). Springer. doi:10.1007/978-981-16-0749-3_57

Rawat, R., Rajawat, A. S., Mahor, V., Shaw, R. N., & Ghosh, A. (2021). Surveillance Robot in Cyber Intelligence for Vulnerability Detection. In *Machine Learning for Robotics Applications* (pp. 107–123). Springer. doi:10.1007/978-981-16-0598-7_9

Rawat, R., Mahor, V., Chirgaiya, S., & Rathore, A. S. (2021). Applications of Social Network Analysis to Managing the Investigation of Suspicious Activities in Social Media Platforms. In *Advances in Cybersecurity Management* (pp. 315–335). Springer. doi:10.1007/978-3-030-71381-2_15

Rawat, R., Mahor, V., Rawat, A., Garg, B., & Telang, S. (2021). Digital Transformation of Cyber Crime for Chip-Enabled Hacking. In *Handbook of Research on Advancing Cybersecurity for Digital Transformation* (pp. 227–243). IGI Global. doi:10.4018/978-1-7998-6975-7.ch012

Rawat, R., Garg, B., Mahor, V., Chouhan, M., Pachlasiya, K., & Telang, S. Cyber Threat Exploitation and Growth during COVID-19 Times. In *Advanced Smart Computing Technologies in Cybersecurity and Forensics* (pp. 85–101). CRC Press.

Mahor, V., Rawat, R., Telang, S., Garg, B., Mukhopadhyay, D., & Palimkar, P. (2021, September). Machine Learning based Detection of Cyber Crime Hub Analysis using Twitter Data. In *2021 IEEE 4th International Conference on Computing, Power and Communication Technologies (GUCON)* (pp. 1-5). IEEE.

Mahor, V., Rawat, R., Kumar, A., Chouhan, M., Shaw, R. N., & Ghosh, A. (2021, September). Cyber Warfare Threat Categorization on CPS by Dark Web Terrorist. In *2021 IEEE 4th International Conference on Computing, Power and Communication Technologies (GUCON)* (pp. 1-6). IEEE. doi:10.1201/9781003140023-6

Rawat, R., Mahor, V., Chirgaiya, S., & Garg, B. (2021). Artificial Cyber Espionage Based Protection of Technological Enabled Automated Cities Infrastructure by Dark Web Cyber Offender. In *Intelligence of Things: AI-IoT Based Critical-Applications and Innovations* (pp. 167–188). Springer. doi:10.1007/978-3-030-82800-4_7

Bhalerao, R., Aliapoulios, M., Shumailov, I., Afroz, S., & McCoy, D. (2019). Mapping the Underground: Supervised Discovery of Cybercrime Supply Chains. *2019 APWG Symposium on Electronic Crime Research (eCrime)*, 1-16. 10.1109/eCrime47957.2019.9037582

Sahoo, S., Mishra, S., Peng, J. C.-H., & Dragicevic, T. (2018). A Stealth Cyber-Attack Detection Strategy for DC Microgrids. *IEEE Transactions on Power Electronics*, *34*(8), 8162–8174. doi:10.1109/TPEL.2018.2879886

Sahoo, S., Peng, J. C.-H., Devakumar, A., Mishra, S., & Dragicevic, T. (2019). On detection of false data in cooperative dc microgrids—A discordant element approach. *IEEE Transactions on Industrial Electronics*, *67*(8), 6562–6571. doi:10.1109/TIE.2019.2938497

Tan, S., Guerrero, J. O., Xie, P., Han, R., & Vasquez, J. C. (2020). Brief Survey on Attack Detection Methods for Cyber-Physical Systems. *IEEE Systems Journal*, *14*(4), 5329–5339. doi:10.1109/JSYST.2020.2991258

Al-Khater, W. A., Al-Maadeed, S., Ahmed, A. A., Sadiq, A. S., & Khan, M. K. (2020). Comprehensive Review of Cybercrime Detection Techniques. *IEEE Access: Practical Innovations, Open Solutions*, *8*, 137293–137311. doi:10.1109/ACCESS.2020.3011259

Chapter 5
Overview of Web Dawdler Outline and FKNN Utilizing Cluster–Based Secret Net

Vinod Mahor
https://orcid.org/0000-0002-2187-6920
IES College of Technology, Bhopal, India

Sadhna Bijrothiya
https://orcid.org/0000-0002-8913-7753
Maulana Azad National Institute of Technology, Bhopal, India

Rakesh Kumar Bhujade
Government Polytechnic, Daman, India

Jasvant Mandloi
Government Polytechnic, Daman, India

Harshita Mandloi
Shri Vaishnav Vidyapeeth Vishwavidyalaya, India

Stuti Asthana
UT Administration of Dadra and Nagar Haveli and Daman and Diu, India

ABSTRACT

Everyone uses the world wide web for their everyday tasks. The WWW is divided into several side by sides, deep-net, and black net. It is dangerous to use the world wide web to obtain the deep or secret-net. In this chapter, the dawdler structure will be used for a faster and safer search. Various types of data will be gathered during the search process and kept in the data. The data categorization procedure will be used to determine the webpage's side by side. The fuzzy k-nearest neighbor approach is used in the arrangement procedure. The fuzzy k-nearest neighbor approach categories the results of the dawdling structure stored in the data. Data will be generated in the form of webpage addresses, page information, and other data by the dawdling structure. the fuzzy k-nearest neighbor arrangement result will result in web side by side data. In this chapter, to focus on many dataset tests, there is as much as 30% of the online surface net, 25% deep-net, 24.5% charter, and 30% secret web.

DOI: 10.4018/978-1-6684-3942-5.ch005

INTRODUCTION

Deep-net and Secret-Net, imperceptible web page, or under net is all terms used to describe the secret web or dark web. Deep-net is a component of the World Wide Web that cannot be readily explored; some categories of secret web or dark web may be found using a conventional web portal, while secret web or dark web cannot be explored in general and requires precise techniques and a different web portal to reach.

The deep-net is distinct since the Secret-Net, despite the fact that the Secret-Net is a subset of the deep-net (M. Balduzzi, V. Ciancaglini, and M. Balduzzi, 2015). The word is given by "Mike Bergman", the organizer of positive Earth According to him, surfing the World Wide Web at this time is comparable to catching angle in the marine: a lot of fish will be captured in the webpages, but the knowledge contained therein will be lost. The majority of content on the World Wide Web network is hidden deep within a dynamic site and ordinary "Search Engines" are unable to locate it.

On the deep-net, traditional web "Search Engines" is unable to discover or retrieve data. The page did not exist until it was animatedly built in response to a precise search. The deep-net has been determined to be larger than the regular web (M. P. Zillman and A. M. H. A. M.S., 2017). The size of the deep-net is estimated to be around 7.5 petabytes on the basis of approximation by the "University of California", Berkeley. A more precise assessment was indicated in a study by He et al, who discovered around 2.5 Lakh existent places crossways the webpage (M. P. Zillman and A. M. H. A. M.S., 2017). The webpage that we use on a daily basis is divided into two categories: common web and surface Net. The secret web or dark web refers to non-web content that cannot be accessed with a standard web portal. The secret web or dark web, which generally includes offensive material or content related with committing crime, such as the selling of guns, illicit narcotics, sex trafficking, mercenaries, cybercrime, terrorists, crypto currency, as well as more than a few other alleged crimes, and has been banned in certain nations (E. Brayton and S. Christopher, 2017). In addition to illegal activity, some hackers utilize disguised online material to protect the organization's identity and operations. Some operations, such as govt. or academic study, employ the secret web or dark web, maybe because each nation has its own privacy laws regarding data secrecy. According to some sources, the surface Net and secret web or dark web are two layers of webpages categorized by the strain side by side of retrieving the si includes offensive material or content related with committing crime, such as the selling of guns, illicit narcotics, sex trafficking, mercenaries, cybercrime, terrorists, crypto-currency, as well as several other alleged crimes, and has been banned in certain nations. te. (A. Lakhani, 2016).

Webs (Nets)

Common Web

A common web site is one that we use to do searches utilising "Search Engines" such as "Google, Bing, Yahoo, and others". The communal web is a subset of the surface Net, where webmasters, administrators, and users frequently utilise actual identities (M. Yadav and N. Goyal, 2015, V. Banos, 2015).

Table 1. Common level of Webs(Net)

Level	Name	Search Engine	Section
L1	Common-Net	CWB (Common Web Browser), ISE (Indexed at Search Engine)	Surface net
L2	Surface-Net	SWC (Surface Net Common), Web Browser	4.0 Percent
L3	Begie-Net	CWB (Common Web Browser), VPN, ISE (Indexed at Search Engine), BSN (Block in Some Nation)	......
L4	Deep-Net	Tor (The Onion Route Browser)	Hidden Web
L5	Charter-Net	Tor (The Onion Route Browser)	96.0 Percent
L6	Secret-Net	Tor (The Onion Route Browser)	......

Surface Net

Surface Net is similar to ordinary web in that it uses actual identities and is searchable. Web portals and "Search Engines" such as "Firefox", "Chrome", "Google, Bing", "Yahoo", and others can be used to conduct searches.

Differences between the common web, the surface Net and which employs more complicated network architectures. Not just for advertising or business, but also for things like email services, human intelligence jobs, MySQL data, online hosting, college campuses, page rank, web identification, and other things. (M. Yadav and N. Goyal, 2015,). According to some sources, webpages such as who is, new grounds, vampire freaks, international social networks, and others are included in the category of surface Net.

Bergie-Net (Hided in Specific Country)

This segment is not part of the surface Net. Bergie Net is the initial side by side of the secret web or dark web, yet it is immobile indexed and accessible through web portals and "Search Engines" in general. Bergie is categorized as a secret web or dark webpage since it is prohibited in some regions. Piracy of film, music, or software is popular among Bergie online users. The "FTP servers, honeypots, google locked results, porn, loaded web servers, much of the World Wide Web, rsc, 4chan, rabbit, and other" forms of Bergie Net (M. Yadav and N. Goyal, 2015,).

Deep-Net

The deep-net is part of the secret web or dark web; in this sector, there are webpages that employ more advanced technology, as well as a webpage that stores study data and secret information. On the World Wide Web, there are many forms of information, such as a celebrity controversy, a hacker organization, sensitive information about the political elite, a world war 3 plot, and so on. This category includes webpages such as sources, mathematical study, and advanced computing. Unlike Bergie Net, this sort of site cannot be viewed by a web portal and is not indexed by "Search Engines" such as Google, Yahoo, and Bing. The suffix. Onion is commonly used to encrypt DNS names for this sort of webpage. This section contains further information as well as discussions of "AI terrorists" hackers, assemblage computer programmer, "shell networking", and other (C. Y. Huang and H. Chang, 2016 J. Christian and S. Hansun, 2016).

Charter-Net (Differences Between Deep and Secret-Net)

Charter Net sits in the middle of the deep and Secret-Nets. There are several webpages in this area that have been designed to be exceedingly sophisticated and, as indicated, not easily accessible. To access it, you'll need a certain web portal. Here you'll find the hidden wiki, elimination box, and forbidden barred literature. The Solid drug trade may be discovered here, and it's evident that secret-net market places aren't extensively documented. On webpages such as doxbin, personal records or doxes may be found. Users are invited to donate "personally identifiable information", such as "social security numbers", "bank routing information", and "credit card information", to Doxbin, a document sharing and online publishing roommates. Solid candy, hidden web, common of "the black market, closed shell system, ghost in the shell", and more online categories (R. Posts, 2017).

Secret-Net

Many previously unknown webpages have been discovered on the Charter Net science, but there are also many criminal webpages as well as well as data about sophisticated tools including digital money, human smuggling, hetman, illicit substances, tetra - acetic technologies, and quantum entanglement, and others. More criminality is discovered in this part, as well as a means to access it. Access to go there is even sold by certain people (R. Posts, 2017, A. Celestini and G. Me, 2017).

Structure for Dawdlers

A web dawdler, often known as a "spider web", is a component of a search engine that allows users to visit online pages and save all of the information contained within them. The web dawdler will retrieve and save all of the url links that are present on each of the visited webpages. The web dawdler operates by providing a source, such as robots.txt, to the server, which then sends all of the resources or data. Page title, page url, anchore, and other meta data are examples of such information (S. J. Kim and J. H. Lee, 2017). A web dawdler structure is a programme that allows you to crawl the World Wide Web. When this was a commonly used web dawdler structure and was built in a variation of programming languages, such as "scrapy ("python"), lucidwork ("python"), frontera ("python"), php dawdler (php), open web spider (php), robo web portal" ("python"), and others. In this chapter, a web dawdler structure based on php and "python" is employed (P. R. E. Indrajit, 2016).

FKNN

The issue of partial truth is dealt with in fuzzy logic, which is an allowance of Boolean algebra. When categorical logic asserts that everyone can be stated in binary numbers system ("0 or 1, black or white, yes or no"), fuzzy logic Boolean truth is replaced at the side by side of truth. Algorithm Fuzzy K Nearest Neighbor (FKNN) is an arrangement approach for objects based on the learning data nearest to the item. FKNN is a data categorization approach that combines the fuzzy algorithm and the KNN Algorithm. A statistical item's participation within every class has a score, similar to the fuzzy theory, which indicates that data can belong to any category through the interval's greatest grade of participation (0, 1) (M. Wan, G. Yang, S. Gai, and Z. Yang, 2017).

By specifying the value of participation of a data on everyone category, the system of fuzzy sets generalizes the conventional FKNN system. The following formula is used:

$$u\left(m,n_i\right) = \frac{\sum_{j=1}^{k} u\left(m_j, y_i\right) * u(m,n_j)^{\frac{-2}{x-1}}}{\sum_{j=1}^{k} d(m,n_j)^{\frac{-2}{x-1}}} \quad (i)$$

Where u(m, ni) is the participation value of data x to category ci, K is the number of a nearest neighbor's used, u(mk, ni) is the participation value neighbouring data in the K neighbor's in the categorization ni, the value 1 if the training data xk corresponds to categorization ci or 0 if it does not, and d(m, nj) is the length between data m and data mk in The distance between the data and its closest neighbour has a substantial influence on the data's value on its neighbor's categorization; the closer the data is to its neighbor's, the greater the data's price on its neighbor's categorization, and vise - versa. (M. Wan, G. Yang, S. Gai, and Z. Yang, 2017). Data with Y dimensions (features) is used to calculate distance. Distance (dissimilarity) b/w two data sets utilized in the FKNN created with:

$$u\left(m_i, n_i\right) = \left(\sum_{l=1}^{y} \left|x_{il} - x_{jl}\right|^{p}\right)^{\frac{1}{p}} \quad (ii)$$

The measurement ("number of features") of the data is N. The cause of distance utilized is p; if "p = 1", the distance used is Manhattan; if "p = 2", the space used is the Euclidean distance. Chebyshev (S. J. Kim and J. H. Lee, 2017, Romil Rawat, Anand Singh Rajawat, Vinod Mahor, 2021) is the distance utilized when p = f.

STUDY METHOD

The dawdler structure and FKNN were used in the study, as shown in the diagram. Test data in the web portal, then use the dawdler structure to store the data to a data that will be categorized using FKNN (M. Plucinski and M. Pietrzykowski, 2017) figure 1 shows the model based crawler SE.

EXECUTION AND OUTCOME

Calculating Every Cluster's Distance Value

When calculating the value of every cluster, the value is based on how difficult it is to get data on the World Wide Web, Table 2 shows the value of variations.

Figure 1. Proposed Architecture

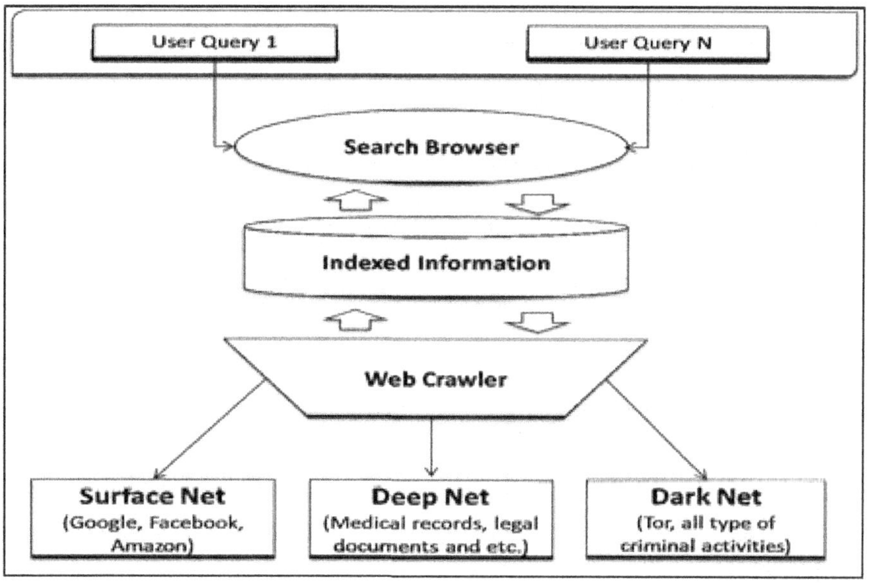

Table 2. Rate of categaries (Section)

S.N.	Section	Rate
L1	Surface-Net	3.1 ≥ Values ≥ 0.1
L2	Begie-Net	0.4 ≥ Values ≥0.6
L3	Deep-Net	0.5 ≥ Values ≥ -3.5
L4	Charter-Net	-3.2 ≥ Values ≥ 0
L5	Secret-Net	-3.4≥ Values ≥-6.1

Locate Data Sample and Data Test

The initial stage was to gather data samples, which were manually collected in the since of phrases often used in the Secret-Net, such as remedies, guns, bit-coin, porn item, illegal porn item, plasma, "heroin", cocaine, "piracy", "terrorism", and others (M. Plucinski and M. Pietrzykowski, 2017).

After that, the illustration data is gathered and entered obsessed by a data.

The following stage is to gather data test, which can be found on numerous webpages that can be found using "Search Engines". Some of the current lists utilise standard DNS names, while others employ cryptonames. The original DNS name is used in the surface Net and web bergie categories, whereas cryptoname is used in the deep-net, web charter, and Secret-Net categories (E. Brayton and S. Christopher, 2017, Romil Rawat, 2021). Table 3 shows the dataset link.

Table 3. Dataset analysis

S.N.	Domain Names
1	http://www.mashable.com
2	http://www.forbes.com
3	http://www.thomsonreuters.com
...	....
28	http://fbichanc6yfagl4l.onion
29	http://ybp4oezfhk24hxmb.onion
30	http://mts7hqqqeogujc5e.onion

Dawdling Procedures and Outcomes

The operation is carried out with the help of a web dawdler structure (Romil Rawat, Vinod Mahor, Sachin Chirgaiya, Rabindra Nath Shaw, 2021). Figure 2 shows an illustration of "web dawdler code" written in python programming language

Figure 2. Python code for web crawler

```
class GameModel:
    def __init__(self,name,type,company,rating,links):
        self.name = name;
        self.type = type;
        self.company = company;
        self.rating = rating;
        self.relatedLinks = links;

    def __str__(self):
        return ("\nName : "+ self.name.encode("UTF-8") +
                "\nType : " + self.type.encode("UTF-8") +
                "\nCompany : " + self.company.encode("UTF-8") +
                "\nRating : "+ self.rating.encode("UTF-8")+"\n");
```

Web dawdling is completed by entering the DNS name into the web dawdler structure. In addition, the web dawdler will deliver "web robot source to a web endpoint" and save all of the data (Vinod Mahor, Romil Rawat, Anil Kumar, Mukesh Chouhan (2021) Figure 3 shows the SQL database.

Cluster Proses and Their Outcomes

After the data has been crawled and saved in the dawdler results data, the FKNN arrangement procedure will be used to cluster the data (M. Plucinski and M. Pietrzykowski, 2017, Romil Rawat, 2021). FKNN algorithm:

- Use the highest and lowest value of the data for each characteristic to normalize the data.
- Using equation, get the K closest neighbors of test data x. (2).
- For each I use equation (1) to get the participation significance u (x, yi), where $1 \leq i \leq C$

Figure 3. M-SQL database based on Crawler

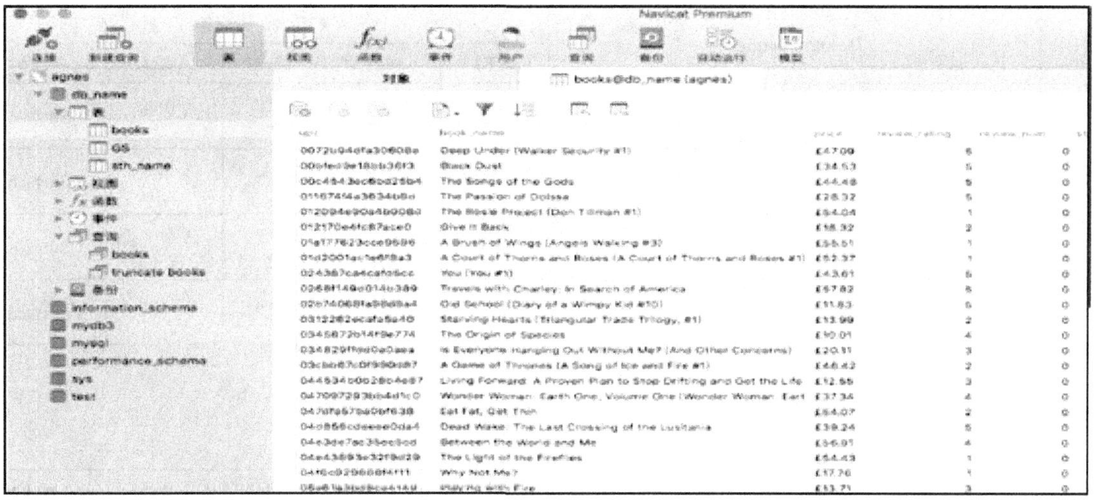

- For every $1 \leq i \leq C$, find the biggest value $v = u(x, y_i)$, where C is the number of kelas.
- Assign the category levels v to me to the ni test data.

The FKNN pseudocode is used in this example (Anand Singh Rajawat, Romil Rawat, Vinod Mahor, Rabindra Nath Shaw, and Ankush Ghosh. 2021, Romil Rawat, Anil Kumar, Mukesh Chouhan, 2021) figure 4 shows the code for FKNN.

The test information in the data was matched to the prior illustration data, and then the arrangement was done using the FKNN approach. Table 4 and table 5 show the outcomes of the categorization method (Romil Rawat, Vinod Mahor, Sachin Chirgaiya, 2021) and figure 5 shows the result analysis, figure 6 shows the centralized secret nets.

CONCLUSION

According to a 30-data-test study, the surface Net accounts for 20percent, Bergie Net for 7.7 percent, deep-net for 20.4percent, charter for 22.7 percent, and Secret-Net for 29.8 percent. Because onion rout-

Figure 4. Code for FKNN

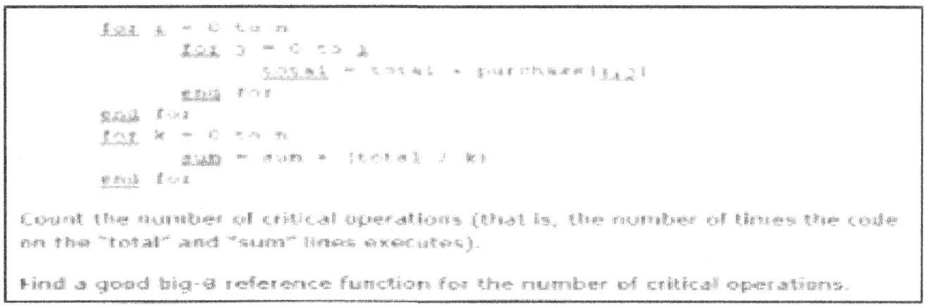

Table 4. Illustration of cluster-based results

S.N.	Domain Names	Cluster Results				
		WF1	WF2	WF3	WF4	WF5
1	http://www.mashable.com	News 2	Social 2.3	Chat 2.5	Group 2.5	Surface
2	http://www.forbes.com	News 2	Social 3	Chat 2	Group 2.6	Surface
3	http://www.thomsonreuters.com	News 2	Social 2.3	Chat 2	Group 2.7	Surface
4	http://www.game.co.uk	News 2	Social 2.3	Chat 2	Group 2.4	Surface

Table 5. Categorize the 30 datasets

S.N.	Domain Names	WF1	WF2	WF3	WF4
1	http://www.mashable.com	1	2	2.5	2.5
2	http://www.forbes.com	1	2	2	2.5
3	http://www.thomsonreuters.com	2	2	2	2.5
4	http://www.game.co.uk	1	1	2	2
5	http://www.game.co.id	1	1	2	2
....	....	....	....	....	....
24	http://poplesxuru7lsr.onion	-4.5	-4.5	-3	-2
25	http://lchudifyeqm4ldjj.onion	-4.5	-4.5	-4	-2
26	http://poplesxuru7lsr.onion	-4.5	-4.5	-4	-4
27	http://bluemoon4vpzulpv.onion	-5	-4.5	-4.5	-4
28	http://fbichanc6yfagl4l.onion	-5	-5	-5	-4
29	http://ybp4oezfhk24hxmb.onion	-6	-5.5	-5	-4
30	http://mts7hqqqeogujc5e.onion	-5.5	-5	-5	-4

Figure 5. Result of 30 dataset based on FKNN

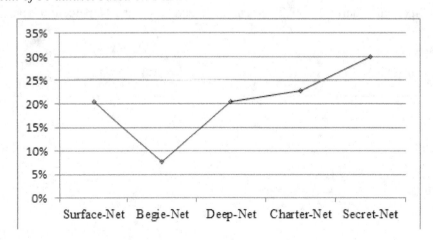

Figure 6. Counterfeiting center on Secret-Net

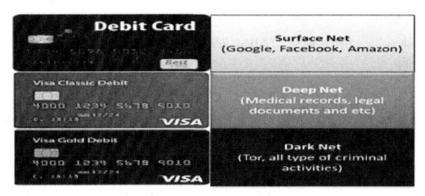

ers are created with several layers and are organized, accessing the Secret-Net requires passing through numerous computers, which takes a long time. Even certain parts of the World Wide Web are unavailable.

Dawdling structures can be useful, but it can be difficult to gain access to precise webpages, such as the deep-net, which is more difficult to reach than the black web. Although the FKNN approach can be effective, there are still certain flaws. Because nothing is definite about the distribution and how to quantify each category, clustering the secret web or dark web is difficult.

Since web dawdlers single access webpages, titles, anchors, and meta-data and not so completely and comprehensively around administration webpages, password security, and additional database information, the reality of the "deals" carried out cannot be known. Some webpages are created but never utilised or have no deals. The World Wide Web may only be used to deceive others. There are a few webpages that are genuinely utilized, and there is a deal.

Bit coin, data fortification for a precise study, and a hacking gang every nation, group, or organization may utilize it to improve the quality of their own. However, some people may exploit it for illegal purposes. Clearly, crime was visible on the Secret-Net. It has been shown by extensive investigation. Some organizations have already acted, such as the "International Law Enforcement Operation on Operation ominous", which was shut down in November 2014 to apprehend the culprits of dark-net users. Similarly, (DARPA) "Defense Advanced Study Project Agency" conducted study on the deep-net search engine until recently ("Memex"). And there are likely to be a slew of additional study and non-profit groups.

REFERENCES

Balduzzi, Ciancaglini, & Balduzzi. (2015). Cybercrime In The Deep Web. *Black Hat Europe 2015*.

Banos, V. (2015). *Web Crawling, Analysis and Archiving*. Aristotle University of Thessaloniki Faculty of Sciences School of Informatics.

Brayton, E., & Christopher, S. (2017). *Number of the Beast. Deep Web*. Available: https://rationalwiki.org/w/index.php

Celestini, A., & Me, G. (2017). Tor Marketplaces Exploratory Data Analysis: The Drugs Case. *Communications in Computer and Information Science*, *630*, 218–229.

Christian, J., & Hansun, S. (2016). *Simulating Shopper Behavior using Fuzzy Logic in Shopping Center Simulation*. ITB J. Publ.

Ciancaglini, Balduzzi, Mcardle, & Rösler. (2015). *Bellow The Surface Exploring the Deep Web Contents*. TrendLabs Res. Pap..

Deep Web. (2014). Available: https://rationalwiki.org/wiki/Deep_web

Huang, C. Y., & Chang, H. (2016). *GeoWeb Crawler: An Extensible and Scalable Web Crawling Framework for Discovering Geospatial Web Resources*. Int. J. GeoInformation.

Indrajit, P. R. E. (2016). *Internet And Information Security, Informatio*. PREINEXUS.

Kim, S. J., & Lee, J. H. (2017). A Study on Metadata Structure and Recommenders of Biological Systems to Support BioInspired Design. *Enginering Appl. Artif. Intell., 57*, 16–41.

Lakhani, A. (2016). *The Ultimate Guide to the Deep Dark Invisible.Web - Darknet Unleashed*. Dark Security and Total Chaos.

Mahor, V., Rawat, R., Kumar, A., & Chouhan, M. (2021). Cyber warfare threat categorization on cps by dark web terrorist. In *2021 IEEE 4th International Conference on Computing, Power and Communication Technologies (GUCON)*, (pp. 1–6). IEEE.

Plucinski & Pietrzykowski. (2017). *Application of the K Nearest Neighbors Method to Fuzzy Data Processing*. West Pomeranian Univ. Technol.

Posts, R. (2017). *The Dark Web Links*. Available: http://www.thedarkweblinks.com

Rajawat, A. S., Rawat, R., Mahor, V., Shaw, R. N., & Ghosh, A. (2021). Suspicious big text data analysis for prediction—on darkweb user activity using computational intelligence model. In *Innovations in Electrical and Electronic Engineering* (pp. 735–751). Springer.

Rawat, Garg, Mahor, Telang, Pachlasiya, & Chouhan. (2021). Organ trafficking on the dark web—the data security and privacy concern in healthcare systems. *Internet of Healthcare Things*, 191.

Rawat, Kumar, Chouhan, Telang, Pachlasiya, Garg, & Mahor. (2021). *Systematic literature review (slr) on social media and the digital transformation of drug trafficking on darkweb*. Available at SSRN 3903797.

Rawat, R., Mahor, V., Chirgaiya, S., & Garg, B. (2021). Artificial cyber espionage based protection of technological enabled automated cities infrastructure by dark web cyber offender. In Intelligence of Things: AI-IoT Based Critical-Applications and Innovations (pp. 167–188). Springer.

Rawat, R., Mahor, V., Chirgaiya, S., Shaw, R. N., & Ghosh, A. (2021). Analysis of darknet traffic for criminal activities detection using tf-idf and light gradient boosted machine learning algorithm. In *Innovations in Electrical and Electronic Engineering* (pp. 671–681). Springer.

Rawat, R., Rajawat, A. S., Mahor, V., Shaw, R. N., & Ghosh, A. (2021). Dark web—onion hidden service discovery and crawling for profiling morphing, unstructured crime and vulnerabilities prediction. In *Innovations in Electrical and Electronic Engineering* (pp. 717–734). Springer.

Wan, M., Yang, G., Gai, S., & Yang, Z. (2017). Two-dimensional discriminant Locality preserving projections (2DDLDP) and its application to feature extraction via fuzzy set. *Multimedia Tools and Applications, 76*(1), 355–371.

Yadav, M., & Goyal, N. (2015). Comparison of Open Source Crawlers - A Review. *International Journal of Scientific and Engineering Research, 6*(9).

Zillman & M.S. (2017). *Deep Web Research and Discovery Resources 2017.* Virtual Private Library.

Chapter 6
Crowdfunded Assassinations and Propaganda by Dark Web Cyber Criminals

Danish Nisarahmed Tamboli
NBN Sinhgad School of Engineering, India

Shailesh Pramod Bendale
https://orcid.org/0000-0002-2055-8410
NBN Sinhgad School of Engineering, India

ABSTRACT

Propaganda has existed for ages, and the internet is merely its newest medium of communication to be misused to promote falsehoods, misinformation, and disinformation. Over time, it has been a successful strategy that nation-states, organizations, and individuals have employed to affect and alter public opinion. Modern propagandists are fast to take advantage of novel communication channels and are eager to use its relative insecurities. Databases and personal devices have been hacked and have also disseminated misinformation more swiftly and extensively via social media outlets and news platforms. This sophisticated strategy is described as cyber propaganda. This has further given rise to anarchists that have developed platforms such as "Assassination Market," where a person or a group of people with similar ideologies can now buy murder.

INTRODUCTION

Propaganda and Hatred

Propaganda can be briefly summarized as "The display of thoughts or activities carried out purposefully by people or organizations with a goal to influence the opinions and behavior of other people or groups for specific purposes via psychological manipulations."

DOI: 10.4018/978-1-6684-3942-5.ch006

Figure 1. Examples of WWI recruitment posters

It is a historic and successful strategy that nations and various organizations have employed to influence and manipulate public opinion on certain topics of interest. Radio stations in Western nations transmitted pro-Western messages to its Eastern counterpart, effectively utilizing them to promote propaganda during the Cold War. (Micro, 2017)

Hate Propaganda is a subset of this very phenomenon, where public advocacy or encouragement of hate against an identified person or group takes place. It usually targets people or property on factors such as color, religion, ethnicity, race, gender identity, mental or physical impairment. (see Figure 1)

While propaganda as a whole has and is used in a wide variety of circumstances, Hate Propaganda is centered mainly around Elections and Wars. To anyone following politics, it's not exactly breaking news that political parties don't like each other more often than not. Take what transpired in the presidential debate of 2020 where former President Trump and President Joe Biden did nothing to disguise their contempt of one another. The discussion for many represented a low moment in the nation's discourse; it was a distillation of a long-developing trend: disliking the opposition party.

The History of Propaganda

The notion that wars gave birth to sophisticated propaganda efforts has caused many folks to assume that propaganda is novel and contemporary. The reality, however, is that propaganda has existed for decades. No one would have mistaken propaganda of being new if, from the very beginning, attempts to mobilize attitudes and beliefs had indeed been named "propaganda". (Micro, 2017)

Before the advent of Athens as a hub of human knowledge, a majority of the people lived under despotisms. There existed no channels or ways to articulate or divulge their sentiments and aspirations as a collective. However, the Greeks, comprised of the citizen class, were mindful of their interests as a collective and well-versed in the city-state's issues and affairs.

Soon differences on religious and political topics spurred the rise of propaganda and counterpropaganda. The strong-minded Athenians, albeit without instruments such as the newspaper, the radio, or the cinema, would employ other potent propaganda techniques to influence mindset and ideas. They used various sports, the theater, law courts, and diverse festivals, and all these created opportunities for utilizing propaganda.

The Greeks utilized theatre for their political and social lessons. One successful device for bringing forth views was oratory, where the Greeks outclassed. Although there were no print presses, a wide variety of handwritten books were distributed throughout the country to mold and limit the population's thoughts.

From then on, anytime a community possessed shared knowledge or a feeling of common interests, it utilized propaganda. Countries adopted strategies similar to those of contemporary propaganda as early as the 16th century. During the rule of the Spanish Armada, Philip II and Queen Elizabeth both planned propaganda in a rather contemporary style.

"Propaganda" as a word allegedly initially was beginning to be used in general language & speech in Europe as a consequence of the campaigns of evangelists of the Catholic church. Pope Gregory XV established the Congregation for the Propagation of the Faith in 1622. It was a committee entrusted with preaching the gospel and governing church matters in heathen regions. Pope Urban VIII layed the foundation of a College of Propaganda to tutor the priests for their missions.

"propaganda" is essentially an old and respectable term; its roots are from Religious activities, which were coupled with propaganda, gaining the attention of the people. In the following decades, the term evolved into a selfish, dishonest, and subversive meaning.

Propaganda has existed far and wide in the Middle Ages and throughout its succeeding historic eras all the way to today. No society has existed without it. Battles between monarchs and Parliament in England were historic battles in which propaganda was engaged. Propaganda was employed as of one the tactics in the struggle of America's independence and the French Revolution.

WWI accentuated the power and success of propaganda. With fascism and communism in the postwar period being the sites of solid radical propaganda. Both communists and fascists aspired to spread their authority outside their respective national lines via propaganda. (Badsey, 2014)

Psychology of Propaganda

Propaganda is a component of a broader functioning of legend and mythmaking, with same psychological processes being taken advantage of, but the key difference lies in propaganda's stories and myths being purposefully constructed. Our early upbringing gives the emotional link of words and visuals with thoughts and attitudes. (Young, 1930) Through suggestions, propagandists play on the connection between our words and visuals. New tales and their elaborations, and depiction of happenings, are meant to stir fear and anxiety and make the population avoid certain things and embrace and love certain other things. Much like our conduct, our anxiety, anger, irritation, avoidance, acceptance, love, and sympathy indicate our allegiance to some specific group and our unfavorable views to others.

The tales and legends with which we are raised are essentially stories of national significance, religion, political parties, and renowned persons in history. Propaganda is a purposeful manufacture of a similar type of content in the interests of collective survival and societal influence. We accept propaganda because it fits into our unconscious minds, which our egos have always satisfied.

Fables and legends are vital to keeping the human spirit because it is the fundamental set of collective beliefs and mindset that is emotionally tuned towards a common goal. Hence, Propaganda is essentially a contemporary method for amplifying the impact of typically unconscious ways individuals sustain their morale. We feed our egos and sustain societal cohesiveness with the help of our idealistic and daydream worlds. The feeling of togetherness that is vital to our spirits is enhanced by giving society the same set of beliefs and mindsets regarding a significant circumstance.

We individually cast onto the society with our views toward a situation. As the inputs and sentimental experience are pretty much the same for most of us, our mindset and responses are likely to be very similar. Through dialogue and observation of others' activities, Society is validated in the projection of one's individual views, and through this, our unconscious inference of collective unity is substantiated. This is how our feeling of collective camaraderie deepens.

Black, Grey and White Propaganda

Black Propaganda is designed to give the appearance that individuals generated; it is aimed to denigrate. (Types Of Propaganda, n.d.) The key component of black propaganda is that the public is unaware somebody is manipulating them and therefore does not realize that they are being influenced to reach to a certain conclusion. It pretends to arise by an origin different as opposed to real one, this is usually connected to clandestine mind games.

Often this origin is disguised or is assigned to phony authorities to promotes lies, falsifications, and deceits. It bases itself on the desire of of content consumers to trust the authenticity of the source. When the creators or transmitters of this form of propaganda campaigns don't completely know the target demographic, their campaigns could end up being misinterpreted, seem dubious, or dwindle entirely.

Many ruling authorities employ it for several purposes. They camouflage its real engagement, by this a state may be even more successful in convincing doubtful target audiences. Political considerations often exist for its deployment. It is needed to mask their involvement in acts can prove to be harmful to its international relations.

On the contrary, White Propaganda is one which displays its origin or nature. This is a highly prevalent style of propaganda and is separated from the former type,which disguises its roots to defame an adversary movement. This usually involves ordinary societal affairs methods and a biased depiction of a subject. We need to take into mind that in various cultures and languages, the word "propaganda" does not carry a bad reputation and meaning. In Russian, propaganda (пропаганда) is a neutral word, analogous to the word "promotion" (of a perspective). White propaganda may be viewed as an recognition of the fact that the society is aware of the attempts being made to influence it.

In certain governments, there is a department dedicated to this. Where, one acknowledges that propaganda is generated, its origin is recognized, and its goals and plans are identified. However, during its lifetime, often white propaganda servers as a camouflage for black propaganda whenever there are attempts to disguise the other.

Finally, Grey Propaganda lies somewhere between Black and White propaganda, with the trustworthy source of the material never explicitly attributed and the sponsor's name being withheld. The purpose of Grey Propaganda is to promote the position of the disguised sponsor in a manner that is more appealing to the target audience, operating under the concept that ideas delivered via ostensibly impartial and unobtrusive means would be more convincing than blatant methods of propaganda. A common method for Grey Propagandists is to disseminate an article in a magazine, disclosing no source. Another technique of Grey Propaganda is anonymous support or providing material help to organizations that advance the propagandist's purpose.

PROPAGANDA TODAY

Today, innovations of genius men and women have created a mechanism of mass communication that has increased the rate and broadened the effect of information and ideologies, enabling propagandists with swift and efficient techniques for propagating their ideologies. This technological enhancement may be utilized in the interests of harmony and international goodwill. Alas, Hitler, Tojo, and others alike chose to grasp this excellent nerve system for narcissistic aims and brutal reasons, thereby extending the function of propaganda in society.

The United Nations were early on sluggish to employ the rapid and effective communication channels for propaganda objectives; Today they are responding blow for blow.

The contemporary evolution of politics too spurred propaganda. Propaganda for promotional activities is crucial in political campaigning in democratic elections. Earlier, Political leaders controlled most nominations, as a result, barely any promotion was required before a prospect candidate was nominated to stand for election. During final elections, one must appeal to the public to vote for him on the basis of their suitability for government and the permanence of their program. Essentially, one must participate in promotional activities as a legit and essential aspect of political battles. (Somerville, 2012)

In democracies, elected elites in authority must elaborate and defend their plans to an audience. By using persuasion, individuals in government aim to harmonize the needs of diverse groups in society. National leaders, presidents, cabinet officials, heads of departments, lawmakers and others alike appeal to the local communities and the country to create a specific direction of policy generally sought and known as public endorsement.

During peacetime, the promotional operations of democracies typically comprise of informing the population of the solutions and services offered by a specific bureau and creating widespread support with regards to the policies with which the bureau is concerned. They aim to make the services "come alive" for the daily citizen, and looking at the long-term, try to make the typical man more aware through official information and marketing. If there is public engagement in the work accomplished in the government's name or on their behalf, informed criticism from the public of government services may be promoted.

Economic shifts in the recent years have drastically increased the amount of propaganda. Under the circumstances of mass production and consumption, propaganda and public affairs have been considerably developed to assist the sale of goods and services and foster goodwill among customers, workers, other organizations, and the public.

Cyber Propaganda and its Platforms

Cyber propaganda may be broadly characterized as employing contemporary technical tools to alter the result of an event or to alter the public's opinion towards a specific viewpoint. (Micro, 2017) Propagandists deploy numerous strategies, such as theft of confidential data and exposure to the public, attacking devices directly, producing and broadcasting fake news, etc. While cyber propaganda primarily targets politicians and prominent individuals, hacktivists often use it to harm private enterprises.

Cyber propaganda tactics range dependent on the particular end aim, ranging from criticizing a prospect victim, influencing the results of an election or voting system, or perhaps even instigating a civil disturbance. We can generally divide cyber propaganda methods into three basic subgroups.

Database Hacking

Cyber criminals may break into secured devices and private datacenters or storage centers to steal important data. The stolen material may be shared selectively, timed to have the an harmful impact. Missions such as these are often state-sponsored and require great effort to implement.

Machine Hacking

A simple approach to modifying an event is to manipulate the origin of the outcome; an instance is manipulating election systems to alter the results. Entities may also force the providers of the electronic voting machines into altering the outcome.

False and Fake News

Posting false or fake news is a strong and highly impactful method that rapidly changes the opinion of the public owing to a rapid news cycle. Phony news entails manufacturing false news pieces, presenting different claims or perhaps even morphed and edited images, and spreading them via prominent social media networks. The material could appear authentic enough that consumers believe content distributes misleading information, which renders offsetting the harm exceedingly tricky.

Online platforms and media allow for free participation and open debate, although typically at the sacrifice of transparency, and are generally available for free (in terms of access) (in terms of access) (in terms of access). Websites and Blogs on the Darkweb, Media platforms, and Twitter, in particular, are strong instruments for electronically organized propaganda. The gate-keeping and fact-checking responsibilities of media are consequently easily bypassed, varied audiences are accessible directly, and unadulterated content is sent at no charge in an instant. Thus, middlemen are no longer needed to reach a group's participants.

In contrast, such channels do not intrinsically provide source validity. Therefore, this requires a while and an active fan following to achieve a reputation as a trusted internet source. However, audiences may be readily deceived and ensnared by these platforms that promote involvement from virtually everyone, fraudulent or real, for example, in the guise of bots. These platforms also permit the quick circulation of visual / voice information, as opposed to in the past where propaganda goods had to be trafficked past borders in VHS (Video Home System) cassettes or CS (Compact disc). For instance, Twitter provides live communication from battle zones, as Rebel groups in Syria publish images instantly out from the fighting zone.

The example demonstrates that such dialogue may provide 'the illusion of legitimacy' and seem to be honest (given the real-time quality). However, it is still controlled, strictly monitored, and transmitted via mediators (inauthentic). The content is often biased (unfair) since it does not present the full picture and therefore is contemptuous since the viewer cannot determine the veracity of the content or is provided with a chosen video.

Darkweb and Tor

Before we get into what Darkweb is, we must understand the Tor Network and its workings. Tor, in brief for 'The Onion Router,' is an open source and freely available software tool for facilitating anonymized interaction. It directs Internet traffic through an unrestricted, international, volunteer overlay network, comprised of greater than 6 thousand relay nodes, for disguising the location of a user as well as usage from anybody undertaking network surveillance or packet analysis. Utilizing Tor makes it harder to track down the Web activity to a user. The intent of Tor is to safeguard an individual's privacy and also one's liberty and ability to conduct confidential communication by maintaining their Web activity unsupervised.

A Tor Browser sends one's online traffic over the onion router network, encrypting it, consisting of a three-layer proxy, simulating segments of an onion (reference to Tor's onion logo and name). Tor Browser links at random to the one of the publicly listed entry nodes that passes the data through a randomly selected middle relay, and ultimately sends out the data through the 3rd and last exit node.

Tor can also be used to access web services that block Tor and can be configured to use bridges. Unlike Tor's entry and exit nodes, bridge IP addresses are not publicly listed, making it difficult for web services, internet service providers or governments to blacklist those IP addresses. This makes Tor a powerful tool for users in countries where there exists heavy censorship and political instability.

The dark web references to websites which are not indexed but are viewable through special web internet browsers. They are considerably smaller in size than the surface web, which is tiny, the dark web a subset of the deep web. Using a sea and glacier analogy, the dark web is the bottom tip of a sunken glacier, with the entire web being the glacier and the open web being the surface above the sea.

However, the dark web is a profoundly hidden part of the deep web that very few ever interact with or even visit. To put it in another way, the deep web comprises everything that exists under the surface, and that still is reachable with the necessary tools, including the dark web. Cracking down the groundwork of the dark web shows a few crucial layers which end up making it an anonymous haven:

No website indexing by general purpose internet search engines. Bing and other renowned search engines cannot recognize or provide findings for websites within the dark web.

"Virtual traffic tunnels" employing a randomized network design.

Inaccessibility by regular browsers owing to the distinct registry operator that is used. Further, It is hidden by other network protocols like firewall and cryptography for added security.

While the image of the dark web is mostly associated with the intent to commit a crime or illegal content, notably "trading" websites wherein visitors may obtain unlawful commodities or services, legitimate parties have also taken use of this framework. Many news portals such as the BBC have a Tor mirror, mainly for access in countries where there is heavy censorship of news and other information. Many Attorneys and Advocates also use the Tor browser during their research and investigations.

CROWDFUNDED ASSASSINATIONS

Cryptocurrencies become an increasingly popular form of digital payment. They have been used as a medium of exchange in return for goods and services, from socks to sushi to drugs. For the past several years, they have been used to purchase murder, too.

On the Azerbaijani Eagles website, one may contract a murder for as low as $5,000. On Slayers Hitmen, one is offered with further possibilities, with a thrashing selling at $2,000 and fatality by torturing costing $50,000.

An anarchist, known by the alias Kuwabatake Sanjuro, back in 2013 built a website known as "Assassination Market," a crowdsourced enterprise that enables anyone to discreetly donate cryptocurrencies towards a bounty in the name of a civil servant - a form of IndieGoGo or Kickstarter for political murders. As per the market's guidelines, when a potential victim on its target list is murdered, Sanjuro anticipates that several individuals will be, any contract killer that can establish that they were involved obtains the accumulated cash.

While today, the site's rewards have remained low but not negligible. The past 11 years that Assassination Market is live on the internet, numerous prospective targets have been nominated individuals. Reward money has been pooled, ranging from 10 to 40 bitcoins against various influential political figures and officeholders, with 124 bitcoins being the greatest reward on the website, targeting Ben Bernanke, who has been a common threat for a great deal of most Cryptocurrency's anti-banking-system believers. With Bitcoin's swiftly growing exchange rates, that's roughly $8 million for his prospect assassin.

Sanjuro's dark goals go further than acquiring the means to contract some electoral murders. He argues that if the market continues and gains enough customers, it will finally authorize the deaths of ample political figures such that none would willingly take office. He states he expects the Assassination Market will abolish "all governments, everywhere."

He feels that this will revolutionize society for good. His handle is common with the unnamed samurai hero in the Akira Kurosawa movie "Yojimbo." Sanjuro selected it in commemoration of Bitcoin's founder and the inventor of Silk Road, an online criminal market, who dubbed himself the Dread Pirate Roberts.

He dreams of a system that would allow a society devoid of conflicts, mass surveillance, nuclear weaponry, military, oppression, financial tampering, and limits to exchanges being firmly within our grasp for simply a few coins per individual. He furthermore feels that as early as just a few politicians are murdered, and they fully comprehend that they have lost the war on confidentiality, the assassinations could indeed cease, allowing him and his camaraderie to move to a phase of tranquility and confidentiality

Verification of Assassinations

Like some other "dark web" websites, Assassination Market works on Tor, a hidden and anonymous network which is created to stop people from tracing a website's visitors or Sanjuro. His decision to utilize solely Cryptocurrencies is aimed at hiding customers, Sanjuro himself, as well as any prospect murderers from getting recognized via the monetary operations. Cryptocurrencies, after all, maybe sent and acquired anonymously without necessarily tying them to any individual.

The website's guidelines advise its visitors that individuals send their cash via a "laundry" system to ensure that the bitcoins are anonymous before adding them to anybody's murder pool.

To adequately demonstrate that a particular assassin is accountable for the demise of a person, The website demands its murderers to produce a text document containing the date and time stamp of the killing prior to the assassination and use a data encryption procedure known as a hash to transform it into a distinct character string. Prior to the murder, the murderer embeds the info in one coin payment or more towards a prospect's prize pool.

Whenever a candidate is assassinated, they may send the text document, which he hashes to verify that the numbers confirm the data supplied prior to the victim's demise. As per Sanjuro's theory, if a file is authentic and accurately predicts the date of execution, the sender has to be involved in the crime. Sanjuro gets 1 percent of the money as a charge for his services. (Vogt, 2013).

FIGHTING FAKE NEWS

The modern digital media ecosystem, developed from the convergence of Technology and Information, portrays a scenario between the press and its viewers is reinvented. (López-Marcos et al, 2021) It provides a dilemma for journalism. In the cyber era, the crowd participates in the creation and spread of news via various media outlets.

With the press and its lack of discipline, fake news, misinformation, deceit and propaganda are rising as the key issues of journalism in a ruthless commercial framework, and maximum absorption of news items. In an environment like this, fact checkers become crucial participants of content validation.

There are several efforts from journalists with regards to the origin of electronic content, internet media and the obstacles it confronts; A crucial aspect is the battle over disinformation and falsehoods disseminated via social media. Thus, it is in requirement of change, fundamental and special abilities that take use of the possibilities which the Data Analysis society brings to the field of investigation and precise reporting.

Fact checkers were originally established in the USA and now have extended overseas. They are amongst the essential themes in journalism in the cyber world, stemming from technology breakthroughs and political and social issues. The standards of the Web, driven by competition and urgency, have affected successful validation of content spreading on the Internet. (Nyhan et al, 2016) The purpose of fact checkers is "to carry out the required measures to determine whether a news item (or piece of information) conforms to reality, has been twisted or is plain false". The job of fact checkers is not constrained to offshoots of conventional reporting, although they do rectify many of its shortcomings. Fact checking is seen as a new milestone which has the power to enhance better public conversation within current media platforms. It is believed that fact checkers only survive and accomplish their work if and when they acquire the faith of the public by the diaphanousness of the methods used and attain diplomatic independence.

Fact Checkers are analyzed depending on the circumstances of name and reputation from validating organizations; many organizations are affiliated to the IFCN, a component of The Poynter Institute for Media Studies, established a few years back, to amalgamate global fact checking news reporters. It is the biggest union of its kind in the globe, its fundamental goals include neutrality, openness and frankness. (Guess, 2015)

As shown in Table 1, An analysis template is used to act as an information collecting device to consistently enforce the collection of data. This spatial analytical sheet, which collects and arranges the data, is put up by examining the following aspects of evaluation: (see Table 1).

CONCLUSION

The internet world affects the way organizations conduct propaganda. Its universality, availability and accessibility and distribution, cheap pricing, and organizational role promote all sorts of fake or legitimate players to reach a larger audience. While also encouraging public discourse about and criticism of propaganda practices. Cyber propaganda differs from analog propaganda with regard to the medium, outlets, styles, viewers, resources, and aims.

The suspicious portion of most individuals would be quite confident that assassination markets are a fraud. Assassination isn't the type of business that exposes itself to public marketing or trusting individu-

Table 1. Fact checking corporate identity & legal history

Legal Identity		Economic Transparency	
Date of Enstablishment		Sources of Funding	
Ownership Bifurcation and Type		Quarterly and Yearly Balances and Results	
Professional Team		Profit Sources and Motive	
Corporate Adertisement, Communication and Transparency			
Visiblity and Advertising	Contact and Points of Interaction	Other Variables	Team structure
Social Media Accounts, Newsletters	Contact Details and Rate of reply	Tone and Design of Fact Checks and other Articles	Background History and Profiles of Employees
Fact Check			
Content		Methodology used	
Themes and Sectors Focused, Geographic focus on Topics, Resources utilitzed		Consultation of Various sources, Citiations, Analysis & Verfification of processes, Correction rates of wrong fact checks	

als based on their web reputations. And the fact that websites openly pledge to take target high-profile individuals adds to its unlikeliness. Viewed in that way, Assassination Markets are simply another site where a fool and his cryptocurrency are quickly split.

And yet, these types of tales - about a vast but hypothetical vision that will probably never be fulfilled - can become real very fast. To take a recent example, the notion of the Silk Road, when it was announced, it appeared absurd to most. Yes, it was theoretically conceivable for individuals to purchase and sell narcotics online. But who, outside a narrow fringe, would utilize it? Of course, we were incorrect - the site functioned effectively for 2 years before being shutdown.

REFERENCES

Badsey, S. (2014, October 8). Propaganda: Media In War Politics. *International Encyclopedia of the First World War (WW1)*. https://encyclopedia.1914-1918-online.net/article/propaganda_media_in_war_politics

Guess, A. M. (2015, March 4). *Fact-checking On Twitter: An Examination Of Campaign 2014*. https://www.americanpressinstitute.org/wp-content/uploads/2015/04/Project-1B-Guess-updated.pdf

López-Marcos, C., & Vicente-Fernández, P. (2021, August 12). *Fact Checkers Facing Fake News And Disinformation In the Digital Age: A Comparative Analysis Between Spain And United Kingdom*. MDPI. https://www.mdpi.com/2304-6775/9/3/36

Micro, T. (2017). *Fake News And Cyber Propaganda: The Use And Abuse Of Social Media - Wiadomości Bezpieczeństwa*. https://www.trendmicro.com/vinfo/pl/security/news/cybercrime-and-digital-threats/fake-news-cyber-propaganda-the-abuse-of-social-media

MicroT. (2017). *Cyber Propaganda 101*. https://www.trendmicro.com/vinfo/es/security/news/cybercrime-and-digital-threats/cyber-propaganda-101

Nyhan, B., & Jason, J. (2016, August 31). *Estimating Fact-checking's Effects - Evidence From a Long-term Experiment During Campaign 2014.* https://www.americanpressinstitute.org/wp-content/uploads/2016/09/Estimating-Fact-Checkings-Effect.pdf

Somerville, K. (2012). *Conclusions: Propaganda, Hate And the Power Of Radio.* SpringerLink. https://link.springer.com/chapter/10.1057/9781137284150_7

Types Of Propaganda - Propaganda. (n.d.). *Types of propaganda - Propaganda.* https://www.american-foreignrelations.com/O-W/Propaganda-Types-of-propaganda.html

Vogt, P. (2013, November 18). *Should We Pay Attention To Assassination Markets?* On the Media | WNYC Studios. https://www.wnycstudios.org/podcasts/otm/articles/should-we-pay-attention-assassination-markets

Young, K. (1930). *Kimball Young: Social Psychology: Chapter 27: Propoganda: PositiveControl Of Public Opinion.* https://brocku.ca/MeadProject/Young/1930/1930_27.html

Section 3
Machine Intelligence for Crime Organization and Analysis

Chapter 7
Neural Net Architecture Strategy Identifying Zero–Day Attacks in the Dark Web

Shruthi J.
BMS Institute of Technology and Management, India

Sumathi M. S.
BMS Institute of Technology and Management, India

Bharathi R.
BMS Institute of Technology and Management, India

Vidya R. Pai
BMS Institute of Technology and Management, India

ABSTRACT

Companies must foresee most critical security threats to keep one step ahead of attackers. Because attackers always refine their techniques to avoid detection and because attackers are persistently imaginative, network traffic analysis solutions have evolved providing organizations with a feasible path forward. Maintaining network visibility has gotten more challenging and time demanding as DevOps, cloud computing, and IoT (internet of things) gain popularity. Network traffic analysis can incorporate its core functionalities to detect malicious intent. The authors developed a unique darknet traffic analysis and network management solution to automate the malicious intent detection process. This strong computational intelligence forensics tool decodes network traffic, viral traffic, and encrypted communication. WANNs, a weight-independent neural network design, can detect zero-day threats. With a sophisticated solution, many businesses can protect their most valuable assets from malicious intent detection on the dark web.

DOI: 10.4018/978-1-6684-3942-5.ch007

INTRODUCTION

Only a small percentage of us have even scratched the surface of what the Internet can provide. A search engine like Google, Yahoo, or Bing only displays 4% of the total information on the internet. Additional 96 percent can only be accessed by specialised research on individual websites, subpages, closed access publications, archives and so on. The Deep Web contains this information (Mo, 2020). Everything we do online, with the exception of the Dark Web-obscured portions of the deep web, may be seen, traced, and, in some cases, monitored. There are three ways to look at the internet as a sea of information.

- **Surface Web:** There are no restrictions on the Surface Web, making it available to everyone. As a whole, it's referred to as the Internet. Search engines like Google, Bing, Yahoo, and more index everything on the Internet's surface (Rawat et al., 2021).
- **Deep Web:** All material that is not publicly available because search engines do not index it can be found in the "Deep Web." To access the deep web, which contains 96% of all internet data, you'll need special authorization.
- **Dark Web:** In the "Dark Web," which is only one percent of the deep web, all illegal activity is taking place.

If you're personal information is discovered on the dark web, there is a good chance that anyone who stumbles across it will be able to access it (Tian et al., 2019). Personal information, bank account information, credit card or debit card information, medical records, credentials, and many other types of data may be included. A company's brand might be tarnished as well as its employees' and shareholders' financial well-being if confidential data is released. When it comes to preventing or mitigating harm from these attacks and data leaks, monitoring the Dark Web is the best option (Rawat et al., 2021)

Monitoring services for the dark web have received a lot of attention in the last two years. However, there is a widespread misunderstanding regarding how or if Dark Web monitoring services work, or even exist at all. Doing so would be a near-impossible undertaking and they would not be able to begin removing data or property that had been illegally obtained (Rajawat et al., 2021). There's sometimes nothing you can do to stop something from being sold or misused once it's on an underground commercial centre. Only publicly available content can be viewed by the Dark Web Monitoring. Just like search engine crawlers can't view anything behind a login or paywall, dark web scanners can't access anything that has been protected from scraping software (Demertzis et al., 2020). Passwords and other identification information, such as social security numbers, are not the focus of their attention.

Monitoring and analysing network traffic is a difficult task, but it is necessary if you want to boost network performance, reduce attack surfaces, increase security, and better manage resources. The Darknet is a marketplace for illegal activities such as viruses, contract killings, poisons, and drugs. "Darknets" or "network telescopes" refer to the internet's unused address space. Darknet traffic does not exchange data with other computers over the internet; instead, it passively takes incoming packets and does not send any of its own (Rawat et al., 2021). A virtual computer network, Tor, allows users to access hidden resources on the dark net. Onion routing of the second generation is implemented using this method. As a result of this kind of routing, a circuit is built up one hop at a time. Because the host is behaving in an unlawful manner, the traffic on the darknet is usually seen as a misconfiguration. To keep tabs on real-time apps, a thorough examination of darknet traffic is needed (Rantos et al., 2019). Cyber security experts and other IT professionals can learn a lot about services that have been targeted by hackers or could be vulnerable to an attack by looking into darknet traffic. Researchers are now concentrating their efforts on monitoring the darknet traffic in order to identify harmful activity, particularly those involving Tor apps. The authors used ML and Deep Learning to accomplish their goal (DL)

RELATED WORK

Researchers S. Lagraa et al., developed an approach to tracking and categorising port scanning activity trends between a clusters of previously surveyed ports. It's stated that this method is fully automated, thanks to the newest graph modelling and text mining tools. It gives cyber security experts and other IT professional's comprehensive information on services that attackers are exploiting or that could be attacked. Using this method, it is easier to identify the targets of attacks, making it more effective. Tests are performed on a large dataset from Darknet or an internet telescope to see if the suggested solution works as expected.

While studying the Darknet's network traffic, the researchers at A. Berman et al. noted the challenges that security investigators and law enforcement face. Although top modelling is a well-known method for semantic analysis of market listings, its ability to record visual images is lagging behind. For the enormous dataset of photos, the researchers suggested an artificial intelligence framework based on the use of both supervised (using CNN) and unsupervised (using LDA) learning approaches. Thus, this strategy is better suited to sifting through darknet information than other methods.

There are many challenges for security services in tracking illegal activity on the Darknet, according to E. F. Fernandez et al. Analyzing a large number of photos from the Darknet takes a long time and is still not very effective. To solve this issue, researchers looked at Semantic Attention Keypoint Filtering (SAKF)-based picture classification methods and proposed a strategy that excluded non-relevant topography at the deep pixel level, allowing them to filter out irrelevant pixels. Bag of Visual Words and Salience Maps are used together in this system. Using the Tor picture as a test case, the researchers validated their technique. According to their findings, dense SIFT descriptors in MobileNet v1, Resnet50, and BoVW outperform other techniques.

The Darknet is currently dominated by cybercrime, illegal drug trading, and crypto currency marketplaces. Research on darknet technologies and specifications is examined in order to point out the challenges in exploiting criminal actions conducted over this network and to draw attention to those gaps. In order to prevent search engines from discovering criminal activity on the Darknet, researchers V. Adewopo et al claim that the network is safeguarded by specialised encryptions and setups. In addition to assisting law enforcement in their pursuit of criminals, this action will help maintain social harmony. Internet crimes were also investigated, including drug dealing and exploitation of Tor users' identities, and researchers proposed a system for inspecting and exploring unnamed online illegal markets.

It was carried out by A. Nastua et al., who carried out an in-depth review of the Tor network. The darknet's advantages and disadvantages are discussed in detail by the authors. One of the most important aspects of the Darknet is its anonymity, which allows its users to engage in any activity, lawful or not, without fear of detection. The writers also discuss the issue of anonymous cryptocurrency payments. This comprehensive study comes to a close with an explanation of what the Darknet will look like in the future.

Table 1. Previous works on darkweb related issues

Author	Objective	Technique Used	Results Obtained
S. Kumar et al.,	using data from darknet traffic to develop an artificial intelligence-based threat detection system	Random Forest	Detects malicious and innocuous network activity, as well as risks that may be lurking in plain sight.
E. Fidalgo et al.,	In order to classify the photos, the SAKF system analyses only the most salient parts of the image.	Machine Learning & DIP	gain of between 1.64% and 15.73%
K. Shahbar et al.,	A network flow-based approach for analysing traffic on the Tor network	Navie Bayes, jRIP	While non-time-related elements have less impact on the mobile platform, they have a greater effect on the PC platform.
Muhammad Bilal Sarwar et al.,	Deep learning-based generalised approach to detecting and classifying darknet traffic	CNN-LSTM	detection of darknet traffic with a 96% accuracy rate and darknet traffic with an 89% accuracy rate
L. Choshen et al.,	System based on natural language processing (NLP) for the detection of legal and illicit Darknet communications	current NLP-based models	The programme compares websites with similar content to determine if the text on the Darknet is legal or illegal.

METHODOLOGY AND MATERIALS

Machine learning algorithms such as neural networks can be successfully utilised in a wide range of industries and the manufacturing process in recent years. A large part of their success is built on their ability to analyse large amounts of data to determine how a system behaves. A great deal of information and future forecasts may be gleaned from data, which can be used to automate a number of processes and give modern industry a major boost in terms of value creation.

Neural Architecture Search

To identify the ideal design of the neural network that outperforms hand-designed models, NAS uses an algorithmic method based on the principle "Better design, Better performance" and NAS helps to reduce the time and expense associated in design testing.

Search space, search strategy, and performance estimation all fall under the umbrella term "NAS."

The NAS technique will create a search space architectural pattern. No matter how complex the branching is, it can be done in any number of ways.

- The search method used to develop a NAS approach determines the search strategy, which can be either a Bayesian optimization or a reinforcement learning approach. This takes into account the amount of time required to construct a model.
- NAS neural architecture model performance metrics convergence is what we use to estimate performance. Depending on the situation, it can assist in improving the model by cascading the findings to the next iteration, or it can simply improvise from scratch on every iteration.
- With NAS, instead of experimenting with huge datasets, NAS takes tiny datasets and improves them, which usually works well with deep learning. NAS has two primary advantages. The narrow search area aids in obtaining a better model in a shorter period of time.

Reinforcement learning, Bayesian optimization, Gradient-based optimization, Sequential model-based optimization, and Evolutionary algorithm are only few of the search methods that have been improved as a result of the improvement in NAS. Efficient NAS and Progressive NAS are two of the most often utilised approaches, each with its own set of processes, benefits, and drawbacks.

Directed graph patterns that link primitive functions together, as well as third-level patterns that encode the connections between them, are all good examples of the type of patterns to look for.

In the NAS subfield of automated machine learning, hyper-parameter optimization is closely associated with reducing programme load and complexity, providing a stable and simple environment, reducing the number of actions required in use, and providing an easy method of learning new things in new places.

Equation for determining the best neural network f* is as follows:

$$f^* = argmin_{f \in F} Cost\left(f\left(\theta^*\right), D_{vol}\right) \qquad (1)$$

$$\theta^* = argmin_{\theta} L\left(f\left(\theta\right), D_{train}\right) \qquad (2)$$

In order to get a model with high accuracy and generalizability beyond the training and testing datasets, the primary priority is to use an adaptive neural network design that adapts to that dataset and precisely coordinates the optimal hyperparameters. NAS strategy design Optimization techniques, learning rate programming, regularisation, and other such hyper parameters are examples of common hyper parameters that can be optimised. That means that with no effort and prior information, they are able to construct the best learning tactics and achieve high performance outcomes.

Meta Learning

An innovative holistic method, Meta learning automates and addresses the difficulty of using machine learning algorithms in a customised way. Machine learning algorithms and hyper parameters can be learned automatically, with the goal of achieving optimal performance. To put it another way, machine learning is a search for an as-of-yet-unknown mapping function between the data inputs and outputs. Parametric properties like algorithm weights and hyper-parametric characteristics limit or expand the search field for viable mapping functions. The following three criteria should be met by any meta-learning system:

- A learning subsystem is required for the system.
- In order to gain experience, it is necessary to make use of information gleaned from metadata associated with the dataset being processed or from previously completed learning tasks in related or unrelated disciplines.
- Dynamic selection of learning bias is required.

In order to get the most out of this meta-learning model, it needs to be tested on a wide variety of learning tasks. Class tags and attribute vectors are connected with each job in supervised learning. The model's ideal settings are as follows:

$$\theta^* = arg_\theta^{min} E_{D-P(D)} \left[L_\theta \left(D \right) \right] \tag{3}$$

In reality, a dataset represents a small portion of the total quantity of data available, even though it appears to be a typical learning process. Often, a dataset D is divided into two parts: a training dataset S and a prediction dataset B for testing and testing predictions.

$$D = \left(S, B \right) \tag{4}$$

Data sets in the D format are made up of two sets of vectors and tags.

$$D = \left\{ \left(x_i, y_i \right) \right\} \tag{5}$$

Multiple B-D training batches should have optimal parameters to maximise the likelihood of detecting true tags.

$$\theta^* = argmax_\theta E_{(x,y) \in D} \left[P_\theta(y \mid x) \right] \tag{6}$$

$$\theta^* = argmax_\theta E_{B \subset D} \left[\sum_{(x,y) \in B} P_\theta(y \mid x) \right] \tag{7}$$

Data samples with unknown tags may benefit from a small set of support for quick learning that can be fine-tuned to reduce prediction error. Because of the limited number of tags that were used to create this false dataset, it is possible to describe quick learning as a "trick" rather than a method.

Dataset

There are a number of factors to consider while selecting, developing, or comparing machine learning approaches in innovative methods. Many publicly available datasets, both real-world and simulated, have been inconsistent in terms of their organisation and standardisation. It is therefore unnecessary to pick and curate specific benchmarks. As a result, in order to conduct a valid comparison experiment, we required a well-known benchmark dataset. In this analysis, we used data from CICDarknet2020, which covers both darknet traffic and the comparable normal traffic from services such as VOIP and Audio-Stream that are implemented or not using Tor and VPN infrastructure (as well as chat and email), P2P file transfers, video streams, and more.

PROPOSED METHOD

This is a completely different issue from the one that neural architecture search attempts to address (NAS). These strategies aim to develop architectures that, once taught, outperform human-designed ones. The answer is never claimed to be inherent to the network's structure. However, no one expects the network to solve the problem without training its weights. NAS networks are incredibly 'trainable'. It is the weights that solve this problem; they found architectures are only better substrates for the weights to reside in.

For structures to encode solutions, weights must be reduced in importance. A more accurate way to evaluate networks is to look at how well they perform if they have weight values derived from a random distribution. When weight sampling is used instead of weight training, performance is reduced to being just a function of the network topology. Fortunately, sampling the weight space is impossible for any but the simplest networks due to the enormous dimension of the problem. We can't efficiently sample high-dimensional weight spaces because of the curse of dimensionality, but we can decrease the number of weight values to one by requiring weight-sharing across all weights. We can get an approximation of network performance in only a few trials by systematic sampling of a single weight value. Using this approximation, the search for ever better architectures can be pushed forward.

Figure 1. WANN overview

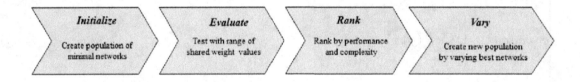

It can be described thusly: the search for these WANNs can be summarised as follows.

- A small number of neural network topologies are constructed in the beginning.
- A new shared weight value is assigned to each network at each deployment during the evaluation process.
- According to their performance and complexity, networks are classified.
- To generate a new population, tournament selection is used to randomly select the top-ranked network topologies.
- Recursively, the method generates topologies of increasing complexity that improve in performance with each generation.

The interpretability of the methods utilised is another critical step in determining the suitable architecture for a specific problem. The model's global interpretability provides a comprehensive view of the system. For example, it's crucial to know how the model decides what to do and how it interacts with other aspects.

Figure 2. Proposed WANN based architecture

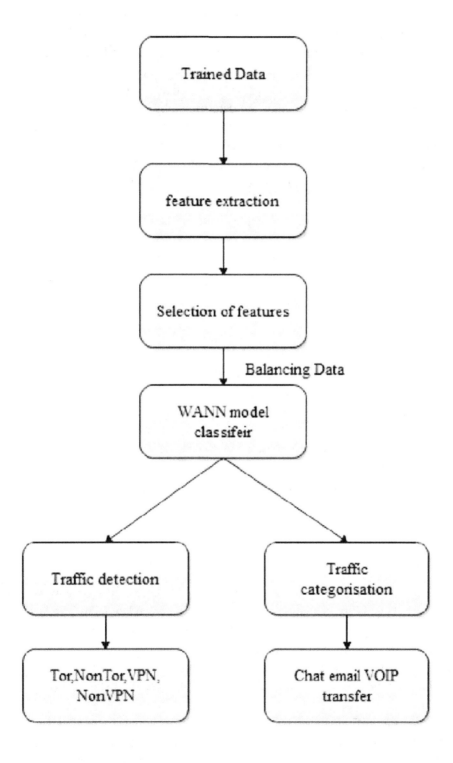

The universal level explanations are based on a generic global representation of the model, which is neither comprehensive nor precise. In the real world, it's nearly impossible to gain a complete grasp of something. As with "local interpretability," the model's reasons for making a specific decision can be examined for a single example of the dataset. Rather than being dependent on a variety of variables, predictions in tiny data sets may simply be linear or monotonous in nature.

It is highly useful to use Shapley values to provide explanations from cooperative/coalitional game theory. Cooperative games' rewards and gains are determined by a mathematical formula that assigns numerical values to groups of participants. The following is how Shapley values are linked to the challenge of understanding WANN architectural structures. A neural network model is being considered as a profit function in a cooperative game in which participants are the dataset's characteristics. Profits are predicted by the model. Using Shapley values, we can see how each feature contributes to the model's overall decision-making process and why.

Finally, the following equation yields the Shapley value of the i-th characteristic of a neural network model.

$$\varphi_i = \sum_{S \in F\{i\}} \frac{|S|!(M - |S| - 1)!}{M!} \left[f_{SU\{i\}} \left(x_{SU\{i\}} \right) - f_S \left(x_s \right) \right] \tag{8}$$

Attributes are represented by F, a subset of which S and M are the sum. When an attribute is present in the prediction, this relationship calculates its contribution and subtracts it when it is not.

SHARP (SHAP) is a strategy that uses Shapley values to explain model decisions. As a linear model, SHAP adds new features by using a method called "extra features contribution."

The reason for the SHAP technique is a local linear approach to model behaviour, which makes intuitive sense. When it comes to specific variables, the model can be very complex, but it is easy to get to a single one. By using Pearson's R correlation table, you may calculate covariance and linear correlation between two sets of independent and dependent variables $\sigma XY = Cov(X,Y) = E(X,Y) E(X)E(Y)$:

$$R = \frac{\sigma_{XY}}{\sigma_X \sigma_Y} \tag{9}$$

However, this technique's inability to detect nonlinear correlations like sinus waves and quadratic curves, together with its inability to analyse the interactions between key factors, led us to choose for a different approach: the predictive power score (PPS). Non-linear and categorical data as well as asymmetric relationships, where one variable informs the other more than the other does in a particular context, are all supported by PPS. Finding patterns in data and choosing out the relevant forecasting variables can be done by scoring the model's success in predicting a variable goal by using an off-sample prediction in the range [0, 1].

It is therefore necessary to find a local explanation of the PPS technique for models capable of operating untrained and then reinforced with training later on. Feature selection must be implemented before the SHAP approach can be used because of the method's sensitivity to model hyper-parameter settings and its general difficulty to deal with large amounts of data. As a result of the enormous number of explanations needed to explain the model's predictions and the inability to accurately distinguish between significant and irrelevant features and distances among data points, the complexity of the problem is increased.

Taking this remark seriously, feature selection was undertaken in order to maintain the most significant aspects without transforming them, in order to limit the number of features while retaining as much valuable information as feasible. It's important to avoid features with poor resolutions because they will make the learning system ineffective, but features that provide meaningful information can make the system both easy and efficient. We want to choose those traits that result in large differences across classes and minor changes within a single class.

Mean absolute error (MAE) was utilised to calculate PPS in numerical variables for feature selection, which is a metric for comparing the estimation or prediction to observed values and is calculated below.

$$MAE = \frac{1}{n}\sum_{i=1}^{n}\left|f_i - y_i\right| = \frac{1}{n}\sum_{i=1}^{n}\left|e_i\right| \tag{10}$$

fi is the actual number, and fi represents an approximation. An inaccuracy in their relationship might be defined as the quotient of these values' absolute values.

The WANN technique was used in conjunction with the Shapley values to reinforce the explanations of the NAS development strategy, after using the PPS technique for feature selection to construct a cyber-security environment with automated solutions that can recognise content from the dark web.

RESULTS

It is important to calculate all of the indices described here in a one-versus-all manner in multi-class categorization. True positives (TP) and false negatives show the extent of misclassification in the confusion matrix. If we have more FPs than FNs, then we have more cases of receiving falsely positive results. On the other hand, we refer to a genuine positive as the number of records for which we receive an accurate positive result (TP). The contrast is what is meant by the term "true negative," or "TN."

For example, sensitivity and specificity are two terms that can be used interchangeably in this context, according to the equations below.

$$TPR = \frac{TP}{TP + FN} \tag{11}$$

$$TNR = \frac{TN}{TN + FP} \tag{12}$$

$$TA = \frac{TP + TN}{N} \tag{13}$$

Using the following formulae, the precision (PRE), recall (REC), and F-score indices are defined:

$$F - Score = 2 X \frac{PRE\, X\, REC}{PRE + REC} \tag{14}$$

$$REC = \frac{TP}{TP + FN} \tag{15}$$

$$PRE = \frac{TP}{TP + FP} \tag{16}$$

The proposed methodology has to be compared against other methodologies by categorising network traffic from Tor, non-Tor VPNs, and non-VPN services. Table 2 shows the categorization results for each method in great detail. The entire CPU time spent since the procedure began, down to the hundredths of a second, was also taken into account, as was memory use as RAM hours (RAM-H). To keep tabs on how well the Linux operating system is using its resources, we wrote a shell script based on the "top" tool.

The following figures show the graphical representation of above said results.

Additionally, ROC curves and class prediction errors for the best-performing algorithm, proposed WANN, are depicted in the following graphs. The proposed algorithm had an accuracy of 90%.

The following image depicts the test dataset's confusion matrix. Model outputs with a high percentage of correct answers (in green squares) and a low percentage of incorrect responses (in light green squares) are clearly superior.

Figure shows the class prediction error curve, which shows how accurate our classifier's predictions are. Each training sample in the fitted classification model is represented by a stacking bar in this graph. Forecasts for each class are represented graphically by the bars (including FN and FP). In order to figure out which classes our classifier had trouble with and, more crucially, which inaccurate responses it produces on a class basis, we employed the class prediction error statistic. Having a clear picture of the strengths and weaknesses of our dataset and the various models helps us make more informed decisions

Table 2. Comparison of results with other classifiers

Classifier	Recall	TT (s)	RAM-H	Precision	F1	Accuracy
Proposed WANN	0.8125	400	0.000125	0.9213	0.9112	0.9512
XGB	0.7500	441.61	0.054	0.9014	0.8990	0.9012
QDA	0.4026	0.71	0.000087	0.6325	0.4394	0.3858
Extra Trees	0.7201	11.61	0.00115	0.8756	0.8762	0.8775
Naïve Bayes	0.1281	0.13	0.00019	0.2303	0.2278	0.2974
Gradient Boosting	0.7106	645.38	0.0681	0.8797	0.8764	0.8801
LDA	0.4400	2.01	0.00025	0.6439	0.6231	0.6497

Figure 3. Performance comparison chart 1

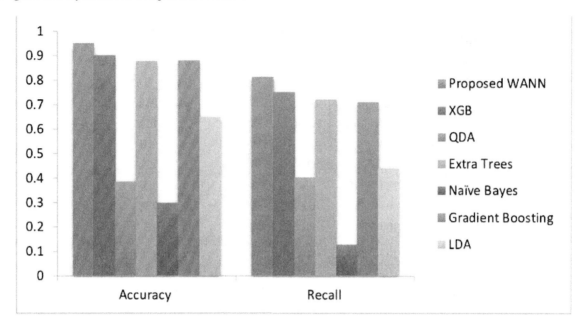

Figure 4. Performance comparison chart 2

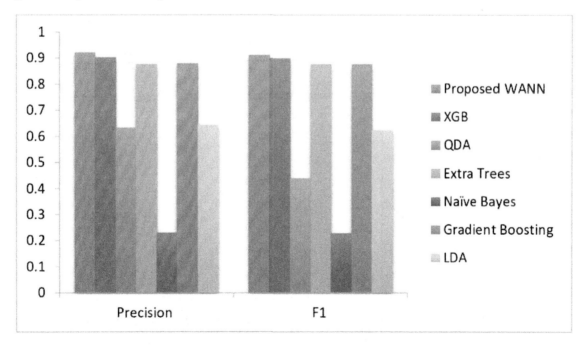

Figure 5. The proposed classifier's confusion matrix

True Class	Predicted Class										
	0	1	2	3	4	5	6	7	8	9	10
0	362	0	65	1	0	2	0	11	0	5	0
1	0	4653	5	14	10	19	0	0	2	122	4
2	8	7	9449	0	3	66	0	306	0	33	0
3	2	30	40	2916	204	25	0	4	211	33	2
4	0	1	32	621	1054	9	0	1	116	3	0
5	2	22	414	34	25	2797	2	63	16	49	0
6	1	0	1	3	3	8	14	1	2	0	0
7	2	0	383	0	0	22	0	14153	0	5	0
8	0	3	0	177	62	2	0	1	775	11	0
9	8	399	300	6	9	59	0	20	6	2053	3
10	0	36	0	0	0	0	0	0	0	19	40

Figure 6. The proposed classifier's prediction error

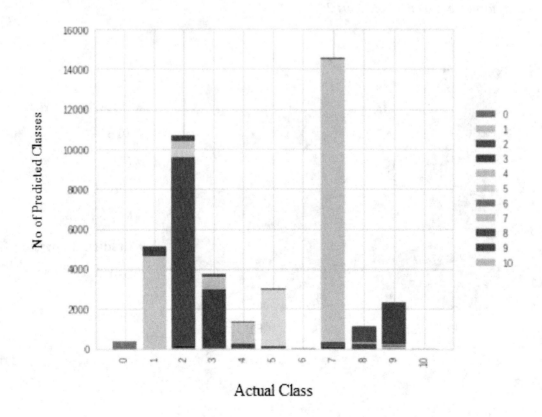

about how to go moving forward. It is possible to produce network architecture that is more advanced than human-designed versions by using NAS to automatically encode search solutions.

CONCLUSION

Computer-aided network traffic analysis was demonstrated in this study, which required minimal resources and produced excellent results. Cyber-attacks frequently cause network traffic flaws or deviations from regular operation; therefore, it is recommended that the advantages of metalearning methodology be exploited and tapped into. On a huge dataset of real-world and simulated hostile network activities, the proposed digital security solution was tested. It was our goal to understand more about how neural network architecture codifies solutions to and represents a certain job without the need for prior knowledge. One of the most exciting aspects of the suggested holistic approach is that it eliminates the requirement for system training by automating and solving the problem of specialisation in the usage of neural network discovering algorithms without the involvement of humans.

An approach to developing interpretable neural networks is presented in this research by directly encoding the answer in network design rather than training its weights. Because it is more resistant to changes in node inputs than existing learning systems, to protect against hostile attacks or even network destruction, the proposed design could serve as a foundation.

REFERENCES

Asad, M., Asim, M., Javed, T., Beg, M. O., Mujtaba, H., & Abbas, S. (2020, July). DeepDetect: Detection of distributed denial of service attacks using deep learning. *The Computer Journal, 63*(7), 983–994. doi:10.1093/comjnl/bxz064

Abbasi, A., Javed, A. R., Chakraborty, C., Nebhen, J., Zehra, W., & Jalil, Z. (2021). ElStream: An ensemble learning approach for concept drift detection in dynamic social big data stream learning. *IEEE Access: Practical Innovations, Open Solutions, 9*, 66408–66419. doi:10.1109/ACCESS.2021.3076264

Javed, Baker, Asim, Beg, & Al-Bayatti. (2020). *AlphaLogger: Detecting motion-based side-channel attack using smartphone keystrokes.* Tech. Rep.

Lagraa, S., Chen, Y., & François, J. (2019, May). Deep mining port scans from darknet. *International Journal of Network Management, 29*(3), e2065. doi:10.1002/nem.2065

Fernandez, E. F., Carofilis, R. A. V., Martino, F. J., & Medina, P. B. (2020). *Classifying suspicious content in Tor Darknet.* Available: https://arxiv.org/abs/2005.10086

Berman, A., & Paul, C. L. (2019). Making sense of Darknet markets: Automatic inference of semantic classifications from unconventional multimedia datasets. *Proc. Int. Conf. Hum.-Comput. Interact*, 230–248. 10.1007/978-3-030-22351-9_16

Adewopo, V., Gonen, B., Varlioglu, S., & Ozer, M. (2019). Plunge into the underworld: A survey on emergence of darknet. *Proc. Int. Conf. Comput. Sci. Comput. Intell. (CSCI)*, 155–159. 10.1109/CSCI49370.2019.00033

Nastuła, A. (2020, April). Dilemmas related to the functioning and growth of Darknet and the onion router network. *J. Sci. Papers Social Develop. Security, 10*(2), 3–10. doi:10.33445ds.2020.10.2.1

Kumar, S., Vranken, H., Dijk, J. V., & Hamalainen, T. (2019). Deep in the dark: A novel threat detection system using darknet traffic. *Proc. IEEE Int. Conf. Big Data (Big Data),* 4273–4279. 10.1109/BigData47090.2019.9006374

Fidalgo, E., Alegre, E., Fernández-Robles, L., & González-Castro, V. (2019, September). Classifying suspicious content in Tor darknet through semantic attention keypoint filtering. *Digital Investigation, 30,* 12–22. doi:10.1016/j.diin.2019.05.004

Choshen, L., Eldad, D., Hershcovich, D., Sulem, E., & Abend, O. (2019). *The language of legal and illegal activity on the Darknet.* Available: https://arxiv.org/abs/1905.05543

Mo, C., Xiaojuan, W., Mingshu, H., Lei, J., Javeed, K., & Wang, X. (2020). A network traffic classification model based on metric learning. *Comput. Mater. Continua, 64*(2), 941–959.

Xiong, B., Yang, K., Zhao, J. Y., & Li, K. Q. (2017, June). Robust dynamic network traffic partitioning against malicious attacks. *Journal of Network and Computer Applications, 87,* 20–31.

Du, C., Liu, S., Si, L., Guo, Y., & Jin, T. (2020). Using object detection network for malware detection and identification in network traffic packets. *Comput. Mater. Continua, 64*(3), 1785–1796.

Rantos, K., Drosatos, G., Demertzis, K., Ilioudis, C., & Papanikolaou, A. (2021). *Blockchain-Based Consents Management for Personal Data Processing in the IoT Ecosystem.* Available online: https://www.scitepress.org/PublicationsDetail.aspx?ID=+u1w9%2fItJqY%3d&t=1

Marin, E., Almukaynizi, M., Nunes, E., & Shakarian, P. Community Finding of Malware and Exploit Vendors on Darkweb Marketplaces. *Proceedings of the 2018 1st International Conference on Data Intelligence and Security (ICDIS),* 81–84.

Almukaynizi, M., Paliath, V., Shah, M., Shah, M., & Shakarian, P. (2018). Finding Cryptocurrency Attack Indicators Using Temporal Logic and Darkweb Data. *Proceedings of the 2018 IEEE International Conference on Intelligence and Security Informatics (ISI),* 91–93.

Cherqi, O., Mezzour, G., Ghogho, M., & el Koutbi, M. (2018). Analysis of Hacking Related Trade in the Darkweb. *Proceedings of the 2018 IEEE International Conference on Intelligence and Security Informatics (ISI),* 79–84.

Dale, M., Miller, J. F., Stepney, S., & Trefzer, M. A. (2016). Evolving Carbon Nanotube Reservoir Computers. In *Unconventional Computation and Natural Computation* (pp. 49–61). Springer.

Rajawat, A. S., Rawat, R., Mahor, V., Shaw, R. N., & Ghosh, A. (2021). Suspicious Big Text Data Analysis for Prediction—On Darkweb User Activity Using Computational Intelligence Model. In *Innovations in Electrical and Electronic Engineering* (pp. 735–751). Springer.

Rawat, R., Mahor, V., Chirgaiya, S., Shaw, R. N., & Ghosh, A. (2021). Sentiment Analysis at Online Social Network for Cyber-Malicious Post Reviews Using Machine Learning Techniques. *Computationally Intelligent Systems and their Applications,* 113-130.

Rawat, R., Mahor, V., Chirgaiya, S., Shaw, R. N., & Ghosh, A. (2021). Analysis of Darknet Traffic for Criminal Activities Detection Using TF-IDF and Light Gradient Boosted Machine Learning Algorithm. In *Innovations in Electrical and Electronic Engineering* (pp. 671–681). Springer.

Rajawat, A. S., Rawat, R., Barhanpurkar, K., Shaw, R. N., & Ghosh, A. (2021). Vulnerability Analysis at Industrial Internet of Things Platform on Dark Web Network Using Computational Intelligence. *Computationally Intelligent Systems and their Applications*, 39-51.

Rajawat, A. S., Rawat, R., Barhanpurkar, K., Shaw, R. N., & Ghosh, A. (2021). Blockchain-Based Model for Expanding IoT Device Data Security. *Advances in Applications of Data-Driven Computing*, 61.

Rawat, R., Dangi, C. S., & Patil, J. (2011). Safe Guard Anomalies against SQL Injection Attacks. *International Journal of Computers and Applications*, 22(2), 11–14.

Rajawat, A. S., Rawat, R., Shaw, R. N., & Ghosh, A. (2021). Cyber Physical System Fraud Analysis by Mobile Robot. In *Machine Learning for Robotics Applications* (pp. 47–61). Springer.

Rawat, R., Rajawat, A. S., Mahor, V., Shaw, R. N., & Ghosh, A. (2021). Dark Web—Onion Hidden Service Discovery and Crawling for Profiling Morphing, Unstructured Crime and Vulnerabilities Prediction. In *Innovations in Electrical and Electronic Engineering* (pp. 717–734). Springer.

Rawat, R., Rajawat, A. S., Mahor, V., Shaw, R. N., & Ghosh, A. (2021). Surveillance Robot in Cyber Intelligence for Vulnerability Detection. In *Machine Learning for Robotics Applications* (pp. 107–123). Springer.

Rawat, R., Mahor, V., Chirgaiya, S., & Rathore, A. S. (2021). Applications of Social Network Analysis to Managing the Investigation of Suspicious Activities in Social Media Platforms. In *Advances in Cybersecurity Management* (pp. 315–335). Springer.

Rawat, R., Mahor, V., Rawat, A., Garg, B., & Telang, S. (2021). Digital Transformation of Cyber Crime for Chip-Enabled Hacking. In *Handbook of Research on Advancing Cybersecurity for Digital Transformation* (pp. 227–243). IGI Global.

Rawat, R., Garg, B., Mahor, V., Chouhan, M., Pachlasiya, K., & Telang, S. Cyber Threat Exploitation and Growth during COVID-19 Times. In *Advanced Smart Computing Technologies in Cybersecurity and Forensics* (pp. 85–101). CRC Press.

Mahor, V., Rawat, R., Telang, S., Garg, B., Mukhopadhyay, D., & Palimkar, P. (2021, September). Machine Learning based Detection of Cyber Crime Hub Analysis using Twitter Data. In *2021 IEEE 4th International Conference on Computing, Power and Communication Technologies (GUCON)* (pp. 1-5). IEEE.

Mahor, V., Rawat, R., Kumar, A., Chouhan, M., Shaw, R. N., & Ghosh, A. (2021, September). Cyber Warfare Threat Categorization on CPS by Dark Web Terrorist. In *2021 IEEE 4th International Conference on Computing, Power and Communication Technologies (GUCON)* (pp. 1-6). IEEE.

Rawat, R., Mahor, V., Chirgaiya, S., & Garg, B. (2021). Artificial Cyber Espionage Based Protection of Technological Enabled Automated Cities Infrastructure by Dark Web Cyber Offender. In *Intelligence of Things: AI-IoT Based Critical-Applications and Innovations* (pp. 167–188). Springer.

Tian, W., Ji, X., Liu, W., Liu, G., Lin, R., Zhai, J., & Dai, Y. (2019). "Defense strategies against network attacks in cyber-physical systems with analysis cost constraint based on honeypot game model," Comput. *Mater. Continua*, *60*(1), 193–211.

Shahbar, K., & Zincir-Heywood, A. N. (2014). Benchmarking two techniques for Tor classification: Flow level and circuit level classification. *Proc. IEEE Symp. Comput. Intell. Cyber Secur. (CICS)*, 1–8.

Blagus, R., & Lusa, L. (2010, December). Class prediction for high-dimensional classimbalanced data. *BMC Bioinformatics*, *11*(1), 1–17.

Pavel, Y. P. P. A. F., & Soares, B. C. (2002). Decision tree-based data characterization for meta-learning. *Proc. IDDM-2002*, 111.

Coulombe, J. C., York, M. C. A., & Sylvestre, J. (2017). Computing with networks of nonlinear mechanical oscillators. *PLoS One*, *12*, e0178663.

Huang, G., Zhu, Q., & Siew, C. (2006). Extreme Learning Machine: Theory and Applications. *Neurocomputing*, *70*, 489–501.

Lekamalage, C. K. L., Song, K., Huang, G., Cui, D., & Liang, K. (2017). Multi layer multi objective extreme learning machine. *Proceedings of the 2017 IEEE International Conference on Image Processing (ICIP)*, 1297–1301.

Tu, E., Zhang, G., Rachmawati, L., Rajabally, E., Mao, S., & Huang, G. (2017). A theoretical study of the relationship between an ELM network and its subnetworks. *Proceedings of the 2017 International Joint Conference on Neural Networks (IJCNN)*, 1794–1801.

Demertzis, K., Iliadis, L. S., & Anezakis, V.-D. (2018). Extreme deep learning in biosecurity: The case of machine hearing for marine species identification. *J. Inf. Telecommun.*, *2*, 492–510.

Demertzis, K., Iliadis, L., Tziritas, N., & Kikiras, P. (2020). Anomaly detection via blockchained deep learning smart contracts in industry 4.0. *Neural Computing & Applications*, *32*, 17361–17378.

Rantos, K., Drosatos, G., Demertzis, K., Ilioudis, C., Papanikolaou, A., & Kritsas, A. (2019). ADvoCATE: A Consent Management Platform for Personal Data Processing in the IoT Using Blockchain Technology. In *Innovative Security Solutions for Information Technology and Communications* (pp. 300–313). Springer.

Chapter 8
Implementation of Machine Learning Techniques for Analyzing Crime and Dark Web Data

Sanjaya Kumar Sarangi
Utkal University, India

Muniraju Naidu Vadlamudi
Institute of Aeronautical Engineering, India

Balram G
Anurag University, India

C. Sasidhar Sarma
Annamacharya Institute of Technology and Science, India

D. Saidulu
Guru Nanak Institutions Technical Campus (Autonomous), India

Sakthidasan Sankaran K.
Hindustan Institute of Technology and Science, India

ABSTRACT

The dark web is a virtually untraceable hidden layer of the internet that is frequently used to store and access secret data. However, a number of situations have been documented in which this platform has been used to covertly undertake illicit and unlawful operations. Traditional crime-solving procedures are inadequate to meet the demands of the current crime environment. Machine learning can be used to detect criminal patterns. Past crime records, social media sentiment analysis, meteorological data, and other sources of data can be used to feed this machine learning technique. Using machine learning, there are five phases to predicting crime. These are data gathering, data classification, pattern recognition, event prediction, and visualization. Using crime prediction technologies, law enforcement agencies can make better use of their limited resources. In this chapter, the authors show the importance of learning the principles of various policies on the dark web and cyber crimes, guiding new researchers through cutting-edge methodologies.

DOI: 10.4018/978-1-6684-3942-5.ch008

INTRODUCTION

A violent crime, according to the FBI, is one that involves the use of force or threats Assault, murder, forcible rape, and robbery are all included in the Uniform Crime Reporting (UCR) programme of the FBI. The FBI's Uniform Crime Reporting (UCR) programme defines each of the offences in this way: When a person intentionally kills another human being, it is referred to as murder. The United States Crime Report (UCR) does not include a homicide or attempted homicide that is classified as an aggravated assault. Forced Rape - Forced rape is when a woman's will is broken and she is sexually assaulted. Attempts or assaults to commit rape by threat or force are not included in this category, even though abuse (without pressure) or other sexual crimes are. To steal something of value from someone else's care, custody, or control, either by force or threat of force, and/or by intimidating the patient, is known as robbery Harassing another person with the intent to inflict severe or aggravated bodily harm is known as aggravated assault. Aggravated assaults are typically committed with a weapon or other means to cause death or serious bodily harm, according to the UCR programme. This category includes attempted aggravated assaults involving firearms, knives, and other weapons that would have resulted in serious bodily harm if completed. Robbery is a crime that includes both aggravated assault and larceny-theft. Sadly, these crimes appear to be on the rise in our society. Using data mining and machine learning, law enforcement officials have been able to reduce crime and improve law enforcement efforts.

Rather than being purely personal acts of thefts, a significant number of hacking activities have evolved into well-organized, financially backed players seeking to make large sums of money. Organizational crime's aims range from direct gain to political benefit in this arena. (W. Tounsi, 2019)

As a result of this shift, enterprises must consider modern and complex approaches in order to stay up with the rapid growth of cyber-attack techniques. As a result, a new generation from in cyber security tools known as Cyber Threat Intelligence is emerging, which is attracting growing research interest and security practitioners alike. An information solution that offers evidence-based information on cyber threats is CTI. Based on the knowledge gathered, organizations can make cyber security decisions, such as those relating to the detection of cyber-attacks, their prevention, and their recovery from cyber-attacks.

Social media platforms are regarded by hackers as essential resources in their quest for knowledge and practice on the Deep and Dark Webs. They trade stolen credit card numbers, violated data, and security breaches over these networks (L. Queiroz et al., 2020). In order to establish and expand, criminal organizations depend on interpersonal connections. Through social networking sites and forums in particular, criminals, such as hacker attacks, are able to disseminate their knowledge and ideas. Members can pursue the posts of other representatives who they believe to be trustworthy or knowledgeable on these websites. Another benefit of being part of a community is that forum members within that community have different specialties and standings based on actions and services. By providing a platform for the spread of cybercriminal networks, forums help to foster an environment where criminal activity can flourish. Due to their importance in detecting and alerting organizations to potential threats, these locations are used by scientists and cyber security professionals (P. Shakarian., 2018). It is also possible to continuously develop new security information technologies by studying these Dark Web hacker communities (Chen P et al.. 2008)

However, how unexpected are different crimes and their underpinning nature? A predictive model has become increasingly necessary as new types of crimes have emerged as a result of social and economic change, say the writers of ref. According to ref. (Rani A and Rajasree., 2019), crime can be predicted and the perpetrator apprehended using the Mahanolobis crime trends and prediction technology and a variational tightly wrapped technique. There were five grants awarded to the United States N.I.J. in 1998(Gorr W and Harris, 2003) for crime predicting the future as a follow-up to crime mapping. Criminal justice organizations in the United States, the Great Britain, the Netherlands, Europe, and Swiss are now using crime forecasting programmes (Rummens A et al., 2017). The ability to detect criminal activity is getting better and better with each trying to pass year thanks to advancements in technology.

Consequently, it has become critical that we can provide a brand powerful new machine to the police and government (a set of programmes) to assist them in criminal investigation. Because the primary purpose of crime forecasting is to predict crimes before they occur, the value of applying crime forecasting techniques is self-evident. Using machine learning algorithms and methods, we aim to make an impact in this paper by predicting both the nature of a crime and the identity of the perpetrator. We had doubts about whether the crime's nature could be predicted before it happened. It's possible to classify every aspect of a crime, despite the fact that it may appear impossible from the outside. As the saying goes, every criminal has a reason for his or her actions. A different way of saying this is that, if we use motive to categorize the types of crimes, we can come up with a list of subtypes. It's possible to establish a database of all recorded crimes by category and visual information of the surrounding area so that Machine learning techniques and computer vision techniques can be used to predict crimes before they occur.

As a first step, the surface web (also known as the open web or clear web) encompasses all websites that can be indexed by search engines (Rajawat et al., 2021). The Deep Web, on the other hand, is a collection of websites that cannot be found through search engines because they are not indexed (or the Invisible Web). A password is required in order to access content on a website that can be accessed by typing in the URL directly into the address bar of the web browser.

A distinction must be made between the "dark web" and the "deep web" by researchers. The Deep Web is a portion of the internet that is inaccessible to search engines due to various technical issues with the way websites operate (Rawat et al., 2021). While the Dark Web is a subcategory of the Deep Web that uses special encryption software to hide users' identities and IP addresses, researchers estimate this to be more than 90% of the entire web.

The Dark Web, or the Dark net, is the most difficult part of the Deep Web to access. In this hidden and encrypted environment, criminals gain an advantage because of the anonymity provided (Rawat et al., 2021). Hackers, both amateur and professional, engage in a wide range of criminal activities, including extortion, network sabotage, and data theft, as well as paedophile networks, human trafficking, terrorism, and the recruitment of extremists, as well as hacked digital media trade, counterfeiting, and murderers for hire.

The Dark Web makes it possible to conceal the identity of users, network traffic, and the data they exchange over it. The Dark Web can only be accessed using special software, such as The Onion Router (TOR) (Rawat et al., 2021), the Invisible Internet Project (I2P), and Freenet. Studies have shown that criminals often use dark networks as their primary operating platform. As an example of Crime-as-a-Service, the Dark Web's marketplaces provide the majority of the items typically found in traditional black markets. Members of Dark Web marketplaces, such as Bitcoin and Monero, use crypto currencies to complete their transactions (Mahor et al., 2021). One way that some cybercriminals help others commit crimes is by acting as providers of cryptocurrency.

The Chapter Organization is as follows:

- Section 1 Provides and Overview of Cybercrimes, Dark web and its history which is helpful to learn the basics of Cybercrimes and Dark web. It also provides the relation of Various Machine Learning techniques with Cybercrimes and Dark web.
- Section 2 gives detailed related work in the field of Machine learning, Cybercrimes and Dark web.
- Section 3 Gives the information about Crime Data Analysis using Machine learning and also explains the data source, Pre-processing, Statistical, Trend and Geographical Analysis of various crimes in Vancouver.
- Section 4 Provides various Challenges and Ethical Concerns in the fields of Machine Learning and Dark web Data analysis and Section 5 Concludes the Work

RELATED WORK

To put it simply, machine learning is the process by which a computer system gains knowledge through the use of precedents. various machine learning algorithms are accessible to clients, and these algorithms will be used with datasets to produce interesting results. However, supervised and unsupervised learning algorithms are two of the most common types of learning algorithms. Supervised learning algorithms use labeled training data to infer information or "the right answer." It is up to the algorithms to predict a specific attribute or set of attributes. Unlabeled class data, on the other hand, is the target of unsupervised learning algorithms, which seek to uncover hidden structures. Algorithms learn more about a dataset as they are tested on a larger number of examples. In the field of data mining, there are five types of machine learning algorithms: These algorithms are using the data's attributes to predict one or more discrete values by one or more of the variables. Algorithms for classifying data One or more observed data can be predicted by these algorithms depending on the types of a dataset (e.g., profit/loss) that take continuous values (such as a percentage). In the procedure of examining the associations among elements, it is a statistical tool (3) Algorithms for Segmentation Analysis — Group or cluster data based on similar properties. (iv) Algorithms for Association Analysis - Identifying connections between various dataset attributes. Algorithms of this type are commonly used in market basket analysis to create association rules. The Web path flow can be summarized using Sequence Analysis Algorithms. (v) Sequence analysis identifies patterns or associations over time by identifying correlations (R. Bermudez et al,. 2011).

To begin, the Surface Web (also known as the "Open Web" or "Clear Web" in other contexts) refers to all websites that are open to the public and can be found via search engines. The Deep Web, on the other hand, is a collection of websites that search engines are unable to index, making them unavailable to the general public (or the Invisible Web). To access the website's content, you'll either need to type its URL into the address bar of your web browser or use a password (E. W. T. Ngai et al,. 2008).

Researchers should distinguish between the Deep Web and the Dark Web. For a variety of reasons, search engines are unable to access certain portions of the internet known as the Deep Web, which are connected to the website's operational duties. Around ninety per cent of the web's content is found on the Deep Web, which is a subcategory of the Interwebz that uses specialised strong encryption to mask users' personalities and Web addresses (R. Liggett et al,. 2019).

Consequently, it is a part of the Darknet known as "the Dark Web," or "the Dark net." Criminal behaviour is more likely to be carried out in secret and encrypted spaces because of the prevalence of anonymity (R. Liggett et al,. 2019). There are a wide range of criminal activities taking place in this area of the internet, including hacking, extortion, network sabotage, and theft of corporate data, as well as numerous other crimes, including child pornography and paedophile networks, drug and arms trafficking, human trafficking, and terrorist recruitment, as well as hacked digital media trade.

It is possible to conceal the identity of the user, traffic patterns, and update over the Dark Web. The Onion Router (TOR), Invisible Internet Project (I2P), and Freenet are some of the only tools available to those outside of the Dark Web who want to browse the Dark Web anonymously (T. J. Holt and A. M. Bossler,. 2020). Studies have shown that criminals often use dark networks as their primary operating platform. CaaS is evident, for example, in Dark Web marketplaces, which sell nearly everything that can be found on a traditional black market (N. Pelton and I. B. Singh, 2019). Members of Dark Web marketplaces, such as Bitcoin and Monero, use cryptocurrencies to complete their transactions. Crypto currency providers may be malicious actors who would like to make life simpler for someone else to involved in illegal activity (G. Hurlburt, 2017). The Dark Web allows users to conceal their online personae, as well as their network traffic and the data they exchange on it. Standard web browsers are unable to provide access to users outside of the Dark Web; only specialized software, such as TOR, I2P, and Freenet, can do so (T. J. Holt and A. M. Bossler,. 2020). It is widely accepted that dark networks are the primary location for criminal activity. Crime-as-a-service (CaaS) can be seen in the Dark Web marketplaces, which offer many of the same goods as traditional black markets. Members of Dark Web marketplaces use cryptocurrencies like Bitcoin and Monero to complete their trades, further obscuring their identities (J. N. Pelton and I. B. Singh, 2019).

Sellers and buyers in dark web marketplaces have varying levels of technical expertise. Hacking tools and malware can be created and sold by a tiny group of extremely knowledgeable vendor, while remaining low knowledgeable vendor purchase from or work together with those to carry out large-scale attacks or breaches of information. Cybercriminals no longer need to be tech-savvy to commit their crimes, as demonstrated by this case study in cybercrime. As a result of this, a number of professional service providers offer additional protection and privacy to their clients in the form of security services. Consequently, the identity of the perpetrator of a cyber attack remains a mystery.

In the field of crime prediction, "Modus Operandi" (Method of Operation) has been used extensively (Grimani et al,. 2020). Some studies show that social media can be used in the data collection process (L. Queiroz etal,.2020). Images from social media were used in University of Alabama research to identify the most wanted criminals, with the goal of catching terrorists in the majority of cases. (E. R. Leukfeldt et al,. 2020) CNN has also used image processing (Convolutional Neural Networks). A crime analysis programme based on image processing was proposed by the Surrey Police Department. There, investigators culled through photos of criminals' shoe prints to narrow the field of potential suspects. According to statistics, criminals' footprints were found at crime scenes in the amounts of 30 to 40 percent on average (S. Aghababaei and M. Makrehchi, 2016). The use of Artificial Intelligence in the detection of crime patterns has also been applied to the financial sector (P. Chitrakar et al,. 2016). A significant number of fraud documentations have been used in financial frauds(N. E. Sawyer and C. W. Monckton,. 1995). Images can be used to detect fake signatures, handwriting, and other forms of identification. Using DNS (Domain Name Server) and HTML content analysis, Easy Solutions Research found that financial institutions' usual phishers can be tracked down. Detecting fraud that follows a predictable pattern was the focus of another study conducted at Beihang University (R. Kumar et al,. 2009). CDR has been used to gather this information (Call Detail Records). Most of these methods for predicting criminal activity had a high rate of accuracy.

Table 1. The quick snap of the(a)creative

Type	Year	Month	Day	Hour	Minute	Hundred _Block	Neighbourhood	X	Y
Other Theft	2004	7	23	12	52	Roboson ST	West end	532689.3	656489
Theft from Vehicle	2004	7	14	18	6	Chestnut ST	Kitsilano	445689.3	124563
Mischief	2004	3	18	9	23	Commercial DR	Grandview	345632.3	145782
Theft from Vehicle	2004	5	21	4	45	Broadway AVE	Wood land	442356.2	456789
Offense against a Person	2004	9	10	3	76	E Broadway	Mount Pleasant	0	0
Offense against a Person	2004	9	9	2	45	Broadway AVE	Grandview	0	0
Mischief	2004	3	3	1	12	39th Avenue	Eastmart	487961.3	567893

CRIME DATA ANALYSIS USING MACHINE LEARNING

Data Source

The city of Vancouver's open data catalogue was used to obtain the original datasets. This project makes use of two sets of data: one on crime, the other on neighborhood. The VPD has been compiling crime statistics since 2003, and new data is added to the database each Sunday morning. Data on the category of crime, as well as the date, moment, and place of incident, can be found in this report. The Geographic Information System (GIS) boundaries of the city's 22 neighborhood areas are included in the neighborhood dataset (GIS). Maps are created by combining information from two different datasets: the crime and the neighborhood.

Preprocessing

An initial preprocessing step involves adding missing values and removing unused columns from the dataset before it can be used as-is. Datasets 1 and 2 are shown in Table 1 and 2.

Statistical Analysis

Crime data is distributed according to every day of the week for the criminal investigation dataset displayed in Figure 1. Every year, 31624 crimes are committed in Vancouver, with 2720 crimes done per month and 90 crimes committed per day. A normal distribution is more likely to be observed in the dataset when the time intervals are increased. After further investigation, it was discovered that the Stanley Cup riot on June 15, 2011, was triggered by an outlier in the daily graph, which had an abnormal maximum value of 650 events at the time.

Table 2. The quick snap of the (b)preprocessed sets of data

Type	Year	Month	Day	Hour	Hundred _Block	Neighbourhood
Other Theft	2004	9	9	13	Roboson ST	West end
Theft from Vehicle	2004	7	12	9	Chestnut ST	Kitsilano
Mischief	2004	3	3	8	Commercial DR	grandview
Theft from Vehicle	2004	5	22	5	Broadway AVE	wood land
Offense against a Person	2004	11	12	6	E Broadway	mount pleasant
Offense against a Person	2004	11	25	4	Broadway AVE	Westview
Mischief	2004	3	4	7	39th Avenue	Southlands
Break and Enter Resident	2004	1	28	8	Vensari ES ST	Kitsilano

Figure 1. In the year, (a) period, (b) day, (c) year, the number of offences

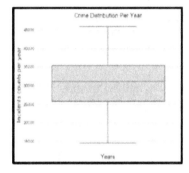 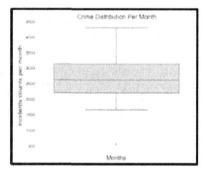 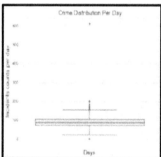

Trend Analysis

Figure 2 shows a general decline in crime from 2003 to 2013, but an increase in 2016 and a slight decline to about 3000 crimes per year in 2018 shows the overall trend.

Figure 3 shows the time-featured heat-map graphs that show the most dangerous times of year are summer and the middle of each month. Weekends and evenings are the most common times for criminal activity. In a heat map, the highest values were found near zero hours when all empty data cells have been filled with zero. because they were all zeros.

Theft from vehicles was the most frequently reported crime, followed closely by mischief. Vehicle theft has decreased significantly in recent years, but there has been an increase in the number of other thefts. In Figure 2, each crime's number and trend are shown.

Geographical Analysis

While there are many ways to depict crime hotspots on a map, choropleth mapping is one of the most commonly used methods (Y. Yu et al,. 2017). Choropleth maps presents the distribution of numerical data by employing dark colours. Crime points can be identified and criminal conduct can be studied

Figure 2. An average of the number of crimes committed each season

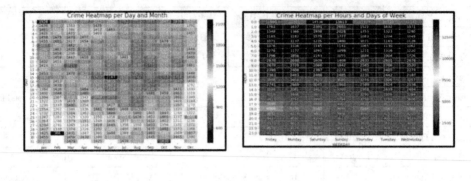

(a)   (b)

using this method. A sophisticated analysis tool for solving crimes is the Geoinformation System (GIS). It aids police officers in making operational and tactical decisions by displaying the locations of crime series on a single map together with relevant geographic data (G. Zhou et al,. 2012).

To begin with, the neighbourhood boundary dataset was converted from UTM to WGS84, known as latitude and longitude, as the first step toward geographic analysis. Because Python has a variety of libraries for visualizing geographic data, it was used to create the map.

The number of crimes committed in each Vancouver neighbourhood was tallied to show the city's crime hotspots. The choropleth map shows the ten most criminally active neighbourhoodsover a 30-day

Figure 3. The violence weather map (a) (b)shows the number of crimes committed each day, month, and week

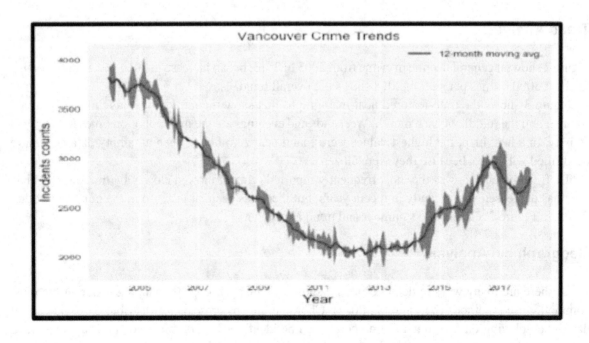

Figure 4. Depicts (a) the number of offenses perpetrated by type and (b) the overall trend

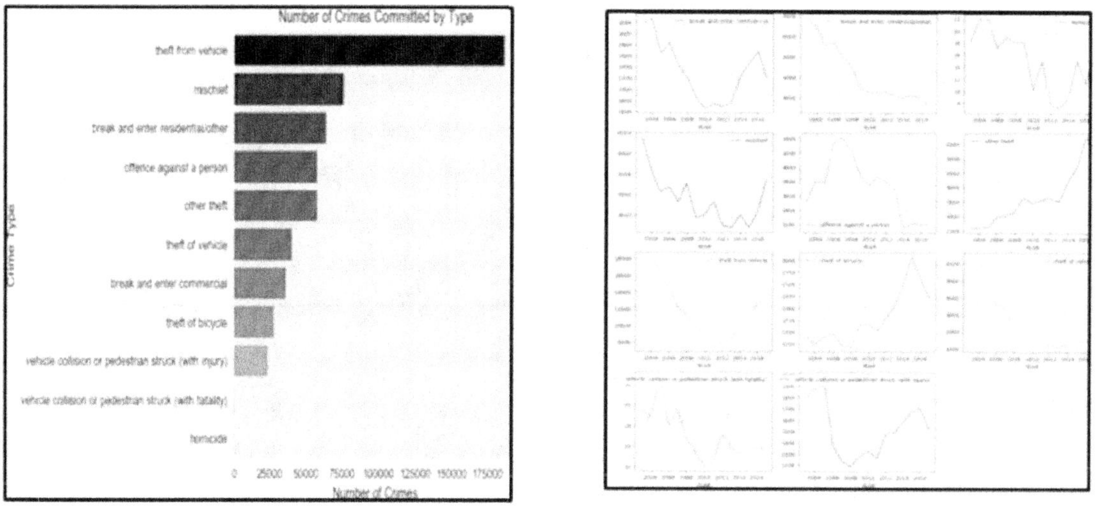

(a)

(b)

period, as shown in Table 3. Figure 5 shows Vancouver's 30-day access point map and spot groupings of events that occurred

Table 3. Top-10 crime-dense neighborhoods

MapID	Name	Density (persquaremiles)
CBD	Downtown	4.6305
SUN	Sunset	4.235
KC	Kensington-CedarCottage	3.265
STR	Strathcona	1.568
RC	Renfrew-Collingwood	2.012
MARP	Marpole	2.456
FAIR	Fairview	1.689
MP	MountPleasant	1.012
KITS	Kitsilano	1.638
OAK	Oakridge	2.056

CHALLENGES AND ETHICAL CONCERNS

Ferguson (R.-H. Ferguson,.2017) dealt with some significant challenges in the linguistics domain when studying Dark Web content:

Figure 5. (a) A hotspot map of Vancouver, and (b) 30-day incident point clusters

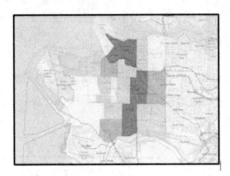 

1. Anonymity can be achieved by the use of ambiguous language in communications between members of a Dark Web community as well as in forum discussions.
2. Weak idiomatic and grammatical context (also intended).
3. Individuals purposefully avoid or restrict the use of specific terms and expressions.
4. Many people from around the world contribute to the Dark Web because they don't follow standard terminology or normative cultural contexts.

Figure 6. Flow chart of the entire work

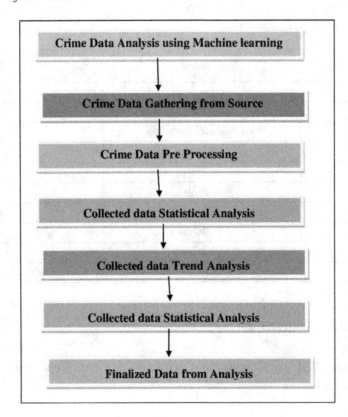

This is similar to Queiroz and Keegan (L. Queirozet and Keegan, 2020), who observed that hackers employ continually evolving and emerging technical terminology with semantic variances, as well as abbreviations and misspellings, which require regular model development to stay up with these changes. Various social networks require different modelling methodologies owing to term changes, which is why a model designed for one network may not perform the same on another. This "Concept Drift" theory was backed by (L. Queirozet and Keegan, 2020) (Akhgar et al,. 2017) because of the above-mentioned shifts in hacker jargon. Additionally, they came up with a plan to counteract this drift by incorporating temporal variables and weights into the model and retraining it.

Another two issues have been added to the CTI field by (Queiroz and Keegan et al,.2020). There are several reasons for this, including a lack of relevant data for researchers to evaluate their models and validate their findings. Concerns about how data should be used ethically are discussed next. In hacking forums and chat rooms, users are not informed explicitly that their data may be used by third parties, as is the case with popular social media platforms (such as Facebook and Twitter) (such as researchers). Obtaining participants' explicit consent for the use of their data in research is also made difficult due to the sheer volume of data that needs to be collected. These factors necessitate that scientists exercise caution when deciding how to make use of the data they've collected.

Akhgar et al. dealt with the following issues in the Dark Web's technical specificity:

1. In general, the web is made up of a variety of different media, including images, videos, and audio.
2. There are a variety of dialects and accents used in the published multimedia, as well as different terminologies.
3. As a result, investigators must frequently wait several weeks before being granted permission to join criminals' social media networks and closed groups. To further their credibility, they must ensure that their online profiles are authentic and that their stories are believable to site administrators.
4. The Dark Web's technical nature makes it difficult to develop crawlers that collect and analyze the necessary data. As a result, researchers must take adequate precautionary measures to protect themselves and their methods and tools from cyber attacks.

Gathering the information from message boards, as according Pastrana et al., poses ethical problems. For moral consideration, research involving human subjects must be reviewed by an Research Ethical Committee(REC). In order to protect the researchers from possible liabilities and to reduce or avoid harm, such reviews are critical. The ethical issues associated with data collection and analysis are distinguished by Pastrana et al. Because of the unique characteristics of each process, they see this division as justifiable. In order to recognize forum behavior as a structure, the information must be collected, while the data must be analyzed in order to understand the human beings associated with the data. There are some technical risks to consider in the first case, such as violating the platform's terms of service or overcoming measures like CAPTCHAs to prevent crawling. Ethics, they say, can justify breaking safety precautions if the benefits outweigh the risks. Using TOR for research, on the other hand, means that the researcher's device will become a network relay.

CONCLUSION

In order to improve the quality of life in a region, crime must be reduced or eliminated if it is at all possible. Old crime data must be used to gain a better understanding of the crimes and criminals, rather than limiting it to criminal records. A person may be unable to clearly examine the vast amount of data available due to the sheer volume of information that must be processed in order to do this analysis, which is why it is necessary to examine these records. Data mining and machine learning techniques must be used in order to gather and analyze data more effectively. This study explored the approaches and techniques that has been utilized to forecast offense & aid rule enforcement. New technologies for offense forecast and anticipation may alter the landscape for rule enforcement authorities. ML has the ability to greatly improve the efficiency and efficacy of rule enforcement agencies. A machine that can learn from past crimes, understand what crime is, and predict exactly future crimes will be connected in the near future to security equipment like sensors and sighting scopes. In this study, Vancouver crime data from the last 10 years were worn in 02 diverse datasets. Predictive mold based on machine learning In order to arrive at crime-prediction results, we used KNN and boosted decision trees. Prediction accuracy can be improved by tailoring both the method and the information to individual applications. In spite of the model's inaccuracy, it serves as the basis for future study.

REFERENCES

Akhgar, P., Bertrand, C., & Chalanouli. (2017). TENSOR: retrieval and analysis of heterogeneous online content for terrorist activity recognition. *Proceedings of the Estonian Academy of Security Sciences*.

Chen, P., Yuan, H. Y., & Shu, X. M. (2008). *Forecasting crime using the ARIMA model*. Paper presented at the 5th international conference on fuzzy systems and knowledge discovery. 10.1109/FSKD.2008.222

Ngai, W. T., Xiu, L., & Chau, D. C. K. (2008). Application of Data Mining Techniques in Customer Relationship Management: A Literature Review and Classification. *Expert Systems with Applications*, 2592–2602.

Leukfeldt, E. R., Kleemans, E. R., & Stol, W. P. (2017). Cybercriminal networks, social ties and online forums: Social ties versus digital ties within phishing and malware networks. *British Journal of Criminology*, *57*(3), 704–722.

Gorr, W., & Harries, R. (2003). Introduction to crime forecasting. *International Journal of Forecasting*, *19*(4), 551–555. doi:10.1016/S0169-2070(03)00089-X

Hurlburt. (2017). Shining light on the dark web. *Computer, 50*(4), 100–105.

Grimani, Gavine, & Moncur. (2020). An evidence syn- thesis of strategies, enablers and barriers for keeping secrets online regarding the procurement and supply of illicit drugs. *International Journal of Drug Policy, 75*.

Zhou, Lin, & Zheng. (2012). A web-based geographical information system for crime mapping and decision support. *IEEE Intl. Conf. on Comput. Problem-Solving (ICCP)*.

Pelton, N., & Singh, I. B. (2019). *Coping with the dark web, cyber-criminals and techno-terrorists in a smart city*. Smart Cities of Today and Tomorrow-Better Technology.

Massy, Queiroz, & Keegan. (2020). Challenges of using machine learning algorithms for cybersecurity: A study of threat-classification models applied to social media communication data. *Cyber Influence and Cognitive Threats*.

Queiroz, Keegan, & Mckeever. (2020). Moving targets: addressing concept drift in supervised models for hacker communication detection. *Proceedings of the 2020 International Conference on Cyber Security and Protection of Digital Services (Cyber Security)*, 1–7. doi:10.1007/978-3-319-95822-4_11

Sawyer & Monckton. (1995). *'Shoe-fit'-a computerized shoe print database*. Academic Press.

Shakarian, P. (2018). Dark-web cyber threat intelligence: From data to intelligence to prediction. *Information (Basel)*, *9*(12), 305. doi:10.3390/info9120305

Chitrakar, P., Zhang, C., Warner, G., & Liao, X. (2016). Social Media Image Retrieval Using Distilled Convolutional Neural Network for Suspicious e-Crime and Terrorist Account Detection. *Multimedia (ISM), 2016 IEEE International Symposium*, 493–498. 10.1109/ISM.2016.0110

Rani, A., & Rajasree, S. (2019). Crime trend analysis and prediction using mahanolobis distance and dynamic time warping technique. *International Journal of Computer Science and Information Technologies*, *5*(3), 4131–4135.

Rummens, A., Hardyns, W., & Pauwels, L. (2017). The use of predictive analysis in spatiotemporal crime forecasting: Building and testing a model in an urban context. *Applied Geography (Sevenoaks, England)*, *86*, 255–261. doi:10.1016/j.apgeog.2017.06.011

Bermudez, R., Gerardo, B., Manalang, J., & Tanguilig, B. (2011). Predicting Faculty Performance Using Regression Model in Data Mining. *Proceedings of the 9th International Conference on Software Engineering Research, Management and Applications*, 68-72.

Liggett, R., Lee, J. R., Roddy, A. L., & Wallin, M. A. (2019). The dark web as a platform for crime: an exploration of illicit drug, firearm, CSAM, and cybercrime markets. The Palgrave Handbook of International Cybercrime and Cyberdeviance.

Kumar, R., Pal, N. R., Chanda, B., & Sharma, J. D. (2009). Detection of fraudulent alterations in ballpoint pen strokes using support vector machines. *India Conference (INDICON), 2009 Annual IEEE*, 1–4. 10.1109/INDCON.2009.5409436

Ferguson, R.-H. (2017). Offline 'stranger' and online lurker: Methods for an ethnography of illicit transactions on the darknet. *Qualitative Research*, *17*(6), 683–698. doi:10.1177/1468794117718894

Rajawat, A. S., Rawat, R., Mahor, V., Shaw, R. N., & Ghosh, A. (2021). Suspicious Big Text Data Analysis for Prediction—On Darkweb User Activity Using Computational Intelligence Model. In *Innovations in Electrical and Electronic Engineering* (pp. 735–751). Springer. doi:10.1007/978-981-16-0749-3_58

Rawat, R., Mahor, V., Chirgaiya, S., Shaw, R. N., & Ghosh, A. (2021). Analysis of Darknet Traffic for Criminal Activities Detection Using TF-IDF and Light Gradient Boosted Machine Learning Algorithm. In *Innovations in Electrical and Electronic Engineering* (pp. 671–681). Springer. doi:10.1007/978-981-16-0749-3_53

Rawat, R., Rajawat, A. S., Mahor, V., Shaw, R. N., & Ghosh, A. (2021). Dark Web—Onion Hidden Service Discovery and Crawling for Profiling Morphing, Unstructured Crime and Vulnerabilities Prediction. In *Innovations in Electrical and Electronic Engineering* (pp. 717–734). Springer. doi:10.1007/978-981-16-0749-3_57

Mahor, V., Rawat, R., Kumar, A., Chouhan, M., Shaw, R. N., & Ghosh, A. (2021, September). Cyber Warfare Threat Categorization on CPS by Dark Web Terrorist. In *2021 IEEE 4th International Conference on Computing, Power and Communication Technologies (GUCON)* (pp. 1-6). IEEE.

Rawat, R., Rajawat, A. S., Mahor, V., Shaw, R. N., & Ghosh, A. (2021). Dark Web—Onion Hidden Service Discovery and Crawling for Profiling Morphing, Unstructured Crime and Vulnerabilities Prediction. In *Innovations in Electrical and Electronic Engineering* (pp. 717–734). Springer.

Aghababaei, S., & Makrehchi, M. (2016). Mining Social Media Content for Crime Prediction. *Web Intelligence (WI), IEEE/WIC/ACM International Conference on,* 526–531.

Tounsi, W. (2019). What is cyber threat intelligence and how is it evolving? In W. Tounsi (Ed.), *Cyber-Vigilance and Digital Trust: Cyber Security in the Era of Cloud Computing and IoT*. ISTE Ltd.

Yu, Y., Wan, X., Liu, G., Li, H., Li, P., & Lin, H. (2017). A combinatorial clustering method for sequential fraud detection. *Service Systems and Service Management (ICSSSM), 2017 International Conference on,* 1–6.

Chapter 9
Image Processing for Criminal Pattern Detection Using Machine Learning in the Dark Web

Sumit Dhariwal
Manipal University Jaipur, India

Avani Sharma
Manipal University Jaipur, India

Biswa Mohan Shaoo
ⓘ https://orcid.org/0000-0002-8368-107X
Manipal University Jaipur, India

ABSTRACT

Data mining has been used to present difficulties in this chapter in order to reduce crime. Crime is a major issue for which we must pay a high price in a variety of ways. Here, the authors look at how machine-learning techniques may be used in an image processing method to aid in the detection of and speed up the investigative process by identifying criminal tendencies. The authors look at the supervised approaches, as well as some enhancements, to help in the identification of criminal trends. They tested their approaches with real-world crime data from a police department, and they were satisfied with the results. They also employed clustering approaches to improve the prediction accuracy of criminal record categorization. They also utilized a clustering approach to assist classify crime records and improve prediction accuracy. They created a weighting system for the characteristics below. The machine-learning framework works with geospatial crime plotting and helps detectives and other law enforcement professionals increase their efficiency. It may also be used to combat terrorism and ensure national security.

DOI: 10.4018/978-1-6684-3942-5.ch009

Figure 1. Each black dot denotes the incidence of a crime in this geospatial map

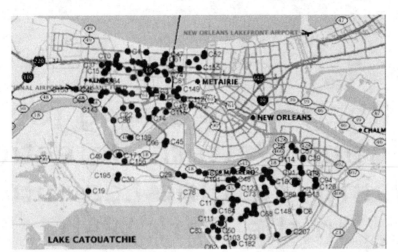

INTRODUCTION

We compare them to data mining systems and the extent to which a person is suspected, which are terms used in criminal justice and police agencies. For a long time, prosecutors in criminology and law enforcement have had the honor of prosecuting wrongdoing. As the use of computerized frameworks for tracking infractions grows, PC information specialists have begun to assist cops and criminal investigators in speeding up the most common method of resolving wrongdoings. We'll use a disciplinary method that combines software engineering and establishing a criminal justice system with an information excavating mindset to establish criminal justice system. To help differentiate cases of wrongdoing, we will use a bunching-based model even more clearly (Chen et al.,2008).

Computer vision is an artificial intelligence area that trains computers to observe and comprehend their environment, giving them a sense of awareness (Shah et al.,2020) and (Patel et al.,2020).

It has a wide range of applications, and its principal role is to analyses environmental data from a camera. Face recognition, number plate recognition, augmented and mixed realities, position determination, and object recognition are just a few of the applications that maybe It is now being investigated whether it is possible to construct mathematical techniques that can be retrieved and used by computers to analyses 3D images using semantics. Image classification is used to identify the image work. (Dhariwal et al., 2020).

MECHANISM FOR REPORTING CRIMES

The statistics on crime frequently pose an intriguing quandary. While certain information is kept private, some is made public. Data about the inmates are frequently available on county or sheriff's websites. Data on narcotics-related offenses and juvenile cases, on the other hand, is generally more limited. Similarly, although the victim's name is typically disguised, information about sex offenders is made public to warn others in the region. As a result, the analyst must deal with all these public vs. private data issues as part of data mining to guarantee that the data mining modeling process does not violate these legal borders (Szeliski et al.,2010). Free text boxes are frequently the most difficult part of data mining for crime data. While free text fields might provide a fantastic narrative line for a newspaper columnist, it's not always easy to turn them into data mining assets. We'll look at how to figure out the most essential aspects of a data-mining model.

Crime Patterns and Data Gathering

To help police solve crimes faster, we'll look at ways to transform criminal data into a data-mining problem (Dhariwal et al.,2019). A group, as we've seen, is a collection of crimes committed in a given geographic region or at a specific crime scene. A cluster is a group of related data elements in data mining - a possible criminal proclivity. As a result, crime patterns will be linked in a one-to-one relationship to appropriate groups or subsets of clusters. As a result, data-mining clustering algorithms can recognize similar but different groups of records. In the remainder of the details, a number of these groups would be beneficial in a crime spree perpetrated by someone or more offenders in our case. The next stage is to determine which variables, depending on this data, provide clustering at its best. Spies will then have access to these clusters, and they will probe further using their domain knowledge. Investigators can focus on the crime spree first thanks to automatic recognition of criminal patterns, and investigating one of these crimes can lead to the resolution of the entire "spree" or, in certain cases, clusters of occurrences. There is little chance of piecing together a whole image of and pieces of material since individual criminal instances are without potential crime patterns. Much of this is now done manually, with the help of computer data analysts and various spreadsheet reports derived from the detectives' own crime logs (Chen et al.,2003).

As a result, classification approaches that rely on previously solved crimes will not be accurate predictors of future criminality. Additionally, the types of offenses evolve throughout the phase; for example, cybercrime on the Internet or offenses committed using a cell phone were not uncommon or widespread previously. As a result, in the future, the clustering method is ideal for detecting new and previously unknown patterns.

SVM TECHNIQUES

We'll look at some of his accomplishments in this field. We'll demonstrate SVM and clustering using a basic example. Take, for example, the oversimplification of criminal records. A criminal data analyst or detective will write a report based on this information, which will be organized in several ways, the first of which will be based on the investigator's knowledge of the most essential characteristic.

Let's just look at Table 1 for an example. As an illustration, Dacoity is a sort of crime, and it will be the most prominent and significant aspect. Rows 1 & 3 depict a modest criminal pattern in which the suspect information and victim characteristics are identical. Because there are numerous features or causes of crime in real life, and only incomplete information on the crime is frequently accessible, data mining may be used to uncover more complicated patterns. A computer data analyst or spy, in most situations, will struggle to identify these patterns with a simple query. As a result, data-mining clustering techniques come in handy when dealing with vast volumes of data as well as noisy or missing data. We proposed the notion of weighting the qualities to account for the various characteristics of various sorts of crimes. This enables dynamically varying weights to be applied to various attributes based on

Table 1. Example of different types of crime

Type of Offense	Suspicious Race	Suspicious Sex	Suspicious Age	Casualty Age	Types of Weapons
Crimes Against Persons	Boy Girls	Male	Young	Elderly	Knife, sharp edge weapon, Murder, violent assault, rape, and dacoity are examples of crimes against persons, often known as personal crimes.
Committing Crimes Against People	Boy	Male	Young	Young	Theft, burglary, vehicle theft, and arson are examples of property crimes that do not result in bodily injury.
Xenophobia	Girls Women Boy	Male	Middle of Age	Elderly	Logical Thinking and Hate crimes are crimes perpetrated against people or property because of biases based on race, gender identity, religion, disability, sexual orientation, or ethnicity.
Moral Offenses	Boy Girls	Male, Female	Young	Middle	There are no complainants or victims. Victimless crimes include prostitution, unlawful gambling, and illegal drug usage.
White-collar crime is a type of criminal activity that occurs when	Boys	Male	Young	Elderly	White-collar crime, in general, causes less worry in the public perception than other sorts of crime; nevertheless, in terms of overall economic value, it is much more damaging to society.
Planned Offence	Boy Girl Women	Male, Female	Young	Middle	Structured organizations are usually involved in the distribution and sale of illegal products and services, as well as other forms of organized crime.
A Sociological Look at Crime	Girl Women Boy	Male, Female	Middle	Young	As previously stated, adolescents, urbanites, the poor, black and brown people, and historically oppressed groups are more likely to be arrested and convicted. others for personal and property crimes.
Robbery	Boy	Male	Middle of Age	Elderly	Pistol, Knife,

the kind of violation. This allows us to solely weigh categorical traits rather than numerical ones that can be readily scaled to weights. By utilizing integral weighting to raise the effective weighting of that variable or attribute, hierarchical features can be replicated as redundant columns (Zang et al., 2010). We haven't come across the usage of weights for clustering anywhere else in the literature because the clustering method prioritizes all features equally.

We included it, however, because of our expert-based or semi-supervised method. Here's an example of a weighting strategy. We cluster datasets for criminal patterns using weighted clustering features and then deliver the conclusions to the detective or domain expert with data on critical qualities.

The researcher first conducts tests on small groups of people before providing professional advice. This iterative method aids in the identification of key characteristics and weights for various types of criminal activity. Based on this information, the domain specialist, i.e., the detective, can forecast future crime trends. For starters, unsolved or future crimes may be classified based on key criteria, with the results presented to investigators for review. Because this activity condenses hundreds of incidents into a handful of smaller ones. It makes it much easier to solve a series of related crimes. A detective's job is made difficult by the difficulty of tracing the criminal pattern.

Another approach is to score the new data set against the current cluster using tracers or known criminal occurrences, and then compare the new cluster to the tracer. Complete this task. Using a tracer to detect something that would not be difficult to detect without the tracer is analogous to using a radioactive tracer to detect something that would not be difficult to detect without the tracer.

The Findings of the CPA (Crime Pattern Analysis)

The planned system is now in use in conjunction with geospatial plots. The crime analyst can then look at findings from a specific geographic location by selecting a period of date and several infractions. The user can choose to view the all-inclusive collection or a specific area of attentiveness within it. The end outcome collection is used as a starting point for data mining. These items are grouped using the attributes and weights provided. Criminal tendencies are likely in developing communities (Dhariwal and Palaniappan.,2020). The resulting clusters are represented on a geospatial map.

The experts must accept that no one approach or combination of methodologies will be able to detect 100% of criminal patterns (which is why we speak in terms of identifiable patterns rather than total patterns). A thief who robs a bank on Friday, a convenience store on Monday, and takes a car on Thursday has most likely changed his identity. That is all there is to it. Only if the suspect was detailed in each event, or if the analyst received intelligence (for example, from a detective, a parole officer, or an assistant) that this criminal was active and possibly committing these crimes, would the analyst want to view these crimes. Such a strategy is known as intelligence-based pattern recognition (Shah et al., 2020).

One of three criteria can be used to determine the likelihood of a pattern:

1. Methodological commonalities discovered after a thorough examination of event reports and narratives.
2. Excessive quantities discovered by threshold analysis, either purposefully or inadvertently.
3. Geographical closeness discovered through crime mapping.

The next sections go through each of these three strategies in depth. In addition, we discuss intelligence-based pattern recognition, hot areas, and criminogenic identification, and cross-judgmental pattern recognition briefly (Li,2012).

Each analyst will devise his or her own technique of daily report evaluation, but here's a common example:

- The analyst gathers all incident reports since the last review at least once a day. 2. While a tangible written report is preferred by most analysts, some analysts work for "paperless" organizations and must rely on electronic reports. The most important aspect is that the analyzer has access to all relevant assertions.
- The consultant does a preliminary scan of the reports, deleting any occurrences that are unlikely to ever establish patent eligibility or that are outside the area of the investor's responsibilities.
- The analyst examines the financial sheet, M.O. The analyst's recollection may prompt him to make connections, however, at the juncture, particularly a strong Mos. resemblance or sign.

Figure 2. A representation of crime clustering with a description highlighting important crime pattern aspects

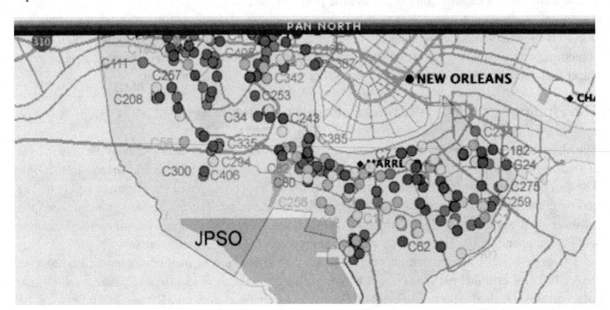

- The current ratio compares their current reports to those obtained by the agency before. The analyst's experience, expertise, intuition, and imagination are the most valuable currency. Analysts gain so much from a competent (King, 2011) information management system or computerized database with strong query capacity and the ability to present results in matrix notation at this stage.

The outcome is depicted in the diagram below. Color-coding is used to identify criminal clusters or patterns. The legend for each group lists the number of total offenses in the set as well as the essential characteristics that define it. (Berghel, 2017) Detectives can utilize this information while investigating suspected criminal gangs.

By watching the court's disposition on these criminal occurrences, whether charges against suspects were admitted or refused, we confirmed our findings regarding the new crime patterns As a result, the starting point for rewriting is crime incident data (some of these crimes already have court decisions/judgments in the system), which is evaluated in terms of essential properties or characteristics or crime variables such as crime perpetrator, victim demographics, and so on (Hurlburt, 2017).

There was no mention of the Court's decision in the clustering procedure. Then, based on their weighting methodologies, we classify crimes into crime clusters (clusters in data mining language), which include probable criminal trends. Detectives now have a list of hundreds of criminal events in fragmented order or one to identify a crime rather than a few predefined ones, thanks to a geographic plot of these criminal patterns (Dhariwal et al., 2012) along with the parameters. that must be measured in order to determine their clusters It's a straightforward task. Sort the items according to their ascending order. In our example, we looked at crime trends (shown in a single color below) as well as the court's personality to ensure that data mining techniques were used.

Table 2. Example of different crime rates of with suspect items

Patterns	A	150 Crime	-Suspect point of entry -Victim's race -Suspicious count -Number of old days	Crimes Against Persons
	B	80 Crime	-Suspect point of entry -Victims Race -Number of old days	Crimes Against Property
	C	50 Crime	-Suspect point of entry -Victim's race -Suspect count -Number of old days	Hate Crimes
	D	30 Crime	-Suspicious race -Suspect average weight -Suspect average height -Suspect average age -Suspect average entry	Crimes Against Morality
	E	20 Crime	-Suspect city -Suspect point of entry -Suspect average weight -Suspect average height -Suspicious average age -Suspicious of old days	White-Collar Crime
	F	10 Crime	-Suspect sex -Suspect point of entry -Suspect city - Suspect average weight -Suspect average height -Suspicious average age	Organized Crime

Machine Learning Concept in Dark-Web

As a result, the dark web, or darknet, as another synonym, is the most difficult-to-reach part of the deep web. Because of this anonymity, suspicious and convicted felons' activities thrive in that hidden and encoded environment (Paganini.,2012).

Inside this part of the browser, novice, and highly qualified hackers, as well as children, undertake various crimes and horrific crimes for fun or profit by extorting ransom, sabotaging networks, or stealing organizations' data. Along with other crimes such as pornography and pedophilia. A system, drug, and weapons trafficking, terrorism and extremist recruitment, terrorist attack planning, hired killers, hacked digital media trading, counterfeit documents, fraud, and a variety of other crimes (Hurlburt, 2017).

CONCLUSIONS AND THE WAY FORWARD

We investigated the possibility of using data mining to uncover criminal trends using clustering techniques. Our contribution was to turn criminal pattern recognition into a machine learning problem, allowing police investigators to use data mining to aid in crime investigation. The scheme was developed using a semi-supervised learning approach based on experts and the weighting of significant factors after the essential characteristics were determined. Because of the large number of instances, our modeling technique was able to find similarities in the task of crime detectives. One of our study's flaws is that crime pattern analysis can only assist investigators, not replace them. Data mining is also vulnerable to the quality of the input data, which may be inaccurate, information may be deleted, and so on. Data entry errors, among other things, could occur. Real-world data mapping for data mining features is a difficult process that frequently necessitates the use of professional data miners and criminal data analysts with in-depth domain knowledge. In the beginning, he'll have to work closely with a spy. One of our study's flaws is that this type of criminal pattern analysis can only help with investigator replacement. In data mining, the quality of the input data, which may be incorrect, is also important. could be deleted, and admissions mistakes could occur, among other things. Furthermore, converting data mining into actual data specialty is not always easy or clear. necessitates the use of expert data on regular basis miners and criminal data analysts are well-versed in the subject at first, they'll need to work with a detective.

REFERENCES

Berghel, H. (2017). Which is more dangerous—The dark web or the deep state? *Computer, 50*(07), 86–91. doi:10.1109/MC.2017.215

Beshiri, A. S., & Susuri, A. (2019). Dark web and its impact in online anonymity and privacy: A critical analysis and review. *Journal of Computer and Communications, 7*(03), 30–43. doi:10.4236/jcc.2019.73004

Chen, H., Chung, W., Qin, Y., Chau, M., Xu, J. J., Wang, G., ... Atabakhsh, H. (2003, May). Crime data mining: an overview and case studies. *Proceedings of the 2003 annual national conference on Digital government research*, 1-5.

Chen, H., Chung, W., Xu, J. J., Wang, G., Qin, Y., & Chau, M. (2004). Crime data mining: a general framework and some examples. *Computer, 37*(4), 50-56.

Chen, H., Thoms, S., & Fu, T. (2008, June). Cyber extremism in Web 2.0: An exploratory study of international Jihadist groups. In *2008 IEEE International Conference on Intelligence and Security Informatics* (pp. 98-103). IEEE. 10.1109/ISI.2008.4565037

Dhariwal, S., & Palaniappan, S. (2020). Image Normalization and Weighted Classification Using an Efficient Approach for SVM Classifiers. *International Journal of Image and Graphics, 20*(04), 2050035. doi:10.1142/S0219467820500357

Dhariwal, S., Raghuwanshi, S., & Shrivastava, S. (2012). Content Based Image Retrieval Using Normalization of Vector Approach to SVM. In *Advances in Computer Science, Engineering & Applications* (pp. 793–801). Springer. doi:10.1007/978-3-642-30111-7_76

Dhariwal, S., Rawat, R., & Patearia, N. (2011). C-Queued Technique against SQL injection attack. *International Journal of Advanced Research in Computer Science, 2*(5).

Hurlburt, G. (2017). Shining light on the dark web. *Computer, 50*(04), 100–105. doi:10.1109/MC.2017.110

King, M. C. (2011, May). The Intelligence Advanced Research Projects Activity-Its BEST and Beyond. In *CLEO: Applications and Technology*. Optical Society of America. doi:10.1364/CLEO_AT.2011.ATuF3

Li, Y., Snavely, N., Huttenlocher, D., & Fua, P. (2012, October). Worldwide pose estimation using 3d point clouds. In *European conference on computer vision* (pp. 15-29). Springer. 10.1007/978-3-642-33718-5_2

Paganini, P. (2012). What is the Deep Web. *A first trip into the abyss. Security affairs.* http://securityaffairs.co/wordpress/5650/cyber-crime/whatis-the-deep-web-a-first-trip-into-the-abyss. html

Patel, H., Prajapati, D., Mahida, D., & Shah, M. (2020). Transforming petroleum downstream sector through big data: A holistic review. *Journal of Petroleum Exploration and Production Technology*, *10*(6), 2601–2611. doi:10.100713202-020-00889-2

Patel, H., Prajapati, D., Mahida, D., & Shah, M. (2020). Transforming petroleum downstream sector through big data: A holistic review. *Journal of Petroleum Exploration and Production Technology*, *10*(6), 2601–2611. doi:10.100713202-020-00889-2

Pelton, J. N., & Singh, I. B. (2019). Coping with the dark web, cyber-criminals and techno-terrorists in a smart city. In *Smart cities of today and tomorrow* (pp. 171–183). Copernicus. doi:10.1007/978-3-319-95822-4_11

Shah, D., Dixit, R., Shah, A., Shah, P., & Shah, M. (2020). A comprehensive analysis regarding several breakthroughs based on computer intelligence targeting various syndromes. *Augmented Human Research*, *5*(1), 1–12. doi:10.100741133-020-00033-z

Yang, L., Liu, F., Kizza, J. M., & Ege, R. K. (2009, March). *Discovering topics from dark websites. In 2009 IEEE symposium on computational intelligence in cyber security.* IEEE.

Zetter, K. (2015). DARPA is developing a search engine for the dark web. *Retrieved*, *11*(15), 2018.

Zhang, Y., Zeng, S., Huang, C. N., Fan, L., Yu, X., Dang, Y., ... Chen, H. (2010, May). Developing a Dark Web collection and infrastructure for computational and social sciences. In *2010 IEEE International Conference on Intelligence and Security Informatics* (pp. 59-64). IEEE. 10.1109/ISI.2010.5484774

Chapter 10
A Fuzzy–GA for Predicting Terrorist Networks in Social Media

Amit Kumar Mishra

Amity School of Engineering and Technology, Amity University, India

Vikram Rajpoot

Madhav Institute of Technology and Science, India

Ramakant Bhardwaj

 https://orcid.org/0000-0002-1538-5615

Amity University, India

Pankaj Kumar Mishra

Amity School of Engineering and Technology, Amity University, India

Pushpendra Dwivedi

iNurture Education Solution Pvt. Ltd., India

ABSTRACT

Global terrorist activities increase with the evolution of various social media sites such as Facebook, Twitter, etc. Various organizations use a wide scope of network capabilities of social media to broadcast their information, propaganda, as well communicate their strategic objectives. So, by analyzing such growing terrorist activity over online social media using mining and analysis, various valuable insights can be predicted. This chapter approaches an effective way of analyzing such activities by identifying nearest nodes in the network. The terrorist network mining algorithm has assisted by successfully achieving terrorist activities and their behavior on nodes of social network using centrality algorithm. The algorithm works in two phases: 1) fuzzification of data to measure centrality between nodes in the network and 2) applying genetic approach for the optimization of data and to increase the searching capability for appropriate cluster centers.

DOI: 10.4018/978-1-6684-3942-5.ch010

INTRODUCTION

Terrorism is an extremely complex worldwide issue, which includes social economy, governmental issues, and society et cetera. A few fear monger occurrences have happened for instance 9/11 capturing and Terrorist Attack as of late, which not just purpose awful effect on the adjacency issues and security of the global group, yet additionally bring results harm and to calamity to the general population and the nation. These occasions have propelled the investigation of fear-based oppressor systems. Furthermore, a considerable measure of researchers regards psychological militant associations as fear monger arranges to look. They generally concentrate on the conduct of psychological oppressors to choose who are the pioneers, guardians or the colleagues. The informal organization is an extremely convoluted framework, including numerous relational connections, for example, blood relationship, promoting relationship, companion relationship, business relationship et cetera. The informal organization is the arrangement of social performing artists and relationship among them. The principal thought of social system investigation is to outline, decide the connection between individuals, gatherings, and association or other data, information handling substances and break down the effect on the associations. Psychological oppressor organize is a unique sort of informal organization with accentuation on both mystery and productivity. A psychological appraiser organize is demonstrated as a general informal organization comprising of hubs and connections between performing artists. The nodes speak to individuals, gathering, and association, while the connections demonstrate the relationship included family, companions, relatives and partners and so on. In this research project we utilize 9/11 seize information, and about them, we consider whether there exists an edge between hubs or not. We utilize contiguous lattice to get a few outcomes. Systems from Social Network Analysis (SNA) and diagram hypothesis can be utilized to recognize enter hubs in the system, which is useful for organizing destabilization purposes, with the goal that brings down the system's effectiveness and power. Lately, an expanding number of researchers think about the focal individual in a system, particularly who is the key part to manage the entire action in the fear-based oppressor organized. Thus, specialists and investigators give careful consideration to the centrality in the systems.

We study static network inside this paper. Existing tools Application is mainly SNA on the static network to discover certain information which is useful. So as to visualize network, we build a graph that is based on composed data, social network analysis primarily studies following key difficulties:

- Vital individual, event, group.
- The relationship amongst each vertex.
- Leaders' identification and followers.
- The node's closeness.
- The vulnerabilities of the network.
- Central actor in the network.
- The effectiveness of n/w and defence of network.

SNA is the utilization of the system hypothesis to interpersonal; organization breaks down as far as social contacts. It contains hubs in the system of connections between the hubs. Social connections powerfully are as genuine disconnected I organizations or be online informal communities Several SNA measures being utilized for an idiom to collaborate among performers, identifying key players and subgroups, discovering topology as well as the quality of a system. As of late SNA has given training in diverse areas. It is basically connected to Information Science, Political Science, Biology, Business Analysis, Economics, Communication Studies, and Intelligence Analysis. Concentrates on the opinion of SNA in Counterterrorism completed up noticeably well famous soon after assaults of 9/11.SNA has extensively the by organizations of the insight and law implementation for accepting the structure of psychological confrontational systems and making procedures to disappoint them by observing examples those are pioneers and covered, in the criminal systems. Some normal of SNA in Counterterrorism is Identification of Key-Player, Discovery of Node and Analysis of Dynamic Network and so on (Hirani et al., 2015).

Social Network Analysis (SNA) and Measures

The Social Network Analysis and measures have been produced significantly more time for informal organization investigating in term of the recognizing key players, discovering design in arranging, the revelation of hub and connection and so on. Centrality is considered thoughts generally in an examination of informal organization for key players distinguishing pieces of proof. Incalculable centrality measures have size. for centrality, including degree, eigenvector centrality, data centrality, impact measure and so on the 3 different natural thought of centrality being proposed by Freeman specifically degree, betweenness, and closeness centrality, those are utilized generally in entering players recognizing in the interpersonal organization. Centrality proposed degree for looking relative significance of degree hub, which is utilized for the most part to define impact made by the hub on neighbouring nodes. In their work, broadened centrality measures degree, closeness, and betweenness to use to gatherings and classes and people. UCINET, a device for making informal organization information discharged than by the Everett and with few of regular SNA centrality measures implied for examination. The recommendation made by Borgatti is a typology of n/w streams relied upon measurements of varying. Everett read about informal communities containing negative ties like for ex. Disdain, dodging and proposed a propel centrality measure, PN centrality for positive and negative ties both (Gupta et al., 2016).

Social Media used by Terrorist Network

Social media is a major element of the modern terrorism. Due to affordability, accessibility, and the broad reach of Social platforms like Facebook, Myspace, Twitter, YouTube, and Tumbler, groups of terrorist have gradually used by the social media to satisfy their mean objectives and broadcast their texts in the borders of the country. Attempts have been made by the range of management and agencies to frustrate the use of social media with the help of terrorist organizations. Today, 90% of systematically organized terrorism of internet carried out from side to side of the social media. By using social media tool, the organizations are active in recruiting novel friends deprived of geographical constraint. The social media is enabling the terror administrations to initiates by sending "friend" requests, audio messages, etc. Like most social networking sites, Twitter excludes activity if consumer's post direct, precise threats of violence in contrast to others but the trick are that does actively monitor the content in the examiner of the above threats. As a substitute, it relies on users to report their notice violations of rules. (Hirani et al., 2015) A social network is an architecture that consists of the set of the node relationships between these nodes. These social networks must be online as well as offline in nature. On further offline social networks is actually life, social networks based on relations of ex-friendship, the locations, events etc (Hirani et al., 2015).

Analysis of Terrorist Network

For examination of the psychological militant system, the system finds from the web by utilizing methodologies, for example, the content-construct discovery of fear-based oppressors with respect to the web. At whatever point a fear-based oppressor organize is recognized, the system persuasive parts and the system pecking order are revealed utilizing an Investigative Data Mining plan. One approach to seeing psychological oppressor activity on the Web is to spy on all movement of the Web destinations related to fear-based oppressor associations so as to distinguish the getting to clients in light of their IP address (Hagberg et al.,2004). In any case, the arrangement was hardly any persuading as these clients don't utilize settled IP locations or URLs. Thus the law authorization organizations endeavoured to distinguish the psychological militants by observing all ISPs movement. After activity examination, the system is preparatory contemplated utilizing Social Network Analysis (SNA) drawing nearer. The recognized fear monger organizes is then concentrated for evaluating promising parts. The investigation of every client is done in the system and the centrality measures are ascertained separately for every hub. The primary centrality measures are degrees (number of direct associations that a hub has), betweenness (the centrality of a person to connect to critical voting demographics) and closeness (a position capacity to screen the data stream and what is going on in the system) (Berzinji et al., 2012).

Destabilization of the Terrorist Network

To know the dynamics of covert n/w, and, any, the network we required to get the basic processes through which networks evolve. Hence, in consideration of this, terrorist n/w roles are being discovered and then accordingly achievement of destabilization is done. The destabilization attended by role calculations execution within n/w. This is generally by knowing the efficacy of network with nodes, serious components of the network, a" Position Role Index" (PRI) and dependence centrality.

- The efficiency of the network, to describe how competent knowledge is being exchanged all over the nodes in the network.
- Critical components of the network, for the discovery the measure centrality of a node.
- In n/w effectiveness is being estimated when a node of that type is disabled from the network.
- PRI is also known as (Position Role Index), highlighted a clear distinction between gatekeepers, and depends on network efficiency.
- Dependence Centrality, for the discovery of node dependency on other nodes of the network (Berzinji et al., 2012).

Tools and Techniques used for SNA in Counterterrorism

A social network is a creation which contains set of nodes and relationships among such nodes. These may be online and also offline in nature. Social networks basically in the social networking sites form, which users allow to relate with other users by sending messages, posting information, videos, likes, and notes on them. On the other hand, social networks those are offline are actual life, social networks created by relations, communication, events etc.

METHODS FOR DATA COLLECTION

Data collection from social network analysis includes the extraction of public and private data, users, groups, and pages, which contain posts, tweets, likes, comments, photos, videos, etc. In social network is available for extracting API and tools from a number of the data. YouTube and a few more. NodeXL, SNA of and UCINET6 are such tools for extracting social network data and further analyzing most of the criminal and terrorist activities using online social networks (Borgatti et al., 2002).

UCINET Tool

Notational Conventions - UCINET is menu-driven Windows program. This implies you pick what you need to do by choosing things from a menu. Menus might be settled, so picking a thing from a menu may call up a submenu with extra decisions, which thusly may call up submenus of their own. Thus, to get to specific decisions, you may need to choose through various menus en route. To speak to the alternatives you should take for a given decision, we utilize edge sections. To reword an old melody (and turn around the significance), UCINET 6.0 is working for speed, not for comfort. Frequently amid the programming of UCINET, we needed to pick between utilizing a quick calculation that utilized a great deal of memory (and in this way lessened the most extreme size of system, it could deal with), and a moderate calculation that spared memory and could deal with substantially bigger data sets. In past variants we attempted to strike a harmony between the two. In this adaptation, we more often than not picked speed. One explanation behind this is it is correctly when working with huge datasets that speed is fundamental: what great is a calculation that can deal with a large number of nodes on the off chance that it takes days to execute? The other reason is that advances in equipment and working framework programming constantly broaden the measure of memory projects can get to, so it appears a misuse of programming time to work out approaches to conserve on memory. One result of menu frameworks is the need to sort out program abilities into classifications and subcategories in a way that is intelligent and fathomable. Obviously, this has turned out to be unthinkable. With just a little exertion one can find a few contending plans for ordering every one of the capacities that UCINET 6.0 offers. None of the plans are impeccable: every doe a rich employment of grouping certain things, however appears to be constrained and subjective with others. The plan we have settled on is no special case. The essential thought is that under "system" we put strategies whose purpose behind being is on a very basic level system theoretic: procedures whose understanding is constrained when connected to non-organize information. A case of such a system is a centrality measure. Conversely, under "devices" we put strategies that are as often as possible utilized by organizing experts, but at the same time are normally utilized as a part of settings having nothing to do with systems. Multidimensional scaling and bunch investigation are cases of such methodology. Unavoidably, obviously, there are systems that are either hard to characterize or for reasons unknown are advantageous to misclassify. The application is made to break down and imagine the informal communities. This product contains a bundle of programming pajek, net draw. Some highlights of this product are: Clustering coefficient, ascertaining the factual measure, computing clicks, figuring confusion - numerous modes and collaboration of the charts, making symmetric lattice, representation by utilizing programming Net draw and E-Net, including Excel manager, network and content. The product arrange is h##. The motivation behind making this product is for understudy and business looks into, and is presented 2006 (Borgatti et al., 2006).

SNA Tool

Social Network Analysis (SNA) is the procedure of research, social structures using systems and diagram hypothesis. It portrays organized structures as far as nodes (singular performing artists, individuals, or things inside the system) and the ties, edges, or (connections or cooperation's) that associate them. Cases of social structures regularly imagined through informal organization examination incorporate web-based social networking systems, images spread, companionship and associated systems, joint effort diagrams, connection, sickness transmission, and sexual connections.

CENTRALITY

Social networks analyzation typically objective to classify and make out rules those are played by the aspirant in the network of the node. The analysis assessments each node relates to the other nodes. In this, centrality measures and goal at the cracking significance of nodes those are relative in a network. To attain this, the centrality of node proceeds into an explanation of how other nodes in the network are related to node through direct relations or undirected relations. There are different measures of centrality to regulate the aim of a node in n/w by taking account relations, diverse aspects among the nodes in n/w of measure centrality.

Centrality is the network properties that have frequently been required to study actors the events in social networks terrorist. The maximum centrality measures those are in this situation are the degree centrality, and closeness centrality, betweenness centrality, and page rank. In the following section, we present common centrality events and a specific centrality of measure, which we denote by closeness centrality.

Degree Centrality

Degree centrality guesses how imperative a node by number analyzation of direct relationships it consumes with other all node pairs in the network. Specifically, the set $\{\pi (s, t) \text{ s.t } |\pi (s, t)| = Dg (s, t)\}$ is calculated for every pair of the nodes s, t $\in$ V dissimilar from v. Then, a number of times ego node v was started on such shortest paths, that is., the size of set $\{\pi (s, t) \text{ s.t } v \in \pi (s, t) \text{ and } |\pi (s, t)| = DG (s, t)\}$ is calculated. Degree Centrality of the node I in the network could be as (Singh et al., 2016),

$$D_i = \frac{\sum_{jTG} A_{ij}}{N - 1}$$

Calculating all degree nodes with all pairs is costly. As an alternative to using paths, as in the original dentition, different alternatives have been measured. One different (Smith et al., 2010) is to only consider when computing betweenness centrality for the node, the network, calculating a result from the nodes directly related it together with edges between them. Other differ and more involve statistical sampling in order to randomly select paths between two random nodes in the network and then to count the number of times ego node appears on the randomly selected path (Ibrahima et al., 2015).

Betweenness Centrality

In Betweenness centrality, betweenness is ascribed to nodes that happen regularly in the most limited ways between different nodes in the systems. Nodes that have a higher probability of being situated on the straightaway between other separate nodes have higher betweenness than different nodes. Such nodes can likewise be depicted as portals. Nodes with high betweenness have a control over information flowing among the others gatherings of nodes in organizing since such nodes regularly go about as extensions. In the fear-based oppressor systems, nodes with high betweenness, as a rule, demonstrate the most critical or included on-screen characters. A performer with a high level of betweenness centrality ordinarily holds a favoured position of the system. Such a hub has more noteworthy and huge control over data engendering inside the system and speaks to a scaffold which can conceivably be a solitary purpose of disappointment. Separating such nodes can adequately disturb the correspondence inside the system. Unique dentitions of betweenness centrality for a conscience hub n figure of most limited ways among all sets of nodes in the system. All the more specifically, the set $\{\pi\ (s,\ t)\ s.t\ |\pi\ (s,\ t)\ | = DG\ (s,\ t)\}$ is figured for each combine of nodes s, t $\in$ V unique in relation to v. At that point, the circumstances the self-image hub v was found in these briefest ways, i.e., the extent of the set $\{\pi\ (s,\ t)\ s.t\ v \in \pi\ (s,\ t)\ and$ $|\pi\ (s,\ t)\ | = DG\ (s,\ t)\}$ is checked. Betweenness centrality G (v) is then figured as takes after:

The betweenness centrality of node I the network can be defined as:

$$B_i = \frac{\sum_{j,kTG} \frac{g_{jk}(i)}{g_{jk}}}{(N-1)(N-2)}$$

Calculating all ways between all sets is expensive. Rather than utilizing geodesic ways, as in the first dentitions, includes options have been considered. One other (Smith, et al., 2010) is when registering betweenness centrality for an inner self-hub, the system coming about because of the node network analysis with it together with the edges between them. Different choices include factual examining with a specific end goal to arbitrarily choose ways between two arbitrary nodes in the system and afterward to tally the circumstances the sense of self-hub shows up on the haphazardly chose way.

Closeness Centrality

Closeness centrality of a hub in a system is another variation for estimating the centrality of a hub. It is a measure of how shut the hub is to every other hub of the system (specifically or in a roundabout way). Closeness centrality measures how rapidly a hub can get to data through different nodes in the system. A hub with a high closeness centrality has a short way to different nodes in the system and can contact them (i.e. The spread data to them) rapidly. Such a hub has high deceivability in the matter of what is going on in the system, and that is on the grounds that the data in the system may normally flow through nodes with high closeness centrality. Regularly, closeness centrality is estimated utilizing the geodesic separation (mostly the way). The hub with the most noteworthy closeness centrality is the one with the fewest separation to every single other hub in the system. One approach to consider the separation of a hub v in a diagram G (V, E) to every other hub is to whole the separations amongst v and each of alternate nodes:

Terrorist networks, it may be useful in identifying the person which can quickly access other persons in the network.

$$C_i = \frac{N-1}{\sum_{jTG} d_{ij}}$$

Estimating closeness centrality for all nodes comes down to an expansiveness first scan of the whole system for each hub. Thus, closeness centrality does not scale and additionally degree centrality. By the by, the acquired outcome considers the system all in all, rather than constraining to a nearby, and conceivably deceptive portion. In (Guofeng et al., 2010), an elective definition of closeness centrality is displayed. The thought is to aggregate when registering closeness centrality for a hub v, for every hub u not quite the same as v, the aftereffect of applying an entirely diminishing positive capacity α to the separation dG(u,v) between nodes has and v, formally:

Pagerank

In the social network is a measure for computing relative importance and ranking the nodes of Page Rank. Using Page Rank in terrorist network analysis overall importance of a person can be determined based on its position in the network. Page rank can be defined as (Xuan et al., 2014):

$$PR(a) = \sum_{bTNb_a} \frac{PR(b)}{L(b)}$$

Algorithm for Discovering Finance Manager

In this part we are representing the algorithm considered to find the node in the network that represents a person having highest degree centrality among all other persons and places, is closest to all other nodes in the betweenness, and has a highest betweenness centrality between the organizations.

In this, we can analyze the node that is operationally most central, active, gateway and controllable in the network. The social network is represented by an undirected graph (V, E) with n vertices composed of the following subgraphs.

- VP, Ep – Number of vertices no and denoted by no graph representing persons as nodes and relations between them.
- (Vo, Eo) – The number of vertices is denoted no. graph representing organizations as nodes and the relations between them.
- (Vpl, Epl) – The number of vertices is denoted Nepal. Total of all nodes in above subsets equals the total number of nodes in an entire graph, i.e., n = np + no + Nepal. In addition to the given

edges in (Vo, Eo), (Vpl, Epl), there are three additional subsets of edges that are a part of the set E in (V, E). These sets of edge sets are (Kang et al., 2011):

1. Ep·o – edges representing relations between persons and organizations.
2. Ep·pl –edges representing relations between persons and places.
3. Eo·pl – edges representing relations between organizations and places.

In terrorist network analysis, it helps in identifying, well connected to some other well-connected terrorist.

$$X_i = \frac{1}{\lambda} \sum_{jTNb_i} A_{ij}.X_j$$

The calculation to find a hub in the system that speaks to a man that is operationally most vital to the system and furthermore nearest to different hubs. The calculation comprises of the accompanying advances.

Nodes are calculated for each VP in the set VP. Degree Centrality is calculated for each VP in VP in the subgraph (VP∪Vpl, Ep·pl); that is,

$$D_i = \frac{\sum_{jTG} A_{ij}}{N-1}$$

Each node is calculated VP in set VP with alternative closeness Centrality (Borgatti et al., 2002).

Betweenness Centrality is calculated for each node VP in VP and with respect to all organizations in Vo; that is, Cb is calculated for each node VP in VP.

$$B_i = \frac{\sum_{j,kTG} \frac{g_{jk}(i)}{g_{jk}}}{(N-1)(N-2)}$$

Once all the centrality scores have been measured as described in above items, the key actors in the social network can be identified.

RELATED WORK

In this section, we present a general idea of research work done in the field of SNA with a broader set of prior research focused on counterterrorism and analysis of criminal networks.

(Matthew Denny has given analysis of Social network for the introduction of various concepts in network theory. Social network analysis (SNA) is one of the most favoured innovations for considering fear monger systems. The SNA method characterizes parts and communication among the on-screen characters inside the informal organization. Diverse measures have been made after some time for separating the casual association in term of perceiving key-players, gather area, finding the plan in the framework, center point, and association disclosure etc. Centrality is one of the normally considered thoughts in casual association examination for recognizing key players. A couple of measures have been created for centrality, including degree, closeness, information centrality, betweenness (Strele et al., 2017). Here centrality metrics and clustering algorithm is used for the analysis of structure of Brazalian Scientific researchers of educational institutions.

(Grando et al., 2016) measures some of the complex networks by analysing vertex centrality of the networks. The analysis measures vertex centrality on the basis of information and sub graphs and eigenvector and gives granularity performance at about 95%. Also the analysis of Socio-spatial data by considering network as bimodal for the user performance at distributed events. The main focus of the participants by measure of matching preference and reality (Atzmueler et al., 2016). There are various computational methods used for the analysis of social networks such as search algorithms. Depth first search algorithm is used for the analysis of social network implemented used singly and double linked lists for measuring connectivity of social networks. It also measures connectivity for the identification of structural properties of networks (Hummon et al., 1990).

(Singh et al., 2016) measures centrality for closed group of adolescent females with their association as individual character lengths. In this paper the author tries to find the high centrality measures from a group of adolescent females in social network to find the correlation between individuals with highest centrality and their character strengths. The character strength can be computed with highest in-degree centrality. Although the individual can be trained for particular character strength hence by finding correlation help for some specific roles within organization or society.

(Kaza et al., 2007) uses some dark network for the analysis of criminal s and terrorist networks. In this paper a more sophisticated dynamic network is analysed and used in large-scale real world narcotic network. Multivariate Cox regression helps the network to identify and prediction of co-offending in future crimes.

(Xu et al., 2017) uses online social networks for the analysis of specific terrorist organizations to obtain various structural features by measuring centrality and prestige of the members. The analysis also reveals for the small groups by clustering subgroups and by using 3-core degree based methods in the online community specific structure can be identified. The structure analysis here has higher cohesion and vitality when compared with other network structures.

(Kalpakis et al., 2018) uses online social network for the understanding of various terrorist activities by predicting terrorism related contents and posts. The paper implements some analysis of textual as well as spatial and temporal investigation in the social network data by identifying various network features and metadata which helps in gathering suspicious activities over Twitter content and finally comparing this content with non-suspended content. It is one of the automation for the early detection and various terrorist activities performed via social networks.

(Al-Zoubi et al., 2017) uses Span profile detection based on the set of publicly available features. The prediction model is analysed on the dataset of 82 Twitter's profiles by applying features selection which is calculated using Information Gain. There are Four classification algorithms implemented for the classification of spam profiles using Decision tree, multilayer perceptron and k-nearest neighbours and Naïve Bayes method.

(Rebollo et al., 2019) uses Big data for the detection of jihadism using Graphs and Fuzzy clustering. This paper focuses on all the leaders and their followers by analysing twitter messages for the prediction of terrorist activities in the network. The architectural model used for the prediction and Big data for the analysis of various public features such as level of activity and the ability of influence others as well as content of twitter messages. The algorithm implemented in the paper works in two phases, first by Graphs for the analysis of various messages propagate in network and then Fuzzy extraction methods and the algorithm successfully detect terrorism activism.

(Venkatagiri et al., 2016) proposed a new trend for predicting terrorist activities in social network using Visual Analytics. In this paper Visual Analysis is combined with some statistical analysis and visually recognize the hidden patterns and trend to predict activities. The prediction is performed on unstructured data extracted from online news articles and twitter posts.

PROPOSED METHODOLOGY

The proposed approach applied here depends in the minimization of diagram or system, hence for this purpose centrality measure have been utilized. Initially, an arrangement of these techniques is set up via preparing information. At that point, these methodology rules are connected to the diagram, which gives a diminished chart with less number of nods. Here in this approach diagram advancement or diminishment of the chart is finished by Algorithms. An info chart is given with N nodes, this diagram is associated diagram. In the chart a hub is speaking to a man, so every hub is having a few properties. In this approach connected strategies on arrange dataset 9/11 terrorist network. So this database is set up for N nodes which have nodes and credits relating to properties. The structure of information associated with each node is shown in Table 3. In this approach, centrality is being set up for enhancement of system. When centrality rules have been arranged then these guidelines is utilized for the lessening of the chart. This strategy is readied utilizing preparing dataset 9/11 ruffians, which have nodes and characteristics. The capacity is utilized for getting ready centrality measures. The enlistment work is the twist that depicts how each position in input space is mapped to a cooperation cost (or level of interest) in the region of 0 and 1. The data space is once in a while implied as the universe of talk, some help name for the essential thought. base on outline got the yield of the first stage, in the midst of the second stage, tree pecking request is delivered by applying estimation for the destabilization of Terrorist Network. The commitments for the computation are upgraded outline (yield of the first stage) and centralities regard.

The centrality measure has numerous compose i.e. degree centrality closeness centrality, betweenness centrality measure and page rank for the chart is utilized for the destabilization of Terrorist Network. We applied proposed strategy on the dataset organize degree centrality, closeness centrality, betweenness centrality and page rank measures. The centrality measure of SNA that ends up being critical in IDM is level of the hub - that is, the measure of further hubs specifically associated with it by the edges. In the chart (arrange) portraying a fear-based oppressor organize, hubs of high degree speak to "all around associated" frequently pioneers.

The proposed algorithm for the destabilization of Terrorist networks in the tool is given as following steps:

Centrality Measures used in Algorithms of the Network

The centrality of a node in a network is interpreted as the importance of the node in the network.

1. Apply on any 'nth' node of the graph 'G' to find the neighbour 'N'.

2. Initialize a node 'J' such that the $K = Æ$
3. Compare the centrality of each node to its neighbour node.
4. The greater condition is true or node of centrality J is greater than of k
5. Then add the node J to root set of K
6. Else If node centrality of J is less than K
7. Then the add node J to root set of the K
8. If both cases are false then ignore the link
9. After calculating root and subsets nodes, find the ladder
10. If a node has no root node, add root of tree T as its main and mark n as the sub of root
11. For root set with the one value, the node is the sub of that set value node
12. For the node with root set with more than one assessment, maximum [N(P1) N(n)] is probable and the root node with the maximum value is set as the root of the node. For N(P1) ∩N(n) = 0, node is overlooked
13. Even then root node set has many values the node is attached to root
14. Repeat steps 1-2 and steps 5-8 for all nodes of graph G
15. Draw tree T.

Distributed Computation of PageRank with Unknown Network Size

This iteration is fully localized, for illustration. In particular, the step size $\alpha(k)$ counts the percentage of updates that have been completed in page s(k), which is inherently known to this page without any global information. Similarly, Hbs(k) is solely decided by the incoming links to page s(k), which is again known to this page. It is also consistent with the observation that every page is only concerned with the rank of neighbouring pages, and returns a sub-PageRank. Subsequently, each neighbouring page detects its updated value in the subpage Rank from page s(k). In summary, the fusion algorithm can also be implemented in a fully distributed way for networks with unknown size. Thus, the remaining problem is to show the convergence of x(k) to the PageRank x. This will be addressed in Section V. Algorithm 2 provides the distributed computation of Page Rank with unknown network size.

1. Initialization: for every i ∈ V, set xi(0) = 0 and s(0) = 0.
2. If s(k) = i, node j ∈ L1 i sends its importance value xj (k) to this node for a local computation as in (28). Node j ∈ L1 i ∪{i} updates its importance value from xj (k) to xj (k + 1).
3. Repeat the process till then the condition is false.
4. End.

Genetic Algorithm Clustering

Genetic algorithm is a concept which is based and inspired from biological evolution. It works very similar and performs selection as in natural selection. Genetic algorithm elements consisting of Individual Chromosome (feasible solution in an optimization problem) and population (which contains set of individuals and maintained in each iteration). It defines fitness function which takes single chromosome as input and generates measure of optimized solution represented in the form of chromosome.

1. Initialize population (preparing the chromosomes)
    a. Find neighbor nodes of each node upto $\sqrt{n}$ level's iteration.
2. Defining Genetic operators
    a. Fusion: takes two unique allele values and combines them into a single allele value, combining two clusters into one.
    b. Fission: takes a single allele value and gives it a different random allele value, breaking a cluster apart.
3. Fitness function
    a. Find nodes with same numbers of neighbor nodes and eliminate the nodes with equal number of neighbor node.

```
For(i=1; i<=n; i++)
{
For(j=i+1; j<=n; j++)
{ if(No.neighbors(i)=No.neighbor(j))
Eliminate node j
}
}
```

4. Crossover
    a. Recombine the clusters by taking union of them.
5. Mutation
    a. Find the most connected node by finding common nodes in clusters.

Fuzzy-GA Approach

For our approach we use data set, network name: The implemented network in the event 9/11, with 61 nodes. For our approach we use data set, network name: The implemented network in the event 9/11, with 61 nodes. After the fuzzification of the dataset, the dataset is being optimized with the help of genetic algorithm The searching capability of genetic algorithms is exploited in order to search for appropriate cluster centers in the feature space such that a similarity metric of the resulting clusters is optimized. The fuzzy – GA algorithm is depicted below.

Step 1: load the adjacency matrix from .csv file
Step 2: pre-processing of dataset
Step 3: compute the various centrality measures (degree, betweenness, closeness, PageRank)
Step 4: calculate the fuzzy centrality
Fuzzy centrality of node i is calculated using below given equation
Fuzzy centrality(i) =

$$\frac{\log\left\{0.2*\mathrm{degree}\left(i\right) + 0.3*\mathrm{Betweenness}\left(i\right) + 0.3*\mathrm{Closeness}\left(i\right) + 0.2*\mathrm{pagerank}\left(i\right)\right\}}{10}$$

Step 5: Fuzzification of dataset based on fuzzy centrality
If (fuzzy centrality<0)
Then fuzzy centrality(i)= 0

Step 6:   Eliminate nodes having fuzzy centrality =0

Step 7:   Apply genetic algorithm for cluster formation

1. Initialize the population
   a. finding neighbors node
2. Fitness value function
   a. Find nodes having same number of neighbors
   b. Eliminate duplicates nodes
3. Crossover
   a. Recombine the clusters
4. Mutation
   a. Find the common node (most connected)

Step 8:   End

Prediction of Terrorists Network on 10 Nodes

We are considering 10 nodes from 9/11 hijackers network dataset. In Table 1, each of the nodes contains value 1 or 0 to show the relation between different nodes in the network. The different Terrorists are notated as T1, T2…..T10 and their names are alias below:

Table 1 (b). Sample 10 terrorist network in dataset

Node	T1	T2	T3	T4	T5	T6	T7	T8	T9	T10
T1	0	0	1	0	0	0	0	0	0	0
T2	0	0	1	1	0	0	0	0	0	0
T3	1	1	0	1	0	0	0	0	0	0
T4	0	1	1	0	1	1	0	1	1	0
T5	0	0	0	1	0	0	0	0	0	0
T6	0	0	0	0	0	0	0	1	1	0
T7	0	0	0	0	0	0	0	0	1	0
T8	0	0	0	0	0	0	0	0	0	0
T9	0	0	0	0	0	1	1	1	0	1
T10	0	0	0	0	0	0	0	1	1	0

T1– MajedMoqed	T2-Khalid Al-Mihdhar	T3- Hani Hanjour
T4-NawafAlhazmi	T5-Salem Alhazmi*	T6-Ahmed Alnami
T7-Ahmed Alghamdi	T8-SaeedAlghamdi*	T9- HamzaAlghamdi
T10- Ahmed Al Haznawi		

Figure 1. Computing different measures on dataset

```
Basic Centrality measures of terrorist network
----------------------------------------------------------------------------------------
S No    NodeId  Terrorist Name              Degree   Betweenness   Closeness   Pagerank
----------------------------------------------------------------------------------------
  1       1     Majed Moqed                   2        0.000         0.025       0.065
  2       2     Khalid Al-Mihdhar             4        0.000         0.033       0.088
  3       3     Hani Hanjour                  6       11.000         0.040       0.143
  4       4     Nawaf Alhazmi                 9       26.000         0.040       0.146
  5       5     Salem Alhazmi*                2        0.000         0.025       0.048
  6       6     Ahmed Alnami                  4        0.000         0.053       0.082
  7       7     Ahmed Alghamdi                2        0.000         0.040       0.061
  8       8     Saeed Alghamdi*               4        0.000         0.067       0.143
  9       9     Hamza Alghamdi                8       17.000         0.061       0.161
 10      10     Ahmed Al Haznawi              3        0.000         0.040       0.061
```

Step 1:   Computation begins after loading of sample dataset.

Step 2:   Different Centrality measures such as Degree, Closeness, Betweenness and Pagerank are considered using MATLAB functions. Fig 1 depicts the basic centrality.

Step 3:   Now, generate the biograph of sample dataset before applying fuzzy. Fig 2 shows the biograph.

Figure 2. BioGraph of sample dataset before applying Fuzzy

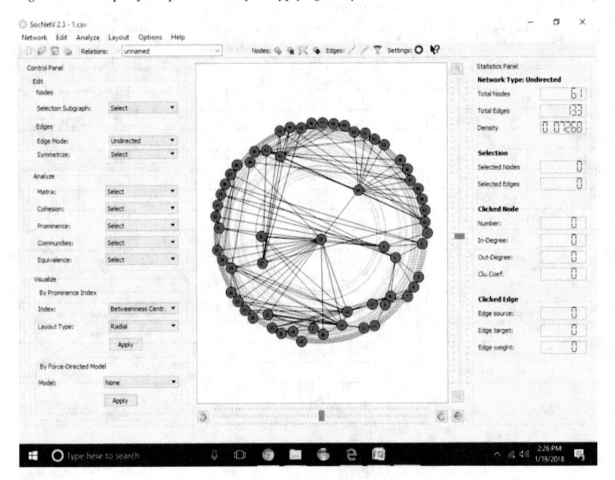

Figure 3. Fuzzy centrality of sample nodes

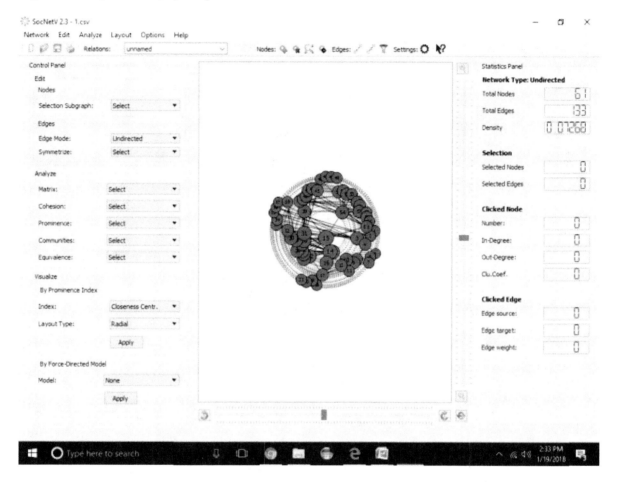

Step 4:   Now Calculate Fuzzy Centrality of each node:
Fuzzy centrality of node i is calculated using below given equation

Fuzzy centrality(i) =

$$\frac{\log\left\{0.2*\text{degree}\left(i\right)+0.3*\text{Betweenness}\left(i\right)+0.3*\text{Closeness}\left(i\right)+0.2*\text{pagerank}\left(i\right)\right\}}{10}$$

For node 1 in our sample database the fuzzy centrality is calculated as
Fuzzy centrality (1) = log{0.2*2 + 0.3*0.000 + 0.3*0.025 + 0.2*0.068}/10
= log {0.4211}/10 = 0.000
Hence fuzzy centrality for node 1 is 0.000. Similarly fuzzy centrality for rest nodes is calculated as shown in figure 3 below.
Step 5:   Applying Fuzzy on dataset
If

Figure 4. BioGraph after applying Fuzzy

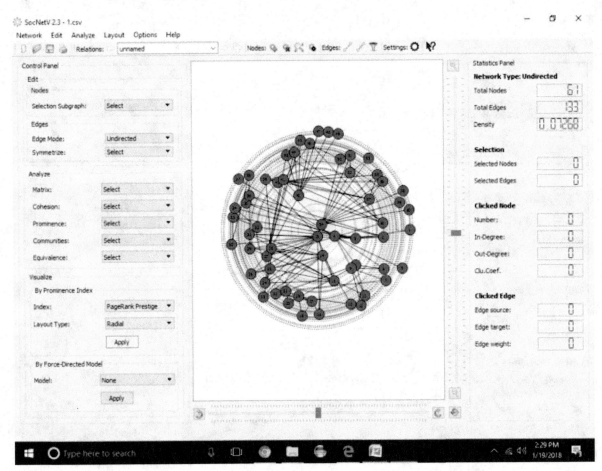

fuzzycentrality(i) < 0

fuzzycentrality = 0

End;

Nodes having fuzzy centrality less than 0 are eliminated in this step.

Step 6:   Generate Biograph after Applying Fuzzy. Fig 4 shows the biograph.

Step 6:   Apply Genetic Algorithm. After applying GA we get the desired results as shown in figure 5.

As we can see that node 4 has higher centrality measures among node 3, 4 &9. The most influencing node in sample dataset is node 4.

EXPERIMENTAL BACKGROUND AND RESULTS ANALYSIS

The 9/11 hijackers network (Mishra, 2021) incorporates 61 nodes (each node is a terrorist involved in 9/11 bombing at World Trade Centers in 2011). Dataset was prepared on the basis of some news report and ties range from 'at school with' to 'on same plane'. The Data consist of mode matrix with 19*19

Figure 5. Results after applying genetic algorithm

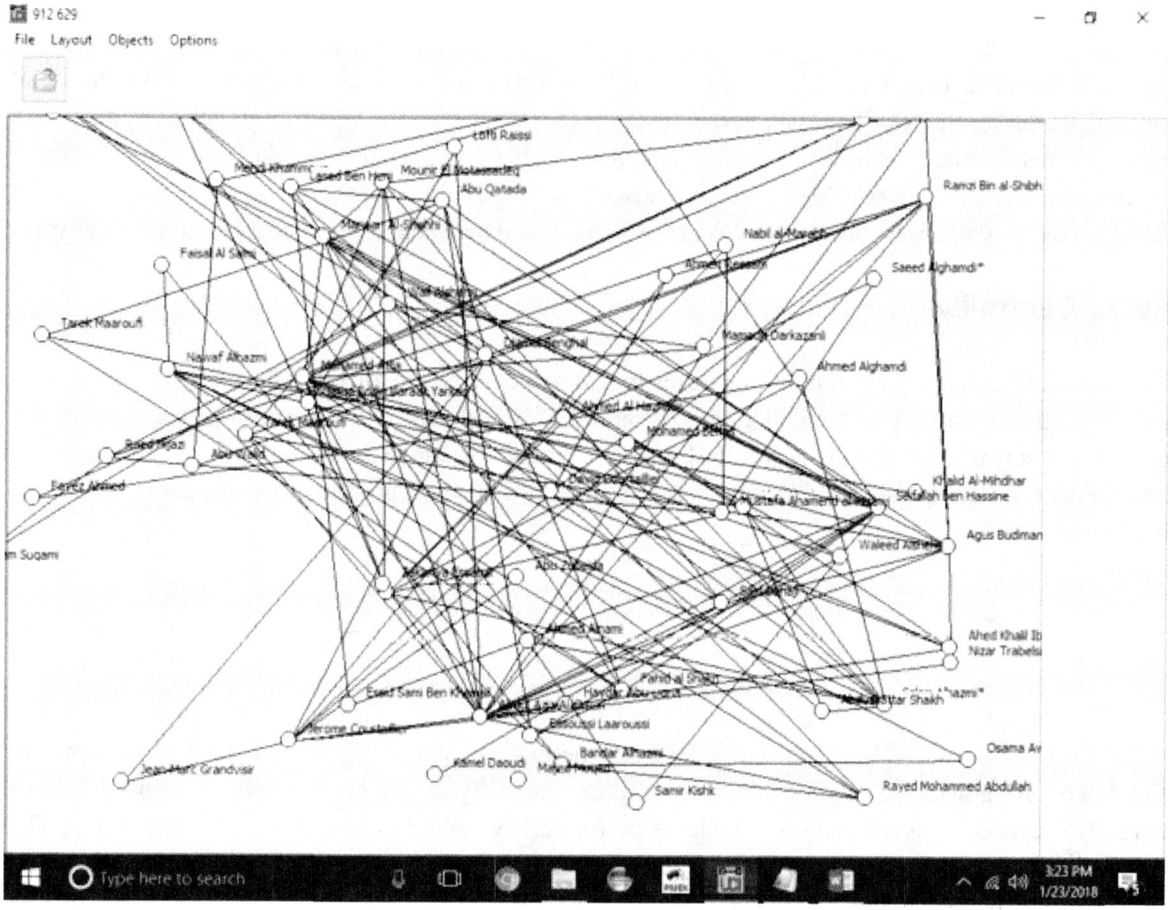

Table 2. Annotations used in 9/11 hijackers' network for attribute nodes and codes

Network Strengths	Ties	Las Vegas Meeting
1 = Trusted Prior Contacts 2 = Other Associates	1 = AA #11 WTC North 2 = AA #77 Pentagon 3 = UA #93 Pennsylvania 4 = UA #175 WTC South 5 = Other Associates	1 = Attended 2 = Did Not Attend

terrorist by terrorist having trusted prior contacts with 1 mode matrix of 61*61 of other involved associates. All the Ties are showed by an undirected and binary matrix, some relations are given as mix of prior contacts such as together trained and financial transactions and together lived and on same plane (Mishra, 2021). Table 2 shows the annotations which are used as attribute nodes and attribute codes.

The Experimental operations and simulations are performed on dataset using 3 tools MATLB, UCI-NET, and SNA. The Simulation in MATLAB starts with the loading of Dataset and then required data preprocessing with some necessary data scaling is done.

Centrality

Centrality measures the nodes in the network are related by direct or undirected relationships. Centrality is considered as network properties which are frequently required to detect actors specially in social network terrorist activities. There are various concepts for the detection of centrality such as by closeness centrality, betweenness centrality, and page rank. In the Table 3, given below are the basic centrality measures across terrorist network, Metric degree shows terrorist activity in the network, Closeness shows the ability of terrorist to access other terrorists in the network and betweenness reveals his control in network.

Fuzzy Centrality

The above table shows the centrality measures for each of the node involved in the network. After computing centrality for each of the node, a fuzzy centrality is performed. There are some fuzzy attributes used in the network for each node which show the value whose range from 0 to 1. Fuzzy centrality for each of the node computed using (1) and Figure 6 shows the fuzzy centrality computed for each of node in the network.

$$FuzzyCentrality(i) = \frac{\log\left[0.2 * degree(i) + 0.3 * betweenness(i) + 0.3 * closeness(i) + 0.2 * pagerank(i)\right]}{10} \tag{1}$$

There are some strongly connected nodes in the network such as Node 54 and Node 15 as shown in Fig 7. This is shown by applying Genetic algorithm centrality on the dataset with an elapsed time of 0.413025 seconds. The connection of nodes is performed by using Fuzzy with Genetic Algorithm. The technique has been executed for 0.215741 seconds which is considered as Elapsed Time. Hence Node Id 15 is the only highly connected node in the network shown in Fig 8.

The Simulation environment for the analysis of centralities in social network analysis using UCINET, the name of 61 terrorists is listed in table 3 with a number assigned to it respectively.

Degree Centrality

In undirected networks, for the network name "9_11_HIJACKERS_CSV" with actors 61 is used and degree centrality index is given as the sum of edges attached to a node u. In directed networks, an index is given as total outbound from node u to all the adjacent matrix nodes (also called "out degree centrality").

If the network is weighted, the DC (degree centrality) score is the sum of weights of outbound edges from node u to all adjacent nodes. To compute in Degree Centrality, use the Degree Prestige measure. DC' is the standardized index (DC divided by N-1 (non-valued nets) or by sum DC (valued nets).

DC range: $0 \leq DC \leq 60$

DC Sum = 263.000

a. Group degree centralization (GDC) of degree centrality:

GDC = 0.184

GDC range: $0 \leq GDC \leq 1$

GDC = 0, when all out-degrees are the same (i.e. regular lattice). GDC = 1, when node completely leads or overshadows other nodes.

Table 3. Basic centrality measures of terrorist network

Node Id	Terrorist Name	Degree	Betweenness	Closeness	Pagerank
1	MajedMoqed	2	0.000	0.001	0.012
2	Khalid Al-Mihdhar	6	2.000	0.002	0.018
3	Hani Hanjour	10	83.500	0.002	0.032
4	NawafAlhazmi	12	160.500	0.002	0.030
5	Salem Alhazmi*	2	0.000	0.001	0.007
6	Ahmed Alnami	4	0.000	0.004	0.013
7	Ahmed Alghamdi	3	10.833	0.004	0.010
8	SaeedAlghamdi*	6	0.000	0.005	0.027
9	HamzaAlghamdi	10	246.167	0.004	0.035
10	Ahmed Al Haznawi	5	225.983	0.005	0.021
11	MohandAlshehri*	4	56.350	0.004	0.020
12	Fayez Ahmed	5	82.850	0.005	0.025
13	ZiadJarrah	11	252.650	0.006	0.045
14	Marwan Al-Shehhi	16	167.617	0.005	0.064
15	Mohamed Atta	18	319.433	0.006	0.062
16	Abdul Aziz Al-Omari*	6	194.167	0.005	0.044
17	WaleedAlshehri	7	139.500	0.004	0.037
18	Wail Alshehri	4	0.000	0.003	0.024
19	SatamSuqami	6	11.167	0.003	0.025
20	RaedHijazi	4	0.000	0.000	0.004
21	Nabil al-Marabh	5	5.833	0.000	0.004
22	Mustafa Ahamend al-Hisawi	4	0.000	0.000	0.003
23	MamounDarkazanli	4	0.000	0.002	0.004
24	ZakariyaEssabar	7	0.000	0.003	0.005
25	Said Bahaji	11	60.100	0.003	0.007
26	Mounir El Motassadeq	6	0.000	0.003	0.005
27	Zacarias Moussaoui	14	424.807	0.004	0.027
28	Ramzi Bin al-Shibh	14	334.017	0.003	0.012
29	AgusBudiman	6	40.167	0.003	0.005
30	Ahed Khalil Ibrahim Samir Al-Ani	2	1.833	0.000	0.004
31	LoftiRaissi	5	0.000	0.000	0.003
32	Rayed Mohammed Abdullah	·6	4.000	0.001	0.008
33	Bandar Alhazmi	3	0.000	0.001	0.005
34	Faisal Al Salmi	3	0.000	0.001	0.005
35	Osama Awadallah	4	0.000	0.000	0.004
36	AbdussattarShaikh	4	0.000	0.000	0.004
37	Mohamed Abdi	1	0.000	0.000	0.003
38	Mohamed Belfas	2	0.000	0.000	0.003
39	ImadEddinBaraatYarkas	7	96.167	0.003	0.010
40	TarekMaaroufi	12	276.481	0.003	0.026
41	Abu Qatada	12	259.481	0.004	0.021
42	DjamalBenghal	16	230.205	0.003	0.035
43	Jerome Courtaillier	8	15.833	0.003	0.018
44	David Courtaillier	6	0.000	0.003	0.015
45	AhmenRessam	4	76.519	0.003	0.010
46	Abu Walid	6	14.667	0.003	0.011
47	Jean Marc Grandvisir	2	0.000	0.002	0.007
48	Abu Zubeida	2	0.000	0.002	0.007
49	NizarTrabelsi	2	0.000	0.002	0.007
50	Haydar Abu Doha	6	65.102	0.003	0.014
51	Mehdi Khammoun	5	1.000	0.002	0.011
52	Mohammed Bensakhria	9	32.324	0.003	0.019
53	Lased Ben Heni	4	0.000	0.002	0.011
54	Essid Sami Ben Khemail	22	359.426	0.003	0.054
55	Seifallah ben Hassine	5	0.167	0.003	0.011
56	EssoussiLaaroussi	5	0.167	0.003	0.011
57	TarekMaaroufi	6	0.000	0.000	0.003
58	Fahid al Shakri	2	0.000	0.002	0.007
59	MadjidSahoune	3	0.000	0.002	0.011
60	Samir Kishk	2	0.000	0.002	0.007
61	KamelDaoudi	8	10.988	0.002	0.010

Figure 6. Nodes connection using Fuzzy centrality

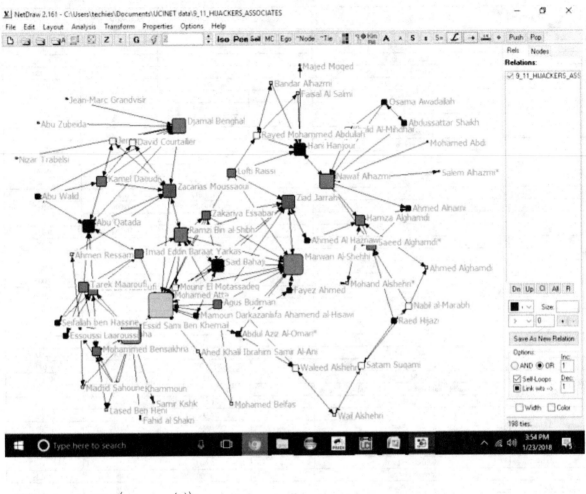

$$C_D(G) = \frac{\sum_v \left(\blacklozenge_G - C_D(v) \right)}{max_H \sum_{v \in H} \left(\blacklozenge_H - C_D(v) \right)}$$

Where ΔG is the maximum degree of any node in G, CD(v)) is the degree of node v in graph G and the maximum is taken over all possible graph of the same Oder (the same number of nodes), i.e., a star.

Betweenness Centrality

In this undirected network using network name 9/11 hijackers and actors is 61 The BC index of a node u is the sum of $\delta(s,t,u)$ for all s,t$\in$ V where $\delta(s,t,u)$ is the ratio of all geodesics between s and t which run through u.

BC' is the standardized index (BC divided by (N-1) (N-2)/2 in symmetric nets or (N-1) (N-2) otherwise. BC range: $0 \le BC \le 1.77e+03$ (Number of pairs of nodes excluding u). BC Sum = 4757.000.

Figure 7. Nodes connection using genetic algorithm centrality

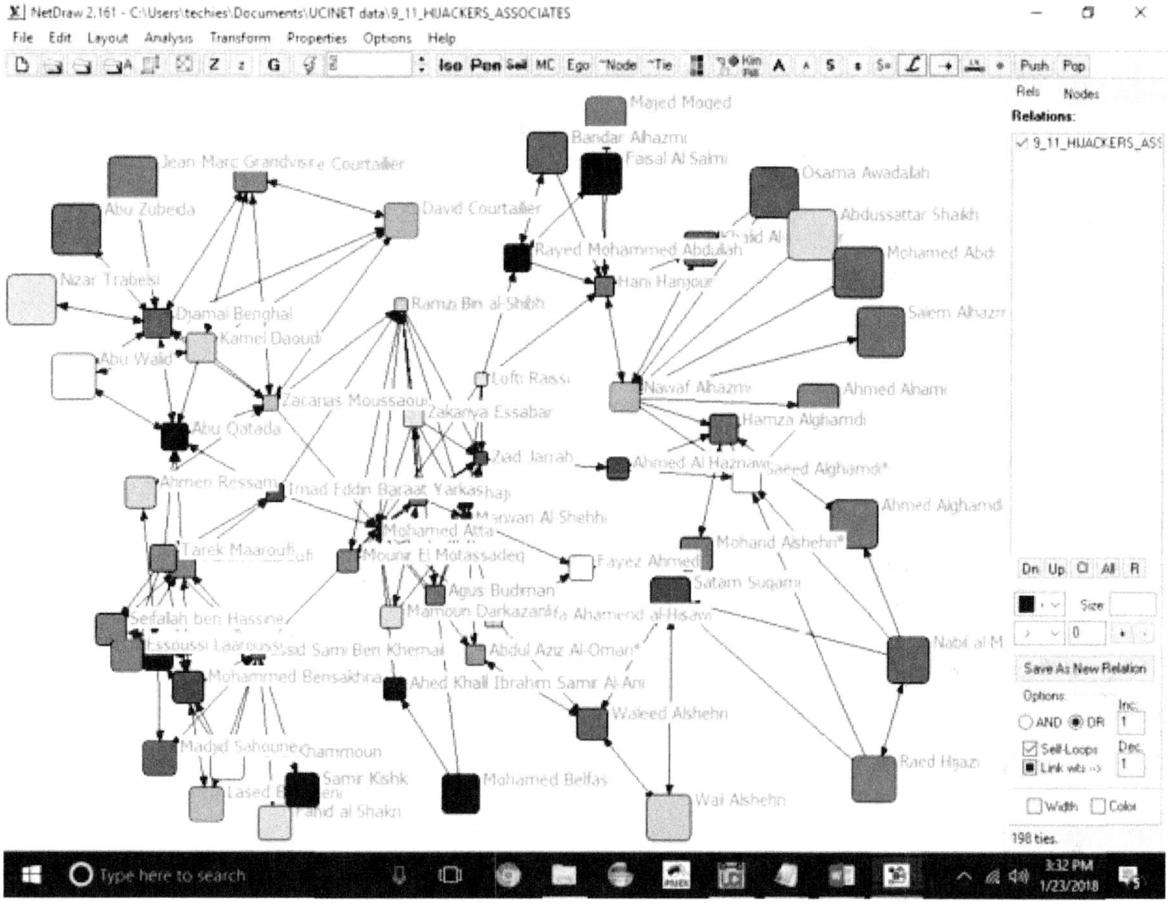

Format Group Betweenness Centralization (GBC)

GBC = 0.469 **GBC range:** $0 \leq GBC \leq 1$ GBC = 0, when all the nodes have exactly the same betweenness index.

GBC = 1, when one node falls on all other geodesics between all the remaining (N-1) nodes. This is exactly the situation realized by a star graph.

Closeness Centrality

In an undirected network, network name "9_11_HIJACKERS.csv" and Actors: 61 is taken. The CC (Closeness Centrality) index is the inverted sum of the geodesic distance from every node u to all extra nodes.

Note: The CC index considers out bound arcs only and isolated nodes are dropped by default. Read the Manual for more. CC' is the standardized index (CC multiplied by (N-1 minus isolates)). CC range: $0 \leq CC \leq 0.0167$ (1 / Number of node pairs excluding u). **CC Sum** = 0.290.

Figure 8. Nodes connection using Fuzzy-GA centrality

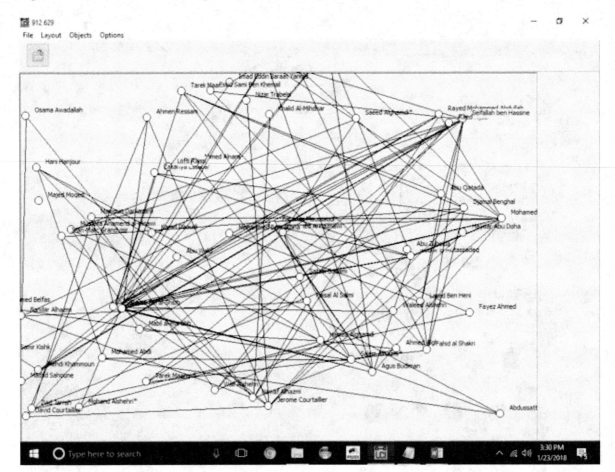

Group Closeness Centralization (GCC)

GCC = 0.326GCC range: $0 \leq$ GCC ≤ 1 GCC = 0, when the lengths of the geodesics are all equal, i.e. a complete or a circle graph.GCC = 1, when one node has geodesic of length 1 to all the other nodes, and the other nodes have geodesics of length 2. to the remaining (N-2) nodes. This is exactly the situation realized by a star graph.

Page Rank Prestige

In undirected networks, in this using Network name:9_11_HIJACKERS.csv and Actors: 61. The PRP is an importance ranking index for each node based on the structure of its incoming links/edges and the rank of the nodes linking to it.

For each node, u proposed algorithms counts all inbound links (edges) to it, but it normalizes each inbound link from a node v by out Degree of v. The Page Rank(PR) values correspond to rule of the normalized link adjacency matrix.

Figure 9. Degree centrality

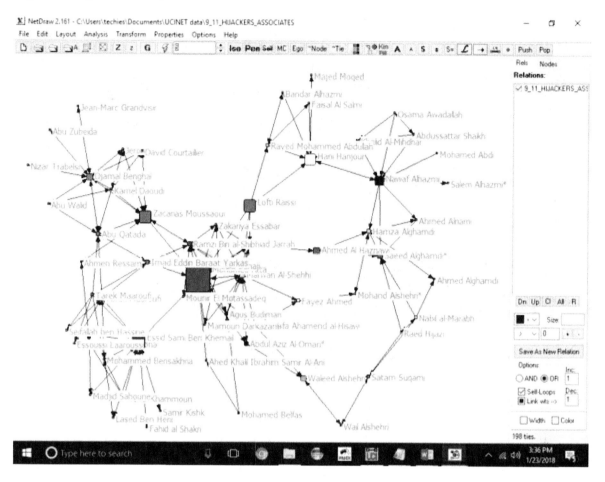

Note: In weighted relations, each backlink to a node u from another node v is considered to have weight=1 but it is normalized by the sum of outbound edge weights of v. Therefore, nodes with high out Link weights give a smaller percentage of their PR to node u.

PRP' is the scaled PRP (PRP divided by max PRP). There calculating values is **PRP range:** (1-d)/N = 0.00246 ≤ PRP Max **PRP = 0.044** (node 15) **Min PRP = 0.005** (node 47) **PRP classes = 55PRP Sum = 0.954 PRP Mean = 0.016 PRP Variance = 0.000.**

Table 4 shows four DC (Degree Centrality) CC (Closeness Centrality) BC (Betweenness Centrality) PR (Page Rank Centrality) centrality measures of terrorists and are calculated using UCINET. By calculating and generating using standard social network techniques in the embassy terrorist data individuals who are key in a network are identified (red nodes) and then removed. After removing useful and important nodes and nodes in the red shape of the disconnected terrorist network. The argument is that the removal of important nodes serves to weaken or break the network as shown in the analysis. However, despite the apparent success of this approach, evidence indicates that this technique is not effective as in the case of dynamic, distributed and a decentralized terrorist network such as 9/11 Hijackers. These types of networks have the ability to heal themselves after the removal of any key member (leader) form the

Figure 10. Betweenness centrality

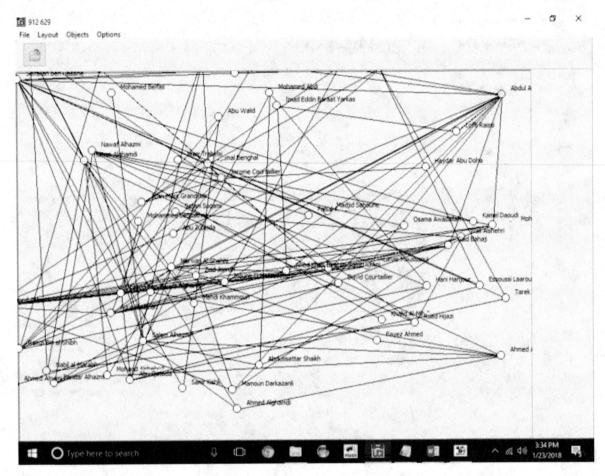

network (Venkatagiri et al., 2016). In fact, leadership removal may make network many dense to the future analysis given in emergence of new leadership that may not be known.

The rate of information flow through the network has been minimized (perhaps to zero).

Figure 11. Closeness centrality

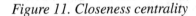

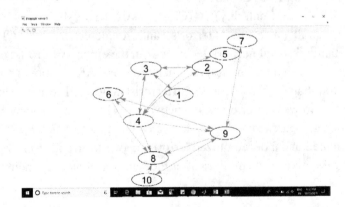

Figure 12. Page Rank Prestige

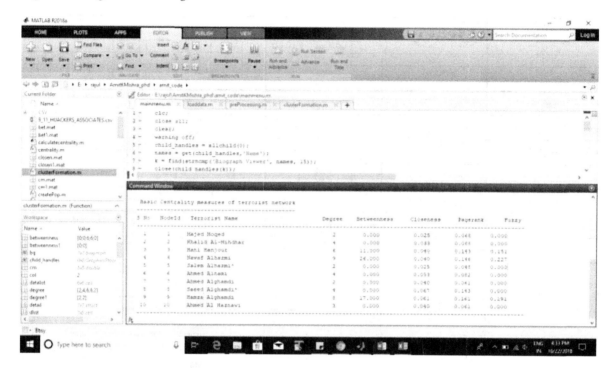

- The network, as a decision making the body, cannot reach a joint consensus.
- The ability of the network to accomplish tasks is totally impaired.
- Based on the above discussion, it is very important to know about the structural properties to gain insight to the following questions in order to not only disconnect but also destabilize these terrorist networks:
- What is the overall network structure?
- Who is the key player in the network?
- What is the efficiency of the network?
- Who is highly connected to whom?
- Who shares most resources to whom?
- Which terrorist, if removed, would highly disrupt the network communication?

These and many more questions could be answered by following the overall structure and dynamics of the terrorist networks.

Two-modulus Network of the Terrorist Organizations

AutoMap software's can be utilized to characterize the ideas and their related information and further change the semantic web to interpersonal organization demonstrate. Before developing terroristic systems, it is important to utilize component grid vocabulary to order the social substances. The component lattice dictionary can be created consequently or self-characterized by the requirements of an investigation. In Figure demonstrated the component grid dictionary produced via AutoMap, where the left section is

Table 4. Shows the value of Centrality

NODE	DC	CC	BC	PR
1	1.000	0.004	0.000	0.006
2	4.000	0.004	41.100	0.017
3	7.000	0.005	370.876	0.029
4	9.000	0.005	250.243	0.038
5	1.000	0.004	0.000	0.006
6	3.000	0.004	0.000	0.013
7	2.000	0.004	2.500	0.010
8	6.000	0.005	123.013	0.024
9	6.000	0.005	105.066	0.025
10	3.000	0.005	182.876	0.012
11	2.000	0.004	18.313	0.009
12	3.000	0.005	47.396	0.012
13	8.000	0.006	231.160	0.024
14	12.000	0.006	134.476	0.036
15	15.000	0.007	894.977	0.044
16	3.000	0.006	76.181	0.011
17	4.000	0.005	125.067	0.016
18	2.000	0.004	0.000	0.010
19	4.000	0.004	66.701	0.018
20	3.000	0.004	17.428	0.013
21	4.000	0.004	24.594	0.018
22	4.000	0.006	104.114	0.014
23	3.000	0.005	0.000	0.010
24	5.000	0.006	0.000	0.015
25	7.000	0.006	4.840	0.020
26	4.000	0.005	0.000	0.012
27	8.000	0.006	368.408	0.022
28	9.000	0.006	96.012	0.025
29	5.000	0.006	42.400	0.016
30	2.000	0.005	15.600	0.009
31	5.000	0.006	421.110	0.017
32	5.000	0.005	41.800	0.020
33	2.000	0.004	0.000	0.010
34	2.000	0.004	0.000	0.010
35	3.000	0.004	0.000	0.014
36	3.000	0.004	0.000	0.014
37	1.000	0.004	0.000	0.006
38	2.000	0.004	0.000	0.009
39	5.000	0.006	0.500	0.016
40	6.000	0.005	72.386	0.020
41	7.000	0.005	31.711	0.021
42	9.000	0.005	88.538	0.030
43	4.000	0.005	199.077	0.012
44	4.000	0.005	0.000	0.012
45	2.000	0.005	0.000	0.008
46	3.000	0.004	28.152	0.010
47	1.000	0.004	0.000	0.005
48	1.000	0.004	0.000	0.005
49	1.000	0.004	0.000	0.005
50	4.000	0.005	0.000	0.015
51	3.000	0.005	28.185	0.012
52	5.000	0.005	1.000	0.018
53	2.000	0.004	7.239	0.009
54	12.000	0.006	0.000	0.043
55	3.000	0.005	447.218	0.011
56	3.000	0.005	0.167	0.011
57	6.000	0.005	0.167	0.020
58	1.000	0.004	31.711	0.006
59	2.000	0.005	0.000	0.009
60	1.000	0.004	0.000	0.006
61	6.000	0.005	0.008	0.018

the name of social substances, and the correct segment is the hub kind of the social elements, including the operator of association individuals and the association On of associations. Select "create component lattice arrange" menu and apply the adjusted vocabulary, and the XML-design archives speaking to the two-modulus system of the fear-based oppressor association will be produced, and the 2D visual impact of the two-modulus organize in ORA is appeared.

The red nodes speak to the general population identified with terroristic associations, the green nodes speak to the associations identified with the terroristic association, and the associations between nodes speak to that there are relations between individuals, associations, or amongst individuals and association. Examination of Human Networks and Their Members Associated information and their interpersonal organization of association individuals are isolated out of the two-modulus arrange information, and the information can be additionally prepared with the system investigation device. UCINET6 is utilized to break down, the system contains 61 nodes, 61 associations, 61 segregated nodes, which represents 20%. The numerous confined nodes show the inadequacy of information. The system thickness and the center system with the exception of the detached nodes has 61 nodes, which thickness is NetDraw2 is utilized to make visual investigation, the strategy for Spring Embedding is embraced to pick similitude and utilize geodesic separation to express, the separation between segments is 10, and the consequence of its system game plan appears in Figure.

The isolated nodes have vertically organized a line, alternate nodes are organized by their separate segments, the nodes of a similar part have a more prominent likeness, which demonstrates a littler geodesic separation in the diagram. It is in this way obvious that there is a generally expansive segment in the information that contains a large portion of the nodes, while the left segments contain a little piece of nodes. The more noteworthy the separation between the chose segments is, the littler the separation between the nodes of a similar segment will be, and the more noteworthy the separation between the parts is, the more clear the structure of the segments in the system will be. Segment acknowledgment calculation in subgroup investigation is chosen to compute the segment numbers and the combination of each segment; consider the segregated nodes a segment, at that point there are 20 segments altogether, among which, there are 7 segments containing more than 3 nodes, and the greatest segment contains 61 nodes, which is the most imperative piece of the system chart. Strong subgroups still exist in the greater parts.

After symmetrical preparing of information, groups revelation calculation investigation comes about are appeared in Table 4, among which, there is one group of the biggest scale, containing all nodes, and performing artists of the littlest scale, containing dataset organize, and among which, the state of the initial individuals' contribution groups appears in Table. Notwithstanding finding the subgroups in systems, the other essential errand of SNA is to distinguish the center individuals in the system. The fundamental strategy is to do centrality examination to the system. The centrality is the quantitative investigation of individual rights 61, and the count comes about are appeared in Table II. From the point of view of the characters distinguished, the vital characters controlled by the centrality have been checked.

Analysis of the Affiliation between Datasets and Networks

As indicated by the information acquired concerning the connection amongst datasets and associations, UCINET6 is utilized to run the system information, organize is developed in arrange, technique for Spring inserting is utilized to make course of action, and there are 61 nodes, which are communicated in red roundabout nodes, and 85 delegate associations, which are communicated in blue box nodes as appeared. The calculation positions a couple of strainers as indicated by the closeness, and lines up the disconnected nodes vertically at a side, to unmistakably demonstrate the few most vital associations in the connection. Notwithstanding the associations related to associations, there are some different associations being placed in a critical position in the system, including all nodes, whose relationship with edges associations makes their position more unmistakable. Through the connection systems, we can break down what number of associations are related with every individual and along these lines recognize the general population assuming an essential part in every association and the association of the biggest normal individuals. There are two approaches to accomplish this examination by utilizing UCINET6: syntax command method and the data processing program method built in the UCINET6.

Here we simply utilize the in-manufactured program of the UCINET6 to work. The table is the half-way consequences of the affiliation degree, and because of constrained space, the table has just demonstrated the initial 10 individuals of the most elevated affiliation degree. The particular count results won't be expounded in view of the mass information. Hierarchical Association Network Association arrange between associations is, for the most part, used to investigate the relationship of the merger and collaboration between associations, the essential associations found from the connection arranges above can likewise be confirmed by the affiliation organize between associations, that is, critical associations ought to likewise be related to more associations in their authoritative affiliation systems, which have demonstrated the most astounding degree or degree centrality in the system chart.

As the related information separated via AutoMap pick the association from the left to one side in the request of the presence of elements, and take the recurrence depiction of the same related information as the force, along these lines in this strategy, it isn't suitable to tell the power of the connections from the symmetry of the connections; while rehashed events of relationship in various settings can be viewed as having extreme relationship. The relationship control is implied by the thickness of the relationship in the framework graphs, and the power regards can in like manner be direct separate on the diagram.

Make centrality examination of the sub mastermind data among affiliations, and along these lines find the inside relationship in the imperative positions. As shown in figure beside the isolated nodes, imagine the framework with the degree centrality as the property, and we can clearly see from the definitive connection orchestrate, that the terroristic affiliations having the most vital level of affiliations (i.e., the most amazing level of centrality) with various affiliations: Majed Moqed Khalid Al-Mihdhar Hani Hanjour Nawaf Alhazmi Salem Alhazmi* Ahmed Alnami et cetera. Here figuring centrality measures in systems examination comes with utilizing proposed calculations utilizing UCINET tool.

DEGREE CENTRALITY MEASURES

Descriptive Statistics

Table5 shows the Actor-by-centrality matrix saved as dataset 9_11_HIJACKERS_ASSOCIATES.In descriptive statistics table actor by centrality matrix saved as dataset 9/11 hijackers dataset and using UCINET6. Calculated values of the network nodes of network Centralization (Outdegree) = 13.139% network centralization (Indegree) = 19.917% network centralization (Outdegree) = 13.139% network centralization (In degree) = 19.917%. In table 3 calculated Mean Std dev, variance SSQ and so on without degree and in degree, Indegree nrm and outdegree nrm.

Figure 13. Degree centrality measures using Ucinet6

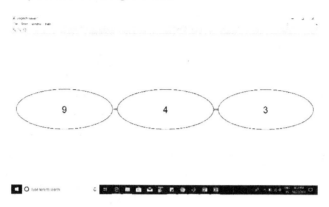

Closeness Centrality Measures

Figure 14. Degree Centrality

Betweenness Centrality

In the three classical centrality measures with 61 actors, the ranking of nodes, Index, and the nodes are calculated according to the node size. The central actors are shown in fig 10and fig 9. To get a better result in the order degree, we show the results in table 5. In the figure, we find results of betweenness centrality very easily.

Table 5. Descriptive statistics actor by centrality matrix

Parameter	1	2	3	4
	Out Degree	**In Degree Nrm**	**OutDegNrm**	**InDeg**
Mean	3.246	3.246	5.410	5.410
Std Dev	2.101	3.006	3.502	5.011
Variance	4.415	9.038	12.264	25.105
SSQ	912.000	1194.000	2533.333	3316.667
MCSSQ	269.311	551.311	748.087	1531.421
EucNorm	30.199	34.554	50.332	57.591
Minimum	0.000	0.000	0.000	0.000
Maximum	11.000	15.000	18.333	25.000
No of Obs	61.000	61.000	61.000	61.000

Figure 15. Closeness centrality

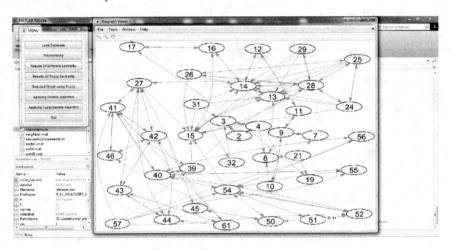

Figure 16. Closeness Centrality measures using UCINET6

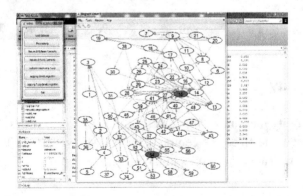

Figure 17. Betweenness centrality

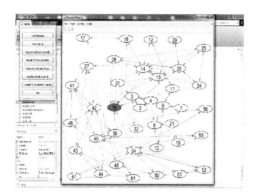

It is not complicated to handle humanly, The local information and many vertices regard as in this only, centrality does not notify separately. Though Betweenness centrality considers global properties of the network, it is hard to use. In this network connection, it is very easy to connect to the network, but our method is fit for anything. If the disconnected network is available in the network nodes, we can calculate and consider the importance of the vertex separately. Another centrality has strict requirements as Betweenness centrality and is also not easy to calculate.

The requirement for the figure is superior.

Descriptive Statistics for Each Measure

Table 6 represents the descriptive statistical value of each measures of given dataset.

CONCLUSION

In this paper, we have initiated a considerable algorithm for centrality measures of terrorist networks which is expected to be most beneficial strategy in finding some patterns in social networks for terrorist activities. For the prediction and analysis of terrorist activities in social networks a dataset of 9/11 hijackers with 61 nodes is considered. We start by analyzing some classical centrality measures and on the basis an adjacency matrix is generated which helps in computing centrality on social networks and another important step is to carry in degree, betweenness and closeness centrality measure and page rank.

The algorithm suggested here is the combinatorial method of applying Fuzzy algorithm to measure centrality between nodes in the network and then optimization using genetic search approach to increase the searching capability for appropriate cluster centers. The algorithm suggested is dynamic and sophisticated to apply on any type of network. Furthermore, the algorithm suggested provides high degree of centrality measure, so the chances of predicting terrorist activities increase with the input adjacency matrix and it can further be used to calculate each node's centrality measure and then analyze rank of these nodes according to the node size and page rank.

Figure 18. Betweenness Centrality measures using UCINET6

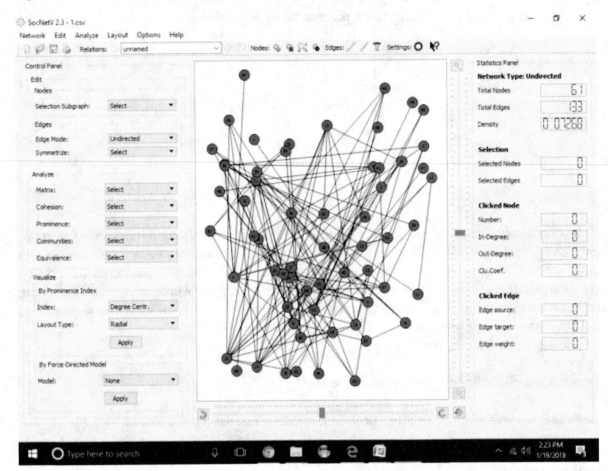

Table 6. Network Centralization Index = 10.19%

1	Mean	69.869	1.974
2	Std Dev	111.050	3.137
3	Sum	4262.000	120.395
4	Variance	12332.194	9.841
5	SSQ	1050044.875	837.918
6	MCSSQ	752263.813	600.294
7	Euc Norm	1024.717	28.947
8	Minimum	0.000	0.000
9	Maximum	424.807	12.000

REFERENCES

Al-Zoubi, Alqatawana, & Faris. (2017). Spam profile detection in social networks based on public features. *8th International conference on information and communication systems (ICICS)*.

Ala, B., & Lisa, A. R. (2012). Detecting Key Players in Terrorist Networks. *2012 European Intelligence and Security Informatics Conference*. 10.1109/EISIC.2012.13

Amit. (2021). 9/11 Hijackers. *IEEE Dataport*. doi:10.21227/ry8q-sj65

Borgatti, Everett, & Freeman. (2002). *Ucinet for Windows: Software for social network analysis*. Academic Press.

Borgatti, S. P., & Everett, M. G. (2006). A graph-theoretic perspective on centrality. *Social Networks, 28*, 466-484.

Borgatti, S. P., Everett, M. G., & Freeman, L. C. (2002). UCINET 6 for Windows. In *Analytic Technologies*. Harvard University Press.

Felipe, G., Noble, D., & Lamb, L. C. (2016). An analysis of Centrality measures for complex and social networks. *IEEE Global Communications Conference 2016*.

Feng, X., Sun, D., Li, Z., & Li, B. (2017). Exploring structural features of terrorist organization's online supporting community via social network modeling. *3rd IEEE International Conference on Computer Communications (ICCC) 2017*.

George, Tsikrika, Gialampoukidis, & Papadopoulos. (2018). Analysis of Suspended Terrorism – Related Content on Social media. Community-Oriented Policing and Technological Innovations, 107-118.

Guofeng & Hong. (2010). *A New Network Core Mining Method based on Node Core Influence Degree*. IEEE.

Hagberg, A., Schult, D., Swart, P., Conway, D., SéguinCharbonneau, L., Ellison, C., & Torrents, J. (2004). *Networkx. High productivity software for complex networks*. https://networkx. lanl. gov/wiki

Hirani, P., & Singh, M. (2015). A Survey on Coverage Problem in Wireless Sensor Network. *International Journal of Computers and Applications, 116*(2), 1–3. doi:10.5120/20305-2347

Hummon & Doreian. (1990). Computational methods for social network analysis. *Social Networks, 12*(4).

Ibrahima, Mendy, Ouya, & Seck. (2015). Spanning graph for maximizing the influence spread in Social Networks. *2015 IEEE/ACM International Conference on Advances in Social Networks Analysis and Mining*.

Kang, U., Papadimitriou, S., Sun, J., & Tong, H. (2011). Centralities in Large Networks: Algorithms and Observations Betweenness. *Proceedings of SIAM International Conference on Data Mining (SDM'2011)*. 10.1137/1.9781611972818.11

Lavanya, V., Sreelakshmi, N., & Mahesh, K. (2016). Visual Analytics of Terrorism Data. *IEEE International Conference on Cloud Computing in Emerging Markets (CCEM)*.

Martin, Hanika, Stumme, & Schaller. (2016). Social event network analysis: Structure, preferences and reality. *IEEE/ACM International Conference on Advances in Social Network Analysis and Mining*.

Matthew. (2014). *Social Network Analysis*. Institute for Social Science Research.

Narotam, S., Varshney, S., & Kapoor, A. (2016). Centrality measures in the close group of adolescent females and their association with individual character strengths. *IEEE/ACM ASONAM 2016*.

Narotam, S., Varshney, S., & Kapoor, A. (2016). Centrality measures in close group of adolescent females and their association with individual character strengths. *ASONAM'16 Proceedings of the 2016 IEEE/ACM International Conference on Advances in Social Networks Analysis and Mining*.

Sanchez, R. C., Puente, C., Palacios, R., & Piriz, C. (2019). Detection of Jihadism in Social networks using big data techniques supported by Graphs and Fuzzy Clustering. Hindwai Complexity.

Saumya, G., & Tiwari, A. (2016, May). Terrorism in the Cyber Space: The New Battlefield. *International Journal of Advanced Research in Computer and Communication Engineering*, *5*(5).

Siddharth, Hu, & Chen. (2007). Dynamic Social Network Analysis of a dark network: Identifying significant facilitators. *IEEE Intelligence and Security Informatics 2007*.

Smith, M., Milic-Frayling, N., Shneiderman, B., Mendes Rodrigues, E., Leskovec, J., & Dunne, C. (2010). *NodeXL: a free and open network overview, discovery and exploration add-in for Excel 2007/2010*. Social Media Research Foundation.

Victor, S., Campose, F., Jose Maria, N. D., & Braga, R. (2017). Data abstraction and centrality measures to scientific social network analysis. *IEEE 21st International Conference on Computer Supported Cooperative Work in Design 2017*.

Xuan, D., Yu, H., & Wang, J. (2014). A novel method of centrality in terrorist network. *2014 Seventh International Symposium on Computational Intelligence and Design*. 10.1109/ISCID.2014.156

Chapter 11
Crime Detection on Social Networks Using AI and ML Techniques

Ranjana Sikarwar
Amity University, India

Harish Kumar Shakya
Amity University, India

Rahul Bharadwaaj
Indian Institute of Information Technology, Bhopal, India

ABSTRACT

Data mining (DM) and machine learning techniques have been used to identify specific patterns and similarities in existing cybercrimes to predict the cyberattacks. Since dealing with big data is a complex task as it requires computationally accurate and efficient techniques, difficulty arises in the analysis of irregular activities on cyberworld. DM techniques offer predictive solutions against cybercrimes and modus operandi. DM methods include classification, association, and clustering while different methods related to machine learning are supervised, semi-supervised, and unsupervised. AI can serve as a smart tool for criminal usage for carrying out malicious activities either by enhancing or changing the existing threats or posing new threats altogether. The expansion of existing threats such as drug trafficking improve frequency of smuggling activities by turning to unmanned underwater vehicles. Also using cheap quadcopter and facial recognition software together could increase the terrorist attacks on civilians.

INTRODUCTION

Cyber relates to everything connecting computers and communication technologies to the internet. Cybersecurity incorporates protocols, technologies, software to protect computers, mobiles, network devices, etc., against cyberattacks (Selamat et al., 2008) (R, 2004). Data mining algorithms help in mining critical

DOI: 10.4018/978-1-6684-3942-5.ch011

information from existing data and detect crime patterns to generate the database for training the system using AI/ML to predict patterns of cybercrime automatically. Web mining or data mining methods are used for cyberattack prediction (Selamat et al., 2008). Cyberattacks can take place either from inside or outside of the network. Different security mechanisms like antivirus, firewalls can't always identify the attacks. Various forms of new attacks cannot be identified by existing security mechanisms or IDS/IPS firewalls (Faghani et al., 2012) (Ahmed & Abulaish, 2013) (Lee & Kim, 2014).

Requirements in Cyber Investigation

This field of investigation encompasses more than just computer forensics. From a flash drive to a worldwide network, this topic embraces digital things along with computers connected wirelessly sharing information over the network. Beyond the electronic data, there are several elements to explore in order to assemble sufficient logical evidence to identify the culprit. An IP address, a user name, or a blog entry might all be used to follow a criminal. This task is challenging due to the extensive technical expertise required to situate a suspect behind a keyboard. Cybercrime investigations are no longer limited to the forensic examination of a single computer. Cybercrime involves the investigation of all linked devices. Many of us learn severely through our own errors, while others prefer to learn from others' mistakes. Those who have undergone forensic analysis and solved challenging difficulties have often attempted a variety of strategies and instruments to tackle challenges. It may be considered selfish not to share the finding of a new forensic item. Common techniques and procedures must be utilized and applied by a community of practitioners in order to become acceptable.

The Idea behind Deep Web and Dark Net

Deep web refers to that part of the web where websites are not indexed just like the ordinary surface internet where websites are easily accessible by the search engines. However, deep web content is also available to the general public using different access methods not just using regular web browsers such as Mozilla Firefox, chrome, safari, etc. Deep web accessibility may require password-encrypted browsers to access the data. It comprises all kind of data that needs special security like medical records, financial records, or any other social media files. This part of the web can't be 'googled' anytime by anybody. Dark web is also a part belonging to the Deep web which can't be reached by regular web browsers. Special browsers such as 'Tor' are needed. The name 'Tor' is a short form of the 'Onion router' which is a far much better and more popular browser with around 2.5 million users daily using it. 'Tor' can help in accessing the Darknet or even smaller subparts of the web also called the Tor network. U.S Government in the 1990s was the first to develop the technology behind the Dark web allowing intelligence bureaus and spies to communicate with each other secretly through messages. The term Dark web is also referred to as Deep web from 2015 due to its anonymous nature and hidden services in Tor's history which couldn't be searched or indexed.

Darknets deal with both legitimate activities such as marketing tracking or performing research on sensitive topics and a large-scale platform for illegal malicious activities. The unprecedented growth of users on online social networks has unfortunately increased the cases of online threats and bullying amongst teenagers resulting in cyberbullying cases, a kind of cyber victimization. A recent study has reported cyberbullying cases among school students. On average 20-40% of cases of cyber victimization have been found according to (Tokunaga, 2010). Cyberbullying is much more harmful than face-to-face bullying because the former can use online platforms 24 by 7 giving chance to the identities of perpetrators of cyberbullying is also hidden.

DARK WEB CRIME USING MACHINE INTELLIGENCE

(Almukaynizi et al., 2018) discussed the DARKMENTION system which uses association rules to find a match between threats on Dark and Deep webs and real-world cyber incidents, thus generating warnings to cybersecurity organizations. The approach presented by (Sapienza et al., 2017) describes a system that matches the text on social media forums and terms used in hackers' discussions on the Dark web. The system makes use of text-mining techniques to match the terms used in posts from cybersecurity experts on social media platforms and hacking forums on the Dark web. (Tavabi et al., 2018) proposed a framework called DarkEmbed which uses language embeddings to represent discussions on the Dark Web and Deep web in low-dimensional vector space. (Arnold et al., 2019) proposed a cyber threat intelligence (CTI) tool to detect cyber threats by monitoring and analyzing discussions on the Dark web identifying any information regarding malicious tools causing vulnerabilities and data breaching. Text feature analysis approach is used to analyze social network data generated from discussions by key actors on breached data on the Dark web. (Ebrahimi et al., 2020) uses a deep learning approach based on using both Transductive Learning (TSVM) and Deep Bidirectional LSTM network for cyber threat detection. (Deliu et al., 2017) discussed different ML methods used for detecting various cyber threats from hacker forums. (Huang et al., 2021) introduced HackerRank approach to identify key hackers with the help of using a combined approach of content analysis (CA) and social network analysis (SNA). (Marin et al., 2018) presented an approach to predict near-future posts of hackers using a sequential rule mining approach. (Deb et al., 2018) used sentimental analysis to predict cyber events. A comparative study on the previous work done by many authors using machine learning and deep learning techniques is shown in table1.

Technical Overview of Dark Web

The Dark Web network comprises an overlaid network often called darknets consisting of many hidden services. These dark networks are accessible using some extraordinary software like tor and Invisible Internet Project(I2P) (Brown, 2016). Tor and I2P software provide anonymity and an encrypted form of data which later was misused as a passage for illegal market trades of guns, drugs, etc., or used as a tool by the terrorists to share disseminate their propaganda or for child abuse material.

Background of Tor Project

The Onion Routing or Tor Project (first generation) was initially created in the mid-'90s by US Naval Research Laboratory and Défense Advanced Research Project Agency (DARPA) to allow secret sharing of messages between operatives of the field and intelligent agencies. In 2002, the Naval Laboratory delivered Tor's source code. Later Electronic Frontier Foundation (EFF) handled Tor's development project and took over the responsibility of maintenance and upgrading the Tor network nowadays. Unlike other tools like I2P (Jardine, 2015), Tor is the most popular tool to provide privacy and anonymity to search and post on the dark web.

Table 1. Comparative study of state-of-art work done on cyber threat detection using machine intelligence

References	Objective of research	Tactics used	Methods and Tools used	Case Study
(Deliu et al., 2017)	Cyber threats are detected more accurately	Word embeddings and classification	SVM, KNN, CNN, word2vec, Glove, Scikit-learn, a python library	Nulled.IO
(Grisham et al., 2017)	Detects key hackers and malware attachments	SNA, Neural Networks, Crawling, Text Classification	Keras, LSTM RNN	Dark web hacker forums in different languages
(Pastrana et al., 2018)	Detects cyberthreat, key actors can predict future key actors	Classification, SNA, Clustering, Prediction	NLP, LDA, K-means, SNA network metrics	Hack forums from CrimeBB datasets
(Tavabi et al., 2018)	Predicting vulnerability exploits	Classification, Crawling, Language Embeddings	SVM, Radial Basis Function (RBF), RF	Deep web and Dark Web sites in 17 different languages
(Zenebe et al., 2019)	Proactive detection of cyber threats and identifying key hackers	Prediction, Visualization, Classification	WEKA, RF, RT, IBM Watson Analytics	University of Arizona's AI Lab dataset
(Sarkar et al., 2018)	Predicting real-world cyberattacks through analyzing forums discussion posts and replies	Classification, Prediction	TS, LOG-REG	53 Dark Web forums
(Ampel et al., 2020)	Classification of hacker exploit source codes	Crawling, Deep Transfer Learning techniques	CBiLSTM models, Convolutional BiLSTM layers	Hacker forums:8 English, 3Russian
(Ebrahimi et al., 2020)	Cyber threat knowledge representation	Classification, crawling,	K-NN, LSTM, SVM, RF, CNN, Generative Adversarial Networks (GAN)	Hacking forums on Dark web
(Koloveas et al., 2021)	Identifying cyber threat-related information	Classification, NoSQL storage, Visualization, social media monitors	MySQL, MongoDB, SVM, K-NN, Word2Vec, spaCy	Notes by Carnegie Mellon University, ExploitDB

Dark Web services are not easily accessible using the format www.abc.com. Rather the dot onion top-level domain (TLD) is specially used to avail these hidden services on the Tor network. These hidden services don't belong to the Internet DNS root.

Tor Directories and Search Engines designed for Tor Network

Tor directory Authorities refers to databases containing information of all active nodes at the network and other database-related knowledge. Router-related information is stored in an encrypted form with a digital signature in the director authorities along with topological knowledge of the network. The administrator of the servers always checks, processes, and verify any information related to nodes to be spread to users for securing the Tor network.

A user connects to the Tor network through the Tor browser which is responsible for communicating with the Tor directory authority. The latter holds the list of all Tor nodes which are available at that particular time. The Tor browser randomly decides the path of all nodes for the user to access the destination server for the user to access the hidden services. Each node knows only the previous node

Table 2. Dark web user groups

Dark Web Legitimate User Groups	Uses
Law Enforcement Agencies (LEA)	Using the web during surveillance activities, receive anonymous tips.
Military	Exchange of confidential messages or data, protecting the identities of working officials
Political Activists or Whistle-Blowers	Act as Whistleblowers to stop injustice from government or business activities

to it and the next node (one-hop knowledge only) of the network. An encryption key is exchanged each time. This mechanism of path selection ensures that even if a single node is not participating it will be difficult to recognize the complete path of the Tor network. During this, it will also select a guard node arbitrarily. Later, it will choose all other nodes which have high bandwidth and are stable nodes. The browser is available on https://www.torproject.org/projects/torbrowser.html.com for Windows, Apple, Linux, MacOS for download. It is available in 16 languages.

Search engines are Tor (website-http://xmh57jrzrnw6insl.onion/ and not Evil (website link-http://hss34r02hsxfogfq.onion/. Onion links can be categorized on the basis of services they provide in the field of drugs, finance, email, etc., which are available in the directory called Hidden wiki. The category of terrorism and child abuse is not included in these. onion links.

Tor Installation

The required file for installation on Windows OS can be downloaded from the list save, open, and run it. Choose the preferred language, then click on install. After finishing the installation process click to connect. For installation on Mac OS firstly download, save and move the .dmg file to the application folder.

Users of Dark Web

The Dark web is a home for both kinds of user activities legitimate as well as criminal ones running in parallel. The legitimate users utilize anonymity and security features while the criminal users perform malicious activities which are illegal in the Dark Web environment. Legal users use Dark Web to hide their identities to provide some secret information about the activities or share confidential data like in research agencies or military, Whistleblowers, political activities or journalists etc. (as shown in table 2 below).

Legitimate Users

General Public-Users

Ordinary users work on the Dark Web to hide their personal details, without being tracked or exposed by any third parties posing risks to their identities. The Tor Project lists some of the causes below to use Tor browsers or other browsers such as I2P or Freenet.

- To protect their identity and privacy from surveillance or personal data and monitoring activities thus making it troublesome for the observers to figure out the identity of the user visiting the websites.
- Protection of privacy and secured communication with the organizations revealing personal details and mailing data to third parties.
- To hide current geolocation on the map.
- To hide the IP address of the working system from being tracked.

IT Industry

Corporate world also come across many cyber threats coming from the environment around them which includes malware attacks, phishing attack, DDOS attacks, hacking of sensitive data of large corporations, and used for sale on the darknet. Corporate assets such as proprietary software are also stolen or placed for extortion in the darknet markets for sale and ransomware. The data contained personal information of the users such as name, contact numbers, birthdate, email addresses, encrypted passwords. Also, in 2016 data of 400,000 accounts was stolen on the µTorrent breach. This stolen data from Yahoo and µTorrent was placed for sale on the darknet's illicit market places. It was detected by an underground research team called Info Armor. In order to provide protection from the above cyber threats following key points needs to be focussed on by a team from the IT industry.

- Protection of all sensitive corporate data using the latest and strong encryption methods and latest intrusion detection systems (IDS).
- Monitoring of network usage of organization and detection of darknet access.
- Observe darknets to detect new trends of attacks and new vulnerabilities.

Journalists

The anonymity services offered by the Dark Web protect the sources of journalists and also avoid state censorship and on occasion arrest. The role of journalists and media professionals is to educate the general public about the criminal usage of the Dark Web. Also, some of the challenges faced by journalists are given by.

- Dark web provides freedom of speech to journalists on sensitive topics.
- The oligarchy of stakeholders in creating an opinion.
- The increase in the number of uncertified journalists.

Activists

Human Rights organizations or political activists also use Dark Webs for carrying out social movements in accordance with protecting human rights. These activist groups can raise their voices anonymously against work labour and other kinds of abuses. To preserve Human Rights, Global Voices highly recommend browsers like Tor which can provide anonymity.

Users with Criminal minds

Different types of illegal activities and abuses take place on dark web networks such as human trafficking, child sex abuse (CSA), criminal trade on the dark marketplace, hired murdering, etc. Other illegal activities also known as 'grey services' includes money laundering activities, discussion on illicit content such as 'bomb marketing techniques' other fora used for meetings and discussions to carry out violent activities and even extremism.

Cyberterrorists

The internet has become a perfect place for cyber terrorists to communicate secretly. Dark web enables encrypted and fast communication between the terrorists to carry out their illegal trade of weapons or train new members to plan new attacks. Dark web is also used as a medium for cyber terrorists to involve new individuals in their plans, exchange information, or propagate information or guidelines for cyber-attacks. The encrypted applications are used by the terrorists to create a room for saving their logistics information, financial support for their activities. Terrorist group activities such as ISIS have increased their propaganda and extremism on the Dark Web. According to (ENISA, 2018) the most serious cyber-threats are DDOS attacks. Furthermore, cyber terrorists are more inclined towards cryptocurrencies now for their funding and marketing on Dark Web to complete their operations. Moreover, cyberterrorists use Dark Web to buy cybercrime services including malware and ransomware for cyberattacks for their own financial gains. In physical terrorist attacks, there is a loss of humans and destruction of property, while in cyberattacks like DDOS attacks many telecommunications, banking, or other application services are hampered and disabled resulting in a chain of events and catastrophic attacks. Cyberthreats when combined with physical attacks such as bombing or slaughter etc., disables the communication systems to control the attacks. Attacks performed by cyber terrorists would cause more destruction to humans' life and properties while attacks performed by cybercriminals is mainly for financial gains.

Hacktivists

This work anonymously uses the dark web and performs data breaching to attack organizations. They are a special form of activists who works in groups driven by socio-political beliefs. Hacktivists also use the dark web for selling sensitive information to support their ideologies whether political or social (Sixgill, 2018). The breached data and sensitive information are disseminated using the Dark Web in order to harm the victims. This sensitive information constitutes databases of personal details of the employees including their ID, phone numbers, email addresses, etc. purchased by other hacktivists in order to harm the enemies. Also, many hacktivists are inspired by terrorist groups for website defacements, malicious code injection, or DDoS attacks.

Cybercriminals

Due to a substantial increase in the number of financial transactions online cybercriminals have become more active. They use Dark Web to buy, sell or exchange illicit materials. The taxonomy of cybercriminals includes many cybercrime stakeholders to cover many crimes like drug and human trafficking, distribution of child abuse material, etc. Dark Web is a safe place and an ideal environment for cybercriminals for trading to earn profit anonymously. The payments on Dark Web are completed using cryptocurrencies like Bitcoin. Apart from sharing illicit goods on the Dark Web, cybercriminals also exchange their opinions, skills, and information.

Insider Threat

Insider threats take place due to the wrong actions or errors done by an individual within an organization. This may cause monetary damage to an organization. Insider threats are executed by either employee with malicious intents or by mistake or blunders caused by the employees. According to a report, most of the losses are due to non-malicious actors (Richardson 2010/2011). Organizations may face threats from their own employees also. According to a survey report of the 15th annual CSI computer crime and security, two types of threat vectors exist employees with malicious aims of harming the organization by leaking data or sensitive information and second employees who have done blunders and are ignorant of it.

Black Hat Hackers

Black Hat hackers are elite hackers or individuals or maybe groups who are expertise in computer skills. These hackers undergo illegal activities with the aim of earning money and may steal or destroy confidential data (Sabillion et al., 2016). The primary focus of virus hacking tool coders is to develop computer viruses/malware/rootkits to sell in the black markets to earn money. Individuals who are not experts in developing such code are the main buyers (Sabillion et al., 2016). Various other malware forms like ransomware and DDoS attacks are designed and implemented using above mentioned malware categories. These types of attacks create a panic amongst the owners by making their services and data unavailable resulting in malfunctioning or causing damage to the IT industry, banking sector, or other large companies. The workstations and all the working systems of the victim are hacked and they have to pay a ransom to the hackers. Such kind of hacking activity is also known as cyber extortion in which hackers gain by earning money through hacking. Furthermore, many hackers make malware just for selling on the Dark Web instead of performing cyberattacks.

State-sponsored Attackers

Cyber Attackers hired and controlled by various countries in terms of peace and war. These sponsored attackers cause harm by unauthorized access to the secrets of state trade, plans, and technology. They cause damage to the critical infrastructure and economy of other target states. The growth in the use of the Dark Web and dark markets has increased the chances of danger and concern for governments. In 2013, millions of yahoo email account data were breached and made available on Dark Web for $300,000. Usually, nation-states and criminals associated with them may cause damage to the economy and cyber defense in multiple ways. For example, cyber espionage is the cheapest way to get the data causing economic and political threats to embarrass a foreign government. According to a report, China-sponsored cybercriminals gain access and steal data from many American companies related to trade and crucial information like designs of important assets. State-sponsored hackers also work like cyber attackers. Cyber-espionage attacks sell the stolen data like credit card numbers or medical history of the patients at a higher price.

Trade and Service Providers and Buyers

Due to the high demands for illicit goods, online trading is growing exponentially. Criminals are earning more and more profit from new customers. All the transactions are performed using cryptocurrencies like those of Bitcoin. The goods sold in illegal trading are explosives, drugs, guns, credit cards, etc. However, many dark markets such as Alpha Bay and Hansa are shut down by LEA's still the cybercriminals find new dark websites to continue with their mission.

Machine Learning for Cybersecurity

Machine learning techniques can be used in different environments in order to protect the digital era from different types of attacks. Machine learning is being used extensively to solve scientific and engineering problems and has supported many applications like computer vision, robot control, speech recognition, and many more (Jordan & Mitchell, 2015). For improving user experiences and recommending products online machine learning algorithms are applied by Amazon, YouTube, Facebook, Google, etc. However, machine learning promotes new ways to analyze vast amounts of data generated, and optimization is achieved through the development of new algorithms. Machine learning is used in cybersecurity to identify security breaches, malware detection and to make organizations aware of the security issues. Also, machine learning is able to alert organizations of higher-level threats and vulnerabilities. Traditional malware detection systems are not able to pace with new variants of attacks that can bypass the network and perform cyber-attacks. Adversaries use machine learning to enhance the attacking capabilities. Devices protecting the network logs and other traces of information. These logs can be managed and maintained into a Security Incident and Event Management (SIEM) system to provide better highlights for cybersecurity professionals. Many security devices already available provide alarm-based responses which rely on signature-based monitoring (Lynn, 2010). Other protection devices such as firewalls, antivirus, Host Intrusion Protection (HIPS), etc. Using only signature detection security may leave many types of attacks undetected. Furthermore, it becomes quite challenging for cybersecurity professionals to detect more advanced malware. The following table 3 shows some of the ML techniques used in different types of attacks.

Models and Methodology of Cybercrime detection using ML Techniques Models

This section describes a model related to cyber threat detection named Detection Maturity Level Model (DML) and the methodology of cybercrime detection using ML techniques.

- **Detection Maturity Level Model (DML)** – DML was firstly introduced by Ryan Stillions in 2014(Stillions, 2014). It's a capability maturity model to measure an organization's maturity in detecting cyber-attacks and responding to it in return as shown in figure 1.

Table 3. Machine learning uses in cybersecurity

Types of Attack	Definition	Use of ML technique
Malware Detection	A kind of software virus spreading infection once get exposed to machine learning vulnerabilities	i) Disclosure of threats ii) Detects malware using either static or dynamic tools iii) Can classify different families of malware
Spam Detection	Detection of unsolicited emails	Honeypot was designed to work using Support Vector machines in order to detect spams on social media platform
Ransomware	Ransomware refers to harmful malware that blocks the victims from accessing their own computer and personal information or data and demands for a ransom payment in return for making their computers free	Machine learning and AI algorithms fight against such types of attacks using their prediction ability. Use of Antiphishing algorithms, Anomaly-based detection methods are also used
ML in phishing	Phishing attacks try to gain control over sensitive details of an individual in an illegitimate way	ML algorithms can predict the pattern of threats in emails by noticing the pattern of header portion and subject matter in the body part of the email.
Intrusion Detection using ML	An intrusion detection system mainly establishes a checkpoint on a system's confidentiality and integrity	ML algorithms use support vector machines to identify malicious activities in the network

Figure 1. Detection Maturity Level Model

METHODOLOGY

The methodology for cybercrime detection using ML techniques is shown in figure 2. Initially, datasets are extracted from the required databases and then pre-processed. After pre-processing of the datasets ML techniques are employed for feature extraction and selection. The selected features are identified which are then fed to the ML-based Classifier models using ML algorithms like SVM, Naïve Bayes, and many other machine learning algorithms to undergo rigorous investigation and analysis. The datasets at the final stage are trained and tested to predict for the malevolent data.

Figure 2. Methodology of cybercrime detection techniques using ML

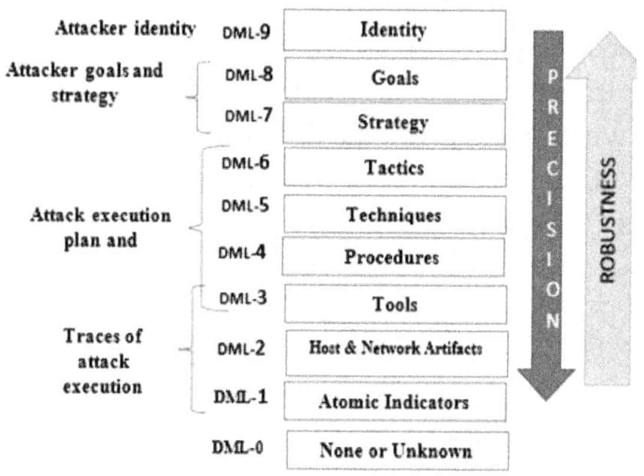

AI in Cybercrime Detection

Many challenges are faced by social media by technology disruption (Brown, 2006) (Hayward, 2012) (Holt & Bossler, 2014). AI Crime (AIC) is a growing interdisciplinary field as given by (King et al., 2020). New technological areas related to cybercrime are discussed in computational (Williams & Burnap, 2016) and Big data era criminology (Chan & Moses, 2017) (Smith et al., 2017). Cybercrimes related to encryption, cryptocurrencies, black marketing and trading on Dark Web called techno crimes are discussed by (Aldridge, 2019) (Munksgaard et al., 2016). AI systems can be used for Anomaly detection like the detection of new malware or fraud transactions. A recent survey by (King et al., 2020) listed a number of threats posed by AI Crime (AIC) such as theft, fraud, forgery, drug trafficking, sexual crimes, etc. Criminals using AI can be categorized as a) Crimes with AI as a tool, b) Crimes with AI as attack surface c) Crimes by AI as an intermediary (Hayward & Maas, 2021).

Crime using AI as a Tool

Using AI as a tool for 'malicious' uses by creating new threats or changing the existing ones to cause more serious types of cybercrimes. AI poses more of the threat by expanding the existing hacking threats to more of enhancing the types of cyberattacks in social media or networks. These types of attacks cover 91% of cybercrimes which start with a phishing email (Bahnsen et al., 2018) - an email asking to click on a link that redirects to websites created by criminals to obtain the personal information for fraud purposes. Moreover, DeepPhish AI (Bahnsen et al., 2018) makes the system learn from existing phishing attacks, avoid spam filters. AI also boosts the Défense against fraudulent emails. One such developed system is 'Panacea'. Furthermore, apart from prevailing threats, AI can develop new threats also. A common example to explain here is called 'Deepfakes' (Citron & Chesney, 2019). GAN applications can forge images, photographs, videos, voices- 'cloned' (Gholipour, 2017). A voice-mimicking software was made to mimic the voice of a CEO asking for the transfer of $243,000 to a fake account (Harwell, 2019). However, it is used mostly for political manipulations.

Using AI as a Platform

Attackers use AI as a surface to spoof systems by exploiting the system vulnerabilities or reverse-engineering them. Also, the training data of a system can be turned into a malicious one. ML systems can be made to malfunction when classifying data. Attackers can also penetrate in the black-box settings of the network. According to Google researchers' image-recognition systems can be made to carry-out free computations for hackers (Elsayed et al., 2019).

Using AI as a Mediator

A random shopping bot was launched on the dark web by a group that shopped for drugs (Kasperkeric 2015). It was found by computer scientists that some of the AI trading agents are successful in marketing scenarios by learning to execute profitable strategies. Strategies such as pinging and spoofing were used for market manipulation. An 'artificial agent' based strategy was used to place false buying orders for market manipulation (Martínez-Miranda et al., 2016).

Cybercrime Detection in Social Media Analysis

Social networking sites like Facebook, Twitter, Instagram, etc are used by people to share news, interests, images, audio, video, etc. cybercriminals misuse these social networking platforms and technologies to conduct cybercrimes like key logger injection, phishing attacks, fake news spread, creation of fake profiles, phishing attacks, etc. Fake links and key logger injection are uploaded by cybercriminals to collect credentials of users like username and passwords. Machine learning algorithms like supervised and unsupervised methods are used to monitor user activities on social media and identify anomalies in case of any malicious posts. Real-time alerts are generated by these machine learning algorithms to identify the malicious activities and criminal profiles on the network. The application of machine learning is to provide automated crime detection and analyze different types of malwares, predict cyberattacks like denial of service and phishing attacks. Data mining techniques can be helpful in the field of cybersecurity for malicious analysis, detecting suspicious activities on social media, detection of intruders in the system and their prevention control mechanisms, blocking spam emails, log analysis of the systems to detect and catch hidden patterns, cyber forensics, identification of phishing links, etc. Machine learning techniques can be used to detect denial of service attacks using IP addresses and linked knowledge. It is helpful in predicting the IP addresses already involved in some malicious activities in cyberspace.

Data mining algorithms such as classification, clustering, association, etc are used to train the data to predict cybercrime on social media and are also useful in cyber forensics. Also, they help in mining critical information from existing data in order to detect threats or crime patterns to create databases for training the system using AI/ML to predict patterns of cybercrimes automatically. Cyberattacks can occur either from inside or outside of the network. Various security mechanisms like antivirus, firewalls cannot always identify the attacks. Existing security mechanisms like IDS/IPS firewall cannot identify the new attacks. Malware is the biggest type of threat which spreads in systems very fast through different methods.

Case Study

One of the largest-scale crimes in the cyber world done through the dark web is sports betting. Betting on sporting events is not a new phenomenon; it exposes a worldwide sector that draws a large audience of people. Match-fixing is widespread in Europe: according to the (ICSS 2017), 34.7 percent of athletes feel a game they are participating in is fixed, and 12.6 percent have participated in a fixed game (ICSS 2017). Organized criminal groups (OCG) recruit and control young athletes who are about to join teams or are juniors, as well as senior players who are nearing the end of their contracts. The main platform used by OCGs and networks to coordinate and advertise all matters of match-fixing is the Dark Web. This is because of the Dark Web's high levels of anonymity and apparent protection from law enforcement.

Betters were charged $25,000–800,000 every game by a website called "BET FIXED MATCH," which claimed to have a global network of 58 sportsmen, officials, and sports agents. The example demonstrates that funding is a dynamic sphere that varies by location. Andrews conducted a two-week conversation through the Dark Web with an accomplished match-fixer named "Frank" to learn more about how these sites functioned, particularly in terms of economics. Frank hosted the site using a "onion" URL that was accessed using the Tor browser, and he utilized Appaloosa Chat to manage the site, which mostly concentrated on American football league matches.

CONCLUSION

This chapter covers AI, ML, and DM techniques to detect different types of cybercrime and cyberattacks, the dark web, and deep web concepts. DM algorithms are applied to identify threats and patterns pertaining to criminal activities. AI and ML techniques are used to train the databases to detect crime patterns automatically. Different types of ransomware which have posed threats to the security of the systems in the past are also been enlisted in this chapter. Deep web data can be accessed only through encrypted credentials as the data behind it consists of sensitive information or records. Darknets deals with both legal and illegal activities. A brief introduction to the 'Tor' browser is also discussed in this chapter.

REFERENCES

Bahnsen, Torroledo, & Camacho. (2018). *DeepPhish: Simulating malicious AI.* Academic Press.

Deb, A., Lerman, K., & Ferrara, E. (2018). Predicting cyber-events by leveraging hacker sentiment. *Information (Basel), 9*(11), 280. doi:10.3390/info9110280

Zenebe, A., Shumba, M., Carillo, A., & Cuenca, S. (2019). Cyber threat discovery from dark web. *Proceedings of the 28th International Conference on Software Engineering and Data Engineering.*

Sapienza, A., Bessi, A., Damodaran, S., Shakarian, P., Lerman, K., & Ferrara, E. (2017). Early warnings of cyber threats in online discussions. *Proceedings of the IEEE International Conference on Data Mining Workshops (ICDMW).* 10.1109/ICDMW.2017.94

Ampel, B., Samtani, S., Zhu, H., Ullman, S., & Chen, H. (2020, November). Labeling hacker exploits for proactive cyber threat intelligence: a deep transfer learning approach. *Proceedings 2020 IEEE International Conference on Intelligence and Security Informatics (ISI)*, 1–6. 10.1109/ISI49825.2020.9280548

Gholipour, B. (2017). New AI Tech Can Mimic Any Voice -. *Scientific American*.

Brown. (2016). Threat Advisory: State of the Dark Web. *AKAMAI Threat Advisory*.

Huang, C., Guo, Y., Guo, W., & Li, Y. (2021). Identifying key hackers in underground forums. *International Journal of Distributed Sensor Networks*, *17*(5). doi:10.1177/15501477211015145

Citron, D. K., & Chesney, R. (2019). *Deep Fakes: A Looming Challenge for Privacy, Democracy, and National Security*. Available: https://scholarship.law.bu.edu/faculty_scholarship/640

Harwell. (2019). *An AI-First: Voice-Mimicking Software Reportedly Used in a Major Theft Technology News*. ndtv.com.

ENISA. (2018). *ENISA Threat Landscape Report 2017–15 Top Cyber-Threats and Trends*. ENISA.

Jardine, E. (2015). *The Dark Web Dilemma: Tor, Anonymity and Online Policing* (Vol. 21). Global Commission on Internet Governance Paper Series.

Marin, E., Almukaynizi, M., Nunes, E., Shakarian, J., & Shakarian, P. (2018). Predicting hacker adoption on dark web forums using sequential rule mining. *Proceedings of the 2018 IEEE Intl Conf on Parallel & Distributed Processing with Applications*, 1183–1190.

Martínez-Miranda, E., McBurney, P., & Howard, M. J. W. (2016). Learning unfair trading: A market manipulation analysis from the reinforcement learning perspective. *Proc. 2016 IEEE Conf. Evol. Adapt. Intell. Syst. EAIS 2016*, 103–109. 10.1109/EAIS.2016.7502499

Ahmed, F., & Abulaish, M. (2013). A generic statistical approach for spam detection in Online Social Networks. *Computer Communications*, *36*(10–11), 1120–1129. doi:10.1016/j.comcom.2013.04.004

Smith, G. J. D., Moses, L. B., & Chan, J. (2017). The challenges of doing criminology in the big data era: Towards a digital and data-driven approach. *British Journal of Criminology*, *57*(2), 259–274. doi:10.1093/bjc/azw096

Elsayed, G. F., Sohl-Dickstein, J., & Goodfellow, I. (2019). Adversarial reprogramming of neural networks. *7th Int. Conf. Learn. Represent. ICLR 2019*, 1–14.

ICSS. (2017). *35% Athletes believe matches at their level were fixed, says forthcoming study*. ICSS. http://theicss.org/2017/07/23/35-athletesbelieve-matches-at-their-level-were-fxed-says-forthcoming-study/

Deliu, I., Leichter, C., & Franke, K. (2017). Extracting cyber threat intelligence from hacker forums: support vector machines versus convolutional neural networks. *Proceedings of the 2017 IEEE International Conference on Big Data (Big Data)*, 3648–3656. 10.1109/BigData.2017.8258359

Grisham, J., Samtani, S., Patton, M., & Chen, H. (2017). Identifying mobile malware and key threat actors in online hacker forums for proactive cyber threat intelligence. *Proceedings of the 2017 IEEE International Conference on Intelligence and Security Informatics (ISI)*, 13–18. 10.1109/ISI.2017.8004867

Chan, J., & Moses, L. B. (2017). Making sense of big data for security. *British Journal of Criminology*, *57*(2), 299–319.

Aldridge, J. (2019). Does online anonymity boost illegal market trading? *Media Culture & Society*, *41*(4), 578–583. doi:10.1177/0163443719842075

Hayward, K. J. (2012). Five spaces of cultural criminology. *British Journal of Criminology*, *52*(3), 441–462. doi:10.1093/bjc/azs008

Kasperkevic, J. (2015). Swiss police release robot that bought ecstasy online. *The Guardian*. Available at: https://www.theguardian.com/world/2015/apr/22/swiss-police-release-robot-random-darknetshopper-ecstasy-deep-web

Hayward, K. J., & Maas, M. M. (2021). Artificial intelligence and crime: A primer for criminologists. *Crime, Media, Culture*, *17*(2), 209–233. doi:10.1177/1741659020917434

Faghani, M. R., Matrawy, A., & Lung, C. H. (2012). A study of Trojan propagation in online social networks. *5th Int. Conf. New Technol. Mobil. Secur. - Proc. NTMS 2012 Conf. Work.*, 6–10. 10.1109/NTMS.2012.6208767

Jordan & Mitchell. (2015). Machine learning: Trends, perspectives, and prospects. *Science, 349*(6245), 255–260.

Williams, M. L., & Burnap, P. (2016). Cyberhate on Social Media in the aftermath of Woolwich: A Case Study in Computational Criminology and Big Data. *British Journal of Criminology*, *56*(2), 211–238. doi:10.1093/bjc/azv059

Miranda, E. M., McBurney, P., & Howard, M. J. W. (2016). Learning unfair trading: a market manipulation analysis from the reinforcement learning perspective. In *Proceedings of the 2016 IEEE conference on evolving and adaptive intelligent systems, EAIS 2016*, (pp. 103–109). Institute of Electrical and Electronics Engineers Inc. 10.1109/EAIS.2016.7502499

Ebrahimi, M., Nunamaker, J. F. Jr, & Chen, H. (2020). Semi-supervised cyber threat identification in darknet markets: A transductive and deep learning approach. *Journal of Management Information Systems*, *37*(3), 694–722. doi:10.1080/07421222.2020.1790186

Almukaynizi, M., Marin, E., & Nunes, E. (2018). DARKMENTION: a deployed system to predict enterprise-targeted external cyberattacks. *Proceedings of the 2018 IEEE International Conference on Intelligence and Security Informatics (ISI)*, 31–36. 10.1109/ISI.2018.8587334

Arnold, N., Ebrahimi, M., & Zhang, N. (2019). Dark-net ecosystem cyber-threat intelligence (CTI) tool. *Proceedings of the IEEE International Conference on Intelligence and Security Informatics (ISI)*, 92–97.

Tavabi, N., Goyal, P., Almukaynizi, M., Shakarian, P., & Lerman, K. (2018). DarkEmbed: exploit prediction with Neural Language models. *Proceedings of the AAAI Conference on Artificial Intelligence*, 7849–7854.

Koloveas, P., Chantzios, T., Alevizopoulou, S., Tryfonopoulos, S., & Tryfonopoulos, C. (2021). INTIME: A machine learning-based framework for gathering and leveraging web data to cyber-threat intelligence. *Electronics (Basel)*, *10*(7), 818. doi:10.3390/electronics10070818

Tokunaga, R. S. (2010). Following You Home from School: A Critical Review and Synthesis of Research on Cyberbullying Victimization. *Computers in Human Behavior, 26*, 277–287. http://ryanstillions. blogspot.com/2014/0 4/the-dml-model 21.html

Munksgaard, R., Demant, J., & Branwen, G. (2016). A replication and methodological critique of the study 'Evaluating drug trafficking on the Tor Network'. *The International Journal on Drug Policy, 35*, 92–96. doi:10.1016/j.drugpo.2016.02.027 PMID:27079624

Robert, R. (2004). A ten-step approach for forensic readiness. *Int J Dig Evi, 2*(3), 313–319.

Richardson, R. (2010/2011). *15th Annual Computer Crime and Security Survey*. Computer Security Institute.

Sabillon, C., Cano, & Serra-Ruiz. (2016). Cybercriminals, cyberattacks, and cybercrime. In 2016 IEEE International Conference on Cybercrime and Computer Forensic (ICCCF) (pp. 1–9). IEEE.

Martin. (n.d.). Taking the high road White hat, black hat: The ethics of cybersecurity. ACM Inroads, 8(1), 33–35.

Sixgill. (2018). *Dark Web Sites as a Platform for Hacktivist Warfare 2018*. Author.

Pastrana, S., Hutchings, A., Caines, A., & Buttery, P. (2018). *Characterizing eve: analysing cybercrime actors in a large underground forum. Research in Attacks, Intrusions, and Defenses.*

Sarkar, S., Almukaynizi, M., Shakarian, J., & Shakarian, P. (2018). Predicting enterprise cyber incidents using social network analysis on dark web hacker forums. *Proceedings of the Cyber Defense Review*, 87–102.

Lee, S., & Kim, J. (2014). Early filtering of ephemeral malicious accounts on Twitter. *Computer Communications, 54*, 48–57. doi:10.1016/j.comcom.2014.08.006

Brown, S. (2006). The criminology of hybrids: Rethinking crime and law in technosocial networks. *Theoretical Criminology, 10*(2), 223–244. doi:10.1177/1362480606063140

Selamat, S. R., Yusof, R., & Sahib, S. (2008). Mapping process of digital forensic investigation framework. *Int. J. Comput. Sci. Netw. Secur., 8*(10), 163–169.

Sharma, A., & Sharma, S. (2012). An intelligent analysis of web crime data using data Mining. *Certif Int J Eng Innov Technol, 2*(3).

Holt, T. J., & Bossler, A. M. (2014). An Assessment of the Current State of Cybercrime Scholarship. *Deviant Behavior, 35*(1), 20–40. doi:10.1080/01639625.2013.822209

King, T. C., Aggarwal, N., Taddeo, M., & Floridi, L. (2020). Artificial Intelligence Crime: An Interdisciplinary Analysis of Foreseeable Threats and Solutions. Springer Netherlands.

Lynn, W. J. (2010). Defending a new domain. *Foreign Affairs, 89*(5).

Chapter 12
Ranking for Better Indexing in the Hidden Web

Sonali Gupta

https://orcid.org/0000-0001-5885-0612

J. C. Bose University of Science and Technology, India

ABSTRACT

WWW is a repository of hyperlinked data sources that contains heterogeneous data in the form of text, audio, video, and metadata. Search engines play an important role in searching information from these data sources. They offer the users an interface to retrieve the data from these resources. The search engines gather, analyze, organize, and handle the data available in these data sources and return thousands of results in the form of web pages. Often the returned web pages include a mixture of relevant and irrelevant information. To return more significant and relevant response pages, a mechanism to rank the returned pages is desirable. Page ranking algorithms play an important role in ranking web pages so that the user could get the relevant result according to the user query. The proposed technique is used to rank the hidden web pages based on the meta information of the pages downloaded by crawler and the calculated value for the chosen parameters.

INTRODUCTION

A lot of information or data is hidden behind the HTML forms on the web. This data is extracted by Hidden Web crawler by automatically filling HTML forms (Bhatia & Gupta, 2012; Gupta & Bhatia, 2014b). Although, the crawlers are made intelligent enough to process the search forms in a specific domain, still the results from the crawlers contain a lot of redundant information and irrelevant results. For Example: when a query such as "job for MBA " is raised on search engine for Surface Web, many results are returned for jobs for MBA in an unrealistic manner to attract the user attention (Lee et al., 2009). An example of the returned web page is shown in Figure 1.

In order to get the more relevant and appropriate results, user has to navigate through the links provided on the result page and when the user proceeds towards the link, these links would turn out to a different link with the same title. query to search "mba" by the user. In case the query is raised at the

DOI: 10.4018/978-1-6684-3942-5.ch012

Figure 1. Result page generated for user's query by a search engine for the Surface Web

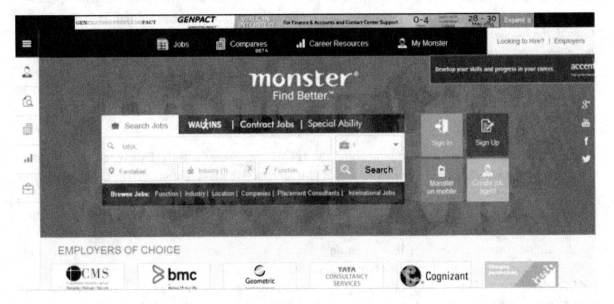

interface offered by a web database of employment domain as in Figure 2, a list of corresponding result is returned in a web page for the raised query

Figure 2. Interface of hidden web database

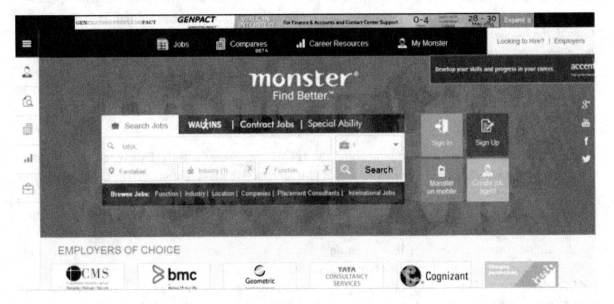

However, the Hidden Web pages are dynamically generated based on the query raised in the search form by the crawler, ranking the results become difficult (Gupta & Bhatia, 2017; Rani & Gupta, 2015).

Figure 3. Example of a web graph that can be used to calculate PageRank

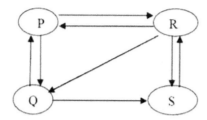

The techniques or algorithms for ranking surface web pages are not directly applicable for ranking of Hidden Web pages due to the lack of hyperlink structure in them (Baeza-Yates & Davis, 2004; E, 2012).

LITERATURE SURVEY

The web page ranking algorithms are applied to rank the search results depending upon their relevance to the search query. The algorithms rank the search results in an order so as to list the most relevant documents at the top of the list amongst the results returned in response to the query string searched in the page returned (E, 2012; Page & Brin, 1998). A web page's ranking for a specific query depends on factors like- its relevance to the word and concepts in the query, its overall link popularity etc. Page ranking algorithm are applied to calculate rank value of each page. Page rank is a numeric value representing how-important a page is on the web. Web page are sorted according to rank value and are returned to the user. To rank a web page different criteria are used by ranking algorithms. For example some algorithms consider the link structure of the web page while others look for the page content to rank the web page.

The popular PageRank algorithm (Page & Brin, 1998) was developed by Larry Page and Sergey Brin in 1996 uses the link structure of the web to determine the importance of the web page. Here a page obtains a higher rank if sum of its back-links is high. PageRank(PR) is the probability of a page being visited by the user. For each web page, Page Rank value for over 25 billion web pages on the WWW is pre-computed. A Simplified version of PageRank is defined in Equation (1)

$$PR(A) = c \sum_{v \in T_a} \frac{PR(v)}{Q(v)}$$

(1)

where A is a web page whose PageRank is to be calculated. TA is the set of pages that point to A and PR(v) is the rank score of page v that point to A. Qv is the number of links from page v and c is a factor used for normalization (so that the total rank of all web pages is constant). Page Rank algorithm can be applied to a web graph with hyperlinks as shown in Figure 3.

Page Rank algorithm assumes that if a page has a link to another page then it votes for that page. Therefore, each inlink to a page raises its importance. Following is a modified version of the PageRank algorithm.

Where PR(A) is PageRank of page A, T1….Tn are all the web pages that link to page A, PR(Ti) is Page rank of page Ti, Q(Ti) is the number of pages to which Ti links to, d is a damping factor which

Figure 4. Hub and authorities

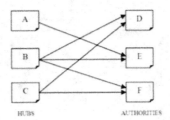

can be set between 0 and 1, PR(Ti)/Q(Ti) = PageRank of Ti distributing to all pages that Ti links to and (1-d) is used to make up for some pages that do not have any out-links to avoid losing some page ranks.

This algorithm is more feasible as it computes rank score at indexing time not at query time. It returns important pages as Rank is calculated on the basis of the popularity of a page. As Pagerank is a query independent algorithm i.e. it precomputes the rank score so it takes very less time. For calculating rank value of a page, it consider the entire web graph, rather than a small subset and thus is less susceptible to localized link spam. The main disadvantage is that it favors older pages, because a new page, even a very good one, will not have many links unless it is part of an existing web site. Also, the algorithm does not consider the content of web page. It does not handle Dangling links, the cases where a page contains a link such that the hypertext points to a page with no outgoing links. The Rank sinks problem occurs when in a network pages get in infinite link cycles. Another problem in PageRank is Spider Traps. A group of pages is a spider trap if there are no links from within the group to outside the group. If a website has circular references, then it reduce the front page's PageRank.

Hypertext Induced Topic Search (HITS) or hubs and authorities is a link analysis algorithm developed by Jon Kleinberg in 1998 to rate Web pages (Kleinberg, 1999). The HITS algorithm is an iterative algorithm developed to quantify each page's value as an authority and as a hub as shown in Figure 4. The premise of the algorithm is that a web page serves two purposes: to provide information on a topic, and to provide links to other pages giving information on a topic.

The algorithm produces two types of pages (Ding et al., 2004)

1. **Authority**: pages that provide important and trustworthy information on a given topic. So an authority is a page that is pointed by many hubs.
2. **Hub**: pages that contain links to authorities" i.e. pointing to many pages.

Weighted Page Rank Algorithm, a modification of the original page rank algorithm, decides the rank score based on the popularity of the pages by taking into consideration the importance of both the in-links and out-links of the pages (Xing & Ghorbani, 2004). This algorithm provides high value of rank to the more popular pages and does not equally divide the rank of a page among its out-link pages. Every out-link page is given a rank value based on its popularity. Popularity of a page is decided by observing its number of in links and out links as shown in Figure 5.

Quality of the pages returned by this algorithm is high as compared to pageRank algorithm. It is also more efficient than pageRank because rank value of a page is divided among it's outlink pages according to importance of that page. But the algorithm considers only link structure not the content of the page, it returns less relevant pages to the user query.

Figure 5. Example of weighted PageRank

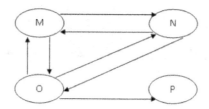

By going through the literature analysis of some of the important web page ranking algorithms it is concluded that each algorithm has some relative strengths and limitation (Gupta & Bhatia, 2018; Liu Zhongbao, 2010; Qian Gao et al., 2013). These methods rank Hidden Web content on basis of source of results of Hidden Web query or on basis of results returned by the query and thus can solve problem of redundant data in the results but still have problem in correctness and relevancy of results.

ALGORITHIM FOR PROPOSED SYSTEM

The Web crawlers crawls the Web and returns a large number of website pages as consequence of client inquiry. To rank a web page, it is parsed to take a note of any hypertext connections on that page that indicates other Web pages (Gupta & Bhatia, 2014a, 2022). At that point parse the pages for new connections, etc., recursively. At the point when the crawler visits a Web page, it concentrates connections to other Web pages. So the crawler puts these URLs toward the end of a line, and keeps crawling to a URL that it expels from the front of the queue.

A step-by-step methodology of the proposed system is given below:

Step 1: A query is fired in the search interface along with the user preference regarding domain of interest.

Step 2: Query term is matched in index and document matched with query term are stored in Seedlist.

Step 3: Download the blacklist.txt document which conveys downloading authorizations furthermore determines the document to barred by crawler. it put limit to the crawler from download the unnecessary pages.

Step 4: Check whether the page has as of new been downloaded or not, via synchronizing the Seedlist and blacklist.

Step 5: To evaluate the ranking gain of a term we would need to know its actual ranking, The Moz Rank and Google Rank of the pages are measured according to the type of document user want in the result. To improve the ranking, a ranking factor is calculated that measures the distance between the two ranked data. Ranking gain factor is key element of ranking processor. Ranking algorithm are intended for proficient execution advancement to bring the pertinent pages.

Step 6: Calculate Spearman factor by the square of difference between Moz Rank and Google Rank using the formula.

Step 7: Then all four factors i.e. Moz Rank, Google Rank, difference square and spearman factor is combined and final rank of each page is computed and rank result are returned to user log.

Figure 6. Moz rank for certain query

SPEARMAN'S RANK CORRELATION COEFFICIENT

Spearman's correlation coefficient measures the strength of association between two factors i.e Google rank and Moz rank. In this work the the differences and square of such differences for calculating the rho or spearman coefficient is taken. This coefficient helps to judge the strong or weak relationship among all the ranked website for performing better and enhanced ranked crawling strategy. The ranking gain factor is then calculated based on the value of ranking distance attained. The work has been influenced by the work in (Bhamidipati & Pal, 2009). The formula for ρ is:

$$\rho = 1 - \frac{6 \sum d_i^2}{n\left(n^2 - 1\right)} \tag{3}$$

Where d_i = difference in paired ranks and n = number of cases.

Moz Rank represents link popularity score. It reflects the importance of any given Web page on the internet pages earn Moz rank by number and quality of other pages that link to them. the higher the quality of incoming link, the higher the Moz rank as shown in Figure 6. Here it takes Moz Rank as one of the input for the improved ranking technique.

Google PageRank (Google pr) is one of the methods uses to determine a page`s relevance or importance. Important pages receive a higher Pagerank and are more likely to appear at the top of the search results. Google Pagerank (PR) is a measure from 0-10 based on backlinks as shown in Figure 7.

Now for the above user query, Table 1 shows the Moz rank as well as Google rank values

Figure 7. Google rank for certain query

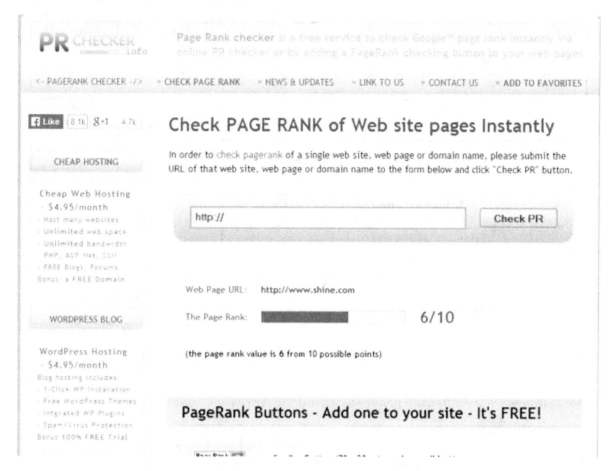

The difference and difference square between moz rank and google rank is then calculated to find the Spearman's coefficient as shown in Table 2.

$$\sum d_i^2 = \mathbf{17.1575}$$

Now r= 1 - {(6*17.1575) / 8(64-1)}
So r= .795744

The Spearman correlation coefficient, r, can take values from +1 to -1. A r of +1 indicates a perfect association of ranks, a r of zero indicates no association between ranks and a r of -1 indicates a perfect negative association of ranks. The closer r is to zero, the weaker the association between the ranks. In the existing approach the ranked result is time consuming and the result given by the search engine to the user are not so relevant.

For calculating new rank score we takes the average among Moz rank, Google rank, difference square and spearman coefficient as shown in Table 3.

Table 1. Moz rank and Google rank values for measuring the ranking score

URL	Moz Rank	Google Rank
http://search.clickjobs.com/jobs/list/q-mba/fdb-1/	2.92	4
http://in.jobrapido.com/?w=mba	4.52	5
http://jobsearch.naukri.com/mba-jobs	4.6	6
http://www.shine.com/job-search/simple/mba/	5.21	6
https://www.freshershome.com/ResultsFromSearch.php?cx=partner-pub-77696816629243 88%3Aton9yxxygmu&cof=FORID%3A 10&ie=ISO-8859-1&q=mba	4.41	2
http://www.vfreshers.com/?s=mba	4.37	3
http://www.indeed.co.in/jobs?q=mba&l=Faridabad%2C+Haryana	4.66	6
http://www.careesma.in/jobs?q=mba&lc=	3.12	5

Table 2. Difference and difference squares for measuring the ranking scored

URL	Moz Rank	Google Rank	d	d^2
http://search.clickjobs.com/jobs/list/q-mba/fdb-1/	2.92	4	1.08	1.1664
http://in.jobrapido.com/?w=mba	4.52	5	.48	.2304
http://jobsearch.naukri.com/mba-jobs	4.6	6	1.74	3.0276
http://www.shine.com/job-search/simple/mba/	5.21	6	0.79	.6421
https://www.freshershome.com/ResultsFromSearch.php?cx=partner-pub-77696816629243 88%3Aton9yxxygmu&cof=FORID%3A10&ie=ISO-8859-1&q=mba	4.41	2	2.21	4.8841
http://www.vfreshers.com/?s=mba	4.37	3	1.37	1.8769
http://www.indeed.co.in/jobs?q=mba&l=Faridabad%2C+Haryana	4.66	6	1.34	1.7956
http://www.careesma.in/jobs?q=mba&lc=	3.12	5	1.88	3.5344

Table 3. Ranked result returned by proposed ranking system

URL	Rank Score
http://search.clickjobs.com/jobs/list/q-mba/fdb-1/	2.220
http://in.jobrapido.com/?w=mba	2.6365
http://jobsearch.naukri.com/mba-jobs	3.6058
http://www.shine.com/job-search/simple/mba/	3.16196
https://www.freshershome.com/ResultsFromSearch.php?cx=partn er-pub-77696816629243 88%3Aton9yxxygmu&cof=FORID%3A10&ie=I SO-8859-1&q=mba	3.02245
http://www.vfreshers.com/?s=mba	2.5106
http://www.indeed.co.in/jobs?q=mba&l=Faridabad%2C+Haryana	3.3128
http://www.careesma.in/jobs?q=mba&lc=	3.11252

RESULT ANALYSIS

In this paper, the algorithm has been evaluated based on the URLs that have been manually chosen initially and included in the file is seedurl.txt. Figure 8 shows the main graphical user interface of the proposed system.

In the interface, we follow the tab named crawler configuration details and click on browse button to upload the seed url file and black list url file. The logs are created in the form of processed pages based on rank score of URL as shown in Figure 9. It will take some time and extract the rank score for proposed approach.

Finally to crawl the log data, we click on Log tab in the interface as shon in Figure 10. The crawled web pages or data is shown in Figure 11. It shows the ranked result in efficient manner which is relevant in user point of view.

Figure 12 compares the relevance of results after they have been ranked by system based on existing ranking methodology, MOZ Rank and the new proposed methodology. It also compares the time taken to rank the results as per their relevance. The Proposed system outperforms the system using the previous approaches mentioned in the literature.

From the graph in Figure 12, it can be concluded that the proposed ranking system returns more relevant results and hence user satisfaction level is high.

Figure 8. Interface of the proposed system

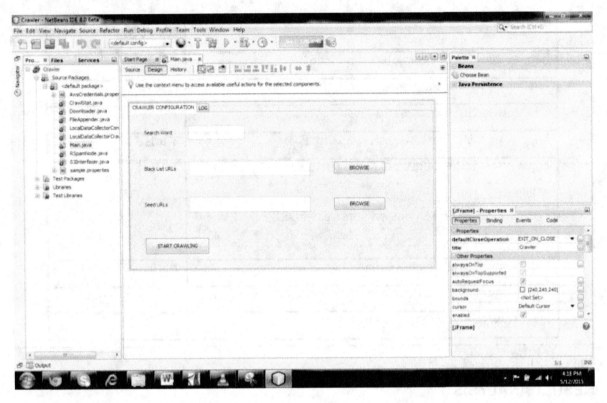

Figure 9. Log Files to upload webpages for ranking

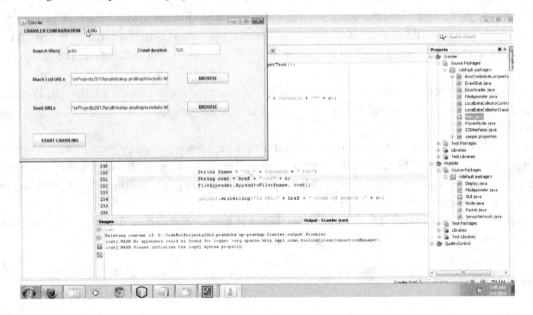

Figure 10. Selecting Log tab for generating processed pages and rank score

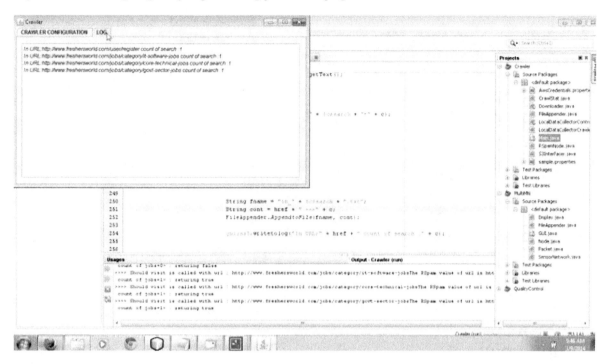

Figure 11. Log Data with ranking and crawling results

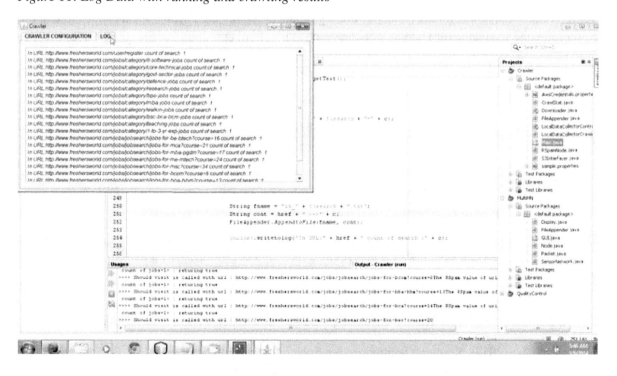

Figure 12. Result graph of survey on relevancy of ranked result set

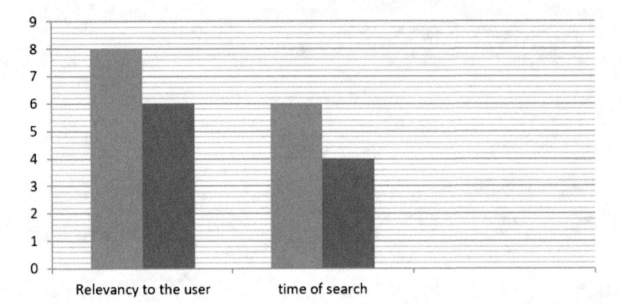

FUTURE WORK

This technique is being implemented on restricted number of website. Some of the website doesn't have moz rank, so it becomes very clear that the coefficient factor is deeply affected by it. Currently the system is working fine on 8 to 10 pages. But the vast WWW cannot barred to work in such limitation. There is also exists some interdependency among inputs of technique. Further we also need to explore better indexing technique for Hidden Web data repository (Rani & Gupta, 2015).

REFERENCES

Baeza-Yates, R., & Davis, E. (2004). Web page ranking using link attributes. *Proceedings of the 13th International World Wide Web Conference on Alternate Track Papers & Posters - WWW Alt. '04*, 328. 10.1145/1013367.1013459

Bhamidipati, N. L., & Pal, S. K. (2009). Comparing Scores Intended for Ranking. *IEEE Transactions on Knowledge and Data Engineering*, *21*(1), 21–34. doi:10.1109/TKDE.2008.111

Bhatia, K. K., & Gupta, S. (2012). Exploring 'hidden' parts of the web: the hidden web. *Fourth International Conference on Advances in Recent Technologies in Communication and Computing (ARTCom2012)*, 305–309. 10.1049/cp.2012.2556

Ding, C. H. Q., Zha, H., He, X., Husbands, P., & Simon, H. D. (2004). Link Analysis: Hubs and Authorities on the World Wide Web. *SIAM Review*, *46*(2), 256–268. doi:10.1137/S0036144501389218

E, M. P. S. M. (2012). Ranking Techniques for Social Networking Sites based on Popularity. *Indian Journal of Computer Science and Engineering (IJCSE) Ranking*, *3*(3), 522–526.

Gao, Q., Su, M. X., & Cho, Y. I. (2013). A multi-agent personalized ontology profile based user preference profile construction method. *IEEE ISR*, 1–4. Advance online publication. doi:10.1109/ISR.2013.6695695

Gupta, S., & Bhatia, K. K. (2014a). A Comparative Study of Hidden Web Crawlers. *International Journal of Computer Trends and Technology*, *12*(3), 111–118. doi:10.14445/22312803/IJCTT-V12P122

Gupta, S., & Bhatia, K. K. (2014b). Deep questions in the "Deep or Hidden" web. *Advances in Intelligent Systems and Computing*, *236*, 821–829. doi:10.1007/978-81-322-1602-5_87

Gupta, S., & Bhatia, K. K. (2017). Optimal query generation for hidden web extraction through response analysis. *The Dark Web: Breakthroughs in Research and Practice*, *2001*, 65–83. doi:10.4018/978-1-5225-3163-0.ch005

Gupta, S., & Bhatia, K. K. (2018). URL-Based Relevance-Ranking Approach to Facilitate Domain-Specific Crawling and Searching. *Studies in Computational Intelligence*, *713*(1), 239–250. doi:10.1007/978-981-10-4555-4_16

Gupta, S., & Bhatia, K. K. (2022). Design of a Parallel and Scalable Crawler for the Hidden Web. *International Journal of Information Retrieval Research*, *12*(1), 1–23. doi:10.4018/IJIRR.289612

Kleinberg, J. M. (1999). Authoritative sources in a hyperlinked environment. *Journal of the Association for Computing Machinery*, *46*(5), 604–632. doi:10.1145/324133.324140

Lee, L.-W., Jiang, J.-Y., Wu, C., & Lee, S.-J. (2009). A Query-Dependent Ranking Approach for Search Engines. *2009 Second International Workshop on Computer Science and Engineering*, 259–263. 10.1109/WCSE.2009.666

Liu, Z. (2010). Research of a personalized search engine based on user interest mining. *2010 International Conference on Intelligent Computing and Integrated Systems*, 512–515. 10.1109/ICISS.2010.5654942

Page, L., & Brin, S. (1998). The anatomy of a large-scale hypertextual Web search engine. *Computer Networks, 30*(1–7), 107–117. doi:10.1016/S0169-7552(98)00110-X

Rani, S., & Gupta, S. (2015). *Novel Indexing Technique for Hidden Web Pages using Semantic Analysis.* Academic Press.

Xing, W., & Ghorbani, A. (2004). Weighted PageRank algorithm. *Proceedings - Second Annual Conference on Communication Networks and Services Research*, 305–314. 10.1109/DNSR.2004.1344743

Chapter 13
Internet of Things Security Challenges and Concerns for Cyber Vulnerability

Shadab Pasha Khan

Oriental Institute of Science and Technology, India

M. A. Rizvi

National Institute of Technical Teachers Training and Research Institute, India

Rehan Khan

Oriental Institute of Science and Technology, India

ABSTRACT

The future is all about machines or devices. Smart devices are strong enough to create a network, establish connections among nodes, and exchange data as and when required. Internet and IoT are two sides of the same coin responsible for ubiquitous connectivity (24x7x365). The modern digital society depends upon IoT in the future to come, which would inherently invite various threats and new challenges due to its diversity. The entire internet is divided into multiple levels (i.e., surface web, deep web, and dark web), which is further explored in terms of providing anonymity. Non-electronic devices can also be connected which then forms the internet of everything (IoE). Security is often ignored by many manufacturers due to the rise in demand which leads to privacy issues. Over the period of time due to IIoT, Industry 4.0, new threats and high-profile IoT-driven cyber-attacks have been identified. For IoT security, we must switch to ML and DL methodologies to identify and resolve new threats and vulnerabilities.

INTRODUCTION

The entire world is moving towards real-time ubiquitous connectivity 24x7x365. All smart devices can be connected to the Internet and make a large network of devices called the Internet of Things (IoT). It is a system of interrelated computing devices, mechanical and digital machines that are embedded

DOI: 10.4018/978-1-6684-3942-5.ch013

with sensors, software, and other technologies with the purpose of exchanging data over the network (Wortmann & Flu¨chter 2015). To connect all smart devices with the Internet, we need IoT Framework, IoT Architecture, and Technologies that will be used to establish communication among devices. The protocols of connectivity and networking used with such devices are generally specific to the application deployed on the IoT. Both personal and business possibilities of IoT are endless. A "thing" in IoT (Internet of things) can refer to a number of things like a person with a heart monitor implant(a medical device), a farm animal accessory(a biochip transponder), an automobile with built-in sensors.

The IoT helps people to live and work smarter. It can automate not just homes but also businesses. Companies can automate processes and can reduce labor costs saving both money and time.

The entire IoT ecosystem is based upon IoT framework, IoT architecture, IoT Communication Protocols, and the latest technologies. The communication protocol is used to establish communication among sensors, actuators, physical objects, and applications. Sensors are one of the basic building blocks of the entire IoT ecosystem, which are used to collect information from the environment based on how the application performs its task. The Internet of things generates huge amounts of data through various devices. These devices belong to various domains which take inputs from the environment through sensors and forward data to the server for further processing. IPv6, Zigbee, LiteOS, OneM2M, DDS, AMQP, CoAP, LoRaWAn are some of the emerging standards in the field of IoT. Various Frameworks like Amazon's Amazon Web Services(AWS) IoT, Arm Mbed IoT (a platform for the development of IoT-based apps for ARM Microcontrollers), Microsoft's Azure IoT suite, Google's Brillio/Weave, and Ericsson's Calvin are available in the field of IoT.

Managing and Monitoring these devices through the Internet is one of the major challenges. As the number of devices increases and more information is shared between devices, these devices become more vulnerable to threats. Security of IoT devices is a must as it can be very dangerous and can lead to various forms of cyberattacks like DDoS, Session Hijacking, MiTM, etc. It can also pose a threat to the other devices connected with them. Several Countermeasures are explored in this chapter, for instance, we can use the concept of Darknet and Tor (The Onion Routing) to improve the security of the IoT devices.(Fernando et al., 2020)

The complete chapter is divided into seven sections. Section 1 consists of IoT & its characteristics, section 2 explores the role of Machine Learning & Deep Learning in IoT Security, section 3 discusses various requirements of IoT, Overview of Attacks is explored in section 4, In section 5 Security of IoT & its challenges are discussed. Different categories of the web are explored in section-6 and at the end, different preventive measures to stop attackers are discussed in section 7.

DARK WEB CRIMES ANALYSIS USING MACHINE LEARNING AND DEEP LEARNING

Machine Learning & Deep Learning plays a key role to detect and reduce the crimes over the dark web. Due to the level of anonymity provided by the Darknet over the dark web, it becomes nearly impossible to track down the cybercriminals, which is why the dark web is infamous for illegal online activities. With the introduction of machine learning, we can now add security to the dark web; so it seems like machine learning can be used to illuminate the dark web. Machine Learning algorithms can be used to detect malicious activity faster and can stop attacks before they get started. It can also help to close zero-day vulnerabilities and other threats that target largely unsecured IoT devices. (Pizzolante et al., 2020)

Machine learning helps us to find out future behaviors based upon past patterns (Jadav et al., 2021). ML algorithms are divided into four categories i.e Supervised Learning, Unsupervised Learning, Semi-Supervised, and Reinforcement Learning. In Supervised Learning, a labeled data set is used in order to predict the future (Zenebe et al., 2019). The generated output is compared with the intended output and if errors are found, train the model. On the other hand, in Unsupervised Learning, an unlabeled dataset is used in order to draw inferences. When the input is neither classified nor labeled, unsupervised learning plays a key role to expose the structure (Kadoguchi et al., 2009). There is one more learning called Semi-Supervised Learning which uses a small amount of labeled data and more amount of unlabelled data in order to draw inferences (K M et al., 2021). Reinforcement Learning is based upon reward-based learning, having its own significance when it comes to handling large amounts of data (Pajooh et al., 2020). In order to distinguish between the deep web and the dark web, illegal activities machine Learning & Deep Learning algorithms can be used in threat analysis, finding the behaviors of attackers, exploring new attacks in the dark web, deep web, and probable solutions to them (Koloveas et al., 2021). The Table 1 shows the work done in the past few years. The comparative details are shown in Table 1.

IoT AND ITS CHARACTERISTICS

In IoT, any smart object having an embedded controller, sensors, and actuators can be connected to the Internet and enable users to get the data from their surroundings. These devices can be deployable in remote locations which are unreachable for human beings such as extreme weather conditions either very low temperature or extremely hot, war zones, uneven hilly areas, etc. These are the following characteristics of IoT. (Atzori et al., 2010)

Ubiquitous Connectivity (24x7)

The prime objective behind the IoT is to get the data from the surroundings and transfer it to the designated server and it is not possible without connectivity. Connectivity plays a very important role in IoT.

Device Identification

To connect the device, we need to identify the device by IPv4 (32 bits) or IPv6 (128 bits). Identification of the device is important and plays a key role in IoT.

Self Adapting Nature in Terms of Complexity

IoT devices must have self-adaptive nature according to the real-time scenario and situation which increases the complexity level at each layer of IoT architecture. Sensors, actuators, controllers, and backbone technologies contribute in order to collect the data from the environment.

IoT Architecture

IoT architecture can be divided into two major categories i.e. Homogeneous and Heterogeneous. Most of the time, all the products belong to multiple manufacturers because of the need for an hour of applications.

Table 1. Related work

S. No.	Authors	Approach	Description	Findings
1	Nazah et al., 2020	Threat Analysis and detection of techniques used by cybercriminals on the dark web.	A comprehensive description of the Darknet threats and challenges.	Dark web services can be used as a weapon to catch the criminals. The unindexed, fragmented, and multilayer structure of the dark web makes it more strenuous to detect crimes.
2	Arabnezhad et al., 2020	Comparison of open aliases vs dark web aliases and linking them with real-world identities with the help of specially developed tools on real scenarios.	A massive-scale experiment on real-world scenarios between-a)two dark forum and b)a dark web forum and a normal forum to link aliases with real internet identities.	Privacy of de-anonymized dark web users can be breached when in standard internet using algorithms which use daily activity profile and writing style.
3	Al-Garadi et al., 2020	Machine learning and deep learning technologies should be used to secure the vulnerabilities in IoT devices.	Machine Learning and Deep Learning methods are important in transforming the security of IoT systems; a thorough review of Machine Learning/Deep Learning methods for the IoT are discussed that can serve as potential future research.	It provides a useful manual that can encourage researchers to advance research in the field of IoT security using Machine Learning/Deep Learning.
4	Kim et al., 2018	Machine Learning predictive models, K-nearest-neighbour, and boosted decision tree are implemented for crime analysis.	Vancouver crime data for the last 15 years was used in two different dataset approaches, KNN and boosted decision tree.	The accuracy was found to be between 39% to 44%. The prediction accuracy can be improved by tuning both the algorithm and data for specific applications. Although this model has low accuracy as a prediction model it provides a preliminary framework for further analysis.
5	Nunes et al., 2016	An operational system for cyber threat intelligence from various social platforms on the darknet and deep web especially from hacker forums, marketplaces offering malicious hacking, which can warn against newly developed cyber threats and cyber-attacks.	The system developed is significantly augmented through the uses of various data mining and machine learning techniques. Preliminary analysis is done on the collected data demonstrating its application to aid a security expert for better threat analysis.	The Machine learning models are able to recall 80% of discussions on forums relating to malicious hacking. Currently, this system on average collects 305 high-quality cyber threat warnings each week.
6	Alnabulsi & Islam, 2019	Examining the dark web forums using the onion routing(tor) and performing affect analysis on the dark web forums which will be useful for measuring the presence of illicit subjects.	dark web forums are analyzed to examine the most common activities in illicit subjects such as drugs, violence, forgery, and piracy.	The results are based on the analysis of three dark web forums which shows that the most common topic of interest is piracy, hacking, drugs, politics, revolution, weapons, and guns.
7	Alharbi et al., 2021	A customized Python Crawler is used to scrape data from the Tor Dark web to analyze the internal structure of the Tor web graph and examine the presence of bow-tie structure as found in the World Wide Web(WWW).	The nodes of the graph represent an individual Tor hidden service while the edge denoted a hyperlink from one service to the other. Various graph metrics are computed and analyzed for both digraphs and undirected graphs.	The graph constructed from the collected data consisted of 48,174 nodes and 1,03,526 edges. When the graph is analyzed it is found that the average distance between two nodes of the graph of the dark web is almost equal to that of the surface web, however, the bow-tie structure differed as IN and LSCC had smaller size and OUT had a bigger size when compared to the surface web.
8	Kawaguchi and Ozawa, 2019	VirusTotal and Gred Engine are used to judge the URLs of the dark web we crawled, to provide a blacklist-based detection software.	A system to collect malicious sites over the dark web is proposed for the safeguard of legitimate users.	The proposed system scored an efficiency of 0.82 accuracy according to the F1- score.
9	Narayanankutty, 2021	SDSec(Software Defined Security) along with MDE(Model-Driven Engineering) has been proposed to be used as an efficient way to reduce large problems to improve security.	SDSec(Software Defined Security) when combined with MDE(Model-Driven Engineering) and with the help of models can address the security issues faced in IoT and self-adaptation of models would ensure that this architecture will improve with time.	The SDSec architecture adapts and improves over time which largely increases the security of IoT systems and can help in achieving end-to-end security in IoT.
10	Zhang et al., 2014	Security issues in the power internet of things are studied and security frameworks are proposed.	Different possible attacks in each layer of IoT are explained along with their countermeasures for the improvement of security.	A global perspective security framework is proposed with security policies and measures considering various kinds of technologies and smart devices.

Security

All smart devices are connected to the Internet so personal or sensitive data could be leaked and compromised. Hence the security of the data, maintaining privacy, establishing trust are some basic dimensions of IoT Security (Ammar et al., 2018). To maintain the security of IoT products, we need to address the issues of Confidentiality, Integrity, Authentication, and Non-Repudiation. (Xu et al., 2015)

REQUIREMENTS OF IoT

Due to the penetration of Next Generation Network i.e. 5G, we are moving towards customer-centric more customized applications to enhance the Quality of life, which will play a significant role in the development of IoT. The basic requirement of IoT is to create a network of interconnected smart devices. Secondly, we want to get access to remote places where we could not reach earlier due to the limitation of connectivity. Third, analysis of the data, once we received the data from the remote places, to draw a meaningful conclusion out of it which will help the whole of mankind.

OVERVIEW OF ATTACKS

The figure 1 above shows the possible attacks in the OSI Model Layer.

Nowadays we are having an explosion in IoT-related products from small toasters to self-driving smart cars and smart buildings. As shown in Figure 1, According to Juniper Research, there are around 46 billion IoT devices, this is an increase of about 200% compared to 2016. This number is expected to jump to 125 billion by 2030 (Source: Martech Advisor).

While this explosion offers a wide range of opportunities for manufacturers and consumers, it also poses major risks in terms of security. Without the security of these devices, hackers will be able to steal data of the users very easily and can even launch attacks on other devices. There are two kinds of attacks, as shown in Figure 1, related to security, Active and Passive. Both Active and Passive attacks can be done on IoT devices. We have some examples of such attacks on IoT devices like Mirai Botnet Attack (also known as Dyn Attack) of 2016 in which the largest DDoS attack ever took place which took down huge portions of Netflix, Twitter, The Guardian, Reddit, and CNN.

The devices like defibrillators and pacemakers of St. Jude Medical had vulnerabilities that allowed hackers to access and manipulate the devices. The Jeep, The Owlet WiFi Baby Heart Monitor, and several webcams had similar vulnerabilities that allowed hackers to access and control them.

Emerging Radio Based RF (Radio Frequency) Attacks

There is a class of threats that utilize the RF (Radio Frequency) attacking vector. It includes attacks on communication vectors like Bluetooth, Bluetooth Low Energy (BLE), radio, Wi-Fi, etc., as these technologies transmit and receive data using radio waves in the RF Spectrum. This attack works by recording the data transmitted from the sender device to the receiver radio device and replaying it at a later time. The vulnerability scans don't look at the RF spectrum and also sidestep firewalls and network-based detection systems. RF-enabled devices offer hackers new opportunities to compromise system security.

Figure 1. Overview of attacks corresponding protocols, functions and threats

LAYERS	PROTOCOLS	FUNCTIONS	THREATS
APPLICATION	FTP, HTTP, DNS,HTTPS, SMTP	USER INTERFACE(UI)	MALWARE, DOS, SMTP ATTACKS, BROWSER HIJACKING
PRESENTATION	JPEG, PNG, MPEG	DATA REPRESENTATION ENCRYPTION	SSL STRIPPING, MALFORMED SSL REQUEST, UNICODE VULNERABILITIES
SESSION	SQL, RPC, NFS	PROCESS TO PROCESS COMMUNICATION	SESSION HIJACKING, DOS
TRANSPORT	TCL, UDP, SSL	END-TO-END COMMUNICATION MANAGEMENT	SYN FLOODING, DESYNCHRONISATION ATTACKS, ENERGY DRAIN ATTACKS
NETWORK	IP, ICMP, ROUTERS	ROUTING DATA, PACKET FORWARDING, WAN DELIVERY	MITM SPOOFING, PING FLOODS, HIJACKING, IP SMURFING
DATALINK	MAC, ETHERNET, BRIDGES	PHYSICAL ADDRESSING, LAN DELIVERY	MAC SPOOFING, TRAFFIC ANALYSIS, SWITCH LOOPING, COLLISION
PHYSICAL	CABLES, FIBRES, PHYSICAL CABLING	TRANSMITTING BITS	WIRETAPPING, JAMMING, TAMPERING, PHYSICAL THREATS

Wireless keyboards and mice are most susceptible to this kind of attack. IoT and other computing devices with WiFi or Bluetooth capabilities have shown vulnerabilities that can be exploited.

SECURITY IN IoT AND ITS CHALLENGES

A vulnerability is a weakness that can be exploited by the hacker to gain access and control the device. The most common vulnerability is weak/easily guessable passwords or even hardcoded passwords. They can be easily brute-forced using a simple Dictionary attack.

Data threats and Data breaches are also possible due to weak security and unsecured, unencrypted networks. Even with just a little bit of data, a lot of information can be available. The more details found about the user, the easier it is to target him.

The IoT devices are also susceptible to Man-in-the-Middle attacks. This is a concept where an attacker or a hacker intercepts a communication between two systems. The attacker can use the captured information for identity theft or other types of fraud.

Hackers can compromise IoT devices connected to the internet and use them to carry out attacks. They commandeer such devices by installing a backdoor or some other malicious code and then use their collective power to target larger targets in DDoS attacks, spamming, or even spying on someone. With just enough information available the attacker can use social engineering to manipulate the targets so they give up credential information. (Liu, X., 2013)

A Layered Approach for Attacks

Architecture of IoT

There isn't a single architecture for IoT which is universally accepted. Architectures vary from researcher to researcher. Many different architectures have been proposed by researchers. Due to enhancements in IoT, many researchers believe that three-layer architecture cannot fulfill the requirements and thus prefer the four-layer architecture. Some even prefer the five-layer architecture five-layer architecture for privacy and security purposes.

Three-layer Architecture

It was proposed in the early stages of the development of IoT and is very basic in nature fulfilling the essentials of IoT.

Perception Layer, Network Layer, and Application Layer are the 3 layers that make up the Three-layer Architecture

1. **Perception layer-** This layer is also known as the sensor layer and has the responsibility to identify things and collect information from them. RFID, 2-D barcode sensors are the kind of sensors integrated with this layer. They collect various information like motion, location, vibration, humidity, etc. (Wu et al., 2010)
2. **Network layer-** This layer is also known as the transmission layer as it works as a crossover between the perception and the application layer. It is highly sensitive to attacks as it transmits the information collected from physical objects with the help of sensors either wired or wirelessly. (Hu and Chen., 2012)
3. **Application layer-** This layer provides services to the applications based on the information collected from the sensors. When used in certain areas, it has vulnerabilities due to the fact that the devices used have weak computational power and a low amount of storage, for instance, a Zigbee. (Zhou and Shi., 2013)

Four-layer Architecture

Due to continuous development in IoT, a Four-layer architecture was introduced as the three-layer architecture was very basic and was unable to fulfill all the requirements of IoT. It has the same three layers as the previous architecture with an extension of one extra layer called the support layer.

1. **Support layer-** To overcome the flaws of the 3 layer Architecture, the support layer was introduced. This layer was primarily added for security in the IoT Architecture. The support layer ensures that the information is sent by an authentic user and is protected from threats. It is also responsible for transmitting information to the network layer. The information can be shared both wired and wireless.

Five-layer Architecture

Though the four-layer architecture played an important role in the development of IoT, it had issues related to storage and security. Therefore a new five-layer architecture was proposed by researchers to make IoT more secure. It had three common layers of the previous architecture namely perception, transport, and application layer, and two extra layers. These extra layers are the Processing layer and the Business layer. (Xueping et al., 2014) This layer has the ability to make IoT more secure.

These new extra layers are explained below:

1. **Processing layer-** This layer is also known as the middleware layer. It processes the information collected from the transport layer and removes supplementary information that has no meaning.
2. **Business layer-** This layer acts as a manager of the whole system and is responsible for the management of and control of the application and the business profit model of IoT. It also manages the user's privacy. Vulnerability in this layer can lead to misuse of the application.

Kinds of Attacks in Different Layers

The different types of attacks in different layers are given below.

Perception Layer

1. **Eavesdropping -** In Eavesdropping, information is stolen by intercepting private communications transmitted over a network. Unsecure networks are vulnerable to this kind of attack.
2. **Fake Node and Malicious -** Fake and malicious nodes of data are added by the attacker to stop transmitting the real information and potential control that can destroy the network.
3. **Replay Attack -** Also known as playback attack, in this attack the attacker intercepts authentic information from the conversation between sender and receiver. The attacker then uses this information as proof of identity and authenticity.
4. **Timing Attack -** Devices with weak computing capabilities are vulnerable to this kind of attack. Attackers extract secrets in the security by observing time taken by several queries, inputs, or cryptographic algorithms.

Network Layer

I. **Denial of Service (DOS) Attack -** A Denial of Service (DoS) attack is an attack meant to shut down a machine or network, making it inaccessible to its intended users. DoS attacks accomplish this by flooding the target with traffic or sending it information that triggers a crash (Rohit et al., 2019).

II. **Man in the middle(MITM) Attack -** In MITM the attacker intercepts or alters the information between the sender and the receiver, according to his needs where the sender and the receiver believe they are directly communicating with each other.

III. **Storage Attack -** In this kind of attack, the attacker accesses or manipulates the information which is stored either in storage devices or in the cloud.

IV. **Exploit Attack -** In exploit attacks the attacker tries to gain control of the system by installing malicious software, backdoors, or by running a sequence of commands.

Application Layer

I. **Cross-Site Scripting (XSS)** - A cross-site scripting vulnerability may be used by attackers to bypass access controls and to inject client-side scripts into web pages viewed by others. (Shiaeles et al., 2019)

II. **Malicious Code Attack -** It is a piece of code written to damage the system or to cause undesirable changes. This could be detected by the antivirus software.

Support Layer

I. **Denial of Service (DoS) Attack -** In this layer too, a DoS attack can be used by the attacker.

II. **Malicious Insider Attack -** It is a kind of attack in which an authorized user accesses the personal information of other users.

Processing Layer

I. **Malware -** It refers to the application of viruses, spyware, adware, Trojan Horses, Worms, etc to steal the confidential information of the users.

Business Layer

I. **Business Logic Attack -** A business logic attack is a flaw in programming which manages the exchange of information between a user interface and the application's supporting database.

II. **Zero-day Attack -** A zero-day is a vulnerability that is either unknown or a patch has not been developed yet. Until the vulnerability is hackers can keep on exploiting.

DEMYSTIFYING WEB

The entire web is divided into three categories i.e. Surface Web, Deep Web and Dark Web.

Figure 2. Demystifying web

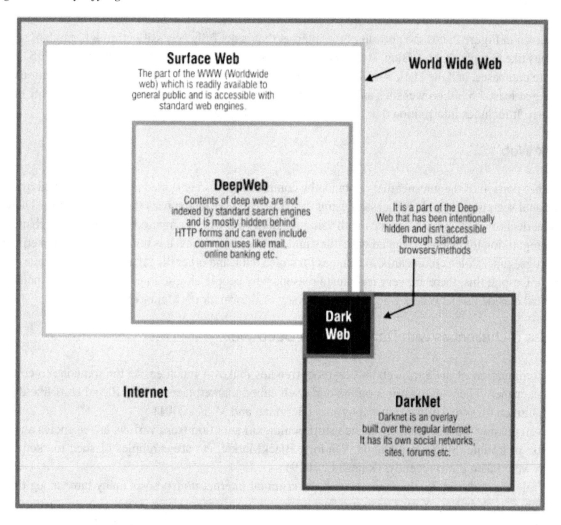

Surface Web

It is that portion of the World Wide Web (WWW) that is readily available to the general public and accessible through standard web search engines like Google, Yahoo, Bing, etc. It is also known as Visible Web, Indexed Web, Indexable Web, or Lightnet and includes a fraction of the internet with approximately 19 Terabytes of information which is just about 4% of the internet, as shown in Figure 2.

Any webpage that requires credentials for access is technically a part of the deep web as a search engine cannot access that information.

Issues & Challenges in Surface Web

The internet is a kind of place where no matter what you do, you always leave digital traces in one form or another. The downside of the surface web is there are trolls, stalkers pornographic content, data exploitation, Identity theft, hacking, intrusion of privacy, etc.

Deep Web

As shown in Figure 2, it is the portion of the internet that is not fully accessible through standard search engines like Google, Yahoo, Bing, etc. It includes pages that are not indexed, fee for service (FFS) sites, private databases, and the Dark web. Deep Web has approximately 7500 Terabytes of information containing at least 4.5 billion websites and most of it is publicly available. It consists of around 96% of the internet. It includes information that is encrypted and is not available publicly.

Dark Web

It is that portion of the internet that contains the content which is encrypted and is not indexed by conventional search engines. It is accessed using the TOR Browser which uses the onion routing. There is a great deal of anonymity that comes with using the dark web when compared to traditional websites. It has a reputation for being associated with illicit and unethical activities. It is home to online marketplaces for drugs, guns, stolen credit cards, exchanges for stolen data, and other illegal activities (Baravalle et al., 2016). Despite this, there are very legitimate reasons why people choose to use the dark web including political dissidents and others who want the privacy of information. (Mahor et al., 2016)

Issues & challenges with Dark Web and Deep Web

The combination of the dark web and cryptocurrencies makes it much easier for someone to commit certain crimes. There are websites on the dark web called marketplaces to buy illegal stuff like drugs, guns, hitmen for hire, child pornography, etc. (Bergman and M. K., 2001)

Even unknowingly stumbling on such stuff could gain attention from various law agencies and can get you in trouble. Silkroad, Valhalla, Pandora, BlackMarket, etc are examples of such marketplaces which were taken down recently. (Rajesh E, 2019)

While the dark web is synonymous with the criminal internet it also hosts many famous legitimate companies such as New York Times and Facebook.

The dark web is full of notorious things, for example, we can find forums that sell exploits of various things for money. There are forums that claim that they have the exploit for various vulnerabilities and sell IoT cyberattacks and such exploits for money.

These websites sell botnets of compromised IoT devices that can be used to launch DDoS attacks. (Bradbury D, 2014)

About Cryptocurrencies

Cryptocurrencies are the most popular modes of transactions on the dark web as they provide convenient methods of obfuscating identities as well as transaction details. Stealth Addresses are used in transactions done via cryptocurrencies on a Blockchain network to hide parties involved in transactions. Bitcoin, Monero, and thorium are the most preferred coins to conduct transactions on the dark web. Recently Litecoin has gained popularity on the dark web as it has faster processing times compared to bitcoin and it also can be stored in offline wallets. It is also kind of "economically feasible" due to its less transaction fee.

Misuse of Bitcoin, IoT & Crime

Cyber Criminals tend to use Bitcoin and other Cryptocurrencies as a payment method because they provide a combination of anonymity, ease of use, and the ability to circumvent international borders and regulations. Fraudsters also use cryptocurrency to launder money. Money launderers can use both Bitcoin mixing services and Bitcoin Exchanges. Random frequency of payments is done to mask illegitimate transactions. Bitcoin mixing allows fraudsters to mask the origin of their ill-gotten proceeds disassociating them from criminal activities to cash out the laundered money safely. (Alghamdi & Selamat, 2022)

In IoT devices, there are some severe threats due to various vulnerabilities. These include DDoS attacks, MITM (Man in the Middle) attacks, sniffing, and spoofing (Peng et al, 2019). For example in some smart security cameras, vulnerabilities could allow hackers to remotely view the camera footage, stream audio output, and can even launch DDoS (Distributed Denial of Service) attacks using the infected device. The same was reported with other IoT devices like Fax Machines, Smart TVs, Smart Bulbs, Smart Homes, and even your Smartphone's microphone.

History of Dark Web

Ian Clarke created a "Freenet" aimed to secure users against government intervention and cyber-attacks along with this the dark web officially appeared in the early 2000s. The U.S. Naval Research funded a project called The Onion Router (TOR) with the intention to allow spies to exchange information completely anonymously. In 2002 they released it into the public domain for everyone to use freely. The reason was simple so that they could remain anonymous and if there were many people using it then distinguishing the messages of the US Military from the other thousands of people would be tedious.

It's called The Onion Router because it uses layers of encryption to maintain anonymity.

Darknet Concepts for IoT Security

It turns out that darknet may actually provide a key to more secure IoT applications. We can run hidden onion services on IoT, that are used in the Tor networking. We can simply understand this as the user transmits a service that is hidden from other nodes on the Tor Network and only devices with the right authentication key are able to actually route and communicate with each other. There are drawbacks to this solution like speed and dependency on each peer node to relay information. This does provide an interesting new approach that may provide new ideas and innovation around the next generation of secure communication and privacy. The IoT network can use the current Tor concept as the current darknet uses it for security purposes instead of criminal.

PREVENTIVE MEASURES OR TECHNIQUES

With the expansion of IoT in the market, the number of potential risks has also expanded. The first wave of IoT attacks started when the Mirai Botnet compromised IoT devices like IP Cameras and routers, forming botnets targeting millions of devices around the world.

Personal information gets collected and stored on these devices such as your name, age, health data, location, etc. which can get stolen by the attackers. IoT devices pose a dangerous threat to everyone's internet safety. Attackers always lookout for new ways to hack systems and gain access to data. Security of the IoT networks should be the foremost priority as such a huge number of devices are connected to them. We can follow some basic common practices like always using strong and unique passwords for all of our devices and should also change them regularly. We should always avoid passwords that are easily guessed such as "password", "abcd123", "qwerty123" or your full name with age or Date of birth.

We must not use unsecured networks with vulnerabilities as they can be easily stolen by attackers.

Layer Wise Attacks Countermeasures

Perception Layer

The most common attacks in this layer are eavesdropping, replay attacks, fake node injection, RFID attacks, hardware tempering, etc. (Ahmed et al., 2017)

The following countermeasures can be taken-

Authentication

Proper authentication of the devices should be done to keep out malicious devices. (Gupta et al., 2016)

Encryption

Data should be encrypted to minimize the risk of data tampering.

RFID attacks can be prevented by the introduction of authentication based on Hash.

For the prevention of eavesdropping, we can use a personalized firewall or a Virtual Private Network (VPN).

Replay attacks can be prevented by tagging each encrypted component with a session ID and a component number. (Mahlous, A. 2019)

Network Layer

The most common types of attacks in the network layer are DoS attacks, MITM, storage attacks, etc. (Chahid et al., 2017)

- **Data Privacy** - Data Privacy in the IoT can be achieved by point-to-point encryption. Confidential data can be achieved by converting data to code that is indecipherable.
- **Data Integrity** - Data Integrity can be achieved by applying cryptographic hash functions to the data. (Tweneboah-Koduah et al., 2017)
- **DoS attacks can pose a serious threat if ignored** - They can be spotted by monitoring the inbound traffic in the networks. Spoofing Prevention can also help in the prevention of DoS attacks, by checking that a source address is consistent with the stated site of origin and by using filters to stop dial-up connections from spoofing. (Ullah et al., 2019)
- **MITM attacks** - The MITM attacks can be prevented by using a strong layer of encryption between the client and the server-side. This point-to-point encryption is the best way to prevent MITM attacks. (Ahemd et al., 2017)

Processing Layer

Cloud attacks are the most common types of attacks in the processing layer as the data is sent to the cloud at this phase. Encryption should be used for securing sensitive data and should always be stored in an encrypted format. We can use web application scanners which can help in detecting a potential attacker.

FRS (Fragmentation Redundancy Scattering)

FRS can be used to minimize the risk of data leakage by scattering the data on different servers into different fragments. The fragmented data won't have any significant information by itself. (Abomhara & Geir M. Køien, 2015)

Application Layer

The risk assessment technique can be used to minimize the risk of threats in the application layer by continuously detecting threats of the system, applying their patches and updates to improve the security of the system. (Pal et al., 2020)

We can use software like Antivirus, Anti-spyware, and Anti-adware so as to maintain the security of the system. Firewalls can also be used to filter unwanted traffic and packets. Firewalls can also help in the prevention of DoS attacks. (Zhang et al., 2014)

CONCLUSION

Security in IoT is of prime importance, it needs to be addressed properly to make it more secure. But due to the heterogeneous architecture of IoT, it is very vulnerable to security threats. In this paper, an honest attempt is made to explore the IoT in terms of its characteristics, architecture, and attacks with regard to different layers of IoT architecture. Security issues and challenges of the Surface web, deep web, and dark web are also discussed. Misuse of Bitcoin, IoT & Criminal activities in the dark web along with issues in cryptocurrency is also discussed.

It tries to identify the most common vulnerabilities and attacks which can affect IoT communication and provides probable preventive measures, which makes the IoT more secure. Different counter strategies were also discussed in order to protect from various attacks.

Further researchers can work on newer forms of threats that are not known or maybe very rarely used by the hackers.

REFERENCES

Abomhara, G. M., & Køien, G. M. (2015). Cyber security and the internet of things: Vulnerabilities, threats, intruders and attacks. *Journal of Cyber Security and Mobility*, 4(1), 65–88. doi:10.13052/jcsm2245-1439.414

Ahemd, M. M., Shah, M. A., & Wahid, A. (2017). IOT security: A layered approach for attacks & defenses. *2017 International Conference on Communication Technologies (ComTech)*. 10.1109/COM-TECH.2017.8065757

Al-Garadi, M. A., Mohamed, A., Al-Ali, A. K., Du, X., Ali, I., & Guizani, M. (2020). A survey of machine and deep learning methods for internet of things (IOT) security. *IEEE Communications Surveys and Tutorials*, *22*(3), 1646–1685. doi:10.1109/COMST.2020.2988293

Alghamdi, H., & Selamat, A. (2022). Techniques to detect terrorists/extremists on the dark web: A Review. *Data Technologies and Applications*. doi:10.1108/DTA-07-2021-0177

Alnabulsi, H., & Islam, R. (2018). Identification of illegal forum activities inside the Dark Net. *2018 International Conference on Machine Learning and Data Engineering (iCMLDE)*. 10.1109/iCML-DE.2018.00015

Ammar, M., Russello, G., & Crispo, B. (2018). Internet of Things: A survey on the security of IoT frameworks. *Journal of Information Security and Applications*, *38*, 8–27. doi:10.1016/j.jisa.2017.11.002

Arabnezhad, E., La Morgia, M., Mei, A., Nemmi, E. N., & Stefa, J. (2020). A light in the dark web: Linking dark web aliases to real internet identities. *2020 IEEE 40th International Conference on Distributed Computing Systems (ICDCS)*. 10.1109/ICDCS47774.2020.00081

Atzori, L., Iera, A., & Morabito, G. (2010). The internet of things: A survey. *Computer Networks*, *54*(15), 2787–2805. doi:10.1016/j.comnet.2010.05.010

Baravalle, A., Lopez, M. S., & Lee, S. W. (2016). Mining the dark web: Drugs and fake ids. *2016 IEEE 16th International Conference on Data Mining Workshops (ICDMW)*. 10.1109/ICDMW.2016.0056

Bergman, M. K. (2001). White Paper: The deep web: Surfacing hidden value. *The Journal of Electronic Publishing: JEP*, *7*(1). Advance online publication. doi:10.3998/3336451.0007.104

Bradbury, D. (2014). Unveiling the dark web. *Network Security*, *2014*(4), 14–17. doi:10.1016/S1353-4858(14)70042-X

Chen, H. (2012). *Dark web*. Integrated Series in Information Systems., doi:10.1007/978-1-4614-1557-2

Fernando, D. W., Komninos, N., & Chen, T. (2020). A study on the evolution of ransomware detection using machine learning and Deep Learning Techniques. *IoT*, *1*(2), 551–604. doi:10.3390/iot1020030

Gupta, K. K., & Shukla, S. (2016). Internet of things: Security challenges for next generation networks. *2016 International Conference on Innovation and Challenges in Cyber Security (ICICCS-INBUSH)*. 10.1109/ICICCS.2016.7542301

Hu, Z. H., & Chen, W. L. (2012). The Security Mechanism for Internet of Things Networks. *Applied Mechanics and Materials*, *220-223*, 3003–3009. . doi:10.4028/www.scientific.net/AMM.220-223.3003

Jadav, N., Dutta, N., Sarma, H. K., Pricop, E., & Tanwar, S. (2021). A machine learning approach to classify network traffic. *2021 13th International Conference on Electronics, Computers and Artificial Intelligence (ECAI)*. 10.1109/ECAI52376.2021.9515039

K, M. A. (2021). Machine learning for anonymous traffic detection and classification. *2021 11th International Conference on Cloud Computing, Data Science & Engineering (Confluence)*. 10.1109/Confluence51648.2021.9377168

Kadoguchi, M., Kobayashi, H., Hayashi, S., Otsuka, A., & Hashimoto, M. (2020). Deep self-supervised clustering of the dark web for Cyber Threat Intelligence. *2020 IEEE International Conference on Intelligence and Security Informatics (ISI)*. 10.1109/ISI49825.2020.9280485

Kawaguchi, Y., & Ozawa, S. (2019). Exploring and identifying malicious sites in dark web using machine learning. *Neural Information Processing*, 319-327. doi:10.1007/978-3-030-36718-3_27

Kim, S., Joshi, P., Kalsi, P. S., & Taheri, P. (2018). Crime Analysis Through Machine Learning. *2018 IEEE 9th Annual Information Technology, Electronics and Mobile Communication Conference (IEMCON)*. 10.1109/IEMCON.2018.8614828

Koloveas, P., Chantzios, T., Alevizopoulou, S., Skiadopoulos, S., & Tryfonopoulos, C. (2021). Intime: A machine learning-based framework for gathering and leveraging web data to Cyber-Threat Intelligence. *Electronics (Basel)*, *10*(7), 818. doi:10.3390/electronics10070818

Liu, X. (2013). Security Risks in the Internet of Things. *Proceedings of the 2012 International Conference on Cybernetics and Informatics Lecture Notes in Electrical Engineering*, 59-64. 10.1007/978-1-4614-3872-4_8

Mahlous, A. (2019). *Internet of Things (IoTs)*. Architecture, Evolution, Threats and Defense.

Mahor, V., Rawat, R., Kumar, A., Chouhan, M., Shaw, R. N., & Ghosh, A. (2021). Cyber Warfare Threat Categorization on CPS by Dark Web Terrorist. *2021 IEEE 4th International Conference on Computing, Power and Communication Technologies (GUCON)*. 10.1109/GUCON50781.2021.9573994

Narayanankutty, H. (2021). Self-adapting model-based SDSEC for IOT networks using machine learning. *2021 IEEE 18th International Conference on Software Architecture Companion (ICSA-C)*. 10.1109/ICSA-C52384.2021.00023

Nazah, S., Huda, S., Abawajy, J., & Hassan, M. M. (2020). Evolution of dark web threat analysis and detection: A systematic approach. *IEEE Access: Practical Innovations, Open Solutions*, *8*, 171796–171819. doi:10.1109/ACCESS.2020.3024198

Nunes, E., Diab, A., Gunn, A., Marin, E., Mishra, V., Paliath, V., ... Shakarian, P. (2016). Darknet and deepnet mining for Proactive Cybersecurity Threat Intelligence. *2016 IEEE Conference on Intelligence and Security Informatics (ISI)*. 10.1109/ISI.2016.7745435

Pajooh, H. H., Rashid, M., Alam, F., & Demidenko, S. (2021). Multi-Layer Blockchain-Based Security Architecture for Internet of Things. *Sensors (Basel)*, *21*(3), 772. doi:10.339021030772 PMID:33498860

Pal, S., Hitchens, M., Rabehaja, T., & Mukhopadhyay, S. (2020). Security Requirements for the Internet of Things: A Systematic Approach. *Sensors (Basel)*, *20*(20), 5897. doi:10.339020205897 PMID:33086542

Peng, K., Li, M., Huang, H., Wang, C., Wan, S., & Choo, K.-K. R. (2021). Security challenges and opportunities for smart contracts in internet of things: A survey. *IEEE Internet of Things Journal*, *8*(15), 12004–12020. doi:10.1109/JIOT.2021.3074544

Pizzolante, R., Castiglione, A., Carpentieri, B., Contaldo, R., D'Angelo, G., & Palmieri, F. (2020). A machine learning-based memory forensics methodology for Tor Browser artifacts. *Concurrency and Computation, 33*(23). Advance online publication. doi:10.1002/cpe.5935

Rajesh, E. (2019). A Research Paper on Dark Web. *International Journal of Emerging Technologies and Innovative Research, 6*(4), 322-327. https://www.jetir.org/papers/JETIREQ06074.pdf

Rohit, M. H., Fahim, S. M., & Khan, A. H. (2019). Mitigating and detecting ddos attack on IOT environment. *2019 IEEE International Conference on Robotics, Automation, Artificial-Intelligence and Internet-of-Things (RAAICON).* 10.1109/RAAICON48939.2019.5

Shiaeles, S., Kolokotronis, N., & Bellini, E. (2019). IOT vulnerability data crawling and analysis. *2019 IEEE World Congress on Services (SERVICES).* 10.1109/SERVICES.2019.00028

Tweneboah-Koduah, S., Skouby, K. E., & Tadayoni, R. (2017). Cyber Security Threats to IoT Applications and Service Domains. *Wireless Personal Communications, 95*(1), 169–185. doi:10.100711277-017-4434-6

Ullah, F., Naeem, H., Jabbar, S., Khalid, S., Latif, M. A., Al-turjman, F., & Mostarda, L. (2019). Cyber security threats detection in internet of things using Deep Learning Approach. *IEEE Access: Practical Innovations, Open Solutions, 7,* 124379–124389. doi:10.1109/ACCESS.2019.2937347

Wortmann, F., & Flüchter, K. (2015). Internet of things. *Business & Information Systems Engineering, 57*(3), 221–224. doi:10.100712599-015-0383-3

Wu, M., Lu, T.-J., Ling, F.-Y., Sun, J., & Du, H.-Y. (2010). Research on the architecture of internet of things. *2010 3rd International Conference on Advanced Computer Theory and Engineering (ICACTE).* 10.1109/ICACTE.2010.5579493

Xu, T., Wendt, J. B., & Potkonjak, M. (2014). Security of IoT systems: Design challenges and opportunities. *2014 IEEE/ACM International Conference on Computer-Aided Design (ICCAD).*10.1109/ICCAD.2014.7001385

Zenebe, A., Shumba, M., Carillo, A., & Cuenca, S. (n.d.). Cyber threat discovery from dark web. *EPiC Series in Computing.* doi:10.29007/nkfk

Zhang, Y., Zou, W., Chen, X., Yang, C., & Cao, J. (2014). The security for power internet of things: Framework, policies, and countermeasures. *2014 International Conference on Cyber-Enabled Distributed Computing and Knowledge Discovery.* 10.1109/CyberC.2014.32

Zhou, Z. W., & Shi, L. (2013). Security Research and Measures for the Internet of Things. *Advanced Materials Research, 748,* 910–914. . doi:10.4028/www.scientific.net/AMR.748.910

Section 4
Online Social Network Applications for Suspicious Pattern Recognition

Chapter 14

Cyber Security for Secured Smart Home Applications Using Internet of Things, Dark Web, and Blockchain Technology in the Future

Vinod Mahor
https://orcid.org/0000-0002-2187-6920
IES College of Technology, Bhopal, India

Sujit Kumar Badodia
https://orcid.org/0000-0003-1630-7261
Shri Vaishnav Vidyapeeth Vishwavidyalaya, India

Anil Kumar
https://orcid.org/0000-0003-4266-2013
School of Computing and IT, Manipal University Jaipur, India

Sadhna Bijrothiya
https://orcid.org/0000-0002-8913-7753
Maulana Azad National Institute of Technology, Bhopal, India

Ankit Temurnikar
https://orcid.org/0000-0002-0416-5289
IES College of Technology, Bhopal, India

ABSTRACT

The need for more comfortable and humane living spaces has accelerated the development of smart homes. Many extremely intelligent houses are part of the internet of things. It operates with the dark web and ensures the privacy of incognito relays and massive data to properly manage customer requests. This increased demand gives rise to a great deal of concern regarding scalability, efficiency, and safety for a smart home system. Detailed data or the lowest levels that can be in a target set are granular data. In this chapter, the authors present the combination of integrating block-chain technology, dark web, and cloud computing in an effective manner. Blockchain technology is decentralized because it can serve processing services. To ensure the safety of the smart home network, the model employs multivariate correlation analysis and the detection of correlations between traffic functions. The performance of the architecture was evaluated with various performance parameters, and blockchain was found to be an effective security solution for future networks on the internet.

DOI: 10.4018/978-1-6684-3942-5.ch014

INTRODUCTION

The "Internet of Things" (IoT) is a collection of devices that "produce," "analyse," and "communicate" massive amounts of vital data and information concerning security and secrecy. Many new IoT networkable gadgets are small and energy-efficient. Because the bulk of available energy and computer systems must be used to develop core applications, providing inexpensive security and privacy support is extremely difficult. (Alam et al., 2012) Robust authentication systems are sometimes too expensive for "Internet of Things" applications due to energy consumption and overhead processes (IoT). Lately, the Dark Web has been discovered as a significant source of high-quality cyber-security data that can be recognised, studied, and transformed into meaningful cyber threat data using the correct methodologies and technology.

Security and data protection must be lightweight, scalable, and distributed to meet IoT requirements. To safeguard users' security, existing approaches frequently expose noisy or partial data, which might hinder some IoT apps from providing personalised services (Xu et al., 2016). Furthermore, numerous cutting-edge security frameworks emphasise the traffic nature and single point of failure, which are not necessarily ideal for IoT due to the scale's difficulties (Lutolf et al., 1992). Blockchain (BC) technology (Shin et al., 2017) potentially addresses Bitcoin's first crypto-currency system's issues in terms of distribution, security, and privacy.

Public Keys are produced and communicated to the network by Bitcoin users identified by changing monetary transactions. This block is where users divide transactions. When a block is completed, BC adds a mining procedure. Miners; attempt to answer a cryptographic riddle that costs resources called the Proof of Work (POW), which first solves the problem by blocking the new BC block (Song et al., 2016). According to (Pishva et al., 2008), introducing BC into IoT is complex. It poses several significant challenges, including high resource demands for the solution of POW, long transaction confirmation latency, and low scalability due to transactions and blocks broadcast across the network. We proposed a new instantiation of BC because the POW concert has been eliminated, and the coins are required. Our suggested framework is built on and distributed on hierarchical structure confidence, keeping with the safety and privacy of BC while being better fitted to the particular demands of the IoT.

We have demonstrated our concepts in a bright house, but we have an agnostic framework that m may apply in different IoT contexts (Singh et al., 2017). The design has three levels: intelligent home, minefield, and minefield centres indicated in Figure 1, service providers, cloud storage, cellphones, and personal PCs form an Overlay network of Smart Homes (Manojkumar et al., 2018.) The Overlay network provides functionality to our design in a peer-to-peer fashion similar to the Bitcoin network. The overlay nodes are based on clusters (CH) to decrease overtime and overtime for the network. The CHS keeps a BC public overlay and two other crucial entries. On the Dark web, cyber attackers plan, organise and discuss attacks. This method allows us to access several sources that malicious attackers choose and uncover issues in real-time, including zero-day issues (Rawat et al., 2021).

The Following is a list of the keys: Request key lists, which are lists of PKs, overlay users who can access data for intelligent homes linked to this cluster; Request key lists, which are lists of PKs of smart households combined into this cluster, can access data. The storage and exchange of data on smart home devices are called "cloud storage." The details of cloud overlay and storage have been investigated. The purpose of this paper is to go through the specifics of our smart home concept in great depth (Sharma et al., 2017). First, we will go through setting up IoT devices and complete transactions. BC enables secure IoT device and data access control on a local and private level. In addition, the BC keeps a permanent record of transactions that can be connected to third parties to provide specific services. The design's safety is based on several factors, including (1) indirect defaults and (2) The smart home and the overlay have different transaction structures. In smart home devices, symmetrical encryption is employed to guarantee lightweight security. We find that the smart home is secret, secure, and accessible, and that may consider critical security threats such as connection attacks (10) and distributed denial of service (DDOS). Finally, we use simulations to illustrate quantitative findings, demonstrating that our approach yields relatively low overheads. The key design sources will be presented in the remainder of the study.

RELATED WORKS

We will explore both current solutions and technology in this part.

The Blockchain is Distributed

Blockchain is a technique that ensures coherence by keeping all members and continuously updating the Blockchain ledger with new transactions. The Blockchain is an accurate, accountable system that prevents transactions from being lost. Bloc-chain maintains transaction legitimacy by storing the transaction's node register and distributing it over the whole network (He et al., 2018). The emergence of the Internet and its cryptographic technology allows all participants to check their transaction liabilities, removing the need for approved third parties and achieving a single point of failure. Continuous records enable data monitoring and fundamentally transparent Blockchain records when data transactions occur across several organisations' own and maintained networks. Anyone with internet access may monitor and analyse all activity.

Furthermore, specific Blockchain networks, like Ethereum, have an "intelligent agreement" capability, generating contracts when specific terms are met. It appears that will preserve Blockchain and IoT technology. The industry, as well as the governmental sector's strong support, has already been received. One of the most exciting aspects of blockchain technology is that data is not maintained in a single, totally decentralised location. It eliminates the necessity for a central string agency and gives individual users control.

Furthermore, Blockchain technology provides supply chain management with traceability and cost savings. It is used to trace the flow of items and their origin, quality, and other factors. The B2B eco-system gains a new level of transparency due to this.

Blockchain is a distributed database that stores data in a structured list manner. The Blockchain contains only genuine transactions, and the network examines the validity and invalidation of the new trade-in of a previous transaction. The Blockchain will be added to the latest data block only after the computer agrees on the transaction's legitimacy (Varatharajan et al., 2019). The consensus within the network is based on different voting techniques and work that is most commonly dependent on how far network users can access and verify transactions contained in the block, and c can permanently add it to the league. It should be simple to alter, using Block-chain verification as a network store participant.

Transactions are part of the corpus. Every block of the book has a header and footer, as seen in Fig. 1. The header section stores high values, with time stamps on the current and previous blocks. The indexing technique is used to get block data (Zheng et al., 2018).

Figure 1. Structure of Block-chain

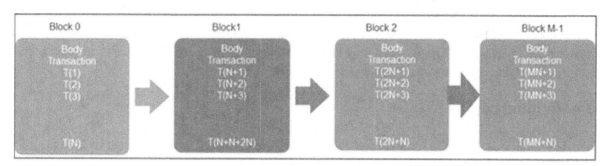

Green Cloud Computing

Green cloud computing is the study and practice of designing, producing, using, and disposing of computers, workstations, and infrastructure components. The main issues are computing resource efficiency and fostering ecologically responsible computer systems (Rawat et al., 2021). Cloud researchers take advantage of enabling a computer system into account. Cloud computing provides a pay-per-use service, which reduces the need for a significant upfront expenditure. The five major components in establishing an efficient smart home are cloud computing, virtualisation, multiple-lease, cloud storage, hypervisors, and the cloud network (Rawat et al., 2021).

It should finish the Service Level Agreement (SLA) for the various services provided by third-party organisations that meet quality standards. Smart homes with all nodes will communicate data through an intelligent gateway to the cloud

Cloud computing provides green computing equipment that is flexible, regionally distributed, cost-effective, and energy-efficient. The consumption of energy and carbon emissions from cloud infrastructure is two major concerns. In a cloud, the process is the primary driver for energy efficiency in terms of existing logic groups or computer resources. There are several techniques to virtualisation that m may use to eliminate energy inefficiency and minimise carbon extractions. According to recent research, a cloud-based migration tool can save carbon emissions by 30% per user.

Various alternative ways also present a cost-effective methodology for calculating service prices and energy-saving solutions. Several elements will be considered when assessing energy consumption, including a single unit task, associated analytical tools, the empirical approach, and various run-time tasks and workload scheduling.

IoT SMART HOME CHALLENGES

Real-life communication raises significant security, confidence, and confidentiality issues. The Internet of Things has already been subjected to several security threats and attacks. Because of the large transmissions, certain attackers can target necessary network data transfers, such as a man-in-the-middle (MitM) assault or a DoS/DDoS attack. The Internet of Things (IoT) raises several unique privacy concerns, including those related to telephone and automotive tracking systems. The data is also actively sent to cloud storage for voice recognition processing.

PROPOSED METHODOLGY

The proposed SH-BlockCC block would combine cloud computation and Blockchain technology to improve the smart home's speed, scalability, and availability. In Figure 3, four elements are shown: the home layer, blockchain network, cloud, and service layer.

Smart Home Layer

A smart home is a collection of intelligent families that includes a variety of Internet of Things (IoT) devices.

Distributed Block-chain Layer

Blockchain has recently attracted the interest of stakeholders in a variety of sectors. Blockchain technology allows for distributed modification of programmes that previously relied on a trustworthy intermediary. It is a distributed directory that efficiently and checkable records various transactions along the chain without a master host. They might implement similar practices under the same service contract without a central authority. Blockchain is a distributed network that allows individuals to communicate empirically without the need for trusted intermediaries (Sukheja et al., 2019).

Blockchain Distribution in Cloud Computing

There was a mistake. Users may store data safely and decentralised using the Cloud Distribution concept. This is accomplished by employing Blockchain capabilities like books, public/private key encryption, and so on, which we described before in this post. Because of the system's decentralised nature, it is impossible to compromise the central servers.

Trust and decentralisation:

Blockchain provides a decentralised framework without a single transactional authority. The nodes in the network should agree when accepting the transaction order to ensure Blockchain confidence (Li et al., 2020).

Complete Privacy

In Blockchain, each user has a key. Can solve various privacy difficulties by storing encrypted user data pieces in cryptocurrency systems (Singh et al., 2016).

Dark Web

This sub-component has been crawling some black websites in depth using the TOR proxy. To do so, the crawler is provided with a list of onion URLs that correspond to cyber communities or markets that offer cybercrime tools and zero-day security defects, and it examines the discussions for relevant information (Rawat et al., 2021).

Figure 2. Smart home architecture (SHA)

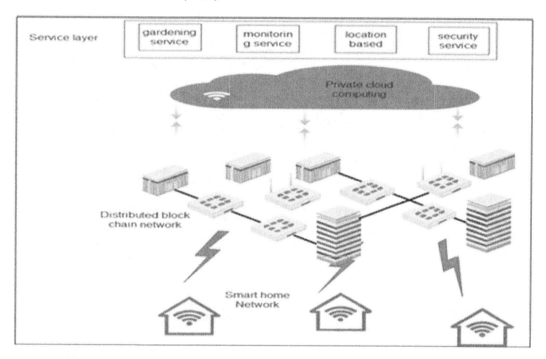

High Quality and Facilitate Usage Resource

With its distributed application, it quickly measures resources. An intelligent agreement, for example, must fulfil a demanding resource algorithm with certain encrypted features. And this request enables a sophisticated computer contract with a resource algorithm to be created on-demand, which automatically pays for the payment when the function is completed.

To summarise, the purpose of blockchain services is to improve qualitative traceability of resource use (Singh et al., 2017) so that SLA can be checked by both clients and reported service providers and the party responsible can determine faults.

Blockchain Transaction Processing in the Smart House

All devices are managed and stored in the local Blockchain via transactions. Local communication between devices or between overlay knots can do this. For some tasks, like shopping and access, monitoring, formation mode, each transaction is programmed,

and removed. The entire Diffie-Hellman algorithm transaction uses a shared key (Sharma et al., 2014). A legitimate transaction is added to construct an intelligent home employing a shared key. The unit is added to the minor is increased by one unit. The weight hacking procedure aims to identify changes in transaction content. Minors are given the device to administer the transaction using a shared key. The children examine the policy heading before handing over the key and requesting permission from the owner. As a result, the device can communicate as long as the key is active. To add a new device to the genesis process, two techniques for data access are used: local access and cloud access. The miner

Figure 3. A look at the smart home, open-source, and cloud-based overlay networks

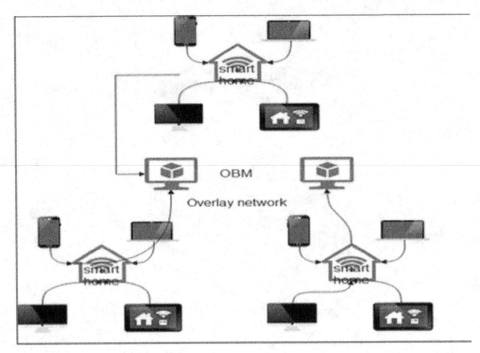

receives an application from the equipment that checks and stores local data for local approval. A miner can request cloud storage information and return it to the cloud.

A transaction is a term used to describe a process. The device requires local authentication. Therefore, miners are dispatched to save the weather device in exchange for authorisation. The key is shared with the local storage device when permission is granted, and the data is saved directly into the local storage. The same blocks are required to store data in the cloud. The user will authenticate the block and hash numbers before storing data. After successful authentication, user data packages are saved in the blocking process in a first-in-first-out (FIFO) order with a hash.

EXPERIMENTAL RESULTS

In a variety of scenarios, the suggested architecture has been carefully studied. An accuracy test of a network traffic attack detection model has been built. With intelligence, the security model analyses the detection of anomalies in the network. The assessment records are presented in this section. In addition, we examine performance in the intelligent and independent home using Blockchain technology.

Performance Evaluation using Blockchain Technology

We compute the smart home and the overlay confidentially for autonomous operation. We evaluate the various models of the proposed performance in this model. Here, two simulators are used:

Cooja: Contiki OS is used to build it, as it is one of the best OSs for a tiny amount of memory and processing power. Cooja is designed for IoT devices with few resources. It emulates different IoT device

Figure 4. Network delay

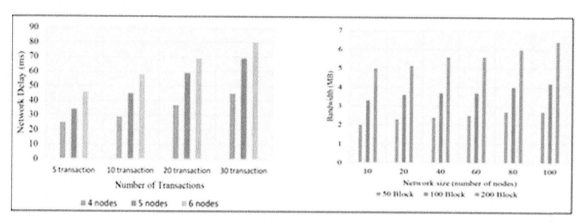

functions, including lighting, heating, and pressure. Netsim: The simulator and emulator for IoT network applications are being tested. We have been testing the performance of overlays here. The suggested blockchain model has overhead and time-consuming computations on a smart home device. Because the local block manager processes all transactions and encrypts them symmetrically and asymmetrically, Cooja and Netsim utilise the local block manager time to evaluate this.

The memory use of SH-BlockCC is shown in Figure 7., which offers a single, two, and five blocks dark web of memory transaction for various block sizes. Increasing the number of transactions per block minimises memory usage. A fixed transaction consumes more memory as the number of blocks increases. According to the findings, less is utilised with stronger memory, and vice versa. If the transaction grows by blocks, a new partnership is automatically created when it reaches the block size limit. However, consumption has been increasing. As a result, storage use is reduced because more transactions are per block.

Scaling the Block-chain

Network overhead is the amount of bandwidth, energy, memory, and time that each sensor node consumes inside a network. To scale the Blockchain, we needed about 100 nodes. In the simulation, m measured

Figure 5. Network overhead

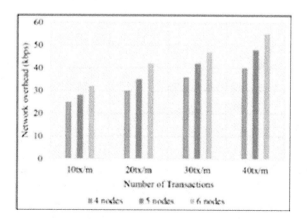

Figure 6. Bandwidth

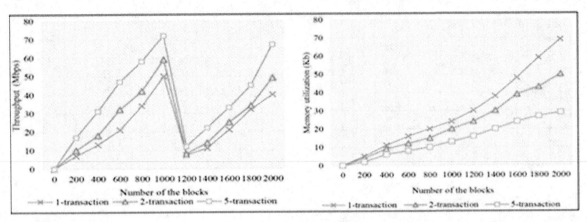

the latency and bandwidth usage per node. We enhance the network size concerning communicated nodes. The delay of different microblock numbers is displayed. Because there are numerous knots in the smaller network, the latency rate is initially low. However, when the web grows in size, the latency rate rises as the nodes take longer to respond. As shown in Fig., network bandwidth consumption is rising with increased network size and block number. Because all blocks are sent to the networks through radio, this is the case. The performance and comparability between our suggested framework and the hardware delay model are shown in Figures 5 and 6. To improve its performance, the suggested architecture incorporates the Blockchain idea.

The contrasts between the supporting framework and the core model of delays and performance are shown in Figures 6 and 7. The suggested architecture incorporates the perforation extension of the Blockchain concept.

Figure 7. Over-all latency and throughput (Normal case)

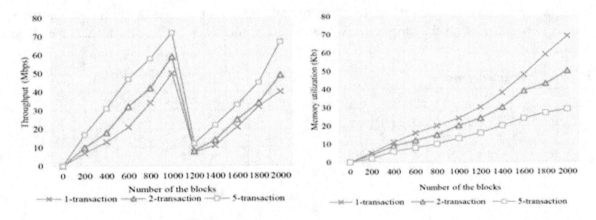

TRP and FPR are performance precision metrics used to determine the suggested model. The FRT (false positive ratio) is a measuring system. The positive and negative probabilities of the TPR-FPR and FR-to-TNR (genuine negative relationship) positive and negative probabilities are calculated. Compared to TRW-CB, NetAD, and MaxEnt, the SH-BlockCC produces superior results. Initial results from a limited number of judgements, primarily on clear web scan, show that nearly all of the obtained URLs include relevant cyber-threat information, with the proportion being higher (as expected) for IoT and dark web (Rawat et al., 2021). In the usual situation, throughput increases, blocks get more prominent, and transactions become larger. It becomes uniform over some time, grows, and gradually recovers.

CONCLUSION

These days, the IoT security business and academics have gotten much attention. Due to their high energy requirements and overhead processing, current security solutions aren't ideal for IoT. We previously recommended leveraging Bitcoin's BC or immutable block ledger to overcome these issues. A smart home idea was utilised as an example in a sample case study. In this article, we outline the numerous vital components of the intelligent home business and various transactions and procedures. We also offered comprehensive security and privacy analysis. Cloud computing expands the smart domain by allowing users to access cloud resources. The efficient broker oversees the selection of energy-efficient service providers and blockchain technology for end-users and peer-to-peer connections that will enable untrustworthy nodes to connect to a cost-effective processing network. Encryption, hacking, underground intelligent home networks and network overlays have all been employed in blockchain technology. The recovery of relevant gathered material from smart buildings for cyber-security via IoT and blockchain technologies and the dark web is among the study goals. Acceptable transactions between device and operator will be made accessible when the policy header and shared widget/minor key authorisation are established. In the intelligent home traffic relations detecting network, we discussed MCA methods. The suggested architecture often includes a network attack and response mechanism in smart homes. Our suggested architecture can efficiently secure an intelligent home because of the receiver operation (ROC), CPU utilisation, overhead transmission time, and overhead network.

REFERENCES

Alam, M. R., Reaz, M. B. I., & Ali, M. A. M. (2012). A review of smart homes—Past, present, and future. *IEEE Transactions on Systems, Man and Cybernetics. Part C, Applications and Reviews*, *42*(6), 1190–1203. doi:10.1109/TSMCC.2012.2189204

He, Q., Xu, Y., Liu, Z., He, J., Sun, Y., & Zhang, R. (2018). A privacy-preserving Internet of Things device management scheme based on Blockchain. *International Journal of Distributed Sensor Networks*, *14*(11), 1550147718808750. doi:10.1177/1550147718808750

Li, X., Jiang, P., Chen, T., Luo, X., & Wen, Q. (2020). A survey on the security of blockchain systems. *Future Generation Computer Systems*, *107*, 841–853. doi:10.1016/j.future.2017.08.020

Lutolf, R. (1992). Smart home concept and the integration of energy meters into a home-based system. *Seventh International Conference on Metering Apparatus and Tariffs for Electricity Supply 1992*, 277–278.

Manojkumar, D., Scholar, P., Kumar, C. A., & Kinathukadavu, C. (2018). *Privacy Policy Multiparty Access Control On Content Sharing Sites*. Academic Press.

Pishva, D., & Takeda, K. (2008). Product-based security model for smart home appliances. *IEEE Aerospace and Electronic Systems Magazine, 23*(10), 32–41. doi:10.1109/MAES.2008.4665323

Rawat, R., Mahor, V., Chirgaiya, S., & Garg, B. (2021). Artificial Cyber Espionage Based Protection of Technological Enabled Automated Cities Infrastructure by Dark Web Cyber Offender. In Intelligence of Things: AI-IoT Based Critical-Applications and Innovations (pp. 167–188). Springer. doi:10.1007/978-3-030-82800-4_7

Rawat, R., Mahor, V., Chirgaiya, S., & Rathore, A. S. (2021). Applications of Social Network Analysis to Managing the Investigation of Suspicious Activities in Social Media Platforms. In *Advances in Cybersecurity Management* (pp. 315–335). Springer. doi:10.1007/978-3-030-71381-2_15

Rawat, R., Mahor, V., Rawat, A., Garg, B., & Telang, S. (2021). Digital Transformation of Cyber Crime for Chip-Enabled Hacking. In *Handbook of Research on Advancing Cybersecurity for Digital Transformation* (pp. 227–243). IGI Global. doi:10.4018/978-1-7998-6975-7.ch012

Rawat, R., Rajawat, A. S., Mahor, V., Shaw, R. N., & Ghosh, A. (2021). Surveillance Robot in Cyber Intelligence for Vulnerability Detection. In *Machine Learning for Robotics Applications* (pp. 107–123). Springer. doi:10.1007/978-981-16-0598-7_9

Sharma, N., & Chirgaiya, S. (2014). A novel approach to Hill cipher. *International Journal of Computers and Applications, 108*(11), 975–8887.

Sharma, V., You, I., & Kul, G. (2017). Socialising drones for inter-service operability in ultra-dense wireless networks using Blockchain. *Proceedings of the 2017 International Workshop on Managing Insider Security Threats*, 81–84. 10.1145/3139923.3139932

Shin, D., Sharma, V., Kim, J., Kwon, S., & You, I. (2017). Secure and efficient protocol for route optimisation in PMIPv6-based smart home IoT networks. *IEEE Access: Practical Innovations, Open Solutions, 5*, 11100–11117. doi:10.1109/ACCESS.2017.2710379

Singh, S., Jeong, Y.-S., & Park, J. H. (2016). A survey on cloud computing security: Issues, threats, and solutions. *Journal of Network and Computer Applications, 75*, 200–222. doi:10.1016/j.jnca.2016.09.002

Singh, S., Sharma, P. K., Moon, S. Y., & Park, J. H. (2017). EH-GC: An efficient and secure architecture of energy harvesting Green cloud infrastructure. *Sustainability, 9*(4), 673. doi:10.3390u9040673

Singh, S., Sharma, P. K., & Park, J. H. (2017). SH-SecNet: An enhanced secure network architecture for the diagnosis of security threats in a smart home. *Sustainability, 9*(4), 513. doi:10.3390u9040513

Song, H., Rawat, D. B., Jeschke, S., & Brecher, C. (2016). *Cyber-physical systems: Foundations, principles and applications*. Morgan Kaufmann.

Sukheja, D., Indira, L., Sharma, P., & Chirgaiya, S. (2019). Blockchain Technology: A Comprehensive Survey. *Journal of Advanced Research in Dynamic and Control Systems, 11*(9), 1187–1203. doi:10.5373/JARDCS/V11/20192690

Varatharajan, A., Latha, C., & Dasig, D. Jr. (2019). Concept of implementing Big data in smart city: Applications, Services, Data Security in accordance with Internet of Things and AI. *International Journal of Recent Technology and Engineering*, *8*(3), 6819–6825. Advance online publication. doi:10.35940/ijrte.C5782.098319

Xu, K., Wang, X., Wei, W., Song, H., & Mao, B. (2016). Toward software-defined smart home. *IEEE Communications Magazine*, *54*(5), 116–122. doi:10.1109/MCOM.2016.7470945

Zheng, S., Apthorpe, N., Chetty, M., & Feamster, N. (2018). User perceptions of smart home IoT privacy. *Proceedings of the ACM on Human-Computer Interaction, 2*(CSCW), 1–20. 10.1145/3274469

Chapter 15
Forecasting the Traits of Cyber Criminals Based on Case Studies

Nandini Bansod

Shri Vaishnav Institute of Forensic Science, Shri Vaishnav Vidyapeeth Vishwavidyalaya, India

Dinesh Baban Kamble

Shri Vaishnav Vidyapeeth Vishwavidyalaya, India

Rina Mishra

Shri Vaishnav Vidyapeeth Vishwavidyalaya, India

Megha Kuliha

Shri Govindram Seksaria Institute of Technology and Science, India

ABSTRACT

The COVID-19 virus has affected every country on the globe; India is amongst the most with over 3.39 billion people who have been infected, and computer use has expanded since. As cybercrime (breaching, spoofing, DDOS assault, and phishing) is one of the most serious problems facing society today, it's crucial to understand what causes such attacks. Although many methods have been proposed to detect cybercrime, criminological theory of crime is one of them. But the most successful method for detecting these malicious activities is machine learning. This is because most of the cyberattacks have some common characteristics which can be identified by machine learning methods. In this context, an approach has been made in the chapter to review machine learning methods to understand the traits of cyber-criminals and crime committed on the dark web along with suitable methods to tackle them.

INTRODUCTION

The internet is probably the most powerful technological invention today and continues to change the daily life of almost everyone in the world. Millions of people use the Internet, and many thousands more

DOI: 10.4018/978-1-6684-3942-5.ch015

enter the Internet daily. Not only has the Internet changed the way we interact with others and learn, but it has also permanently changed the way we live. As internet and computer technology continues to flourish; cyber guilty mind person has found ways to use this technology as a tool for their deviant actions. Cybercrime is a new type of crime that is committed using information or related technology. Cybercrime is different and more brutal than traditional / common crimes because crimes are committed electronically which makes it difficult to track and identify such type of cybercriminals. The most common type of cybercrime includes, data breach, cyber threat, identity theft, DDos attack etc. (Scarpitti et al., 2009) Within the realm of crime, there are several common theories that aim to explain why some people engage in illegitimate activity, while others avoid it. However, these theories were intended to explain the crimes committed in the 'real world', they are also applicable to cybercrime type of threat. These theories include differential association theory, community learning theory, low self-control theory, general strain theory, hypothesis of frustration anger, general work theory, crime prevention theory and rational choice theory. This chapter will consider the characteristics of the above ideas, to identify the most common causes of cybercrime.

Criminological Theories for the Prediction of Criminal Profiling Based on Traits

Edwin Sutherland's social learning theory is a conventional theory of crime and has been utilized to explain the various traits of criminal behaviors. This theory concretizes within it four fundamental premises that include differential association, definitions, differential reinforcement, and imitation (Burruss et al.,2012) (Agnew,1992).

A different relationship refers to people who have acquired the motives and skills for committing crimes by associating or being exposed to others who are already involved in crime (i.e., associating with a rebellious peer group). Different reinforcement means rewards associated with certain criminal behavior. These criminal behaviors are often learned through the process of imitation, which occurs when people learn actions and behaviors by observing and listening to others. Thus, when a person commits a crime, he imitates such acts and sees others participate in them (Agnew,1992). About cybercrime, research has found that social learning theory can explain the development and ongoing problem of software piracy related crime. (Hinduja and Kooi, 2013)In their software crime research, (Burruss et al.,2012), reported that people who engage in software crime, learn, and later adopt the wrong behavior. Software crime requires skill and knowledge to be achieved and a deviant group of people initially learn these skills from professionals. Another theory i.esocial control theory assumes that people can see the advantages of crime and are capable of inventing and executing all sorts of criminal acts on the spot—without special motivation or prior training. It assumes that the impulse to commit crime is resisted because of the costs associated with such behavior.

Even though social learning theory explains the importance of external factors influencing criminal involvement, the low self-control theory states that low self-control is an important factor in crime. The theory was developed primarily by forensic scientists Michael Gottfredson and Travis Hirschi. They have shown that their theory of self-control can explain all forms of crime, (Hinduja and Kooi, 2013) People with low self-control were characterized by risk, poor eyesight, impulsiveness and prefer simple and easy jobs. These factors limit a person's ability to accurately calculate the consequences of a crime. According to this principle, crime is viewed to an end, and the ability to curb such cravings is related to self-control. Therefore, those who are inclined to get involved in crime should lack adequate self-control. Also, a person with low self-control acts recklessly- without much thought and based on what they are doing. This puts them at risk as they do not consider the consequences of their actions. Finally, low-income people are self-centered and have no empathy for others (Burruss et al.,2012). According to Gottfredson and Hirschi, low self-esteem occurs at the beginning of social interactions when caregivers work effectively in their care. Thus, negligent parents and careless parents may fail to associate with their child to properly delay self-gratification, concern for the feelings of others, and control of their own desires. As a result, youths with low self-control tend to become more prone to crime, and their criminal tendencies persist in later life. Symptoms of low self-esteem can be applied to other simple forms of computer crime, including cyber bullying, hacking, posting obscene material etc.

General Strain theory (GST) is a part of the social structure theories of crime, which "fit the positivist mode in that they contend that social forces push or influence people to commit crime", social pushes include depression, failure to achieve good value goals (e.g., money), loss of valuable assets, and introduction of negative values (e.g., physical abuse) etc, such social forces lead to negative emotions and propel the person to engage in wrongful conduct.

According to (Agnew,1992), depression is not a major cause of crime but of negative emotions such as anger and frustration. This is directly related to the frustration-anger hypothesis developed by Yale University psychologists. They believed that anger comes before frustration, and frustration can be seen in both aggressive and non-violent behavior (Kevin, 2013). In addition, these negative feelings required responsive responses to alleviate internal stress. Dealing with distorted behavior and violence can be especially true for young people because of their limited resources and inability to escape from tragic places. In their article, (Patchin & Hinduja, 2011) they concluded that general strain theory could be used to explain illegal behavior such as cyberbullying among teens. Cyberbullying is an ongoing and growing phenomenon in which teens use electronic medium to harass or intimidate their peers in a deliberate attempt to harm or directly. There are some unique features in offline digital setting, such as: anonymity, endless communication, and permanent stay. This new technology allows victims to be attacked at any time and the anonymity of cyber bullies makes it difficult to spot them. (Agnew,1992) points out that depression causes people to feel angry, frustrated, depressed, and the pressure to act. In response to this pressure, victims respond by seeking to take corrective action to alleviate the bad feelings. Therefore, for some victims, cyberbullying is one of the most effective behavioral interventions for adolescents (Patchin & Hinduja, 2011) Together, the theory of common sense and the hypothesis of frustration anger, provides insight into how people, especially young people, respond and respond to negative stress, whether it be bullying or deviant behavior to reduce stress.

Routine Activity Theory was developed by Cohen and Felson to initially fill in the gaps in existing models that had failed to adequately address crime trends since the end of World War II. Cohen and Felson gave routine activity theory emphasized crime occurs when three elements converge: (i) a motivated offender, (ii) a suitable target, and (iii) the absence of a capable guardian (Bradford, 2013). A motivated criminal is a person who is determined to commit a crime when the opportunity arises. The appropriate target is the one indicated by the offender (e.g., credit card information). In addition, a competent caregiver covers anything that hinders the hijacker's ability to get targeted (e.g., anti-virus, encryption). With the increasing use of the internet, criminals have found new opportunities to make their victims in a new environment. Researchers have reported some support in applying theory of common occupational theory in computer crime research (Kevin, 2013). People whose jobs put them in a situation where they can deal with criminals are at greater risk of harassment. Studies have shown that time spent on the Internet, overuse of online banking and online shopping, and risky online behavior put people at greater risk for criminals. People with these actions are more likely to be targeted for identity theft. In addition, a lack of antivirus and network security are associated with increased vulnerability (Van Wilsem, 2011). Therefore, routine activity theory can be used, to some extent, to describe certain types of computer crimes.

Early detection of cybercrime and accurate prediction of attack development depends on the future actions available to the attackers, their intentions, and their motive — that is, the cybercriminal's "profile" that describes the criminal organization (men's rea) of the perpetrator. Typically, an "attacker profile" is a set of attacker qualities — both internal as motivations and skills, and externally as existing financial support and tools used. The description of the attacker profile allows us to determine the type of perpetrator and the complexity of the opposition ratings and may greatly simplify the attacker's annotation process when investigating security incidents. Cybercrime is increasing day by day; this chapter provides insight into cybercrime profiles from crime perspectives. There is a need for a technical approach to a theoretical way to detect cybercrime before it happens. A machine learning algorithm can be used in this area to predict online attacks based on a set of data and cybercrime and criminal features. If we try to understand the threat of cybercrime by combining technology with theory, such situations can be easily solved. By using multiple algorithms in machine learning, we can predict cyber-attacks. Some of those approaches have been reviewed in this chapter, which will assist law enforcement agencies in dealing with cyber incidents.

Dark Wcb Related Crime and their Prediction using Various Machine Learning Algorithm

Digitalization has contributed significantly in the rapid proliferation of several forms of cyberattacks as technology has advanced. As most people are concerned about web security, this has become a critical problem. They move online to comply with their demands. As the Internet has grown in the mid-to-late 1990s, it began to transform so many things on a worldwide scale. The most significant change arrived in the form of rapid communication As long as you have an Internet connection, You can chat to anyone. The major source of worry is that the Internet was not developed with aspects such as privacy and anonymity in mind. As a result, everything may be monitored or traceable. But Some individuals are particularly worried about their privacy, and one such group existed in the mid-1990s. The Federal Government of the United States was a group of persons. A group of mathematicians and computer scientists. Working for the Naval Research Laboratory (NRL), a branch of the US Navy, began development of a novel concept known as Onion Routing. It allows us to communicate anonymously in both directions when the source and destination cannot be discovered by a third party (Chertoff et al.,2017) Overlay Network is used to do this. A network that is established on top of another network is known as an overlay network. That is the situation in our instance. The network is the Internet. The traffic in this case is routed over an overlay network, as depicted in Fig.-1

A Darknet is defined as a network that uses the onion routing technology. The Dark Web emerged because of the convergence of all these distinct darknets. People at NRL eventually believed that for the network to be anonymous, it required to be accessible to everyone, not only the US Government. As a result, the NRL was obliged to open source its own Onion routing system, which is Now the Onion Router (TOR) (Ciancaglini, et al., 2013).

As depicted in Fig. 2, the World Wide Web (www) is divided into three sections: the Surface Web, the Deep Web, and the Dark Web. The Surface Web, often known as the visible or indexed web, is eas-

Figure 1. Overlay network

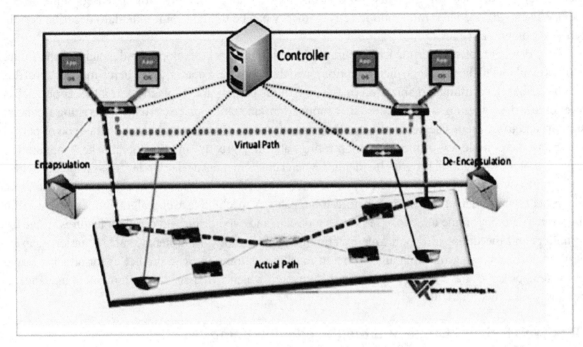

ily accessible to the public using regular web search engines. Surface online search engines provide just 0.03 percent of results.

The Deep Web (Mirea et al., 2019) is the inverse of the surface web in that it is inaccessible to the general public. It's also referred to as the Invisible or Hidden web. It is believed that the deep and dark web account for 96 percent of the Internet. It's usually used for keeping things private. Netflix, internet banking, web mail, dynamic websites and databases, and anything password or paywall protected are examples of deep web sites.

The Dark Web (Naseem et al., 2016) which also refers to World Wide Web material but is not a part of the surface web, is likewise inaccessible by browsers that are ordinarily used to access the surface web. It evolved with the help of the United States Military, who utilized it to connect with intelligence assets stationed afar without being identified. The dark web is the area of the internet where most of the illicit and unpleasant activity occurs. The Dark Web is also utilized as an unlawful platform for Terrorism, Hacking and Fraud Services, Phishing and Scams, Child Pornography, and other criminal activities. The Dark Web is a subset of the Deep Web. The Dark Web offers concealed services.

The Dark Web is the epicenter of criminal attacks (Van Hout & Bingham, 2013). because it provides anonymity and serves as a bridge to the world of crime. Some of the most notable crimes that have occurred in recent years are drug trafficking, human trafficking, informational leakage, child pornography, proxying, fraud, bit coin scam, arms trafficking, onion cloning, contract killer, torture and revenge porn. (Foltz, 2013) (Lacson & Jones, 2016)(Finklea et al., 2017)(da Cunhaet al., 2020)

The Dark Web may be used to perform a variety of cyberthreats. The most significant disadvantage of the Dark Web is its anonymity, which increases the attacker's confidence and makes it easier to assault the intended victim (Cambiasoet al., 2019) Some of the notable cyber threats are correlation attack, congestion attack, timing attack on TOR, traffic and timing attack, traffic fingerprinting attack,

Figure 2. Layers of internet

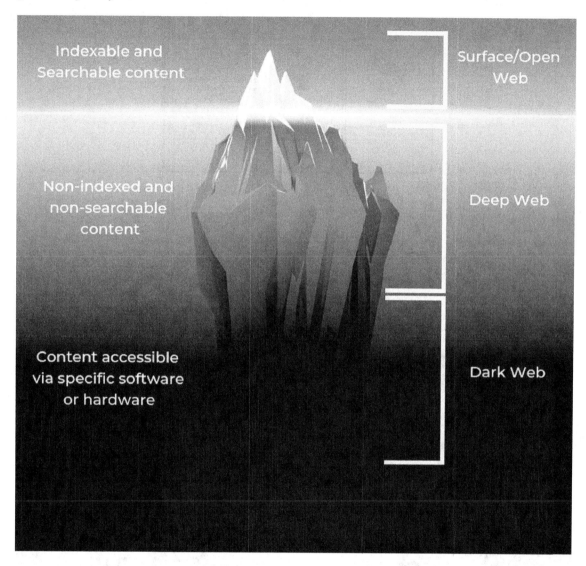

distributed denial of service attack, hidden service attack, phishing, man in middle attack, SQL injection attack, dark web and malware and credential misuse, etc.

The Dark Web offers secret services that are terminated with an onion extension. For example, Facebook provides a secret service. Duck Duck Go is another search engine example. To reach the Dark Web, you must use specialized browsers. The Onion Router (TOR), Free Net, Riffle, Invisible Internet Project (I2P), and Whonix have been some of the browsers designed to directly access the Dark Web. Because of the dark web's obscurity, it is an ideal setting for all types of severe unlawful activity, providing significant technological challenges for law enforcement organizations to investigate crimes committed on it. However, throughout the last decade, several investigations have been able to bring down unlawful networks that operate on the dark web.one such effort was conducted by (da Cunha et al., 2020) In their study they obtained the pedophile ring data directly from the dark web internet forum

Figure 3. Showing illegal cyber act on dark web (Balaji, N., 2020)

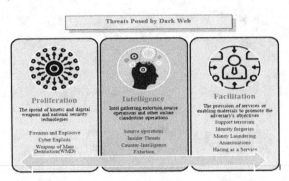

Figure 4. Cyber threats on dark web (Balaji, 2020)

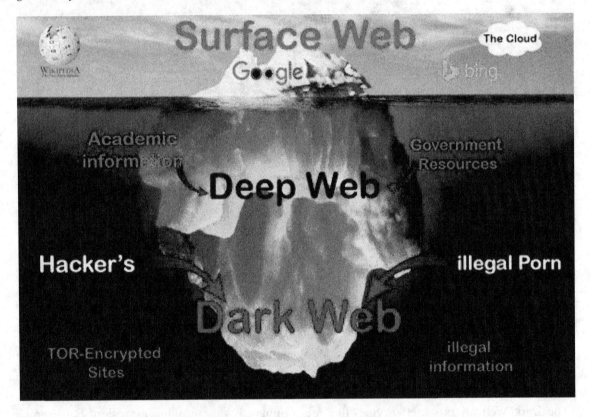

or message board investigated during Operation Darknet– i.e., an online discussion site where individuals could interact in the form of posted messages and files in conversations known as topics or threads. After that various mathematical calculation was used to track the offenders using their activity on dark web. (da Cunha et al., 2020)

Another technique to predict criminal behaviors is to slow down the Silk Road, where criminals engage in illegal activity. One such well-known move was carried out by North American authorities, who confiscated a significant internet black market responsible for the trade of illicit substances. (da Cunha et al., 2020)

RESULTS

Summary on theoretical background in some cyber-attack where characteristics features can be used as a data set to forecast the cyber criminals and suggested machine learning and artificial intelligence method which can be used for future prediction.

Cosmos Bank Cyber-attack

Hacking (Malware attack) under organized crime According to the report of UN security council the crime was committed by the North Korea people. Characteristics of cybercriminal:

- First, this crime was committed by group of members.
- Criminals in this case have a wide area network.
- They were specifically trained to the act.
- Criminals have a centralized authority as the they were the money mule- people who serve as intermediaries for criminals and criminal organizations — acting on behalf of operators abroad.
- Then data of bank users was sold on dark web to fulfill their malicious intention. (Sangvai,2020)

UIDAI Aadhaar Software Hacked

- The purpose of criminal in this case to sell the data of users and Gain Profit for finance.
- Data breaching is possible if person have been skilled to do so.
- It's a type of organized crime where data was first breached and then sold further to be misused. (Pali et al., 2020)

Canara Bank ATM Case

- Hackers used skimming devices to steal information and stolen amounts of up to 20 lakh rupees.
- Criminals had preplanned strategies for doing this act.
- They might be a localized technical person who has the knowledge about the location and vulnerably of the ATM. (Dhawan, 2019)

Justdial Data Breaching Case

- Criminal having the knowledge about the just dial website that it was running on unprotected application.
- In this case hackers can easily breach the details of users.

Unacademy, Big Basket and Haldi ram User Data Breach

- Offenders in this case hacked the high security website and breached around 11 million users' data and sold this data on dark web.
- The purpose of the offenders is to gain financial profit.
- They are highly skilled person. (Singh, 2021).

The Google Attack, 2020

- The attacker used several networks to spoof 167 Mpps (millions of packets per second) to 180,000 exposed CLDAP, DNS, and SMTP servers, which would then send large responses to us.
- This demonstrates the volumes a well-resourced attacker can achieve: This was four times larger than the record-breaking 623 Gbps attack from the Mirai botnet a year earlier.
- It shows that attackers are now highly skilled and have wide area network to do so.
- This type of activity is conduct by organized criminal
- They have well proper management and other hierarchical arrangement to perform such act. (Nicholson, 2021) (Yuchong & Qinghui, 2021)

Mobi Kwik Data Breach

- According to reports, the data breach affected 3.5 million customers, revealing know-your-customer records including addresses, phone numbers, Aadhaar cards, and PAN cards, among other things.
- Attackers might be used these data to sell on dark web and deep web.
- The whole purpose of attacker is to gain money.
- They to have a wide area network and perform such act in a preplanned manner.

Indian Bank Phishing Attack

- As per the findings of Bank's security department, the phishers have sent more than 1,00,000 emails to account holders of UTI Bank as well as other banks. "
- The attacker in this case was internal person
- Who is aware about the activity of the bank? And having the skilled knowledge about the same. (Singh, 2007) (Alkhalil et al., 2021)

Online Credit Card Fraud on E-Bay

- The modus operandi of the accused was to hack into the eBay India website and make purchases in the names of credit cardholders.
- The accused was a BCA student along with his friend.
- They are skilled and unsatisfied with their regular life.
- For gaining money and fulfilling their lavish need they did this crime. **(Krebs, 2015)**

Discussion

Table 1. Criminological theories and traits of criminal which can be used as a feature for their forecasting

Criminological theories	Traits
Self-control theory	1. poor eyesight, 2. impulsiveness, 3. prefer simple, 4. self-satisfaction and 5. easy jobs
Differential association theory	1. Motive, 2. skills, 3. revenge
Routine activity theory	1. Rationality, 2. motivated to commit crime, 3. suitable target and 4. the absence of capable guardians
General strain theory	1. Failure to achieve positively valued goals. 2. Removal of positive stimuli. 3. Introduction of negative stimuli.
Social learning theory	1. Interaction and cognition, 2. surrounding behavior, and 3. Peer environment

CONCLUSION

Predicting crimes before they occur is simple to understand, but it takes a lot more than understanding the concept to make it a reality. This chapter has written to assist researchers aiming to make crime prediction a reality and implement such advanced technology in real life. These new technologies have resulted in the emergence of a new sort of crime known as cybercrime. Criminal conduct can be described by both criminological theories and machine learning algorithm. In this chapter, efforts have been made to review criminological theory and machine learning methods that can be used by researchers and law enforcement to forecast cybercrime.

Table 2. For above mentioned cases here are some reported machine learning algorithm to track them

Cyber Crime	Data set	Machine learning algorithm and artificial intelligence technique	References
Data Breaches	**Not mentioned**	1. The framework semantically relates threats, 2. Deep Learning-Driven Cyber Threat Intelligence Modeling (deep feature extractor (DFE), CTI-driven detection (CTIDD) and CTI-attack type identification (CTIATI) 3. Random Forest Algorithm	**(Kumar, et al., 2021) (Noor et al.,2019) & (prathap, et al., 2021)**
Phishing	Phishing Websites Dataset by Mohammad, Rami et al	1. A recurrent neural network method 2. List-based approach 3. Visual similarity-based approach: Some methods use visual similarities by analyzing text content, text format, HTML, CSS, and images of web pages to identify phishing websites 4. Logistic regression, decision tree, random forest, Ada boost, SVM, KNN, neural networks, gradient boosting, and XGBoost 5.	**(Dutta et al.,2021) (Basit et al.,2020)**
DDOS attack	CICIDS 2017 benchmark dataset	1. multiple regression analysis 2. random forest algorithm 3. WEKA	**(Peneti & E, 2021) (Saini et al . 2020)**
Child pornography	binary labeled dataset (VIC International)	1. convolutional neural networks (CNN) 2. PhotoDNA Hash (PDNA) 3. term-frequency inverse-document-frequency (TF-IDF) 4. **Character-Based Quantization** 5. **Logistic Regression** 6. **Long Short-Term Memory network**	**(The internet watch foundation)**
Drug trafficking on dark web	databases of Google Scholar, IEEE Xplore, ScienceDirect, Springer, Scopus, and ACM Digital Library	1. random forest, 2. decision tree, and 3. support vector machine 4. Naive Bayes(NB), logistic regression (LOG-REG) algorithms	**(Li et al., 2019)**

Table 3. Summary of machine learning method reported for the detection of cybercrime and criminal

References	Type of cyber crime	Feature	Method	Advantage
(Tamir et al., 2021)	General crime at Chicago Police Department's CLEAR (Citizen Law Enforcement Analysis and Reporting) system	nature, location, time, description, and severity of the reported crime	Random forest, K-nearest neighbours (KNN), Adaptive Boost (AdaBoost), and artificial neural network (NN)	• An impressive accuracy of 90.77. • better performance in terms of precision, recall and F-1 scores • Methods can be used in large metropolitan cities to determine which police calls need imminent attention and manage their resources accordingly. • It would also help them plan which areas of the city would require more police involvement in the future.
(Arora et al., 2019)	Cybercrime on social media for ex. Hate speech	Synonyms, Age, Location, Gender, Hashtags, and Sarcasm	RF	• Detecting cyber threats automatically
(Ghasem et al., 2015)	phishing, spamming, cyberbullying and cyberstalking	write prints, behaviors, unique vocabularies, and related email header information of an email	Anti-Cyberstalking Email System (ACES), **Informative Feature Selection (IFS)**	novel robust feature selection approach to select informative features, aiming to improve the performance
(Bilen and Ozer et al.,2021)	All type of cyber crime	age, gender, income, occupation, harm, and attack methods	The Support Vector Machine Linear for type of attack The Logistic Regression for attacker prediction	• One of the key advantages of this study is using actual data and it is a preliminary step towards profiling for people having similar features with the attacked victims. • Another advantage of the this is predicting what the cyber-attack method will be and whether its perpetrator can be detected. • Their results show that any exposure to cyber-crimes reduces as the level of education and income increases.
(Fachkha, 2013)	Distributed Denial of Service (DDoS) Attack	intensity/rate (packets/ sec) and size (estimated number of used compromised machines/bots).	moving average, weighted moving average, exponential smoothing, and linear regression	• better understanding of the scale and speed of DDoS attacks.

REFERENCES

Agnew, R. (1992). Foundation for a General Strain Theory of Crime and Delinquency. *Criminology*, *30*(1), 47–88. doi:10.1111/j.1745-9125.1992.tb01093.x

Alkhalil, Z., Hewage, C., Nawaf, L., & Khan, I. (2021). Phishing Attacks: A Recent Comprehensive Study and a New Anatomy. *Frontiers of Computer Science*, *3*, 563060. Advance online publication. doi:10.3389/fcomp.2021.563060

Arora, T., Sharma, M., & Khatri, S. K. (2019). Detection of Cyber Crime on social media using Random Forest Algorithm. *2019 2nd International Conference on Power Energy, Environment, and Intelligent Control (PEEIC),* 47-51.

Balaji, N. (2020) *How To Access Dark Web Anonymously and know its Secretive and Mysterious Activities.* GB Hackers on Security. https://gbhackers.com/how-to-access-deep-anonymous-web-and-know-its-secretive-and-mysterious-activities/)

Basit, A., Zafar, M., Liu, X., Javed, A. R., Jalil, Z., & Kifayat, K. (2020). A comprehensive survey of AI-enabled phishing attacks detection techniques. *Telecommunication Systems.* Advance online publication. doi:10.100711235-020-00733-2 PMID:33110340

Bilen, A., & Özer, A. B. (2021). Cyber-attack method and perpetrator prediction using machine learning algorithms. *PeerJ. Computer Science, 7,* e475. doi:10.7717/peerj-cs.475 PMID:33954249

Bradford, W. R. (2013). Online routines and identity theft victimization: Further explaining routine activity theory beyond direct-control offenses. *Journal of Research in Crime and Delinquency, 50*(2), 216–238. doi:10.1177/0022427811425539

Burruss, G. W., Bossler, A. M., & Holt, T. J. (2012). Assessing the Mediation of a Fuller Social Learning Model on Low Self-Control's Influence on Software Piracy. *Crime and Delinquency, 59*(8), 1157–1184. doi:10.1177/0011128712437915

Cambiaso, E., Vaccari, I., Patti, L., & Aiello, M. (2019). *Darknet Security: A Categorization of Attacks to the Tor Network.* ITASEC.

Chertoff, M. (2017). A public policy perspective of the Dark Web. *Journal of Cyber Policy, 2*(1), 26–38. doi:10.1080/23738871.2017.1298643

Ciancaglini, V., Balduzzi, M., Goncharov, V., & McArdle, R. **(2013).** Deep web and Cybercrime It's Not All About TOR. *Trend Micro,* 2-21.

da Cunha, B. R., MacCarron, P., Passold, J. F., dos Santos, L. W. Jr, Oliveira, K. A., & Gleeson, J. P. (2020). Assessing police topological efficiency in a major sting operation on the dark web. *Scientific Reports, 10*(1), 73. Advance online publication. doi:10.103841598-019-56704-4 PMID:31919365

Dhawan, S. (2019). *Canara bank ATM fraud: Here is the bank's reply and new safety features to keep your money safe.* The Financial Express. Retrieved February 17, 2022, from https://www.financialexpress.com/money/canara-bank-atm-fraud-here-is-the-banks-reply-and-new-safety-features-to-keep-your-money-safe/1686396/

Dutta, A. K. (2021). Detecting phishing websites using Machine Learning Technique. *PLoS One, 16*(10), e0258361. Advance online publication. doi:10.1371/journal.pone.0258361 PMID:34634081

Fachkha, C., Bou-Harb, E., & Debbabi, M. (2013). Towards a forecasting model for distributed denial of service activities. *2013 IEEE 12th International Symposium on Network Computing and Applications,* 110–117. 10.1109/NCA.2013.13

Finklea, K. (2017). *Dark Web, CRS report.* Legal Reference Services.

Foltz, R. (2013). Silk road and migration. Encyclopedia of global human migration. doi:10.1002/9781444351071.wbeghm484

Ghasem, Z., Frommholz, I., & Maple, C. (2015). *Machine Learning Solutions for controlling Cyberbullying and Cyberstalking*. Academic Press.

Hinduja, S., & Kooi, B. (2013). Curtailing cyber and information security vulnerabilities through situational crime prevention. *Security Journal*, *26*(4), 383–402. doi:10.1057j.2013.25

Kevin, R. C. (2013). Toward a conceptual model of motive and self-control in cyber-aggression: Rage, reward and recreation. *Journal of Youth and Adolescence*, *42*(5), 751–771. doi:10.100710964-013-9936-2 PMID:23526207

Krebs, B. (2015). How scammers use eBay as a personal ATM. *The Sydney Morning Herald*. https://www.smh.com.au/technology/how-scammers-use-ebay-as-a-personal-atm-20151104-gkq3aq.html

Kumar, P., Gupta, G. P., Tripathi, R., Garg, S., & Hassan, M. M. (2021). DLTIF: Deep Learning-Driven Cyber Threat Intelligence Modeling and Identification Framework in IoT-Enabled Maritime Transportation Systems. *IEEE Transactions on Intelligent Transportation Systems*, 1–10. doi:10.1109/TITS.2021.3122368

Lacson, W., & Jones, B. (2016). The 21st century Dark Net market: Lessons from the fall of silk road. *International Journal of Cyber Criminology*, *10*(1), 40–61.

Li, J., Xu, Q., Shah, N., & Mackey, T. K. (2019). A Machine Learning Approach for the Detection and Characterization of Illicit Drug Dealers on Instagram: Model Evaluation Study. *Journal of Medical Internet Research*, *21*(6), e13803. doi:10.2196/13803 PMID:31199298

Mirea, M., Wang, V., & Jung, J. (2019). The not so dark side of the darknet: A qualitative study. *Security Journal*, *32*(2), 102–118. doi:10.105741284-018-0150-5

Naseem, I., Kashyap, A. K., & Mandloi, D. (2016). Exploring anonymous depths of invisible web and the digi underworld. *International Journal of Computer Applications, NCC*, (3), 21–25.

Nicholson, P. (2021, December 9). *Five Most Famous DDoS Attacks and Then Some*. A10 Networks. https://www.a10networks.com/blog/5-most-famous-ddos-attacks/

Noor, U., Anwar, Z., Malik, A. W., Khan, S., & Saleem, S. (2019). A machine learning framework for investigating data breaches based on semantic analysis of adversary's attack patterns in threat intelligence repositories. *Future Generation Computer Systems*, *95*, 467–487. doi:10.1016/j.future.2019.01.022

Pali, I., Krishania, L., Chadha, D., Kandar, A., Varshney, G., & Shukla, S. (2020). *A Comprehensive Survey of Aadhar & Security Issues*. arXiv, 1–12.

Patchin, J. W., & Hinduja, S. (2011). Traditional and non-traditional bullying among youth: A test of general strain theory. *Youth & Society*, *43*(2), 727–751. doi:10.1177/0044118X10366951

Peneti, S., & E, H. (2021). DDOS Attack Identification using Machine Learning Techniques. *2021 International Conference on Computer Communication and Informatics (ICCCI)*, 1-5.

Prathap, M. R., Nandhini, K. M., Vairavel, K. S., & Suraj, M. V. (2021). Detection of Data Breaching Websites using Machine Learning. *2021 International Conference on Advancements in Electrical, Electronics, Communication, Computing and Automation (ICAECA)*, 1-6. 10.1109/ICAECA52838.2021.9675712

Saini, P., Behal, S., & Bhatia, S. (2020). Detection of DDoS Attacks using Machine Learning Algorithms. *The Internet Watch Foundation - Eliminating Child Sexual Abuse Online.*

Sangvai, R. (2020). Responding to Cyber Attack on ATM and SWIFT Payment Gateway by Cosmos Cooperative Bank Pune A Change Management Exercise. *MuktShabd Journal, 9*(7), 633–640.

Scarpitti, F. R., Nielsen, A. L., & Miller, J. M. (2009). A Sociological Theory of Criminal Behavior. In Crime and Criminals Contemporary and Classic Readings in Criminology (2nd ed.). New York: Oxford University Press.

Singh, N. (2007). Online banking Fraud Using Phishing. *Journal of Internet Banking and Commerce, 12*, 1–27.

Singh, S. (2021). 10 Biggest Cyber Attacks on Indian Companies. *The420CyberNews.* https://www.the420.in/10-major-cyber-attacks-on-indian-companies-that-are-eye-openers-check-the-full-list-here/

Tamir, A., Watson, E., Willett, B., Hasan, Q., & Yuan, J.-S. (2021). Crime Prediction and Forecasting using Machine Learning Algorithms. *International Journal of Computer Science and Information Technologies, 12*(2), 26–33.

Van Hout, M. C., & Bingham, T. (2013). 'Silk Road', the virtual drug marketplace: A single case study of user experiences. *The International Journal on Drug Policy, 24*(5), 385–391.

Van Wilsem, J. (2011). Worlds tied together. Online and non-domestic routine activities and their impact on digital and traditional threat victimization. *European Journal of Criminology, 8*(2), 115–127.

Yuchong, L., &Qinghui, L. (2021). A comprehensive review study of cyber-attacks and cyber security; Emerging trends and recent developments. *Energy Reports, 7*, 8176-8186. https://doi.org/10.1016/j.egyr.2021.08.126

Chapter 16
Dark Web for the Spread of Illegal Activities Using Tor

Vinod Mahor
iD https://orcid.org/0000-0002-2187-6920
IES College of Technology, Bhopal, India

Sadhna Bijrothiya
iD https://orcid.org/0000-0002-8913-7753
Maulana Azad National Institute of Technology, Bhopal, India

Rakesh Kumar Bhujade
Government Polytechnic, Daman, India

Jasvant Mandloi
Government Polytechnic, Daman, India

Harshita Mandloi
Shri Vaishnav Vidyapeeth Vishwavidyalaya, India

Stuti Asthana
UT Administration of Dadra and Nagar Haveli and Daman and Diu, India

ABSTRACT

The dark web has been in existence since about the emergence of the internet. There is still a wealth of material indexed on the web that is freely available to anyone with internet connection, regardless of region. There is even more information and data that is concealed and needs specific rights to access. Tor is well-known and extensively used anonymity software that is built on the Tor network and provides secrecy over the vulnerable web. The personal data defense is generally beneficial. This chapter provides a brief summary of established methods to gain access to this section of the web as well as examples of its talents being abused.

DOI: 10.4018/978-1-6684-3942-5.ch016

INTRODUCTION

Every webpages s and services that a common internet browser has collected are included in the Internet, which is utilized on a regular basis by both private operators and commercial enterprises and organizations. The incoming and outgoing connections connect these sites and portals to one another. Indexing robots crawler these pages utilizing links that lead to them as well as connections to other webpages from their pages (Amika, 2016).

These pages should be static, placed on servers, and include visible HTML code. Every time you make a modification to the web portal or a page, new material is uploaded to the server. As a result, the entire process is transparent and open to the public. The DNS Domain Name System) database, which links hostnames to IP addresses, is another component of the Internet.

DNS servers are used to offer transparency, regulate information flow, and protect users from spam and unwanted material. Increased control and monitoring of Internet users in terms of information and material they generate, as well as portals they visit, has led in the emergence of a unique version of the Web with a higher degree of privacy.

Many people are aware that anything printed on the Internet may be seen in some form or another indefinitely. As a result, even the ordinary user comes to the conclusion that the self-appointed black Web, or deep Web, should be used for at least some of their operations. The "dark-web"is a worldwide network that requires special technology to reach, setup, or authorization, and which frequently uses network technologies, end points that aren't main stream.

(Arslani, M. 2015) The html code for "dark-web" pages is produced dynamically depends on consequences of material acquired from their own databases, unlike the indexed area of the Internet, which has static sites "visible Internet". This way of constructing an independent web site prevents indexing robots from crawling the site. This is precisely one of the reasons why the general Internet browser does not index these pages (Goodman, 2015). On the other hand, black web a sites have a lot of content that is utilised for everyday publication and publicity distribution (Abbasi & Chen; 2005). Textual files, both steady and transient, and file systems, and different types of mixture can be found in these forums. The collection of such a wide range of content kinds poses a number of distinct issues not found when spearing index able files. A "dark-web"forum crawler, on the other hand, must weigh the pros and cons of various collection-update tactics. As a result, harmful users have leveraged the concept of high anonymity in communication and work to address a variety of illicit operations, ranging from rental services to "drug trafficking and firearms to human trafficking".

The following is a breakdown of the paper's structure. The second section explains the theoretic underpinning of the dark-web, as well as alternative access methods and parallels and contrasts with the visible Internet. From the user's perspective, the third section shows how to use "dark-web"services. Also shown are instances of various unlawful behaviors that may be discovered by scanning the dark web. The study's main results are discussed in the fourth section. The last portion includes a reference list that was sometimes used collect data about the "dark-web"and illegal activities on it (BBC. 2014).

DARK-WEB AND DEEP WEB

In reference to without indexed portions of the Web, the terms black web and deep web are often used interchangeably in the publications and in everyday speech: dark and deep web. The phrase "dark-web"

Figure 1. Model of webs

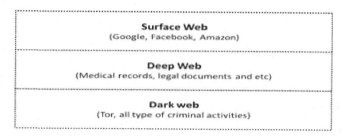

refers to anything that Google and other public Internet browsers do not index and hence cannot return as a search result. These might be little things like forum comments that are only visible to listed users, private YouTube content that may only be accessed through a forwarded link or "Facebook posts" that are only viewable to friends. Research journals, as well as a range of other similar goods, need a membership fee to see. (BBC. 2015).

In the deep-web, there is a subset known as the dark-web, which is used to advertise or disseminate illegal behaviour. Websites that facilitate criminal activity are typically concealed behind them. The onion route is a search engine browser for criminal and other activities (Cekerevac, Z., Dvorak, Z., & Cekerevac, P. 2016).). Because the "dark-web" is virtually fully anonymous, it is used by groups who want to stay concealed from government institutions and law enforcement authorities. Money transactions are conducted using a specifically constructed digital currency called Bitcoin to further secure users of such networks. The institution that administers payments, bitcoin transfers, and their change to traditional currency drifts supports the creation and encryption of the currency.

One method of gaining access to the "dark-web" is via the utilization of the Tor "The Onion Router" network, which was built with the primary intention of functioning as a gateway to this portion of the Internet. Tor spreads signals over almost 6,000 servers in order to mask the user's IP address. Tor is free software (Ciancaglini, V., Balduzzi, M., McArdle, R., & Rosler, M. 2015). As seen in Figure 1, the client application progressively assembles a link b/w the source and destination of data packets that is formed of encrypted connections b/w randomly selected server nodes in order to build a secret and secure connection inside the Tor network.

This relationship develops in stages, with each server simply being aware of which servers packets have been delivered from and whether the domain will be used to route them to. This is accomplished by encrypting each step by a unique key. Once the link is established, many software programmes may be used to send various sorts of data (Romil Rawat, Anand Singh Rajawat, Vinod Mahor, Rabindra Nath Shaw, and Ankush Ghosh 2021).

Apart from Tor-a, which is used to exchange files in most circumstances, the IIP ("Invisible Internet Project") system Level is utilised to offer unidentified message b/w applications.

Its level is capable of supporting a wide range of protocols and applications. A specific encryption is used to safeguard every recognized connection b/w two or more users, by studying network flow data and comparing the featurs and security afforded by "Tor browser" and IIP, it was discovered that IIP is extra resilient to attacks (Romil Rawat, Vinod Mahor, Sachin Chirgaiya, Rabindra Nath Shaw, and Ankush Ghosh 2021).

Freenet is a similar technology that is straightforward and more than accessible to the general public. The programme establishes a connection in the background while the user accesses it through the browser. On the network, the user can select the level of security. P2P is used for all communication and file sharing, and each time a connection is established, a new route is formed. As a result, every revisiting of pages takes longer than in the other above-mentioned industries and machineries.

The facts that around 3.2Lakh German's use some type of "dark-web" net prove the service's attractiveness, according to the police. According to the data, more than three million people throughout the world access the dark web's material. When compared to the visible online, the quantity of material saved on the "dark-web" is forty times bigger, totaling around 750 terabytes. The majority of the material is maintained in specialised databases, which are the property of organization's and people (Cook, J. 2014). According to this, the visible portion of the web accounts for around 4% of the total, with the other 96% belonging to the dark-web.

OTHER WORK "DARK-WEB" SERVICES MIGHT BE USED

Other forms of terroristic actions on the Internet have been discovered via various sorts of study. These are propaganda, recruitment and training ("encouraging people to join the Jihad or other terrorist organisations, and receiving online training"), fundraising ("transferring funds, conducting credit card fraud, and other money laundering activities"), communications ("disseminating instruction, resources, and support via email, digital photographs, and chat sessions"), and targeting ("conducting online surveillance and identifying vulnerable individuals"). Aside from these categories, "dark-web" service stations are used for a variety of additional crimes (Europol. 2014, Falconer, J. 2012). The following paragraphs explain some of the instances gathered from various sources.

Silk Road, a gateway for drug and other illicit commodities trafficking, is one of the instances of "dark-web" utilization revealed by fit anti-drug organizations. Ross Ulbrich, a 28-year-old programmer who went by the moniker Dread Pirate Roberts, was the company's creator and proprietor. On his laptop, there was a lot of proof. From 2011 to 2013, he built a dollar 1.2 billion business solely via the use of a laptop and the Internet. Ulbricht was found guilty on all 7 counting, containing one accusation of currency valeting, narcotics trafficking, and computer hacking, after only three weeks on trial. we were identified after the authorities obtained a message from 2010 in which he was recommending interested individuals to the Silk Road, signed a different identity "altoid", and requested professionals in the bitcoin community to be the top developers, as well as giving the address for communication (Goodman, M. (2015). It' site functioned in the same way as any other online shopping platform. Postal firms delivered the ordered products. For terms of enhancing services to clients, we must first understand their needs; postal corporations do not inspect the contents of shipments, creation this procedure of sending a particularly convenient option for illicit commerce. If competent authorities determine that it is frequently utilised for these sorts of deliveries, the postal firm may face complications (Knibbs, K. 2014, Lukovic, M. 2014).

Ulbricht was arrested a month after this day and closure of the site, the doorway resurfaced on Current version of the dark-web has been released, demonstrating the tenacity of those who deal with such crimes. The site swiftly grew in popularity, with an average of 1.5 lakh users per month besides once-a-month revenue of roughly $8.2 million as per FBI estimates, proceeds from the selling of goods and services. The labour site was shut down after a year, and the administrator, Blake Bent-hall, was jailed. That barely continued an hour before the portal was restarted and continued to function, Next time around, it's in edition 3.0. This data indicates the dark-web's robustness and the resilience of its gateways (Mergen, L. 2015).

The "Silk Road" had a companion location, The Arsenal, until 2012, that specialized in the selling of weapons, dull and shrill objects for harming and slaughter. After a length of time, the same facility was shut down owing to low attendance. Weapons and ammunition are sold in a alike fashion on other websites, particular of which agreement delivery throughout the world under the slogan "We deliver internationally, since everyone has the right to self-defense" (Mitrovic, M. 2016). Everything from fire-arms to C4 explosives may be discovered. Toys; several additional gadgets, and Home equipment are typically placed in particular containers in order to pass through x-ray inspection.

Distribution of pornographic material in the field of photography is prohibited. In the United Kingdom, a similar campaign was launched. 650 persons were arrested in this action for various sorts of youngster misuse, ranging since the custody of child porno-graphic photos to pan-daring (Mitrovic, M. 2016). In Northern Ireland, 37 persons were detained in 2015 on suspicion of pedophilia and the dissemination of teenager pornography via the onion route.

Around are cases that suggest the "dark-web" is an ideal location for cybercrime. Users may purchase a wide range of viruses on this site. Simultaneously, website users may become victims of numerous forms of malware spread via phishing. Vawtrak, a banking Trojan spread by e-mail, is one such piece of malware (N1. 2015). The Crypto Locker malwares are another significant category of Trojan that can be discovered on the dark web. After accessing the victim's data, the virus encrypts them. After "encrypt-ing files, the victim is sent to a page where they are requested to pay a fee in order to restore control of their information". Payment requests and information needed to complete businesses are frequently written in the victim's local philological. Tor's purpose in these transactions is to host payment sites so that bitcoin transactions may be completed (PC. 2015, Sancho, D. 2015).

Aside from viruses, interested parties may pay "hackers" to carry out different forms of "hacker" assaults on their behalf on the dark-web. Rates range from a few hundred dollars to several thousand dollars, depending on the task's complexity and danger. Hackers offer a variety of services, ranging from school assessment rectification to the theft of access codes for different functions and key authoritative data. The Chinese organization Hidden Lynx claims to have hundreds of competent "cyber" thieves who got into "Google", "Adobe", and "Lockheed Martin's computer systems.

Professional assassin services are available for those with more malevolent motives and a real readi-ness to go down in the dark world of the dark web. One of the scenarios given in is of a person with moral and "extremely flexible business ethics", who is an allegedly "verified mercenary with eight-year experience" who provides services that are only remunerated upfront in Bitcoins. Only exchanging information on the victim is permitted during communication with such individuals. All interactions, as well as any email correspondence, are required to be encrypted. It will be erased if any part of the message is not encrypted (Spalevic, Z., Ilic, M., & Palevic, M. 2016).

Lovecraft is another website that provides similar services. According to the advertisement, the or-ganization's members are former Foreign Legion troops and mercenaries. "The greatest location to keep your issue is grave," says the organization's motto. The security and privacy of client communications are of utmost importance to this portal. Identification information such as the recipient's name, home and work addresses, as many photographs and details as possible about whom the victim is, as well as the licence plate, description, and photograph of the vehicle used are all required. Service fees range between $ 3,000 to $ 180,000, depending on the victim's common choice and socioeconomic background. When asked how long it takes to prepare for a job and go to a target, a team of assassins replies that it takes around two months, depending on the agreement. They also add that the cost of airline tickets, weapons, and housing is not included in the initial charge. There are various means of murder available on Cthulhu's website, varying from the conventional to torture and abuse to bombings. It goes without saying that the cost of killing a commoner differs from that of killing a public figure, political figure, or member of law enforcement.

There have been several instances when children have been utilised to make money. Europol detained 184 people in 2011 in collaboration with thirteen other nations. Counterfeit money may be purchased on the dark web. A guarantee is nearly always offered in addition to the money, as well as a description of the manufacturing process demonstrating that, as the vendors claim, counterfeit money is manufactured in the same way as real money. All counterfeit currencies are accessible, however the quality and number varies. In these kinds of deals, a 600 US dollar may get you a 2,500 counterfeit, and a 500 euro can get you a 2,000 counterfeit. All transactions are made with the understanding that they would be subjected to routine inspections, including ultraviolet light (Todorovic, A. 2015). Of course, Bitcoin is used to pay for counterfeit money in numerous circumstances.

It is possible to get data on a variety of identities, credit card numbers, bank account numbers, and even information on online auctions. You may buy data on many other people's credit cards, addresses, and other private data through Transatlantic Carding, which operates on the so-called "dark web". The cost varies from $7 to $90. The price determines the quality of information. Accounts, on the other hand, are sold in one of two ways. The first way is purchasing a single account and providing complete information on the account's balance. Another option is to buy a huge number of accounts, of which only a small percentage are likely to be legitimate. Because the consumer has visibility into the quantity of cash in the account, the first option is significantly more cost-effective, as it provides a greater guarantee that the monies invested will be repaid, as well as the extra money made. There is also the option of purchasing real debit and credit cards from various banks (Vijesti. 2015).

On the "dark-web", there are several sites purporting to sell passports and identification documents. The cost of these services is determined by both the country in which the papers are generated and the vendor. It's tough to check the legitimacy of these documents, "especially when it comes to citizenship". These facilities can also be used to defraud immigrants who are desperate to get citizenship in the nation where they are currently residing. The cost of passports, driver's licences, and identification cards in Australia, for example, is 800 euros on the Fake ID website. The most costly paperwork is for the United States, while the cheapest is for Malaysia (Zetter, K. 2013, Vijesti. 2015).

In adding to the aforementioned, the "dark-web" is home to some of the most strange activities, such as human organ trafficking. According to some sources, a kidney "costs $ 200,000, a heart costs $120,000, a liver costs $150,000, and a pair of eyes costs $1500". Additionally, a variety of beauty items made from human flesh and skin are available for purchase (N1, 2015; Falconer, 2012, Vinod Mahor, Romil Rawat, Anil Kumar, Mukesh Chouhan 2021). In addition, a wide range of themes that cater to diverse fetishes may be found. Horrifying images of passengers' last words and conversations on a crashed plane, convicts on the day of death ("for example, the electric chair in a Texas prison"), or pornographic films in which ladies crush tiny creatures with heels are among the contents. Furthermore, there are various proposals in which people give themself up as food or participate in other types of homicide. On the dark web, there is a well-known site known as Red Room, where victims are subjected to violence and executions, which are recorded in real time ().

Extremists too use the Internet to spread ideologies that give religious justifications for their crimes. The "Internet has established a "physical tie b/w individuals and a virtual religious community", according to a survey of 172 participants engaging in the worldwide Salafi Jihad. The Internet appeals to lonely people by allowing them to interact with those who have something in common with them. Terrorists benefit from such a virtual society in a variety of ways. It no longer has any links to any country, emphasising the importance of battling the far opponent (e.g., the United States) above the close opponent. Furthermost "potential Jihad recruits who are not Islamic scholars are drawn to internet chat groups because they support radical, abstract", yet basic answers. Terrorists' identities are also protected by the anonymity of Internet cafés. The Internet, on the other hand, cannot directly touch Jihad since Jihad dedication requires a long duration of "face-to-face" connection (Anand Singh Rajawat, Romil Rawat, Vinod Mahor, Rabindra Nath Shaw, and Ankush Ghosh. 2021).

Furthermore, most previous research on terrorists' use of the Internet involve a manual technique to examine large amounts of data. Such a strategy does not "scale well with the rapid expansion of the Internet and the frequent change of terrorists" online individualities. The US Government designated Alneda.com as a terrorist web site that named itself the "Center for Islamic Studies and Research" and gave material to "Al Qaeda" (Mitrovic, M. 2016).

Terrorists utilise the Internet to share motivational tales and operational specifics with one another in order to build terrorist organisations. They provide analysis and comments on current events on their websites, which are accessible to the media and non-members alike. Among the calls for Muslims to fly to Pakistan and Afghanistan was one from Azzam.com, which referred to them as "Jewish-backed American Crusaders." Another website, Qassam.net, solicited donations for the purpose of purchasing AK-47 assault rifles. Web portals on the Dark Web are protected in a number of ways, depending on their purpose. One of the most efficient approaches is to observe the behaviour of visitors who do not adhere to the established routine. The first thing administrators do when they see strange visitor behaviour is to launch a basic inquiry. If a visitor can only see the current row in the text and not the preceding rows, they are being monitored, according to the message (Sancho, D. 2015, Vijesti. 2015).

Next, on the visitor's computer, a programme called a key logger is installed, which will record every keystroke the visitor makes. The advantage of this technique is that administrators may keep total control over all visitor activity until they have determined who the visitors are and what they are trying to accomplish.

THE ONION ROUTE (ToR)

With the goal of providing users with anonymity while using the Internet, TOR is an open-source software project that has grown into one of the most extensively used anonymous networks in the world. Specifically, this is performed by encrypting the original message many times in order to conceal the user's identity and protect their privacy (Romil Rawat, Bhagwati Garg, Vinod Mahor, Shrikant Telang, Kiran Pachlasiya, and Mukesh Chouhan. (2021). TLS is one of the most widely used security protocols across a wide range of networking settings, including the TOR network, and is one of the most secure. Specifically, it is implemented at the transport level of the TCP/IP networking paradigm. In conventional TLS, the AES encryption technique is employed to preserve confidentiality, while Diffie-Hellman is used to establish and exchange keys (Romil Rawat, Anil Kumar, Mukesh Chouhan, SHRIKANT TELANG, Kiran Pachlasiya, Bhagwati Garg, and Vinod Mahor 2021).

As a result of these security measures, "it is not feasible for an analyst to monitor and extract the features of TOR traffic using traffic analysis tools in order to identify the activities of TOR users. Out of 4.39 billion internet users globally, the total number of directly connected TOR clients every day is expected to be roughly 2.06 million", according to a statistic developed by the TOR project (Vinod Mahor, Sachin Chirgaiya, and Bhagwati Garg. 2021).

CONLUSION

The Internet is universally acknowledged as a resource for finding information about everything and everyone. Anyone who has ever used an Internet service, input data, or registered an account is recorded in one of the databases. Aside from the data provided by a variety of services, large-scale trading of various sorts of items is conducted on a regular basis, even across nations on opposite sides of the globe. When you consider that the visible section of the Internet only makes up 4% of what's there, a high amount of contacts, information, and transactions may appear little in compared to what's in the deep web. In this chapter, aspect makes it difficult for ordinary people to gain access to services that exist outside the visible realm. The fact that the "dark-web" is not indexed is exploited by various illicit products sellers for profit. It is frequently used by numerous terrorist organizations, in addition to monetary motives, to promote philosophy and announcement, as well as to engage in "arms and human trafficking". Apart from terrorist groups, the "dark-web" is used by a vast number of individuals for other forms of trafficking and illicit operations. Some of the instances of use detailed in the book surely "lead to the conclusion that" there is still a lot of untapped and hidden territory on the Internet.

REFERENCES

Amika. (2016). *Deep web – hidden underworld of the Internet.* b92 Blog. Retrieved October 20, 2016, from http://blog.b92.net/text/26912/DEEP-WEB-%E2%80%93- skriveno-podzemlje-Interneta/

Arslani, M. (2015). *Dark internet: Underworld, which offers everything from guns to organs.* Express. Retrieved November 11, 2016, from http://www.express.hr/tehno/mracni-internet-kriminalno-podzemlje-koje-nudi-sve-od-oruzja-do-organa-635

BBC. (2014). *Child abuse image investigation leads to 660 arrests.* BBC News. Retrieved September 19, 2016, from www.bbc.com/news/uk-28326128

BBC. (2015). *50 arrests in NI online abuse images probe in past year, say police.* BBC News. Retrieved October 20, 2016, from www.bbc.com/news/uk-northernireland-31896685

Cekerevac, Z., Dvorak, Z., & Cekerevac, P. (2016). Is the "dark web" deep and dark? *FBIM Transactions,* 1-12.

Ciancaglini, V., Balduzzi, M., McArdle, R., & Rosler, M. (2015). *Below the Surface: Exploring the Deep Web.* Trend Micro.

Cook, J. (2014). FBI Arrests Former SpaceX Employee, Alleging He Ran The 'Deep Web' Drug Marketplace Silk Road 2.0. *Business Insider.* Retrieved October 15, 2016, from www.businessinsider.com/fbi-silk-road-seizedarrests-2014-11

Europol. (2014). *Operation Rescue*. Europol. Retrieved September 19, 2016, from www. europol.europa. eu/content/operation-rescue

Falconer, J. (2012). *Mail-order drugs, hitmen & child porn: A journey into the dark corners of the deep web*. Insider. Retrieved October 30, 2016, from http://thenextweb.com/ insider/2012/10/08/mail-order-drugs-hitmen-child-porn-a-journey-into-the-dark corners-of-the-deep-web/

Goodman, M. (2015). Most of the web is invisible to Google. Kere's what it contains. *Popular Science*. Retrieved November, 18, 2016, from https://www.popsci.com/dark web-revealed.

Knibbs, K. (2014). *Silk Road 3 Is Already Up, But It's Not the Future of Darknet Drugs*. Gizmodo. Retrieved October 15, 2016, from https://gizmodo.com/silk-road-3-isalready-up-butits-not-the-future-of-da-1655512490

Lukovic, M. (2014). *Deep internet - Drugs, murders, pornography - what is hidden in the black hole web?* Before After. Retrieved September 18, 2016, from http://www. beforeafter.rs/tehnologija/deep-internet/

Mergen, L. (2015). *On anonymous networking in Haskell: announcing Tor and IIP for Haskell*. Luctor et Emergen. Retrieved October, 3, 2016, from: http://www. leonmergen.com/haskell/privacy/2015/05/30/on-anonymous-networking-in haskellannouncing-tor-and-IIP-for-haskell.html

Mitrovic, M. (2016). *Dark secrets of global network*. New Energy (Nova Energija). Retrieved November 01, 2016, from http://www.novaenergija.net/

2015). *Darknet - the dark side of internet surfing. N1 SCI-TECH portal Zagreb*. Retrieved September 18, 2016, from http://rs.n1info.com/a50647/Sci-Tech/Sve-o Deep-Web-ili-Darknetu.html

PC. (2015). Definition of: surface Web. *PC Magazine Encyclopedia*. Retrieved November 20, 2016, from http://www.pcmag.com/encyclopedia/ term/52273/surface-web

Sancho, D. (2015). *Steganography and Malware: Why and How*. TrendLabs Security Intelligence Blog. Retrieved October 30, 2016, from http://blog.trendmicro.com/ trendlabs-security-intelligence/steganography-and-malware-why-and-how/

Spalevic, Z., Ilic, M., & Palevic, M. (2016). Electronic Tracking Of Postal Services. In *Proceedings of 3rd the International Scientific Conference on ICT and e-Business Related Research – Sinteza* (pp. 479-485). Belgrade: University Singidunum. 10.15308/Sinteza-2016-479-485

Todorovic, A. (2015). *What is deep and dark web, you need to take care and how to protect myself?* Kompijuteraš. Retrieved November, 18, 2016, from https://kompjuteras. com/sta-je-deep-dark-web-trebam-li-se-brinuti-kako-da-se-zastitim/

Vijesti. (2015). *Dark internet: There are hackers, sellers of human organs, and weapons*. Vijesti online. Retrieved October 30, 2016, from https://www.vijesti.me/techno/tamni-internet-tu-su-hakeri-prodavci-ljudskih-organa-oruzja-828308

Zetter, K. (2013). How the Feds Took Down the Silk Road Drug Wonderland. *Wired*. Retrieved October 20, 2016, from: www.wired.com/2013/11/silk-road

Mahor, R. Kumar, & Chouhan. (2021). Cyber warfare threat categorization on cps by dark web terrorist. In *2021 IEEE 4th International Conference on Computing, Power and Communication Technologies (GUCON)* (pp. 1–6). IEEE.

Rajawat, Rawat, Mahor, Shaw, & Ghosh. (2021), Suspicious big text data analysis for prediction—on darkweb user activity using computational intelligence model. In *Innovations in Electrical and Electronic Engineering* (pp. 735–751). Springer.

Rawat, Garg, Mahor, Telang, Pachlasiya, & Chouhan. (2021). Organ trafficking on the dark web—the data security and privacy concern in healthcare systems. *Internet of Healthcare Things, 191*.

Rawat, Kumar, Chouhan, Telang, Pachlasiya, Garg, & Mahor. (2021). *Systematic literature review (slr) on social media and the digital transformation of drug trafficking on darkweb*. Available at SSRN 3903797.

Rawat, M. Chirgaiya, & Garg. (2021). Artificial cyber espionage based protection of technological enabled automated cities infrastructure by dark web cyber offender. In Intelligence of Things: AI-IoT Based Critical-Applications and Innovations (pp. 167–188). Springer.

Rawat, Mahor, Chirgaiya, Shaw, & Ghosh (2021). Analysis of darknet traffic for criminal activities detection using tf-idf and light gradient boosted machine learning algorithm. In *Innovations in Electrical and Electronic Engineering* (pp. 671–681). Springer.

Rawat, Rajawat, Mahor, Shaw, & Ghosh. (2021). Dark web—onion hidden service discovery and crawling for profiling morphing, unstructured crime and vulnerabilities prediction. In *Innovations in Electrical and Electronic Engineering* (pp. 717–734). Springer.

Compilation of References

Abbasi, A., Javed, A. R., Chakraborty, C., Nebhen, J., Zehra, W., & Jalil, Z. (2021). ElStream: An ensemble learning approach for concept drift detection in dynamic social big data stream learning. *IEEE Access: Practical Innovations, Open Solutions, 9*, 66408–66419. doi:10.1109/ACCESS.2021.3076264

Abomhara, G. M., & Køien, G. M. (2015). Cyber security and the internet of things: Vulnerabilities, threats, intruders and attacks. *Journal of Cyber Security and Mobility, 4*(1), 65–88. doi:10.13052/jcsm2245-1439.414

Abu Saleh, M. (2019). Crime Data Analysis in Python using K Means clustering. *International Journal for Research in Applied Science and Engineering Technology, 7*(4), 151–155. doi:10.22214/ijraset.2019.4027

Adewopo, V., Gonen, B., Varlioglu, S., & Ozer, M. (2019). Plunge into the underworld: A survey on emergence of darknet. *Proc. Int. Conf. Comput. Sci. Comput. Intell. (CSCI)*, 155–159. 10.1109/CSCI49370.2019.00033

Agarwal,, R., & Verma,, O. P. (2019). An efficient method for image forgery detection based on trigonometric transforms and deep learning. *Multimedia Tools and Applications*.

Aghababaei, S., & Makrehchi, M. (2016). Mining Social Media Content for Crime Prediction. *Web Intelligence (WI), IEEE/WIC/ACM International Conference on*, 526–531.

Aghajani, G., & Ghadimi, N. (2018). Multi-objective energy management in a micro-grid. *Energy Reports, 4*, 218–225. doi:10.1016/j.egyr.2017.10.002

Agnew, R. (1992). Foundation for a General Strain Theory of Crime and Delinquency. *Criminology, 30*(1), 47–88. doi:10.1111/j.1745-9125.1992.tb01093.x

Ahemd, M. M., Shah, M. A., & Wahid, A. (2017). IOT security: A layered approach for attacks & defenses. *2017 International Conference on Communication Technologies (ComTech)*. 10.1109/COMTECH.2017.8065757

Ahmed, F., & Abulaish, M. (2013). A generic statistical approach for spam detection in Online Social Networks. *Computer Communications, 36*(10–11), 1120–1129. doi:10.1016/j.comcom.2013.04.004

Akhgar, P., Bertrand, C., & Chalanouli. (2017). TENSOR: retrieval and analysis of heterogeneous online content for terrorist activity recognition. *Proceedings of the Estonian Academy of Security Sciences*.

Ala, B., & Lisa, A. R. (2012). Detecting Key Players in Terrorist Networks. *2012 European Intelligence and Security Informatics Conference*. 10.1109/EISIC.2012.13

Alam, M. R., Reaz, M. B. I., & Ali, M. A. M. (2012). A review of smart homes—Past, present, and future. *IEEE Transactions on Systems, Man and Cybernetics. Part C, Applications and Reviews, 42*(6), 1190–1203. doi:10.1109/TSMCC.2012.2189204

Al-Ansi, A., Al-Ansi, A. M., Muthanna, A., Elgendy, I. A., & Koucheryavy, A. (2021). Survey on Intelligence Edge Computing in 6G: Characteristics, Challenges, Potential Use Cases, and Market Drivers. *Future Dark Web, 13*(5), 118.

Aldridge, J. (2019). Does online anonymity boost illegal market trading? *Media Culture & Society, 41*(4), 578–583. doi:10.1177/0163443719842075

Al-Garadi, M. A., Mohamed, A., Al-Ali, A. K., Du, X., Ali, I., & Guizani, M. (2020). A survey of machine and deep learning methods for internet of things (IOT) security. *IEEE Communications Surveys and Tutorials, 22*(3), 1646–1685. doi:10.1109/COMST.2020.2988293

Alghamdi, H., & Selamat, A. (2022). Techniques to detect terrorists/extremists on the dark web: A Review. *Data Technologies and Applications.* doi:10.1108/DTA-07-2021-0177

Alhakami, W., ALharbi, A., Bourouis, S., Alroobaea, R., & Bouguila, N. (2019). Network anomaly intrusion detection using a nonparametric bayesian approach and feature selection. *IEEE Access, 7*, 52181–52190.

Alkhalil, Z., Hewage, C., Nawaf, L., & Khan, I. (2021). Phishing Attacks: A Recent Comprehensive Study and a New Anatomy. *Frontiers of Computer Science, 3*, 563060. Advance online publication. doi:10.3389/fcomp.2021.563060

Al-Khater, W. A., Al-Maadeed, S., Ahmed, A. A., Sadiq, A. S., & Khan, M. K. (2020). Comprehensive Review of Cybercrime Detection Techniques. *IEEE Access: Practical Innovations, Open Solutions, 8*, 137293–137311. doi:10.1109/ACCESS.2020.3011259

Almukaynizi, M., Grimm, A., Nunes, E., Shakarian, J., & Shakarian, P. (2017). Predicting cyber threats through hacker social networks in darkweb and deepweb forums. In *Proceedings of the 2017 International Conference of The Computational Social Science Society of the Americas* (pp. 1-7). ACM. 10.1145/3145574.3145590

Almukaynizi, M., Marin, E., & Nunes, E. (2018). DARKMENTION: a deployed system to predict enterprise-targeted external cyberattacks. *Proceedings of the 2018 IEEE International Conference on Intelligence and Security Informatics (ISI)*, 31–36. 10.1109/ISI.2018.8587334

Almukaynizi, M., Paliath, V., Shah, M., Shah, M., & Shakarian, P. (2018). Finding Cryptocurrency Attack Indicators Using Temporal Logic and Darkweb Data. *Proceedings of the 2018 IEEE International Conference on Intelligence and Security Informatics (ISI)*, 91–93.

Alnabulsi, H., & Islam, R. (2018). Identification of illegal forum activities inside the Dark Net. *2018 International Conference on Machine Learning and Data Engineering (iCMLDE)*. 10.1109/iCMLDE.2018.00015

Alsafi, Abduallah, & Pathan. (2019). IDPS: An Integrated Intrusion Handling Model for Cloud. *Networking and International Architecture.*

Al-Shaer, E. S., Wei, J., Hamlen, K. W., & Wang, C. (2019). *Autonomous Cyber Deception: Reasoning, Adaptive Planning, and Evaluation of Honey Things.* Springer. doi:10.1007/978-3-030-02110-8

Al-Zoubi, Alqatawana, & Faris. (2017). Spam profile detection in social networks based on public features. *8th International conference on information and communication systems (ICICS).*

Ambika, N. (2020). Improved Methodology to Detect Advanced Persistent Threat Attacks. In Quantum Cryptography and the Future of Cyber Security (pp. 184-202). IGI Global.

Ambika, N. (2021). An Improved Solution to Tackle Cyber Attacks. In *Advanced Controllers for Smart Cities* (pp. 15–23). Springer.

Amika. (2016). *Deep web – hidden underworld of the Internet.* b92 Blog. Retrieved October 20, 2016, from http://blog. b92.net/text/26912/DEEP-WEB-%E2%80%93- skriveno-podzemlje-Interneta/

Amir, N., Latif, R., Shafqat, N., & Latif, S. (2020). Crowdsourcing Cybercrimes through Online Resources. *2020 13th International Conference on Developments in eSystems Engineering (DeSE),* 158-163. 10.1109/DeSE51703.2020.9450747

Amit. (2021). 9/11 Hijackers. *IEEE Dataport.* doi:10.21227/ry8q-sj65

Ammar, M., Russello, G., & Crispo, B. (2018). Internet of Things: A survey on the security of IoT frameworks. *Journal of Information Security and Applications, 38,* 8–27. doi:10.1016/j.jisa.2017.11.002

Ampel, B., Samtani, S., Zhu, H., Ullman, S., & Chen, H. (2020, November). Labeling hacker exploits for proactive cyber threat intelligence: a deep transfer learning approach. *Proceedings 2020 IEEE International Conference on Intelligence and Security Informatics (ISI),* 1–6. 10.1109/ISI49825.2020.9280548

Arabnezhad, E., La Morgia, M., Mei, A., Nemmi, E. N., & Stefa, J. (2020). A light in the dark web: Linking dark web aliases to real internet identities. *2020 IEEE 40th International Conference on Distributed Computing Systems (ICDCS).* 10.1109/ICDCS47774.2020.00081

Arnold, N., Ebrahimi, M., & Zhang, N. (2019). Dark-net ecosystem cyber-threat intelligence (CTI) tool. *Proceedings of the IEEE International Conference on Intelligence and Security Informatics (ISI),* 92–97.

Arora, T., Sharma, M., & Khatri, S. K. (2019). Detection of Cyber Crime on social media using Random Forest Algorithm. *2019 2nd International Conference on Power Energy, Environment, and Intelligent Control (PEEIC),* 47-51.

Arslani, M. (2015). *Dark internet: Underworld, which offers everything from guns to organs.* Express. Retrieved November 11,2016, from http://www.express.hr/tehno/mracni-internet-kriminalno-podzemlje-koje-nudi-sve-od-oruzja-do-organa-635

Asad, M., Asim, M., Javed, T., Beg, M. O., Mujtaba, H., & Abbas, S. (2020, July). DeepDetect: Detection of distributed denial of service attacks using deep learning. *The Computer Journal, 63*(7), 983–994. doi:10.1093/comjnl/bxz064

Atlam, H. F., Walters, R. J., & Wills, G. B. (2018). Fog computing and the dark web of things: A review. *Big Data and Cognitive Computing, 2*(2), 10.

Atzori, L., Iera, A., & Morabito, G. (2010). The internet of things: A survey. *Computer Networks, 54*(15), 2787–2805. doi:10.1016/j.comnet.2010.05.010

Badsey, S. (2014, October 8). Propaganda: Media In War Politics. *International Encyclopedia of the First World War (WW1).* https://encyclopedia.1914-1918-online.net/article/propaganda_media_in_war_politics

Baeza-Yates, R., & Davis, E. (2004). Web page ranking using link attributes. *Proceedings of the 13th International World Wide Web Conference on Alternate Track Papers & Posters - WWW Alt. '04,* 328. 10.1145/1013367.1013459

Bahnsen, Torroledo, & Camacho. (2018). *DeepPhish: Simulating malicious AI.* Academic Press.

Balaji, N. (2020) *How To Access Dark Web Anonymously and know its Secretive and Mysterious Activities.* GB Hackers on Security. https://gbhackers.com/how-to-access-deep-anonymous-web-and-know-its-secretive-and-mysterious-activities/)

Balduzzi, Ciancaglini, & Balduzzi. (2015). Cybercrime In The Deep Web. *Black Hat Europe 2015.*

Banos, V. (2015). *Web Crawling, Analysis and Archiving.* Aristotle University of Thessaloniki Faculty of Sciences School of Informatics.

Baravalle, A., Lopez, M. S., & Lee, S. W. (2016). Mining the dark web: Drugs and fake ids. *2016 IEEE 16th International Conference on Data Mining Workshops (ICDMW)*. 10.1109/ICDMW.2016.0056

Barnum, S. (2012). Standardizing cyber threat intelligence information with the structured threat information expression (stix). *Mitre Corporation*, *11*, 1–22.

Basit, A., Zafar, M., Liu, X., Javed, A. R., Jalil, Z., & Kifayat, K. (2020). A comprehensive survey of AI-enabled phishing attacks detection techniques. *Telecommunication Systems*. Advance online publication. doi:10.100711235-020-00733-2 PMID:33110340

BBC. (2014). *Child abuse image investigation leads to 660 arrests*. BBC News. Retrieved September 19, 2016, from www.bbc.com/news/uk-28326128

BBC. (2015). *50 arrests in NI online abuse images probe in past year, say police*. BBC News. Retrieved October 20, 2016, from www.bbc.com/news/uk-northernireland-31896685

Berghel, H. (2017). Which is more dangerous—The dark web or the deep state? *Computer*, *50*(07), 86–91. doi:10.1109/MC.2017.215

Bergman, M. K. (2001). White Paper: The deep web: Surfacing hidden value. *The Journal of Electronic Publishing: JEP*, *7*(1). Advance online publication. doi:10.3998/3336451.0007.104

Berman, A., & Paul, C. L. (2019). Making sense of Darknet markets: Automatic inference of semantic classifications from unconventional multimedia datasets. *Proc. Int. Conf. Hum.-Comput. Interact*, 230–248. 10.1007/978-3-030-22351-9_16

Berman, D. S., Buczak, A. L., Chavis, J., & Corbett, C. L. (2019). A Survey of Deep Learning Methods for Cyber Security. *Information (Basel)*, *10*(122), 1–35. doi:10.3390/info10040122

Bermudez, R., Gerardo, B., Manalang, J., & Tanguilig, B. (2011). Predicting Faculty Performance Using Regression Model in Data Mining. *Proceedings of the 9th International Conference on Software Engineering Research, Management and Applications*, 68-72.

Beshiri, A. S., & Susuri, A. (2019). Dark web and its impact in online anonymity and privacy: A critical analysis and review. *Journal of Computer and Communications*, *7*(03), 30–43. doi:10.4236/jcc.2019.73004

Bhalerao, R., Aliapoulios, M., Shumailov, I., Afroz, S., & McCoy, D. (2019). Mapping the Underground: Supervised Discovery of Cybercrime Supply Chains. *2019 APWG Symposium on Electronic Crime Research (eCrime)*, 1-16. 10.1109/eCrime47957.2019.9037582

Bhamidipati, N. L., & Pal, S. K. (2009). Comparing Scores Intended for Ranking. *IEEE Transactions on Knowledge and Data Engineering*, *21*(1), 21–34. doi:10.1109/TKDE.2008.111

Bharati & Sarvanaguru. (2018). Crime Prediction and Analysis Using Machine Learning. *International Research Journal of Engineering and Technology*, *5*(9), 1037–1042.

Bhatia, K. K., & Gupta, S. (2012). Exploring 'hidden' parts of the web: the hidden web. *Fourth International Conference on Advances in Recent Technologies in Communication and Computing (ARTCom2012)*, 305–309. 10.1049/cp.2012.2556

Bilen, A., & Özer, A. B. (2021). Cyber-attack method and perpetrator prediction using machine learning algorithms. *PeerJ. Computer Science*, *7*, e475. doi:10.7717/peerj-cs.475 PMID:33954249

Birajdar, G., & Mankar, V. (2013). Digital image forgery detection using passive techniques: A survey. *Digital Investigation*, *10*(3), 226–245. doi:10.1016/j.diin.2013.04.007

Blagus, R., & Lusa, L. (2010, December). Class prediction for high-dimensional classimbalanced data. *BMC Bioinformatics, 11*(1), 1–17.

Borgatti, Everett, & Freeman. (2002). *Ucinet for Windows: Software for social network analysis.* Academic Press.

Borgatti, S. P., & Everett, M. G. (2006). A graph-theoretic perspective on centrality. *Social Networks, 28,* 466-484.

Borgatti, S. P., Everett, M. G., & Freeman, L. C. (2002). UCINET 6 for Windows. In *Analytic Technologies.* Harvard University Press.

Bradbury, D. (2014). Unveiling the dark web. *Network Security, 2014*(4), 14–17. doi:10.1016/S1353-4858(14)70042-X

Bradford, W. R. (2013). Online routines and identity theft victimization: Further explaining routine activity theory beyond direct-control offenses. *Journal of Research in Crime and Delinquency, 50*(2), 216–238. doi:10.1177/0022427811425539

Brayton, E., & Christopher, S. (2017). *Number of the Beast. Deep Web.* Available: https://rationalwiki.org/w/index.php

Brown. (2016). Threat Advisory: State of the Dark Web. *AKAMAI Threat Advisory.*

Brown, S. (2006). The criminology of hybrids: Rethinking crime and law in technosocial networks. *Theoretical Criminology, 10*(2), 223–244. doi:10.1177/1362480606063140

Burruss, G. W., Bossler, A. M., & Holt, T. J. (2012). Assessing the Mediation of a Fuller Social Learning Model on Low Self-Control's Influence on Software Piracy. *Crime and Delinquency, 59*(8), 1157–1184. doi:10.1177/0011128712437915

Cai, Y., Li, D., & Wang, Y. (2020, February). Detection and Analysis Framework of Anomalous Dark web Crime Data Based on Edge Computing. In *2020 International Conference on Inventive Computation Technologies (ICICT)* (pp. 28-31). IEEE. 10.1109/ICICT48043.2020.9112412

Cambiaso, E., Vaccari, I., Patti, L., & Aiello, M. (2019). *Darknet Security: A Categorization of Attacks to the Tor Network.* ITASEC.

Cao, G., Chen, Y., Zong, G., & Chen, Y. (n.d.). Detection Of Copy-Move Forgery in Digital Image Using Locality Preserving Projections. *8th International Congress On Image And Signal Processing (Cisp).* 10.1109/CISP.2015.7407949

Cekerevac, Z., Dvorak, Z., & Cekerevac, P. (2016). Is the "dark web" deep and dark? *FBIM Transactions,* 1-12.

Celestini, A., & Me, G. (2017). Tor Marketplaces Exploratory Data Analysis: The Drugs Case. *Communications in Computer and Information Science, 630,* 218–229.

Chan, J., & Moses, L. B. (2017). Making sense of big data for security. *British Journal of Criminology, 57*(2), 299–319.

Chaojun, G., Jirutitijaroen, P., & Motani, M. (2015). Detecting false data injection attacks in ac state estimation. *IEEE Transactions on Smart Grid, 6*(5), 2476–2483. doi:10.1109/TSG.2015.2388545

Chen, H., Chung, W., Xu, J. J., Wang, G., Qin, Y., & Chau, M. (2004). Crime data mining: a general framework and some examples. *Computer, 37*(4), 50-56.

Chen, P., Yuan, H. Y., & Shu, X. M. (2008). *Forecasting crime using the ARIMA model.* Paper presented at the 5th international conference on fuzzy systems and knowledge discovery. 10.1109/FSKD.2008.222

Chen, H. (2008). IEDs in the Dark Web: Genre classification of improvised explosive device web pages. In *IEEE International Conference on Intelligence and Security Informatics* (pp. 94-97). IEEE. 10.1109/ISI.2008.4565036

Chen, H. (2012). *Dark web.* Integrated Series in Information Systems., doi:10.1007/978-1-4614-1557-2

Chen, H., Chung, W., Qin, Y., Chau, M., Xu, J. J., Wang, G., ... Atabakhsh, H. (2003, May). Crime data mining: an overview and case studies. *Proceedings of the 2003 annual national conference on Digital government research*, 1-5.

Chen, H., Thoms, S., & Fu, T. (2008, June). Cyber extremism in Web 2.0: An exploratory study of international Jihadist groups. In *2008 IEEE International Conference on Intelligence and Security Informatics* (pp. 98-103). IEEE. 10.1109/ISI.2008.4565037

Cherqi, O., Mezzour, G., Ghogho, M., & el Koutbi, M. (2018). Analysis of Hacking Related Trade in the Darkweb. *Proceedings of the 2018 IEEE International Conference on Intelligence and Security Informatics (ISI)*, 79–84.

Chertoff, M. (2017). A public policy perspective of the Dark Web. *Journal of Cyber Policy*, 2(1), 26–38. doi:10.1080/23738871.2017.1298643

Chitrakar, P., Zhang, C., Warner, G., & Liao, X. (2016). Social Media Image Retrieval Using Distilled Convolutional Neural Network for Suspicious e-Crime and Terrorist Account Detection. *Multimedia (ISM), 2016 IEEE International Symposium*, 493–498. 10.1109/ISM.2016.0110

Choshen, L., Eldad, D., Hershcovich, D., Sulem, E., & Abend, O. (2019). *The language of legal and illegal activity on the Darknet*. Available: https://arxiv.org/abs/1905.05543

Christian, J., & Hansun, S. (2016). *Simulating Shopper Behavior using Fuzzy Logic in Shopping Center Simulation*. ITB J. Publ.

Ciancaglini, Balduzzi, Mcardle, & Rösler. (2015). *Bellow The Surface Exploring the Deep Web Contents*. TrendLabs Res. Pap..

Ciancaglini, V., Balduzzi, M., Goncharov, V., & McArdle, R. **(2013).** Deep web and Cybercrime It's Not All About TOR. *Trend Micro*, 2-21.

Ciancaglini, V., Balduzzi, M., McArdle, R., & Rosler, M. (2015). *Below the Surface: Exploring the Deep Web*. Trend Micro.

Citron, D. K., & Chesney, R. (2019). *Deep Fakes: A Looming Challenge for Privacy, Democracy, and National Security*. Available: https://scholarship.law.bu.edu/faculty_scholarship/640

Cook, J. (2014). FBI Arrests Former SpaceX Employee, Alleging He Ran The 'Deep Web' Drug Marketplace Silk Road 2.0. *Business Insider*. Retrieved October 15, 2016, from www.businessinsider.com/fbi-silk-road-seizedarrests-2014-11

Coulombe, J. C., York, M. C. A., & Sylvestre, J. (2017). Computing with networks of nonlinear mechanical oscillators. *PLoS One*, 12, e0178663.

da Cunha, B. R., MacCarron, P., Passold, J. F., dos Santos, L. W. Jr, Oliveira, K. A., & Gleeson, J. P. (2020). Assessing police topological efficiency in a major sting operation on the dark web. *Scientific Reports*, 10(1), 73. Advance online publication. doi:10.103841598-019-56704-4 PMID:31919365

Dale, M., Miller, J. F., Stepney, S., & Trefzer, M. A. (2016). Evolving Carbon Nanotube Reservoir Computers. In *Unconventional Computation and Natural Computation* (pp. 49–61). Springer.

Deb, A., Lerman, K., & Ferrara, E. (2018). Predicting cyber-events by leveraging hacker sentiment. *Information (Basel)*, 9(11), 280. doi:10.3390/info9110280

Deep Web. (2014). Available: https://rationalwiki.org/wiki/Deep_web

Dehghani, M., Khooban, M. H., & Niknam, T. (2016). Fast fault detection and classification based on a combination of wavelet singular entropy theory and fuzzy logic in distribution lines in the presence of distributed generations. *International Journal of Electrical Power & Energy Systems*, 78, 455–462. doi:10.1016/j.ijepes.2015.11.048

Dehghani, M., Khooban, M. H., Niknam, T., & Rafiei, S. M. R. (2016). Time-varying sliding mode control strategy for multibus low-voltage microgrids with parallel connected renewable power sources in islanding mode. *Journal of Energy Engineering*, *142*(4), 05016002. doi:10.1061/(ASCE)EY.1943-7897.0000344

Dehghantanha, A., Conti, M., & Dargahi, T. (2018). *Cyber threat intelligence*. Springer International Publishing. doi:10.1007/978-3-319-73951-9

Deliu, I., Leichter, C., & Franke, K. (2017). Extracting cyber threat intelligence from hacker forums: support vector machines versus convolutional neural networks. *Proceedings of the 2017 IEEE International Conference on Big Data (Big Data)*, 3648–3656. 10.1109/BigData.2017.8258359

Demertzis, K., Iliadis, L. S., & Anezakis, V.-D. (2018). Extreme deep learning in biosecurity: The case of machine hearing for marine species identification. *J. Inf. Telecommun.*, *2*, 492–510.

Demertzis, K., Iliadis, L., Tziritas, N., & Kikiras, P. (2020). Anomaly detection via blockchained deep learning smart contracts in industry 4.0. *Neural Computing & Applications*, *32*, 17361–17378.

Demertzis, K., Tsiknas, K., Takezis, D. S., & Iliadis, L. (2021). Darknet traffic big-data analysis and network management for real-time automating of the malicious intent detection process by a weight agnostic neural networks framework. *Electronics (Basel)*, *10*(7), 1–25. doi:10.3390/electronics10070781

Dhariwal, S., & Palaniappan, S. (2020). Image Normalization and Weighted Classification Using an Efficient Approach for SVM Classifiers. *International Journal of Image and Graphics*, *20*(04), 2050035. doi:10.1142/S0219467820500357

Dhariwal, S., Raghuwanshi, S., & Shrivastava, S. (2012). Content Based Image Retrieval Using Normalization of Vector Approach to SVM. In *Advances in Computer Science, Engineering & Applications* (pp. 793–801). Springer. doi:10.1007/978-3-642-30111-7_76

Dhariwal, S., Rawat, R., & Patearia, N. (2011). C-Queued Technique against SQL injection attack. *International Journal of Advanced Research in Computer Science*, *2*(5).

Dhawan, S. (2019). *Canara bank ATM fraud: Here is the bank's reply and new safety features to keep your money safe.* The Financial Express. Retrieved February 17, 2022, from https://www.financialexpress.com/money/canara-bank-atm-fraud-here-is-the-banks-reply-and-new-safety-features-to-keep-your-money-safe/1686396/

Dhivya, S., Sangeetha, J., & Sudhakar, B. (2020). Copy-move forgery detection using SURF feature extraction and SVM supervised learning technique. *Soft Computing*, *24*(19), 14429–14440. doi:10.100700500-020-04795-x

Ding, C. H. Q., Zha, H., He, X., Husbands, P., & Simon, H. D. (2004). Link Analysis: Hubs and Authorities on the World Wide Web. *SIAM Review*, *46*(2), 256–268. doi:10.1137/S0036144501389218

Ding, D., Han, Q.-L., Xiang, Y., Ge, X., & Zhang, X.-M. (2018). A survey on security control and attack detection for industrial cyber-physical systems. *Neurocomputing*, *275*, 1674–1683. doi:10.1016/j.neucom.2017.10.009

Du, C., Liu, S., Si, L., Guo, Y., & Jin, T. (2020). Using object detection network for malware detection and identification in network traffic packets. *Comput. Mater. Continua*, *64*(3), 1785–1796.

Dutta, A. K. (2021). Detecting phishing websites using Machine Learning Technique. *PLoS One*, *16*(10), e0258361. Advance online publication. doi:10.1371/journal.pone.0258361 PMID:34634081

E, M. P. S. M. (2012). Ranking Techniques for Social Networking Sites based on Popularity. *Indian Journal of Computer Science and Engineering (IJCSE) Ranking, 3*(3), 522–526.

Ebrahimi, M., Nunamaker, J. F. Jr, & Chen, H. (2020). Semi-supervised cyber threat identification in darknet markets: A transductive and deep learning approach. *Journal of Management Information Systems*, 37(3), 694–722. doi:10.108 0/07421222.2020.1790186

Elaskily, M., Aslan, H., Elshakankiry, O., Faragallah, O., El-Samie, F., & Dessouky, M. (2020). A novel deep learning framework for copy-move forgery detection in images. *Multimedia Tools and Applications*, 79(27-28), 19167–19192. Advance online publication. doi:10.100711042-020-08751-7

Elsayed, G. F., Sohl-Dickstein, J., & Goodfellow, I. (2019). Adversarial reprogramming of neural networks. *7th Int. Conf. Learn. Represent. ICLR 2019*, 1–14.

ENISA. (2018). *ENISA Threat Landscape Report 2017–15 Top Cyber-Threats and Trends*. ENISA.

Esmalifalak, M., Liu, L., Nguyen, N., Zheng, R., & Han, Z. (2014). Detecting stealthy false data injection using machine learning in smart grid. *IEEE Systems Journal*, 11(3), 1644–1652. doi:10.1109/JSYST.2014.2341597

Europol. (2014). *Operation Rescue*. Europol. Retrieved September 19, 2016, from www. europol.europa.eu/content/operation-rescue

Fachkha, C., Bou-Harb, E., & Debbabi, M. (2013). Towards a forecasting model for distributed denial of service activities. *2013 IEEE 12th International Symposium on Network Computing and Applications*, 110–117. 10.1109/NCA.2013.13

Fachkha, C., & Debbabi, M. (2015). Darknet as a source of cyber intelligence: Survey, taxonomy, and characterization. *IEEE Communications Surveys and Tutorials*, 18(2), 1197–1227. doi:10.1109/COMST.2015.2497690

Faghani, M. R., Matrawy, A., & Lung, C. H. (2012). A study of Trojan propagation in online social networks. *5th Int. Conf. New Technol. Mobil. Secur. - Proc. NTMS 2012 Conf. Work.*, 6–10. 10.1109/NTMS.2012.6208767

Falconer, J. (2012). *Mail-order drugs, hitmen & child porn: A journey into the dark corners of the deep web*. Insider. Retrieved October 30, 2016, from http://thenextweb.com/ insider/2012/10/08/mail-order-drugs-hitmen-child-porn-a-journey-into-the-dark corners-of-the-deep-web/

Felipe, G., Noble, D., & Lamb, L. C. (2016). An analysis of Centrality measures for complex and social networks. *IEEE Global Communications Conference 2016*.

Feng, X., Sun, D., Li, Z., & Li, B. (2017). Exploring structural features of terrorist organization's online supporting community via social network modeling. *3rd IEEE International Conference on Computer Communications (ICCC) 2017*.

Ferguson, R.-H. (2017). Offline 'stranger' and online lurker: Methods for an ethnography of illicit transactions on the darknet. *Qualitative Research*, 17(6), 683–698. doi:10.1177/1468794117718894

Fernandez, E. F., Carofilis, R. A. V., Martino, F. J., & Medina, P. B. (2020). *Classifying suspicious content in Tor Darknet*. Available: https://arxiv.org/abs/2005.10086

Fernando, D. W., Komninos, N., & Chen, T. (2020). A study on the evolution of ransomware detection using machine learning and Deep Learning Techniques. *IoT*, 1(2), 551–604. doi:10.3390/iot1020030

Ferraro, Giordani, & Serafini. (2019). fclust: An R Package for Fuzzy Clustering. *The R Journal*, 11(1), 1 - 5.

Fidalgo, E., Alegre, E., Fernández-Robles, L., & González-Castro, V. (2019, September). Classifying suspicious content in Tor darknet through semantic attention keypoint filtering. *Digital Investigation*, 30, 12–22. doi:10.1016/j.diin.2019.05.004

Finklea, K. (2017). *Dark Web, CRS report*. Legal Reference Services.

Foltz, R. (2013). Silk road and migration. Encyclopedia of global human migration. doi:10.1002/9781444351071. wbeghm484

Foroutan, S. A., & Salmasi, F. R. (2017). Detection of false data injection attacks against state estimation in smart grids based on a mixture Gaussian distribution learning method. IET Cyber-Phys. *Syst. Theory Appl., 2*(4), 161–171. doi:10.1049/iet-cps.2017.0013

Fridrich, J. (1999). Methods for Tamper Detection in Digital Images. *Proc. of ACM Workshop on Multimedia and Security*, 19–23.

Gao, Q., Su, M. X., & Cho, Y. I. (2013). A multi-agent personalized ontology profile based user preference profile construction method. *IEEE ISR*, 1–4. Advance online publication. doi:10.1109/ISR.2013.6695695

George, Tsikrika, Gialampoukidis, & Papadopoulos. (2018). Analysis of Suspended Terrorism – Related Content on Social media. Community-Oriented Policing and Technological Innovations, 107-118.

Ghasem, Z., Frommholz, I., & Maple, C. (2015). *Machine Learning Solutions for controlling Cyberbullying and Cyberstalking*. Academic Press.

Gholipour, B. (2017). New AI Tech Can Mimic Any Voice -. *Scientific American*.

Gia, T. N., Qingqing, L., Queralta, J. P., Zou, Z., Tenhunen, H., & Westerlund, T. (2019, September). *Edge AI in smart farming IoT: CNNs at the edge and fog computing with LoRa. In 2019 IEEE AFRICON*. IEEE.

Giraldo, J., Urbina, D., Cardenas, A., Valente, J., Faisal, M., Ruths, J., Tippenhauer, N. O., Sandberg, H., & Candell, R. (2018). A survey of physics-based attack detection in cyber-physical systems. *ACM Computing Surveys, 51*(4), 1–36. doi:10.1145/3203245 PMID:31092968

Gonzalez, R., & Woods, R. (n.d.). *Digital Image Processing* (2nd ed.). Addison-Wesley.

Goodman, M. (2015). Most of the web is invisible to Google. Kere's what it contains. *Popular Science*. Retrieved November, 18, 2016, from https://www.popsci.com/dark web-revealed.

Gorr, W., & Harries, R. (2003). Introduction to crime forecasting. *International Journal of Forecasting, 19*(4), 551–555. doi:10.1016/S0169-2070(03)00089-X

Grimani, Gavine, & Moncur. (2020). An evidence syn- thesis of strategies, enablers and barriers for keeping secrets online regarding the procurement and supply of illicit drugs. *International Journal of Drug Policy, 75*.

Grisham, J., Samtani, S., Patton, M., & Chen, H. (2017). Identifying mobile malware and key threat actors in online hacker forums for proactive cyber threat intelligence. *Proceedings of the 2017 IEEE International Conference on Intelligence and Security Informatics (ISI)*, 13–18. 10.1109/ISI.2017.8004867

Guess, A. M. (2015, March 4). *Fact-checking On Twitter: An Examination Of Campaign 2014*. https://www.american-pressinstitute.org/wp-content/uploads/2015/04/Project-1B-Guess-updated.pdf

Guofeng & Hong. (2010). *A New Network Core Mining Method based on Node Core Influence Degree*. IEEE.

Gupta, K. K., & Shukla, S. (2016). Internet of things: Security challenges for next generation networks. *2016 International Conference on Innovation and Challenges in Cyber Security (ICICCS-INBUSH)*. 10.1109/ICICCS.2016.7542301

Gupta, S., & Bhatia, K. K. (2014a). A Comparative Study of Hidden Web Crawlers. *International Journal of Computer Trends and Technology, 12*(3), 111–118. doi:10.14445/22312803/IJCTT-V12P122

Gupta, S., & Bhatia, K. K. (2014b). Deep questions in the "Deep or Hidden"web. *Advances in Intelligent Systems and Computing, 236*, 821–829. doi:10.1007/978-81-322-1602-5_87

Gupta, S., & Bhatia, K. K. (2017). Optimal query generation for hidden web extraction through response analysis. *The Dark Web: Breakthroughs in Research and Practice, 2001*, 65–83. doi:10.4018/978-1-5225-3163-0.ch005

Gupta, S., & Bhatia, K. K. (2018). URL-Based Relevance-Ranking Approach to Facilitate Domain-Specific Crawling and Searching. *Studies in Computational Intelligence, 713*(1), 239–250. doi:10.1007/978-981-10-4555-4_16

Gupta, S., & Bhatia, K. K. (2022). Design of a Parallel and Scalable Crawler for the Hidden Web. *International Journal of Information Retrieval Research, 12*(1), 1–23. doi:10.4018/IJIRR.289612

Habibi, M. R., & Baghaee, H. R. (2020). Detection of false data injection cyber-attacks in DC microgrids based on recurrent neural networks. *IEEE Journal of Emerging and Selected Topics in Power Electronics.*

Hagberg, A., Schult, D., Swart, P., Conway, D., SéguinCharbonneau, L., Ellison, C., & Torrents, J. (2004). *Networkx. High productivity software for complex networks.* https://networkx. lanl. gov/wiki

Hameed, A. R., Islam, S., Ahmad, I., & Munir, K. (2021). Energy-and performance-aware load-balancing in vehicular fog computing. *Sustainable Computing: Informatics and Systems, 30*, 100454. doi:10.1016/j.suscom.2020.100454

Harwell. (2019). *An AI-First: Voice-Mimicking Software Reportedly Used in a Major Theft Technology News.* ndtv.com.

Hayward, K. J. (2012). Five spaces of cultural criminology. *British Journal of Criminology, 52*(3), 441–462. doi:10.1093/bjc/azs008

Hayward, K. J., & Maas, M. M. (2021). Artificial intelligence and crime: A primer for criminologists. *Crime, Media, Culture, 17*(2), 209–233. doi:10.1177/1741659020917434

He, Q., Xu, Y., Liu, Z., He, J., Sun, Y., & Zhang, R. (2018). A privacy-preserving Internet of Things device management scheme based on Blockchain. *International Journal of Distributed Sensor Networks, 14*(11), 1550147718808750. doi:10.1177/1550147718808750

He, S., He, Y., & Li, M. (2019). Classification of illegal activities on the dark web. In *2nd International Conference on Information Science and Systems* (pp. 73-78). ACM. 10.1145/3322645.3322691

He, Y., Mendis, G. J., & Wei, J. (2017). Real-time detection of false data injection attacks in smart grid: A deep learning-based intelligent mechanism. *IEEE Transactions on Smart Grid, 8*(5), 2505–2516. doi:10.1109/TSG.2017.2703842

Hinduja, S., & Kooi, B. (2013). Curtailing cyber and information security vulnerabilities through situational crime prevention. *Security Journal, 26*(4), 383–402. doi:10.1057j.2013.25

Hirani, P., & Singh, M. (2015). A Survey on Coverage Problem in Wireless Sensor Network. *International Journal of Computers and Applications, 116*(2), 1–3. doi:10.5120/20305-2347

Holt, T. J., & Bossler, A. M. (2014). An Assessment of the Current State of Cybercrime Scholarship. *Deviant Behavior, 35*(1), 20–40. doi:10.1080/01639625.2013.822209

Huang, C. Y., & Chang, H. (2016). *GeoWeb Crawler: An Extensible and Scalable Web Crawling Framework for Discovering Geospatial Web Resources.* Int. J. GeoInformation.

Huang, C., Guo, Y., Guo, W., & Li, Y. (2021). Identifying key hackers in underground forums. *International Journal of Distributed Sensor Networks, 17*(5). doi:10.1177/15501477211015145

Huang, G., Zhu, Q., & Siew, C. (2006). Extreme Learning Machine: Theory and Applications. *Neurocomputing, 70,* 489–501.

Hummon & Doreian. (1990). Computational methods for social network analysis. *Social Networks, 12*(4).

Hurlburt. (2017). Shining light on the dark web. *Computer, 50*(4), 100–105.

Hurlburt, G. (2017). Shining light on the dark web. *Computer, 50*(04), 100–105. doi:10.1109/MC.2017.110

Hu, Z. H., & Chen, W. L. (2012). The Security Mechanism for Internet of Things Networks. *Applied Mechanics and Materials, 220-223,* 3003–3009. . doi:10.4028/www.scientific.net/AMM.220-223.3003

Ibrahima, Mendy, Ouya, & Seck. (2015). Spanning graph for maximizing the influence spread in Social Networks. *2015 IEEE/ACM International Conference on Advances in Social Networks Analysis and Mining.*

ICSS. (2017). *35% Athletes believe matches at their level were fixed, says forthcoming study.* ICSS. http://theicss. org/2017/07/23/35-athletesbelieve-matches-at-their-level-were-fxed-says-forthcoming-study/

Indrajit, P. R. E. (2016). *Internet And Information Security, Informatio.* PREINEXUS.

Jadav, N., Dutta, N., Sarma, H. K., Pricop, E., & Tanwar, S. (2021). A machine learning approach to classify network traffic. *2021 13th International Conference on Electronics, Computers and Artificial Intelligence (ECAI).* 10.1109/ECAI52376.2021.9515039

Jardine, E. (2015). *The Dark Web Dilemma: Tor, Anonymity and Online Policing* (Vol. 21). Global Commission on Internet Governance Paper Series.

Javed, Baker, Asim, Beg, & Al-Bayatti. (2020). *AlphaLogger: Detecting motion-based side-channel attack using smartphone keystrokes.* Tech. Rep.

Jordan & Mitchell. (2015). Machine learning: Trends, perspectives, and prospects. *Science, 349*(6245), 255–260.

K, M. A. (2021). Machine learning for anonymous traffic detection and classification. *2021 11th International Conference on Cloud Computing, Data Science & Engineering (Confluence).* 10.1109/Confluence51648.2021.9377168

Kadoguchi, M., Hayashi, S., Hashimoto, M., & Otsuka, A. (2019). Exploring the dark web for cyber threat intelligence using machine leaning. In *IEEE International Conference on Intelligence and Security Informatics (ISI)* (pp. 200-202). IEEE. 10.1109/ISI.2019.8823360

Kadoguchi, M., Kobayashi, H., Hayashi, S., Otsuka, A., & Hashimoto, M. (2020). Deep self-supervised clustering of the dark web for Cyber Threat Intelligence. *2020 IEEE International Conference on Intelligence and Security Informatics (ISI).* 10.1109/ISI49825.2020.9280485

Kai, K., Cong, W., & Tao, L. (2016). Fog computing for vehicular ad-hoc networks: paradigms, scenarios, and issues. *The Journal of China Universities of Posts and Telecommunications, 23*(2), 56-96.

Kang, L., & Cheng, X. (2010). Copy-Move Forgery Detection in Digital Image. In *3rd International Congress on Image and Signal Processing.* IEEE Computer Society. 10.1109/CISP.2010.5648249

Kang, U., Papadimitriou, S., Sun, J., & Tong, H. (2011). Centralities in Large Networks: Algorithms and Observations Betweenness. *Proceedings of SIAM International Conference on Data Mining (SDM'2011).* 10.1137/1.9781611972818.11

Karaman, M., Catalkaya, H., Gerehan, A. Z., & Goztepe, K. (2016). Cyber operation planning and operational design. *Cyber-Security and Digital Forensics,* 21.

Kasperkevic, J. (2015). Swiss police release robot that bought ecstasy online. *The Guardian*. Available at: https://www. theguardian.com/world/2015/apr/22/swiss-police-release-robot-random-darknetshopper-ecstasy-deep-web

Kaur, G., & Kumar, M. (2015, September). Study of Various Copy Move Forgery Attack Detection In Digital Images. *International Journal Of Research In Computer Applications And Robotics*, *3*(9), 30–34. doi:10.5120/21082-3764

Kaur, M., & Sharma, R. (2013). Optimization of Copy Move Forgery Detection Technique. *International Journal of Advanced Research in Computer Science and Software Engineering*, *3*(4).

Kawaguchi, Y., & Ozawa, S. (2019). Exploring and identifying malicious sites in dark web using machine learning. In *International Conference on Neural Information Processing* (pp. 319-327). Springer. 10.1007/978-3-030-36718-3_27

Kelkar, A., & Dick, C. (2021, September). A GPU Hyperconverged Platform for 5G Vran and Multi-Access Edge Computing. In *2021 IEEE Canadian Conference on Electrical and Computer Engineering (CCECE)* (pp. 1-6). IEEE. 10.1109/CCECE53047.2021.9569133

Kevin, R. C. (2013). Toward a conceptual model of motive and self-control in cyber-aggression: Rage, reward and recreation. *Journal of Youth and Adolescence*, *42*(5), 751–771. doi:10.100710964-013-9936-2 PMID:23526207

Khraisat, A., Gondal, I., & Vamplew, P. (2019). An anomaly intrusion detection system using C5 decision tree classifier. In *Trends and applications in knowledge discovery and data mining* (pp. 149–155). Springer.

Kim, S. J., & Lee, J. H. (2017). A Study on Metadata Structure and Recommenders of Biological Systems to Support BioInspired Design. *Enginering Appl. Artif. Intell.*, *57*, 16–41.

Kim, S., Joshi, P., Kalsi, P. S., & Taheri, P. (2018). Crime Analysis Through Machine Learning. *2018 IEEE 9th Annual Information Technology, Electronics and Mobile Communication Conference (IEMCON)*. 10.1109/IEMCON.2018.8614828

King, T. C., Aggarwal, N., Taddeo, M., & Floridi, L. (2020). Artificial Intelligence Crime: An Interdisciplinary Analysis of Foreseeable Threats and Solutions. Springer Netherlands.

King, M. C. (2011, May). The Intelligence Advanced Research Projects Activity-Its BEST and Beyond. In *CLEO: Applications and Technology*. Optical Society of America. doi:10.1364/CLEO_AT.2011.ATuF3

Kleinberg, J. M. (1999). Authoritative sources in a hyperlinked environment. *Journal of the Association for Computing Machinery*, *46*(5), 604–632. doi:10.1145/324133.324140

Knibbs, K. (2014). *Silk Road 3 Is Already Up, But It's Not the Future of Darknet Drugs*. Gizmodo. Retrieved October 15, 2016, from https://gizmodo.com/silk-road-3-isalready-up-butits-not-the-future-of-da-1655512490

Kohli, P., Sharma, S., & Matta, P. (2021, April). Security Challenges, Applications and Vehicular Authentication Methods in VANET For Smart Traffic Management. In *2021 2nd International Conference on Intelligent Engineering and Management (ICIEM)* (pp. 327-332). IEEE.

Kohli, P., Sharma, S., & Matta, P. (2021, March). Security of Cloud-Based Vehicular Ad-Hoc Communication Networks, Challenges and Solutions. In *2021 Sixth International Conference on Wireless Communications, Signal Processing and Networking (WiSPNET)* (pp. 283-287). IEEE. 10.1109/WiSPNET51692.2021.9419406

Koketsurodrigues, T., Liu, J., & Kato, N. (2021). Offloading Decision for Mobile Multi-Access Edge Computing in a Multi-Tiered 6G Network. *IEEE Transactions on Emerging Topics in Computing*.

Koloveas, P., Chantzios, T., Alevizopoulou, S., Tryfonopoulos, S., & Tryfonopoulos, C. (2021). INTIME: A machine learning-based framework for gathering and leveraging web data to cyber-threat intelligence. *Electronics (Basel)*, *10*(7), 818. doi:10.3390/electronics10070818

Krebs, B. (2015). How scammers use eBay as a personal ATM. *The Sydney Morning Herald.* https://www.smh.com.au/technology/how-scammers-use-ebay-as-a-personal-atm-20151104-gkq3aq.html

Kumar, S., Vranken, H., Dijk, J. V., & Hamalainen, T. (2019). Deep in the dark: A novel threat detection system using darknet traffic. *Proc. IEEE Int. Conf. Big Data (Big Data),* 4273–4279. 10.1109/BigData47090.2019.9006374

Kumar, P., Gupta, G. P., Tripathi, R., Garg, S., & Hassan, M. M. (2021). DLTIF: Deep Learning-Driven Cyber Threat Intelligence Modeling and Identification Framework in IoT-Enabled Maritime Transportation Systems. *IEEE Transactions on Intelligent Transportation Systems,* 1–10. doi:10.1109/TITS.2021.3122368

Kumar, R., Pal, N. R., Chanda, B., & Sharma, J. D. (2009). Detection of fraudulent alterations in ball-point pen strokes using support vector machines. *India Conference (INDICON), 2009 Annual IEEE,* 1–4. 10.1109/INDCON.2009.5409436

Kurien, N. A., Danya, S., Ninan, D., Raju, C. H., & David, J. Accurate and Efficient Copy-Move Forgery Detection. *9th International Conference on Advances in Computing and Communication (ICACC). ,* (2019).10.1109/ICACC48162.2019.8986157

Lacson, W., & Jones, B. (2016). The 21st century Dark Net market: Lessons from the fall of silk road. *International Journal of Cyber Criminology, 10*(1), 40–61.

Lagraa, S., Chen, Y., & François, J. (2019, May). Deep mining port scans from darknet. *International Journal of Network Management, 29*(3), e2065. doi:10.1002/nem.2065

Lakhani, A. (2016). *The Ultimate Guide to the Deep Dark Invisible.Web - Darknet Unleashed.* Dark Security and Total Chaos.

Lakshmanaprabu, Shankar, Ilayaraja, Nasir, & Chilamkurti. (2019). Random forest for big data classification in the internet of things using optimal features. *International Journal of Machine Learning and Cybernetics, 10,* 2609 - 2618.

Lavanya, V., Sreelakshmi, N., & Mahesh, K. (2016). Visual Analytics of Terrorism Data. *IEEE International Conference on Cloud Computing in Emerging Markets (CCEM).*

Lee, L.-W., Jiang, J.-Y., Wu, C., & Lee, S.-J. (2009). A Query-Dependent Ranking Approach for Search Engines. *2009 Second International Workshop on Computer Science and Engineering,* 259–263. 10.1109/WCSE.2009.666

Lee, S., & Kim, J. (2014). Early filtering of ephemeral malicious accounts on Twitter. *Computer Communications, 54,* 48–57. doi:10.1016/j.comcom.2014.08.006

Lekamalage, C. K. L., Song, K., Huang, G., Cui, D., & Liang, K. (2017). Multi layer multi objective extreme learning machine. *Proceedings of the 2017 IEEE International Conference on Image Processing (ICIP),* 1297–1301.

Leukfeldt, E. R., Kleemans, E. R., & Stol, W. P. (2017). Cybercriminal networks, social ties and online forums: Social ties versus digital ties within phishing and malware networks. *British Journal of Criminology, 57*(3), 704–722.

Liao, Z., Peng, J., Huang, J., Wang, J., Wang, J., Sharma, P. K., & Ghosh, U. (2020). Distributed probabilistic offloading in edge computing for 6g-enabled massive dark web of things. *IEEE Dark Web of Things Journal, 8*(7), 5298-5308.

Liggett, R., Lee, J. R., Roddy, A. L., & Wallin, M. A. (2019). The dark web as a platform for crime: an exploration of illicit drug, firearm, CSAM, and cybercrime markets. The Palgrave Handbook of International Cybercrime and Cyberdeviance.

Li, J., Xu, Q., Shah, N., & Mackey, T. K. (2019). A Machine Learning Approach for the Detection and Characterization of Illicit Drug Dealers on Instagram: Model Evaluation Study. *Journal of Medical Internet Research, 21*(6), e13803. doi:10.2196/13803 PMID:31199298

Lin, C., Han, G., Qi, X., Guizani, M., & Shu, L. (2020). A distributed mobile fog computing scheme for mobile delay-sensitive applications in SDN-enabled vehicular networks. *IEEE Transactions on Vehicular Technology, 69*(5), 5481–5493. doi:10.1109/TVT.2020.2980934

Liu, X. (2021, October). Resource Allocation in Multi-access Edge Computing: Optimization and Machine Learning. In *2021 IEEE 12th Annual Information Technology, Electronics and Mobile Communication Conference (IEMCON)* (pp. 0365-0370). IEEE.

Liu, L., Chen, C., Pei, Q., Maharjan, S., & Zhang, Y. (2021). Vehicular edge computing and networking: A survey. *Mobile Networks and Applications, 26*(3), 1145–1168. doi:10.100711036-020-01624-1

Liu, X. (2013). Security Risks in the Internet of Things. *Proceedings of the 2012 International Conference on Cybernetics and Informatics Lecture Notes in Electrical Engineering*, 59-64. 10.1007/978-1-4614-3872-4_8

Liu, Y., Zhang, H., Long, K., Zhou, H., & Leung, V. C. (2021). Fog Computing Vehicular Network Resource Management Based on Chemical Reaction Optimization. *IEEE Transactions on Vehicular Technology, 70*(2), 1770–1781. doi:10.1109/TVT.2021.3051287

Liu, Z. (2010). Research of a personalized search engine based on user interest mining. *2010 International Conference on Intelligent Computing and Integrated Systems*, 512–515. 10.1109/ICISS.2010.5654942

Li, X., Jiang, P., Chen, T., Luo, X., & Wen, Q. (2020). A survey on the security of blockchain systems. *Future Generation Computer Systems, 107*, 841–853. doi:10.1016/j.future.2017.08.020

Li, Y., Snavely, N., Huttenlocher, D., & Fua, P. (2012, October). Worldwide pose estimation using 3d point clouds. In *European conference on computer vision* (pp. 15-29). Springer. 10.1007/978-3-642-33718-5_2

López-Marcos, C., & Vicente-Fernández, P. (2021, August 12). *Fact Checkers Facing Fake News And Disinformation In the Digital Age: A Comparative Analysis Between Spain And United Kingdom.* MDPI. https://www.mdpi.com/2304-6775/9/3/36

Lukovic, M. (2014). *Deep internet - Drugs, murders, pornography - what is hidden in the black hole web?* Before After. Retrieved September 18, 2016, from http://www. beforeafter.rs/tehnologija/deep-internet/

Lutolf, R. (1992). Smart home concept and the integration of energy meters into a home-based system. *Seventh International Conference on Metering Apparatus and Tariffs for Electricity Supply 1992*, 277–278.

Lynn, W. J. (2010). Defending a new domain. *Foreign Affairs, 89*(5).

Maddikunta, P. K. R., Pham, Q. V., Prabadevi, B., Deepa, N., Dev, K., Gadekallu, T. R., & Liyanage, M. (2021). Industry 5.0: A survey on enabling technologies and potential applications. *Journal of Industrial Information Integration*, 100257.

Maher, F., Azrak, A., Sedik, A., Dessowky, M., Ghada, M., Banby, E., Khalaf, A., Elkorany, A., Fathi, E., & Samie, E. An efficient method for image forgery detection based on trigonometric transforms and deep learning. *Multimedia Tools and Applications*. Advance online publication. doi:10.100711042-019-08162-3,2020

Mahlous, A. (2019). *Internet of Things (IoTs).* Architecture, Evolution, Threats and Defense.

Mahor, R. Kumar, & Chouhan. (2021). Cyber warfare threat categorization on cps by dark web terrorist. In *2021 IEEE 4th International Conference on Computing, Power and Communication Technologies (GUCON)* (pp. 1–6). IEEE.

Mahor, V., Rawat, R., Kumar, A., & Chouhan, M. (2021). Cyber warfare threat categorization on cps by dark web terrorist. In *2021 IEEE 4th International Conference on Computing, Power and Communication Technologies (GUCON),* (pp. 1–6). IEEE.

Mahor, V., Rawat, R., Kumar, A., Chouhan, M., Shaw, R. N., & Ghosh, A. (2021). Cyber Warfare Threat Categorization on CPS by Dark Web Terrorist. *2021 IEEE 4th International Conference on Computing, Power and Communication Technologies (GUCON).* 10.1109/GUCON50781.2021.9573994

Mahor, V., Rawat, R., Kumar, A., Chouhan, M., Shaw, R. N., & Ghosh, A. (2021, September). Cyber Warfare Threat Categorization on CPS by Dark Web Terrorist. In *2021 IEEE 4th International Conference on Computing, Power and Communication Technologies (GUCON)* (pp. 1-6). IEEE.

Mahor, V., Rawat, R., Kumar, A., Chouhan, M., Shaw, R. N., & Ghosh, A. (2021, September). Cyber Warfare Threat Categorization on CPS by Dark Web Terrorist. In *2021 IEEE 4th International Conference on Computing, Power and Communication Technologies (GUCON)* (pp. 1-6). IEEE. doi:10.1201/9781003140023-6

Mahor, V., Rawat, R., Telang, S., Garg, B., Mukhopadhyay, D., & Palimkar, P. (2021, September). Machine Learning based Detection of Cyber Crime Hub Analysis using Twitter Data. In *2021 IEEE 4th International Conference on Computing, Power and Communication Technologies (GUCON)* (pp. 1-5). IEEE.

Mahor, V., Rawat, R., Telang, S., Garg, B., Mukhopadhyay, D., & Palimkar, P. (2021, September). Machine Learning based Detection of Cyber Crime Hub Analysis using Twitter Data. In *2021 IEEE 4th International Conference on Computing, Power and Communication Technologies (GUCON)* (pp. 1-5). IEEE. 10.1109/GUCON50781.2021.9573736

Maind, R., Khade, A., & Chitre, D. (2014). Image Copy Move Forgery Detection Using Block Representing Method. *International Journal Of Soft Computing And Engineering, 4*(2).

Malik, U. M., Javed, M. A., Zeadally, S., & ul Islam, S. (2021). Energy efficient fog computing for 6G enabled massive IoT: Recent trends and future opportunities. *IEEE Dark web of Things Journal.*

Manandhar, K., Cao, X., Hu, F., & Liu, Y. (2014). Detection of faults and attacks including false data injection attack in smart grid using Kalman filter. *IEEE Transactions on Control of Network Systems, 1*(4), 370–379. doi:10.1109/TCNS.2014.2357531

Mangat, S. S., & Kaur, H. (2016). Improved copy-move forgery detection in image by feature extraction with KPCA and adaptive method. *2nd International Conference on Next Generation Computing Technologies (NGCT).* 10.1109/NGCT.2016.7877501

Manojkumar, D., Scholar, P., Kumar, C. A., & Kinathukadavu, C. (2018). *Privacy Policy Multiparty Access Control On Content Sharing Sites.* Academic Press.

Marin, E., Almukaynizi, M., Nunes, E., Shakarian, J., & Shakarian, P. (2018). Predicting hacker adoption on dark web forums using sequential rule mining. *Proceedings of the 2018 IEEE Intl Conf on Parallel & Distributed Processing with Applications,* 1183–1190.

Marin, E., Almukaynizi, M., Nunes, E., Shakarian, J., & Shakarian, P. (2018). *Predicting hacker adoption on darkweb forums using sequential rule mining.* In *Intl Conf on Parallel & Distributed Processing with Applications, Ubiquitous Computing & Communications, Big Data & Cloud Computing, Social Computing & Networking, Sustainable Computing & Communications (ISPA/IUCC/BDCloud/SocialCom/SustainCom).* IEEE.

Marin, E., Almukaynizi, M., Nunes, E., & Shakarian, P. Community Finding of Malware and Exploit Vendors on Darkweb Marketplaces. *Proceedings of the 2018 1st International Conference on Data Intelligence and Security (ICDIS),* 81–84.

Martin, Hanika, Stumme, & Schaller. (2016). Social event network analysis: Structure, preferences and reality. *IEEE/ACM International Conference on Advances in Social Network Analysis and Mining.*

Martin. (n.d.). Taking the high road White hat, black hat: The ethics of cybersecurity. ACM Inroads, 8(1), 33–35.

Martínez-Miranda, E., McBurney, P., & Howard, M. J. W. (2016). Learning unfair trading: A market manipulation analysis from the reinforcement learning perspective. *Proc. 2016 IEEE Conf. Evol. Adapt. Intell. Syst. EAIS 2016*, 103–109. 10.1109/EAIS.2016.7502499

Massy, Queiroz, & Keegan. (2020). Challenges of using machine learning algorithms for cybersecurity: A study of threat-classification models applied to social media communication data. *Cyber Influence and Cognitive Threats*.

Mattern, T., Felker, J., Borum, R., & Bamford, G. (2014). Operational levels of cyber intelligence. *International Journal of Intelligence and CounterIntelligence*, *27*(4), 702–719. doi:10.1080/08850607.2014.924811

Matthew. (2014). *Social Network Analysis*. Institute for Social Science Research.

Mehrdad, S., Mousavian, S., Madraki, G., & Dvorkin, Y. (2018). Cyber-physical resilience of electrical power systems against malicious attacks: A review. *Curr. Sustain. Renew. Energy Rep.*, *5*(1), 14–22. doi:10.100740518-018-0094-8

Mergen, L. (2015). *On anonymous networking in Haskell: announcing Tor and IIP for Haskell*. Luctor et Emergen. Retrieved October, 3, 2016, from: http://www. leonmergen.com/haskell/privacy/2015/05/30/on-anonymous-networking-in haskellannouncing-tor-and-IIP-for-haskell.html

Micro, T. (2017). *Fake News And Cyber Propaganda: The Use And Abuse Of Social Media - Wiadomości Bezpieczeństwa*. https://www.trendmicro.com/vinfo/pl/security/news/cybercrime-and-digital-threats/fake-news-cyber-propaganda-the-abuse-of-social-media

MicroT. (2017). *Cyber Propaganda 101*. https://www.trendmicro.com/vinfo/es/security/news/cybercrime-and-digital-threats/cyber-propaganda-101

Miller, S., El-Bahrawy, A., Dittus, M., Graham, M., & Wright, J. (2020). Predicting Drug Demand with Wikipedia Views: Evidence from Darknet Markets. In *Proceedings of the web conference* (pp. 2669-2675). ACM. 10.1145/3366423.3380022

Mirea, M., Wang, V., & Jung, J. (2019). The not so dark side of the darknet: A qualitative study. *Security Journal*, *32*(2), 102–118. doi:10.105741284-018-0150-5

Mitrovic, M. (2016). *Dark secrets of global network*. New Energy (Nova Energija). Retrieved November 01, 2016, from http://www.novaenergija.net/

Mo, C., Xiaojuan, W., Mingshu, H., Lei, J., Javeed, K., & Wang, X. (2020). A network traffic classification model based on metric learning. *Comput. Mater. Continua*, *64*(2), 941–959.

Mohammadi-Ivatloo, B., Shiroei, M., & Parniani, M. (2011). Online small signal stability analysis of multi-machine systems based on synchronized phasor measurements. *Electric Power Systems Research*, *81*(10), 1887–1896. doi:10.1016/j.epsr.2011.05.014

Mungekar, A., Solanki, Y., & Swarnalatha, R. (2020). Augmentation of a SCADA based firewall against foreign hacking devices. *Iranian Journal of Electrical and Computer Engineering*, *10*(2), 1359–1366. doi:10.11591/ijece.v10i2.pp1359-1366

Munksgaard, R., Demant, J., & Branwen, G. (2016). A replication and methodological critique of the study 'Evaluating drug trafficking on the Tor Network'. *The International Journal on Drug Policy*, *35*, 92–96. doi:10.1016/j.drugpo.2016.02.027 PMID:27079624

2015). *Darknet - the dark side of internet surfing*. N1 SCI-TECH portal Zagreb. Retrieved September 18, 2016, from http://rs.n1info.com/a50647/Sci-Tech/Sve-o Deep-Web-ili-Darknetu.html

Narayanankutty, H. (2021). Self-adapting model-based SDSEC for IOT networks using machine learning. *2021 IEEE 18th International Conference on Software Architecture Companion (ICSA-C)*. 10.1109/ICSA-C52384.2021.00023

Narotam, S., Varshney, S., & Kapoor, A. (2016). Centrality measures in close group of adolescent females and their association with individual character strengths. *ASONAM'16 Proceedings of the 2016 IEEE/ACM International Conference on Advances in Social Networks Analysis and Mining.*

Narotam, S., Varshney, S., & Kapoor, A. (2016). Centrality measures in the close group of adolescent females and their association with individual character strengths. *IEEE/ACM ASONAM 2016.*

Naseem, I., Kashyap, A. K., & Mandloi, D. (2016). Exploring anonymous depths of invisible web and the digi underworld. *International Journal of Computer Applications, NCC,* (3), 21–25.

Nastuła, A. (2020, April). Dilemmas related to the functioning and growth of Darknet and the onion router network. *J. Sci. Papers Social Develop. Security, 10*(2), 3–10. doi:10.33445ds.2020.10.2.1

Nazah, S., Huda, S., Abawajy, J., & Hassan, M. M. (2020). Evolution of dark web threat analysis and detection: A systematic approach. *IEEE Access: Practical Innovations, Open Solutions, 8,* 171796–171819. doi:10.1109/ACCESS.2020.3024198

Ngai, W. T., Xiu, L., & Chau, D. C. K. (2008). Application of Data Mining Techniques in Customer Relationship Management: A Literature Review and Classification. *Expert Systems with Applications,* 2592–2602.

Nguyen, H. H., Yamagishi, J., & Echizen, I. (2019). Capsule-Forensics: Using Capsule Networks To Detect Forged Images And Videos. *IEEE International Conference on Acoustics, Speech and Signal Processing (ICASSP).* 10.1109/ICASSP.2019.8682602

Nicholson, P. (2021, December 9). *Five Most Famous DDoS Attacks and Then Some.* A10 Networks. https://www.a10networks.com/blog/5-most-famous-ddos-attacks/

Noor, U., Anwar, Z., Malik, A. W., Khan, S., & Saleem, S. (2019). A machine learning framework for investigating data breaches based on semantic analysis of adversary's attack patterns in threat intelligence repositories. *Future Generation Computer Systems, 95,* 467–487. doi:10.1016/j.future.2019.01.022

Nunes, E., Diab, A., Gunn, A., Marin, E., Mishra, V., Paliath, V., ... Shakarian, P. (2016). Darknet and deepnet mining for Proactive Cybersecurity Threat Intelligence. *2016 IEEE Conference on Intelligence and Security Informatics (ISI).* 10.1109/ISI.2016.7745435

Nyhan, B., & Jason, J. (2016, August 31). *Estimating Fact-checking's Effects - Evidence From a Long-term Experiment During Campaign 2014.* https://www.americanpressinstitute.org/wp-content/uploads/2016/09/Estimating-Fact-Checkings-Effect.pdf

Ozay, M., Esnaola, I., Vural, F. T. Y., Kulkarni, S. R., & Poor, H. V. (2015). Machine learning methods for attack detection in the smart grid. *IEEE Transactions on Neural Networks and Learning Systems, 27*(8), 1773–1786. doi:10.1109/TNNLS.2015.2404803 PMID:25807571

Paganini, P. (2012). What is the Deep Web. *A first trip into the abyss. Security affairs.* http://securityaffairs.co/wordpress/5650/cyber-crime/whatis-the-deep-web-a-first-trip-into-the-abyss. html

Page, L., & Brin, S. (1998). The anatomy of a large-scale hypertextual Web search engine. *Computer Networks, 30*(1–7), 107–117. doi:10.1016/S0169-7552(98)00110-X

Painuly, S., Sharma, S., & Matta, P. (2021, April). Future Trends and Challenges in Next Generation Smart Application of 5G-IoT. In *2021 5th International Conference on Computing Methodologies and Communication (ICCMC)* (pp. 354-357). IEEE.

Pajooh, H. H., Rashid, M., Alam, F., & Demidenko, S. (2021). Multi-Layer Blockchain-Based Security Architecture for Internet of Things. *Sensors (Basel), 21*(3), 772. doi:10.339021030772 PMID:33498860

Pali, I., Krishania, L., Chadha, D., Kandar, A., Varshney, G., & Shukla, S. (2020). *A Comprehensive Survey of Aadhar & Security Issues.* arXiv, 1–12.

Pal, S., Hitchens, M., Rabehaja, T., & Mukhopadhyay, S. (2020). Security Requirements for the Internet of Things: A Systematic Approach. *Sensors (Basel)*, *20*(20), 5897. doi:10.339020205897 PMID:33086542

Pastrana, S., Hutchings, A., Caines, A., & Buttery, P. (2018). *Characterizing eve: analysing cybercrime actors in a large underground forum. Research in Attacks, Intrusions, and Defenses.*

Patchin, J. W., & Hinduja, S. (2011). Traditional and non-traditional bullying among youth: A test of general strain theory. *Youth & Society*, *43*(2), 727–751. doi:10.1177/0044118X10366951

Patel, H., Prajapati, D., Mahida, D., & Shah, M. (2020). Transforming petroleum downstream sector through big data: A holistic review. *Journal of Petroleum Exploration and Production Technology*, *10*(6), 2601–2611. doi:10.100713202-020-00889-2

Pavel, Y. P. P. A. F., & Soares, B. C. (2002). Decision tree-based data characterization for meta-learning. *Proc. IDDM-2002*, 111.

PC. (2015). Definition of: surface Web. *PC Magazine Encyclopedia*. Retrieved November 20, 2016, from http://www.pcmag.com/encyclopedia/ term/52273/surface-web

Pelton, J. N., & Singh, I. B. (2019). Coping with the dark web, cyber-criminals and techno-terrorists in a smart city. In *Smart cities of today and tomorrow* (pp. 171–183). Copernicus. doi:10.1007/978-3-319-95822-4_11

Pelton, N., & Singh, I. B. (2019). *Coping with the dark web, cyber-criminals and techno-terrorists in a smart city.* Smart Cities of Today and Tomorrow-Better Technology.

Peneti, S., & E, H. (2021). DDOS Attack Identification using Machine Learning Techniques. *2021 International Conference on Computer Communication and Informatics (ICCCI)*, 1-5.

Peng, K., Li, M., Huang, H., Wang, C., Wan, S., & Choo, K.-K. R. (2021). Security challenges and opportunities for smart contracts in internet of things: A survey. *IEEE Internet of Things Journal*, *8*(15), 12004–12020. doi:10.1109/JIOT.2021.3074544

Pishva, D., & Takeda, K. (2008). Product-based security model for smart home appliances. *IEEE Aerospace and Electronic Systems Magazine*, *23*(10), 32–41. doi:10.1109/MAES.2008.4665323

Pizzolante, R., Castiglione, A., Carpentieri, B., Contaldo, R., D'Angelo, G., & Palmieri, F. (2020). A machine learning-based memory forensics methodology for Tor Browser artifacts. *Concurrency and Computation*, *33*(23). Advance online publication. doi:10.1002/cpe.5935

Plucinski & Pietrzykowski. (2017). *Application of the K Nearest Neighbors Method to Fuzzy Data Processing.* West Pomeranian Univ. Technol.

Posts, R. (2017). *The Dark Web Links.* Available: http://www.thedarkweblinks.com

Prathap, M. R., Nandhini, K. M., Vairavel, K. S., & Suraj, M. V. (2021). Detection of Data Breaching Websites using Machine Learning. *2021 International Conference on Advancements in Electrical, Electronics, Communication, Computing and Automation (ICAECA)*, 1-6. 10.1109/ICAECA52838.2021.9675712

Qiao, M., Sung, A., Liu, Q., & Ribeiro, B. (2011). A novel approach for detection of copy-move forgery. *Fifth International Conference on ADVCOMP (Advanced Engineering Computing and Applications in Sciences.*

Queiroz, Keegan, & Mckeever. (2020). Moving targets: addressing concept drift in supervised models for hacker communication detection. *Proceedings of the 2020 International Conference on Cyber Security and Protection of Digital Services (Cyber Security),* 1–7. doi:10.1007/978-3-319-95822-4_11

Qureshi, A., & Deriche, M. (2014). *A review on copy move image forgery detection techniques.* IEEE SSD International Multi-Conference on Systems, Signals and Devices. doi:10.1109/SSD.2014.6808907

Rajawat, A. S., Rawat, R., Barhanpurkar, K., Shaw, R. N., & Ghosh, A. (2021). Blockchain-Based Model for Expanding IoT Device Data Security. *Advances in Applications of Data-Driven Computing,* 61.

Rajawat, A. S., Rawat, R., Barhanpurkar, K., Shaw, R. N., & Ghosh, A. (2021). Vulnerability Analysis at Industrial Internet of Things Platform on Dark Web Network Using Computational Intelligence. *Computationally Intelligent Systems and their Applications,* 39-51.

Rajawat, Rawat, Mahor, Shaw, & Ghosh. (2021), Suspicious big text data analysis for prediction—on darkweb user activity using computational intelligence model. In *Innovations in Electrical and Electronic Engineering* (pp. 735–751). Springer.

Rajawat, A. S., Rawat, R., Mahor, V., Shaw, R. N., & Ghosh, A. (2021). Suspicious big text data analysis for prediction—on darkweb user activity using computational intelligence model. In *Innovations in Electrical and Electronic Engineering* (pp. 735–751). Springer.

Rajawat, A. S., Rawat, R., Mahor, V., Shaw, R. N., & Ghosh, A. (2021). Suspicious Big Text Data Analysis for Prediction—On Darkweb User Activity Using Computational Intelligence Model. In *Innovations in Electrical and Electronic Engineering* (pp. 735–751). Springer. doi:10.1007/978-981-16-0749-3_58

Rajawat, A. S., Rawat, R., Shaw, R. N., & Ghosh, A. (2021). Cyber Physical System Fraud Analysis by Mobile Robot. In *Machine Learning for Robotics Applications* (pp. 47–61). Springer. doi:10.1007/978-981-16-0598-7_4

Rajesh, E. (2019). A Research Paper on Dark Web. *International Journal of Emerging Technologies and Innovative Research, 6*(4), 322-327. https://www.jetir.org/papers/JETIREQ06074.pdf

Rani, S., & Gupta, S. (2015). *Novel Indexing Technique for Hidden Web Pages using Semantic Analysis.* Academic Press.

Rani, A., & Rajasree, S. (2019). Crime trend analysis and prediction using mahanolobis distance and dynamic time warping technique. *International Journal of Computer Science and Information Technologies, 5*(3), 4131–4135.

Rantos, K., Drosatos, G., Demertzis, K., Ilioudis, C., & Papanikolaou, A. (2021). *Blockchain-Based Consents Management for Personal Data Processing in the IoT Ecosystem.* Available online: https://www.scitepress.org/PublicationsDetail.aspx?ID=+u1w9%2fItJqY%3d&t=1

Rantos, K., Drosatos, G., Demertzis, K., Ilioudis, C., Papanikolaou, A., & Kritsas, A. (2019). ADvoCATE: A Consent Management Platform for Personal Data Processing in the IoT Using Blockchain Technology. In *Innovative Security Solutions for Information Technology and Communications* (pp. 300–313). Springer.

Rawat, Garg, Mahor, Telang, Pachlasiya, & Chouhan. (2021). Organ trafficking on the dark web—the data security and privacy concern in healthcare systems. *Internet of Healthcare Things,* 191.

Rawat, Kumar, Chouhan, Telang, Pachlasiya, Garg, & Mahor. (2021). *Systematic literature review (slr) on social media and the digital transformation of drug trafficking on darkweb.* Available at SSRN 3903797.

Rawat, M. Chirgaiya, & Garg. (2021). Artificial cyber espionage based protection of technological enabled automated cities infrastructure by dark web cyber offender. In Intelligence of Things: AI-IoT Based Critical-Applications and Innovations (pp. 167–188). Springer.

Rawat, Mahor, Chirgaiya, Shaw, & Ghosh (2021). Analysis of darknet traffic for criminal activities detection using tf-idf and light gradient boosted machine learning algorithm. In *Innovations in Electrical and Electronic Engineering* (pp. 671–681). Springer.

Rawat, R., Mahor, V., Chirgaiya, S., & Garg, B. (2021). Artificial cyber espionage based protection of technological enabled automated cities infrastructure by dark web cyber offender. In Intelligence of Things: AI-IoT Based Critical-Applications and Innovations (pp. 167–188). Springer.

Rawat, R., Mahor, V., Chirgaiya, S., Shaw, R. N., & Ghosh, A. (2021). Sentiment Analysis at Online Social Network for Cyber-Malicious Post Reviews Using Machine Learning Techniques. *Computationally Intelligent Systems and their Applications*, 113-130.

Rawat, Rajawat, Mahor, Shaw, & Ghosh. (2021). Dark web—onion hidden service discovery and crawling for profiling morphing, unstructured crime and vulnerabilities prediction. In *Innovations in Electrical and Electronic Engineering* (pp. 717–734). Springer.

Rawat, D. B., & Bajracharya, C. (2015). Detection of false data injection attacks in smart grid communication systems. *IEEE Signal Processing Letters*, 22(10), 1652–1656. doi:10.1109/LSP.2015.2421935

Rawat, R., Dangi, C. S., & Patil, J. (2011). Safe Guard Anomalies against SQL Injection Attacks. *International Journal of Computers and Applications*, 22(2), 11–14. doi:10.5120/2558-3511

Rawat, R., Garg, B., Mahor, V., Chouhan, M., Pachlasiya, K., & Telang, S. Cyber Threat Exploitation and Growth during COVID-19 Times. In *Advanced Smart Computing Technologies in Cybersecurity and Forensics* (pp. 85–101). CRC Press.

Rawat, R., Mahor, V., Chirgaiya, S., & Garg, B. (2021). Artificial Cyber Espionage Based Protection of Technological Enabled Automated Cities Infrastructure by Dark Web Cyber Offender. In *Intelligence of Things: AI-IoT Based Critical-Applications and Innovations* (pp. 167–188). Springer. doi:10.1007/978-3-030-82800-4_7

Rawat, R., Mahor, V., Chirgaiya, S., & Rathore, A. S. (2021). Applications of Social Network Analysis to Managing the Investigation of Suspicious Activities in Social Media Platforms. In *Advances in Cybersecurity Management* (pp. 315–335). Springer. doi:10.1007/978-3-030-71381-2_15

Rawat, R., Mahor, V., Chirgaiya, S., Shaw, R. N., & Ghosh, A. (2021). Analysis of darknet traffic for criminal activities detection using tf-idf and light gradient boosted machine learning algorithm. In *Innovations in Electrical and Electronic Engineering* (pp. 671–681). Springer.

Rawat, R., Mahor, V., Chirgaiya, S., Shaw, R. N., & Ghosh, A. (2021). Analysis of Darknet Traffic for Criminal Activities Detection Using TF-IDF and Light Gradient Boosted Machine Learning Algorithm. In *Innovations in Electrical and Electronic Engineering* (pp. 671–681). Springer. doi:10.1007/978-981-16-0749-3_53

Rawat, R., Mahor, V., Rawat, A., Garg, B., & Telang, S. (2021). Digital Transformation of Cyber Crime for Chip-Enabled Hacking. In *Handbook of Research on Advancing Cybersecurity for Digital Transformation* (pp. 227–243). IGI Global. doi:10.4018/978-1-7998-6975-7.ch012

Rawat, R., Rajawat, A. S., Mahor, V., Shaw, R. N., & Ghosh, A. (2021). Dark web—onion hidden service discovery and crawling for profiling morphing, unstructured crime and vulnerabilities prediction. In *Innovations in Electrical and Electronic Engineering* (pp. 717–734). Springer.

Rawat, R., Rajawat, A. S., Mahor, V., Shaw, R. N., & Ghosh, A. (2021). Dark Web—Onion Hidden Service Discovery and Crawling for Profiling Morphing, Unstructured Crime and Vulnerabilities Prediction. In *Innovations in Electrical and Electronic Engineering* (pp. 717–734). Springer. doi:10.1007/978-981-16-0749-3_57

Rawat, R., Rajawat, A. S., Mahor, V., Shaw, R. N., & Ghosh, A. (2021). Surveillance Robot in Cyber Intelligence for Vulnerability Detection. In *Machine Learning for Robotics Applications* (pp. 107–123). Springer. doi:10.1007/978-981-16-0598-7_9

Richardson, R. (2010/2011). *15th Annual Computer Crime and Security Survey*. Computer Security Institute.

Robert, R. (2004). A ten-step approach for forensic readiness. *Int J Dig Evi*, 2(3), 313–319.

Rodrigues, T. K., Liu, J., & Kato, N. (2021). Application of Cybertwin for Offloading in Mobile Multi-access Edge Computing for 6G Networks. *IEEE Dark web of Things Journal*.

Rodriguez, M. Z. (2019). *Clustering algorithms: A comparative approach*. PLOS.

Rohit, M. H., Fahim, S. M., & Khan, A. H. (2019). Mitigating and detecting ddos attack on IOT environment. *2019 IEEE International Conference on Robotics, Automation, Artificial-Intelligence and Internet-of-Things (RAAICON)*. 10.1109/RAAICON48939.2019.5

Rummens, A., Hardyns, W., & Pauwels, L. (2017). The use of predictive analysis in spatiotemporal crime forecasting: Building and testing a model in an urban context. *Applied Geography (Sevenoaks, England)*, 86, 255–261. doi:10.1016/j.apgeog.2017.06.011

Sabillon, C., Cano, & Serra-Ruiz. (2016). Cybercriminals, cyberattacks, and cybercrime. In 2016 IEEE International Conference on Cybercrime and Computer Forensic (ICCCF) (pp. 1–9). IEEE.

Sahoo, S., Mishra, S., Peng, J. C.-H., & Dragicevic, T. (2018). A Stealth Cyber-Attack Detection Strategy for DC Microgrids. *IEEE Transactions on Power Electronics*, 34(8), 8162–8174. doi:10.1109/TPEL.2018.2879886

Sahoo, S., Peng, J. C.-H., Devakumar, A., Mishra, S., & Dragicevic, T. (2019). On detection of false data in cooperative dc microgrids—A discordant element approach. *IEEE Transactions on Industrial Electronics*, 67(8), 6562–6571. doi:10.1109/TIE.2019.2938497

Saini, P., Behal, S., & Bhatia, S. (2020). Detection of DDoS Attacks using Machine Learning Algorithms. *The Internet Watch Foundation - Eliminating Child Sexual Abuse Online*.

Samtani, S., Li, W., Benjamin, V., & Chen, H. (2021). Informing Cyber Threat Intelligence through Dark Web Situational Awareness: The AZSecure Hacker Assets Portal. *Digital Threats: Research and Practice*, 2(4), 1–10. doi:10.1145/3450972

Sanchez, R. C., Puente, C., Palacios, R., & Piriz, C. (2019). Detection of Jihadism in Social networks using big data techniques supported by Graphs and Fuzzy Clustering. Hindwai Complexity.

Sancho, D. (2015). *Steganography and Malware: Why and How*. TrendLabs Security Intelligence Blog. Retrieved October 30, 2016, from http://blog.trendmicro.com/ trendlabs-security-intelligence/steganography-and-malware-why-and-how/

Sangvai, R. (2020). Responding to Cyber Attack on ATM and SWIFT Payment Gateway by Cosmos Cooperative Bank Pune A Change Management Exercise. *MuktShabd Journal*, 9(7), 633–640.

Sapienza, A., Bessi, A., Damodaran, S., Shakarian, P., Lerman, K., & Ferrara, E. (2017). Early warnings of cyber threats in online discussions. *Proceedings of the IEEE International Conference on Data Mining Workshops (ICDMW)*. 10.1109/ICDMW.2017.94

Sarkar, S., Almukaynizi, M., Shakarian, J., & Shakarian, P. (2018). Predicting enterprise cyber incidents using social network analysis on dark web hacker forums. *Proceedings of the Cyber Defense Review*, 87–102.

Sarkar, S., Almukaynizi, M., Shakarian, J., & Shakarian, P. (2019). Mining user interaction patterns in the darkweb to predict enterprise cyber incidents. *Social Network Analysis and Mining*, 9(1), 1–28. doi:10.100713278-019-0603-9

Saumya, G., & Tiwari, A. (2016, May). Terrorism in the Cyber Space: The New Battlefield. *International Journal of Advanced Research in Computer and Communication Engineering, 5*(5).

Sawyer & Monckton. (1995). *'Shoe-fit'-a computerized shoe print database.* Academic Press.

Scarpitti, F. R., Nielsen, A. L., & Miller, J. M. (2009). A Sociological Theory of Criminal Behavior. In Crime and Criminals Contemporary and Classic Readings in Criminology (2nd ed.). New York: Oxford University Press.

Schäfer, M., Fuchs, M., Strohmeier, M., Engel, M., Liechti, M., & Lenders, V. (2019). BlackWidow: Monitoring the dark web for cyber security information. *11th International Conference on Cyber Conflict (CyCon),* 1-21. 10.23919/CYCON.2019.8756845

Selamat, S. R., Yusof, R., & Sahib, S. (2008). Mapping process of digital forensic investigation framework. *Int. J. Comput. Sci. Netw. Secur., 8*(10), 163–169.

Shahbar, K., & Zincir-Heywood, A. N. (2014). Benchmarking two techniques for Tor classification: Flow level and circuit level classification. *Proc. IEEE Symp. Comput. Intell. Cyber Secur. (CICS),* 1–8.

Shah, D., Dixit, R., Shah, A., Shah, P., & Shah, M. (2020). A comprehensive analysis regarding several breakthroughs based on computer intelligence targeting various syndromes. *Augmented Human Research, 5*(1), 1–12. doi:10.100741133-020-00033-z

Shah, S. D. A., Gregory, M. A., & Li, S. (2021). Cloud-native network slicing using software defined networking based multi-access edge computing: A survey. *IEEE Access: Practical Innovations, Open Solutions, 9,* 10903–10924. doi:10.1109/ACCESS.2021.3050155

Shakarian, P. (2018). Dark-web cyber threat intelligence: From data to intelligence to prediction. *Information (Basel), 9*(12), 305. doi:10.3390/info9120305

Sharma, A., & Sharma, S. (2012). An intelligent analysis of web crime data using data Mining. *Certif Int J Eng Innov Technol, 2*(3).

Sharma, S., Agarwal, P., & Mohan, S. (2020, December). Security challenges and future aspects of fifth generation vehicular adhoc networking (5G-VANET) in connected vehicles. In *2020 3rd International Conference on Intelligent Sustainable Systems (ICISS)* (pp. 1376-1380). IEEE.

Sharma, S., Ghanshala, K. K., & Mohan, S. (2019, September). Blockchain-based dark web of vehicles (IoV): an efficient secure ad hoc vehicular networking architecture. In *2019 IEEE 2nd 5G World Forum (5GWF)* (pp. 452-457). IEEE.

Sharma, B., & Nandi, G. (2014). A Study on Digital Image Forgery Detection. *International Journal of Advanced Research in Computer Science and Software Engineering, 4*(11).

Sharma, N., & Chirgaiya, S. (2014). A novel approach to Hill cipher. *International Journal of Computers and Applications, 108*(11), 975–8887.

Sharma, V., You, I., & Kul, G. (2017). Socialising drones for inter-service operability in ultra-dense wireless networks using Blockchain. *Proceedings of the 2017 International Workshop on Managing Insider Security Threats,* 81–84. 10.1145/3139923.3139932

Shaukat, K., Luo, S., Chen, S., & Liu, D. (2020). Cyber Threat Detection Using Machine Learning Techniques: A Performance Evaluation Perspective. *2020 International Conference on Cyber Warfare and Security (ICCWS),* 1-6. 10.1109/ICCWS48432.2020.9292388

Shiaeles, S., Kolokotronis, N., & Bellini, E. (2019). IOT vulnerability data crawling and analysis. *2019 IEEE World Congress on Services (SERVICES)*. 10.1109/SERVICES.2019.00028

Shi, J., Du, J., Wang, J., Wang, J., & Yuan, J. (2020). Priority-aware task offloading in vehicular fog computing based on deep reinforcement learning. *IEEE Transactions on Vehicular Technology*, *69*(12), 16067–16081. doi:10.1109/TVT.2020.3041929

Shin, D., Sharma, V., Kim, J., Kwon, S., & You, I. (2017). Secure and efficient protocol for route optimisation in PMIPv6-based smart home IoT networks. *IEEE Access: Practical Innovations, Open Solutions*, *5*, 11100–11117. doi:10.1109/ACCESS.2017.2710379

Siddharth, Hu, & Chen. (2007). Dynamic Social Network Analysis of a dark network: Identifying significant facilitators. *IEEE Intelligence and Security Informatics 2007*.

Singh, S. (2021). 10 Biggest Cyber Attacks on Indian Companies. *The420CyberNews*. https://www.the420.in/10-major-cyber-attacks-on-indian-companies-that-are-eye-openers-check-the-full-list-here/

Singh, N. (2007). Online banking Fraud Using Phishing. *Journal of Internet Banking and Commerce*, *12*, 1–27.

Singh, S., Jeong, Y.-S., & Park, J. H. (2016). A survey on cloud computing security: Issues, threats, and solutions. *Journal of Network and Computer Applications*, *75*, 200–222. doi:10.1016/j.jnca.2016.09.002

Singh, S., Sharma, P. K., Moon, S. Y., & Park, J. H. (2017). EH-GC: An efficient and secure architecture of energy harvesting Green cloud infrastructure. *Sustainability*, *9*(4), 673. doi:10.3390u9040673

Singh, S., Sharma, P. K., & Park, J. H. (2017). SH-SecNet: An enhanced secure network architecture for the diagnosis of security threats in a smart home. *Sustainability*, *9*(4), 513. doi:10.3390u9040513

Sivakumar, R. R., & K. S. (2021). Real Time Crime Detection Using Deep Learning Algorithm. *2021 International Conference on System, Computation, Automation and Networking (ICSCAN)*, 1-5. 10.1109/ICSCAN53069.2021.9526393

Sixgill. (2018). *Dark Web Sites as a Platform for Hacktivist Warfare 2018*. Author.

Smith, G. J. D., Moses, L. B., & Chan, J. (2017). The challenges of doing criminology in the big data era: Towards a digital and data-driven approach. *British Journal of Criminology*, *57*(2), 259–274. doi:10.1093/bjc/azw096

Smith, M., Milic-Frayling, N., Shneiderman, B., Mendes Rodrigues, E., Leskovec, J., & Dunne, C. (2010). *NodeXL: a free and open network overview, discovery and exploration add-in for Excel 2007/2010*. Social Media Research Foundation.

Sodhro, A. H., & Zahid, N. (2021). AI-Enabled Framework for Fog Computing Driven E-Healthcare Applications. *Sensors (Basel)*, *21*(23), 8039. doi:10.339021238039 PMID:34884048

Somerville, K. (2012). *Conclusions: Propaganda, Hate And the Power Of Radio*. SpringerLink. https://link.springer.com/chapter/10.1057/9781137284150_7

Song, H., Rawat, D. B., Jeschke, S., & Brecher, C. (2016). *Cyber-physical systems: Foundations, principles and applications*. Morgan Kaufmann.

Spalevic, Z., Ilic, M., & Palevic, M. (2016). Electronic Tracking Of Postal Services. In *Proceedings of 3rd the International Scientific Conference on ICT and e-Business Related Research – Sinteza* (pp. 479-485). Belgrade: University Singidunum. 10.15308/Sinteza-2016-479-485

Sukheja, D., Indira, L., Sharma, P., & Chirgaiya, S. (2019). Blockchain Technology: A Comprehensive Survey. *Journal of Advanced Research in Dynamic and Control Systems*, *11*(9), 1187–1203. doi:10.5373/JARDCS/V11/20192690

Sun, C., Wu, X., Li, X., Fan, Q., Wen, J., & Leung, V. C. (2021). Cooperative Computation Offloading for Multi-Access Edge Computing in 6G Mobile Networks via Soft Actor Critic. *IEEE Transactions on Network Science and Engineering*.

Suresh Kumar, K., Radha Mani, A. S., Sundaresan, S., & Ananth Kumar, T. (2021). Modeling of VANET for Future Generation Transportation System Through Edge/Fog/Cloud Computing Powered by 6G. *Cloud and IoT-Based Vehicular Ad Hoc Networks*, 105-124.

Tamir, A., Watson, E., Willett, B., Hasan, Q., & Yuan, J.-S. (2021). Crime Prediction and Forecasting using Machine Learning Algorithms. *International Journal of Computer Science and Information Technologies*, 12(2), 26–33.

Tan, S., Guerrero, J. O., Xie, P., Han, R., & Vasquez, J. C. (2020). Brief Survey on Attack Detection Methods for Cyber-Physical Systems. *IEEE Systems Journal*, 14(4), 5329–5339. doi:10.1109/JSYST.2020.2991258

Tanzeela, Q., Hayat, K., Khan, S. U., & Madani, S. (2013). Survey on blind image forgery detection. *IET Image Processing*.

Tavabi, N., Goyal, P., Almukaynizi, M., Shakarian, P., & Lerman, K. (2018). DarkEmbed: exploit prediction with Neural Language models. *Proceedings of the AAAI Conference on Artificial Intelligence*, 7849–7854.

Thakur, S., Kaur, R., Chadha, R., & Kaur, J. (2016). A Review Paper on Image Forgery Detection in Image Processing. *IOSR Journal of Computer Engineering*, 18(4), 86-89.

Tian, W., Ji, X., Liu, W., Liu, G., Lin, R., Zhai, J., & Dai, Y. (2019). "Defense strategies against network attacks in cyber-physical systems with analysis cost constraint based on honeypot game model," Comput. *Mater. Continua*, 60(1), 193–211.

Todorovic, A. (2015). *What is deep and dark web, you need to take care and how to protect myself?* Kompijuteraš. Retrieved November, 18, 2016, from https://kompjuteras.com/sta-je-deep-dark-web-trebam-li-se-brinuti-kako-da-se-zastitim/

Tokunaga, R. S. (2010). Following You Home from School: A Critical Review and Synthesis of Research on Cyberbullying Victimization. *Computers in Human Behavior*, 26, 277–287. http://ryanstillions.blogspot.com/2014/0 4/the-dml-model 21.html

Tounsi, W. (2019). What is cyber threat intelligence and how is it evolving? In W. Tounsi (Ed.), *Cyber-Vigilance and Digital Trust: Cyber Security in the Era of Cloud Computing and IoT*. ISTE Ltd.

Tounsi, W., & Rais, H. (2018). A survey on technical threat intelligence in the age of sophisticated cyber attacks. *Computers & Security*, 72, 212–233. doi:10.1016/j.cose.2017.09.001

Trifonov, R., Manolov, S., Yoshinov, R., Tsochev, G., Nedev, S., & Pavlova, G. (2018). Operational Cyber Threat Intelligence supported by Artificial Intelligence methods. *International Conference on Information Technologies (InfoTech-2018)*, 20-21.

Tu, E., Zhang, G., Rachmawati, L., Rajabally, E., Mao, S., & Huang, G. (2017). A theoretical study of the relationship between an ELM network and its subnetworks. *Proceedings of the 2017 International Joint Conference on Neural Networks (IJCNN)*, 1794–1801.

Tweneboah-Koduah, S., Skouby, K. E., & Tadayoni, R. (2017). Cyber Security Threats to IoT Applications and Service Domains. *Wireless Personal Communications*, 95(1), 169–185. doi:10.100711277-017-4434-6

Types Of Propaganda - Propaganda. (n.d.). *Types of propaganda - Propaganda*. https://www.americanforeignrelations.com/O-W/Propaganda-Types-of-propaganda.html

Ullah, F., Naeem, H., Jabbar, S., Khalid, S., Latif, M. A., Al-turjman, F., & Mostarda, L. (2019). Cyber security threats detection in internet of things using Deep Learning Approach. *IEEE Access: Practical Innovations, Open Solutions*, 7, 124379–124389. doi:10.1109/ACCESS.2019.2937347

Van Hout, M. C., & Bingham, T. (2013). 'Silk Road', the virtual drug marketplace: A single case study of user experiences. *The International Journal on Drug Policy, 24*(5), 385–391.

Van Wilsem, J. (2011). Worlds tied together. Online and non-domestic routine activities and their impact on digital and traditional threat victimization. *European Journal of Criminology, 8*(2), 115–127.

Varatharajan, A., Latha, C., & Dasig, D. Jr. (2019). Concept of implementing Big data in smart city: Applications, Services, Data Security in accordance with Internet of Things and AI. *International Journal of Recent Technology and Engineering, 8*(3), 6819–6825. Advance online publication. doi:10.35940/ijrte.C5782.098319

Victor, S., Campose, F., Jose Maria, N. D., & Braga, R. (2017). Data abstraction and centrality measures to scientific social network analysis. *IEEE 21st International Conference on Computer Supported Cooperative Work in Design 2017.*

Vijesti. (2015). *Dark internet: There are hackers, sellers of human organs, and weapons.* Vijesti online. Retrieved October 30, 2016, from https://www.vijesti.me/techno/tamni-internet-tu-su-hakeri-prodavci-ljudskih-organa-oruzja-828308

Vogt, P. (2013, November 18). *Should We Pay Attention To Assassination Markets?* On the Media | WNYC Studios. https://www.wnycstudios.org/podcasts/otm/articles/should-we-pay-attention-assassination-markets

Wang, X. Y., Wang, C., Wang, L., Jiao, L. X., Yang, H. Y., & Niu. (2020). A fast and high accurate image copy-move forgery detection approach. Multidimensional Systems and Signal Processing. Advance online publication. doi:10.1007/s11045-019-00688-x

Wan, M., Yang, G., Gai, S., & Yang, Z. (2017). Two-dimensional discriminant Locality preserving projections (2DDLDP) and its application to feature extraction via fuzzy set. *Multimedia Tools and Applications, 76*(1), 355–371.

Williams, M. L., & Burnap, P. (2016). Cyberhate on Social Media in the aftermath of Woolwich: A Case Study in Computational Criminology and Big Data. *British Journal of Criminology, 56*(2), 211–238. doi:10.1093/bjc/azv059

Wortmann, F., & Flüchter, K. (2015). Internet of things. *Business & Information Systems Engineering, 57*(3), 221–224. doi:10.100712599-015-0383-3

Wu, M., Lu, T.-J., Ling, F.-Y., Sun, J., & Du, H.-Y. (2010). Research on the architecture of internet of things. *2010 3rd International Conference on Advanced Computer Theory and Engineering (ICACTE).* 10.1109/ICACTE.2010.5579493

Wu, Y., Abd-Almageed, W., & Natarajan, P. (2018). Detecting copy-move image forgery with source/target localization. *Proceedings of the European Conference on Computer Vision (ECCV),* 168–184. 10.1007/978-3-030-01231-1_11

Xing, W., & Ghorbani, A. (2004). Weighted PageRank algorithm. *Proceedings - Second Annual Conference on Communication Networks and Services Research,* 305–314. 10.1109/DNSR.2004.1344743

Xiong, B., Yang, K., Zhao, J. Y., & Li, K. Q. (2017, June). Robust dynamic network traffic partitioning against malicious attacks. *Journal of Network and Computer Applications, 87,* 20–31.

Xuan, D., Yu, H., & Wang, J. (2014). A novel method of centrality in terrorist network. *2014 Seventh International Symposium on Computational Intelligence and Design.* 10.1109/ISCID.2014.156

Xu, K., Wang, X., Wei, W., Song, H., & Mao, B. (2016). Toward software-defined smart home. *IEEE Communications Magazine, 54*(5), 116–122. doi:10.1109/MCOM.2016.7470945

Xu, T., Wendt, J. B., & Potkonjak, M. (2014). Security of IoT systems: Design challenges and opportunities. *2014 IEEE/ACM International Conference on Computer-Aided Design (ICCAD).* 10.1109/ICCAD.2014.7001385

Yadav, J., & Dongre, N. (2017). Analysis of Copy-Move Forgery Detection in Digital Image. *International Journal of Engineering Development and Research, 5*(1).

Yadav, M., & Goyal, N. (2015). Comparison of Open Source Crawlers - A Review. *International Journal of Scientific and Engineering Research*, 6(9).

Yadav, T., & Rao, A. M. (2015). Technical aspects of cyber kill chain. In *International Symposium on Security in Computing and Communication* (pp. 438-452). Springer. 10.1007/978-3-319-22915-7_40

Yang, H. Y., Qi, S. R., Niu, Y., & Wang, X. Y. (2019). Copy-move forgery detection based on adaptive keypoints extraction and matching. *Multimedia Tools and Applications*, 78(24), 34585–34612. Advance online publication. doi:10.100711042-019-08169-w

Yang, L., Liu, F., Kizza, J. M., & Ege, R. K. (2009, March). *Discovering topics from dark websites. In 2009 IEEE symposium on computational intelligence in cyber security*. IEEE.

Young, K. (1930). *Kimball Young: Social Psychology: Chapter 27: Propoganda: PositiveControl Of Public Opinion.* https://brocku.ca/MeadProject/Young/1930/1930_27.html

Yousefpour, A., Fung, C., Nguyen, T., Kadiyala, K., Jalali, F., Niakanlahiji, A., & Jue, J. P. (2019). All one needs to know about fog computing and related edge computing paradigms: A complete survey. *Journal of Systems Architecture*, 98, 289–330. doi:10.1016/j.sysarc.2019.02.009

Yu, Y., Wan, X., Liu, G., Li, H., Li, P., & Lin, H. (2017). A combinatorial clustering method for sequential fraud detection. *Service Systems and Service Management (ICSSSM), 2017 International Conference on*, 1–6.

Yuchong, L., &Qinghui, L. (2021). A comprehensive review study of cyber-attacks and cyber security; Emerging trends and recent developments. *Energy Reports, 7*, 8176-8186. https://doi.org/10.1016/j.egyr.2021.08.126

Zenebe, A., Shumba, M., Carillo, A., & Cuenca, S. (n.d.). Cyber threat discovery from dark web. *EPiC Series in Computing.* doi:10.29007/nkfk

Zenebe, A., Shumba, M., Carillo, A., & Cuenca, S. (2019). Cyber threat discovery from dark web. *Proceedings of the 28th International Conference on Software Engineering and Data Engineering.*

Zetter, K. (2013). How the Feds Took Down the Silk Road Drug Wonderland. *Wired*. Retrieved October 20, 2016, from: www.wired.com/2013/11/silk-road

Zetter, K. (2015). DARPA is developing a search engine for the dark web. *Retrieved, 11*(15), 2018.

Zhang, H., & Zou, F. (2020). A Survey of the Dark Web and Dark Market Research. In *IEEE 6th International Conference on Computer and Communications (ICCC)* (pp. 1694-1705). IEEE.

Zhang, D., Yu, F. R., & Yang, R. (2021). Blockchain-Based Multi-Access Edge Computing for Future Vehicular Networks: A Deep Compressed Neural Network Approach. *IEEE Transactions on Intelligent Transportation Systems*, 1–15. doi:10.1109/TITS.2021.3110591

Zhang, Y., Zeng, S., Huang, C. N., Fan, L., Yu, X., Dang, Y., ... Chen, H. (2010, May). Developing a Dark Web collection and infrastructure for computational and social sciences. In *2010 IEEE International Conference on Intelligence and Security Informatics* (pp. 59-64). IEEE. 10.1109/ISI.2010.5484774

Zhang, Y., Zou, W., Chen, X., Yang, C., & Cao, J. (2014). The security for power internet of things: Framework, policies, and countermeasures. *2014 International Conference on Cyber-Enabled Distributed Computing and Knowledge Discovery.* 10.1109/CyberC.2014.32

Zheng, S., Apthorpe, N., Chetty, M., & Feamster, N. (2018). User perceptions of smart home IoT privacy. *Proceedings of the ACM on Human-Computer Interaction, 2*(CSCW), 1–20. 10.1145/3274469

Zhou, Lin, & Zheng. (2012). A web-based geographical information system for crime mapping and decision support. *IEEE Intl. Conf. on Comput. Problem-Solving (ICCP).*

Zhou, Z. W., & Shi, L. (2013). Security Research and Measures for the Internet of Things. *Advanced Materials Research, 748,* 910–914. . doi:10.4028/www.scientific.net/AMR.748.910

Zillman & M.S. (2017). *Deep Web Research and Discovery Resources 2017.* Virtual Private Library.

About the Contributors

Romil Rawat is currently working as Assistant Professor in Shri Vaishnav Vidyapeeth Vishwavidyalaya, Indore, India. He attended several research programs and received research grants from USA, Germany, Italy and UK. The Author has research alignment towards Cyber Security, IoT, Dark Web Crime analysis and investigation techniques, and working towards tracing of illicit anonymous contents of cyber terrorism and criminal activities. He also chaired International Conferences and Hosted several research events including National and International Research Schools, PhD colloquium, Workshops, training programs. He also published several Research Patents.

Shrikant Telang is currently working as Assistant Professor in Shri Vaishnav Vidyapeeth Vishwavidyalaya, Indore, India. He attended several research programs. The Author has research alignment towards Cyber Security, IoT, Dark Web Crime analysis and investigation techniques, and working towards tracing illicit anonymous contents of cyber terrorism and criminal activities. He also joins International Conferences and several research events including National and International Research Schools, Workshops, training programs. He also published several Research Patents.

P. William is working as an Assistant Professor, Department of Information Technology, Sanjivani College of Engineering, SPPU Pune. He received his Bachelor of Engineering in Computer Science and Engineering from CSVTU, Bhilai in 2013 and Master of Technology in Computer Science and Engineering from CSVTU, Bhilai in 2017. He is currently pursuing his Ph. D. in the Department of Computer Science and Engineering from School of Engineering & Information Technology, MATS University, Raipur. He has published many papers in Scopus indexed journals and IEEE Conferences. His field of research includes Natural Language Processing, Machine learning, Soft Computing, Cyber Security and Cloud Computing. He has been associated with numerous Multi-National Companies including IBM, TCS etc. and Educational Groups. A focused and hardworking professional with experience in taking Corporate Trainings. He is a Life Member of Quality Circle Forum of India (QCFI) and member of various other professional bodies.

Upinder Kaur is working as an Assistant Professor in the Department of Computer Science and Engineering, Akal University, Bathinda, Punjab, India. She received her Ph. D. Degree at Department of Computer Science and Applications, Kurukshetra University, Kurukshetra. She is in teaching since October 2006. She holds Master of Technology (M. Tech.) degree in Computer Science and Engineering from MMEC, Mullana, Ambala, India. Her main research interests are in the areas of Distributed Computing, Distributed Data Structures, Cloud Computing, Data Science and Analytics, ML/DL. Currently working on the research issues in applications of deep learning in agriculture and health care. She has attended many National and International Conferences/workshops and she has more than 25 research papers in national / international journals and conferences. She has also a member of IEEE, ACM and supervising three Ph.D. Scholars and several graduate and undergraduate students in multi-cloud domain and data science in agriculture and deep learning in bio-signals.

Om Kumar C.U. has specialized in the domain of Cyber Security at Anna University, Chennai (2016-2020) for obtaining a Ph.D. His B.Tech in CSE (2006-10) and M.Tech in CSE (2011-2013) with First class with Distinction were from colleges affiliated to JNTU- Anantapur. Hisinitial stint at Teaching was at SRM- Easwari Engineering College, Chennai from (2013-2016) proved my teaching potential and made me choose Teaching as my profession. His research interest spans across IoT and Deep Learning in particular. Major research contributions have been published by 3 SCI journals (Journal of Super Computing Springer, Computer Communications Elsevier, Computational Intelligence Wiley). He holds 6 Scopus publications as of date. Have published two books pertaining to Anna university syllabus of CSE. Received accolades through acknowledgment from Oxford publications for reviewing the book titled 'Programming and Data Structures' by Dr. Thareja. He is a peer-review member of Concurrency and Computation Wiley, Microprocessor and MicroSystem Elsevier, and Automated Intelligence and Humanized Computing Springer. He is an editorial member of Medicon and Machine Learning Research journals.

* * *

Karim Ishtiaque Ahmed, faculty at Bahrain Training Institute, Higher Education Council, Ministry of Education, Bahrain, holds Master's degree in computer science. His previous work experience includes working as a Sr. Software Engineer at a CMM level 5 company. His expertise includes SAP and EAI technologies. Author has in depth knowledge of Cloud Computing, Machine Learning and various programming languages like C, C++, Java and .NET.

Stuti Asthana is acting as Independent Researcher and Analyst in the domain of Artificial Intelligence. In 2019, she received doctoral degree, Doctor of Philosophy with specialization in Artificial Intelligence from Suresh Gyan Vihar University (NAAC "A" Grade), Jaipur, India. In 2012, she received Master's degree, Master of Technology with specialization in Computer Science and Engineering from Rajiv Gandhi Prodhyogiki Vishwavidhyalaya, Bhopal, M.P., India. Within the period of her doctoral-level studies at the Doctor of Philosophy of Computer Engineering, she has demonstrated herself extraordinary as disciplined and dedicated research scholar. As an unwavering dedicated researcher, she has published 12 Research Papers in various reputed Web of Science, SCOPUS, DBLP indexed International Journals and flagship international Scopus Indexed Conferences. Her doctoral research investigates the design and development of Multiscript Handwriting Recognition Using Neural Network. She is an active Editorial Board member for various reputed international journals. She has also published National and International Patents in the areas of Data Mining, Machine Learning, IoT and Neural Network.

Sujit Badodia is currently working as Assistant Professor in Shri Vaishnav Vidyapeeth Vishwavidyalaya, Indore, India. He attended several research programs from national level. Prof. Badodia Currently pursuing PhD from Institute of Engineering Technology, Devi Ahilya Vishvavidyalaya Indore. His research is in cyber security, social sensing, and deep learning.

Nandini Bansod is working as an assistant professor at SVVV since last 5 year. She has expertise in the field of forensic toxicology, cyber forensics.

Ramakant Bhardwaj is working as Associate Professor, Department of Mathematics, Amity University Kolkata India. He has published about 170 research papers in reputed journals. Six mathematics books have been published in his co-authorship. Dr Bhardwaj delivered lectures in many international, national conferences and workshop as WCE 2010, Imperial college London (UK), ICFPTA-09 Changhua University Taiwan, ICFPTA-07 Chiang Mai University Thailand, ICEAST-07 Bangkok .10 students have been awarded PhD in his supervision and five are working now.

Rakesh Kumar Bhujade completed Ph.D. in Artificial Intelligence in 2016 and currently working as Head of the Information Technology Department in Government Polytechnic, Daman. He has published 01, Australian Government Patent, 05 Indian patents, 03 Books, 02 AWS Global Certifications, 01 Research Grant (TEQIP III) and more than 30 papers in Scopus Indexed International Journal/ Conferences. He also acted as Advisory Board member in many International Journals and conferences.

Sumit Dhariwal has a Bachelor of Engineering degree and Master of Technology degree. He obtained a BE degree in Rajiv Gandhi Technical University's Computer Science and Engineering Branch in 2008 and he obtained an MTech degree. Samrat Ashok of Technological Institute's Information & Technology Branch in 2011. Since 2018 he is now the Research Scholar of the Malaysia University of Science and Technology of the Department of Information and Technology in Malaysia. He worked as Assistant Professor in Technical Universities. And the author has also contributed a lot in the conference of the International Conference and Conference on the National & International Journal Journals.

Pushpendra Dwivedi is a research scholar with specialization in the field of Malware Analysis and Wireless Body Area Network. A dedicated, resourceful, and innovative Academician and Researcher with 8+ years of extensive experience with a proven track record in areas of Computer Science and pedagogy, and research.

Balram G. received a Master of Technology in Computer Science and Engineering from Jawarharlal Nehru Technological University, Hyderabad in 2010, and is Pursuing Ph.D. in Computer Science and Engineering with a major specialization on Internet of Things from KL Deemed to be University. He is working as an Assistant Professor in the Department of CSE Since 2012. He is the facilitator at the Internet of Things Technical Club under the CSE Department and TREAURER of CSI Hyderabad Chapter. He is acting as Single Point of Contact for Smart India Hackathon. He is received "Best Educationist" Award from International Institute for Education and Management, New Delhi and he also received "Inspire Faculty" Award from Infosys Limited, Hyderabad. He is having two patent and two copy rights.

Ravindrababu Jaladanki completed his M.Tech in Digital Systems and Computer Electronics from J..N.T University, Hyderabad. He completed Ph.D in J.N.T.U. Hyderabad, and a Life member of ISTE. Presently working as Associate Professor in Electronics and Communications Engineering Department, P.V.P. Siddhartha Institute of Technology, Kanuru, Vijayawada, Andhra Pradesh. He has 21 years of experience in teaching. He published around 32 papers in various national /International Journals and Conferences.

Sakthidasan Sankaran K. is a Professor in the Department of Electronics and Communication Engineering at Hindustan Institute of Technology and Science, India. He received his B.E. degree from Anna University in 2005, M.Tech. Degree from SRM University in 2007 and Ph.D. Degree from Anna University in 2016. He is a Senior Member of IEEE and member in various professional bodies. He is an active reviewer in Elsevier Journals and editorial board member in various international Journals.

His research interests include Image Processing, Wireless Networks, Cloud Computing and Antenna Design. He has published more than 65papers in Referred Journals and International Conferences. He has also published three books to his credits.

Dinesh Baban Kamble currently working as an Assistant Professor at Shri Vaishanav Institute of Forensic Science, SVVV, Indore. Completed Master Degree in Forensic Science from Mumbai University in 2014. Qualified UGC-NET in Dec. 2014 and UGC-NET(JRF) in June 2015 also Qualified UGC-SET in 2016. Now perusing PhD in Forensic Toxicology.

Imran Khan is working as Faculty Member, Bahrain Training Institute, Higher Education Council, Ministry of Education, Bahrain. Worked as Lecturer at Sirt University, Ministry of Education, Libya, Asst. Professor under Osmania University and JNTUH colleges, Corporate Trainer in programming languages like C, C++, JAVA, PHP, presently involve in different IOT and Machine Learning projects.

Rehan Khan is a student at the Oriental Institute Of Science and Technology, from the Department of Computer Science and Engineering - Data Science. A tech savvy and Pentesting enthusiast. He is a Developer with freelancing experience in the field of Software Development. He is having various certifications in the field of Penetration Testing/Hacking/Ethical Hacking/Cyber Security, Android Development, Programming from various platforms like Udemy, Oracle, Coursera, etc. along with several badges from Google Cloud.

Priya Kohli received her undergraduation degree from H.N.B.G.U in 2015 and postgraduation degree from Graphic Era Hill University, Dehradun, India in 2018. She is currently serving as an Assistant Professor at GEHU, Dehradun and research scholar at Graphic Era Deemed To Be University, Dehradun, India. Her research area comprises of Wireless sensors, Vehicular communication, IoE, Industry 5.0, wireless networking, security, privacy.

Megha Kuliha is currently working as an Assistant Professor in the department of Information Technology at SGSITS, Indore, having more than 15 Years of Teaching and Research Experience. Her area of Research focussed on Data Mining, IoT, Block Chain, and Analytics.

Anil Kumar is currently working as Assistant Professor in Department of Computer Science & Engineering, School of Computing and IT at Manipal University Jaipur, Rajasthan, India, He worked as Assistant Professor in Government Engineering College, Bharatpur, Rajasthan and Hindustan College of Science & Technology, Mathura, UP, India. He has more than 10 Years of experience in teaching UG and PG students. His area of Interest includes Software Engineering, Soft Computing, Machine Learning, Cyber Security and Algorithm Design. He is currently a member of reputed technical societies like IEEE, CSI, IAENG.

Thenmozhi M. is an Assistant Professor in Department of English, School of Social Sciences and Languages at VIT, Vellore. She did Ph. D. in English, on the "Feministic Perspectives in the Select Works of Amrita Pritam", VIT. She has ten years of teaching experience and also served in Guangdong University of Technology, China (International Faculty Exchange Programme) in 2018. She has presented many papers in National and International conferences of repute widely in the areas of Literature, ELT and Gender issues. Her several papers and book chapters have been published in National/International Journals. She is a NLP (Neuro Linguistics Programming) trainer and has Conducted Faculty Development Programs in NLP, Soft Skills and workshop for Techniques in Teaching English Language. She is a motivational speaker and she has many more projects in mind for future.

Sumathi M. S. (Manjari Suryanarayana) is Assistant professor in Electronic and Telecommunication Engineering department at BMS Institute of Technology, Avallahalli, Bangalore. She obtained her Bachelor's degree in Electronics and Communication, in 2006 and Then she obtained her Master's degree in VLSI & Embedded Systems, in 2009 and perused doctoral degree in the year 2021, from Visvesvaraya Technological University, India. She has guided more than 15 UG project. She has published more than 20 papers in international conference and journal. She has delivered many motivational and technical talk for the welfare of the students. Her specializations includes embedded systems, wireless sensor networks and robotics. Her current research interests are wireless sensor networks.

Vinod Mahor is currently working as Assistant Professor in IES College of Technology, Bhopal, Madhya Pradesh India. He attended several research programs From IIT, NIT, NITTTR and other organization. The Author has research alignment towards Cyber-security, IoT, Dark Web Crime research and investigative tactics, as well as efforts to trace unlawful anonymous materials of cybercrime and criminal operations He also presided over national international conferences.

Harshita Mandloi completed her ME from Information Technology Department of Institute of Engineering &Technology (IET), a UTD of Devi Ahilya University, Indore, Madhya Pradesh, India. She has more than 13 year of teaching experience at UG and PG level presently working as Assistant professor in in CSE Department of Shri Vaishnav Vidyapeeth Vishwavidyalaya Indore. She has published 2 international and one national paper in the reputed journal of CSE & IT.

Jasvant Mandloi is research scholar at Information Technology Department of Institute of Engineering &Technology (IET), a UTD of Devi Ahilya University, Indore, Madhya Pradesh, India and the author of 6 refereed publications. He was Head of the department at one of the prestigious Engineering college of Central India. He was secretary of CSI Indorechapter for year 2016-17. He served as National Co-Coordinator for Vidyarthi Vigyan Mantahn (A Project for School Level Students by Vigyan Bharati, an NGO working for National Science Movement). He has done his graduation in Information Technology from JIT Borawan Madhya Pradesh in year 2006. He has received Master's degree MTech IT from UTD RGPV Bhopal in year 2008.He has membership of technical association ISTE and CSE and received awards at National level from IBM and NEN India. He has recently cleared the UPSC interview and get selected as T&P officer in the Daman Technical Department. His areas of research interest are Blockchain, Smart Contract, Cloud computing, Cybersecurity and Machine learning.

Priya Matta, Associate Professor, Department of Computer Science and Engineering, Graphic Era (Deemed to be University), received her graduate degree from HNB Garhwal University, Post graduate from IGNOU and GEU, India in 2000, 2003 and 2010. She recieved her Ph.D. in computer science and engineering with Graphic Era University, India. Her current research interests include Internet-of-Things and Information Security. She has 30 publications in top quality international conferences and journals. She is a member of several professional bodies, including IEEE, CSTA (Association for Computing Machinery) and IAENG. She is a recipient of the Eminent Research Award (Computer Science & Engineering Engineering) of the Graphic Era University three times.

Sonam Mehta is currently working as Assistant Professor. She is a research scholar, pursuing PhD from Devi Ahilya Vishwavidyalaya, Indore, Madhya Pradesh, India.

Amit Kumar Mishra awarded best paper in COVID-19 by MPCOST Bhopal (Govt Of MP), did PhD from Banasthali Vidyapeeth, Tonk, Rajasthan. Currently working as Associate Professor, Department of Computer Science and Engineering, Amity School of Engineering and Technology, Amity University, Madhya Pradesh. He has attended several international conferences and international workshops worldwide. He published book chapters in Taylors Francis, CRC press. He has published more than seven research papers in reputed journals and more than 10 papers in international conferences. Eleven students have done M.Tech in his guidance. Delivered invited lecturer in national and international event.

Pankaj Mishra is currently working as an Associate Professor of Applied Physics and central Ph.D Coordinator, Amity University Madhya Pradesh, Gwalior. Dr. Mishra has teaching and research experience of almost 20 years. He is pursuing D.Sc from Barkatullah University, Bhopal and He completed Ph.D. from Rani Durgavati University, Jabalpur. His experience in different domains of Physics and Electronics has produced number of International and National Publications, includes the regular referred papers in journals, conference, seminars. He has published 70 research papers in International Journals (SCI & Scopus) and in proceedings of National/International conferences. He has received Gold medal for his meritorious performance in Post-Graduation. His research interest is electret and thin film technology in the field of microelectronics. He has filed fifteen patents and completed one research project funded by MPCST, Bhopal. He has written 5 book chapters and also coauthored one book in Engineering Physics. Under his supervision two Ph.D has been awarded and four research scholars are working in the area of Microelectronics. He is reviewer of many SCI and Scopus Journal. He is a life member of IEEE, IEAT and many repute body of research and Guest Editor of Materials Today Proceedings. He is a life member of IETE, India and Senior Member of IEEE, USA.

Rina Mishra is currently working as an Assistant Professor at Shri Vaishnav Vidyapeeth Vishwavidyalaya, Indore, India. She has research alignment towards cryptography and steganography, and is currently working on cyber crime analysis and detection on an online social network. She attended various research and training programmes and published several research papers.

Ambika N. is a MCA, MPhil, Ph.D. in computer science. She completed her Ph.D. from Bharathiar University in the year 2015. She has 16 years of teaching experience and presently working for St. Francis College, Bangalore. She has guided BCA, MCA and M.Tech students in their projects. Her expertise includes wireless sensor network, Internet of things, cybersecurity. She gives guest lectures in her expertise. She is a reviewer of books, conferences (national/international), encyclopaedia and journals. She is advisory committee member of some conferences. She has many publications in National & international conferences, international books, national and international journals, and encyclopaedias. She has some patent publications (National) in computer science division.

Syed Imran Patel is a Lecturer, Education Program Manager, and Lead Internal Verifier at Bahrain Training Institute, HEC, EDUC-Information System Training Programs, Ministry of Education, Bahrain, with over 13 years of experience in programming and networking. He contributes to the Quality Assurance Committee, the Grade and Credit Transfer Committee, and the Curriculum Development Committee with his knowledge.

He designed and developed the curriculum for Information and Communication Technology and IT Technical Workshop subjects in Bahrain Training Institute's Extended Diploma in IT and Orientation Program.

Vikram Rajpoot is working as an Assistant Professor in Department of Information Technology Madhav Institute of Technology & Science Gwalior. He received his B.E. in Information Technology from MITS Gwalior in 2010, M. Tech in Information Technology from SATI, Vidisha in 2012 and PhD in Frequent Pattern Mining from MGCGV Chitrakoot University, Satna in 2019. He has more than nine years of teaching experience, and his fields of interest are Frequent Pattern Mining and Machine Learning.

Murtaza Rizvi obtained his Doctorate in Computer Science from Maulana Azad National Institute of Technology (MANIT) Bhopal. Dr. Rizvi has also achieved Master's degree in Electronics and Post Graduate Diploma in Computer Applications from Aligarh Muslim University, Aligarh and Master's of Business Administration (MBA) from Barkatullah University Bhopal. Presented Research in an International Conference at University of California San Francisco, USA where it was rated second. He was honoured to chair one of the session of an International conference organized by World Congress on Education (WCE 2013) held in London. Dr. Rizvi has more than 28 years of experience in the field of Computer Science and Applications as faculty (Associate Professor) in National Institute of Technical Teachers' Training and Research, Bhopal (NITTTR) a Govt. Of India Institute. He has published approximately 140 research papers in reputed International Journals and International Conferences across the globe out of which 16 are SCI indexed. Also published Monographs by Lambert Publisher Germany. One patent against his name on ATM security. Also has copyright on facial Recognition Algorithm and Computer vision based automatic attendance calculation and updating system. He has attended many International/ National Conferences in India and abroad to present his papers. He was invited in many International conferences as keynote speaker, session chair and invited talk. He has delivered expert lecture in various organizations on latest topic of Computer Science and quality of education and research methodology. He is a registered guide in many Technical Universities in the faculty of Computer Sc. and Applications and as penal examiner of Ph. D and master's thesis. He is also consultant to various Institutes for the quality improvement. Besides, he is also on various committees outside the Institute. A book named "Computer and Communication a Practical Manual for Internet Café" for NCERT New Delhi India written by him is another feather to his cap. He has authored 10 chapters in edited books published by international publishers like IGI, and CRC Press. Also, developed many curriculum of Computer Sc. for BE, diploma and MBA for various states. He made valuable academic visits to USA, UK, Germany, Switzerland, Singapore, France, Japan, Hong Kong, Macau, Holland, Dubai, Sharjah. Turkey and Malasiya. He is having strong National and International Linkages with Institutions, organizations and professionals/individuals. He is Member of Advisory/Editorial/Reviewer board of International journals like International Journal of Engineering and Science, International Journal of Networking and Parallel Computing. He is also Member Technical Programme Committee (TPC) of International Conferences organized by Institutions and Organizations in India and abroad. Many International Professional bodies and societies have offered him honorary memberships.

Biswa Mohan Sahoo is a Senior IEEE member and received his B.Tech and M.Tech degree in computer science and engineering from Biju Patnaik University of Technology, Odisha, India and PhD degree in computer science and engineering from Indian Institute of Technology (ISM), Dhanbad, India. He is currently working as an Assistant Professor at Amity University, Uttar Pradesh, India. He has published more than 20 articles in prestigious international peer review journals and conferences in the area of Wireless Sensor Networks, Swarm Intelligence and IoT. His currently focus on artificial intelligence approaches on sensor networks. His research interest area is wireless sensor network with Evolutionary Algorithm and Artificial intelligence.

Avani Sharma completed Ph.D from NIT, Rajasthan and M.Tech from LNMIIT. She research area include Internet of Things, Soft Security for IoT, MANET Security and Machine Learning. She has published research articles in various international conferences and journals. She is currently working as an Assistant Professor in Manipal University Jaipur, India.

Sachin Sharma, Associate Dean, International Affairs and Associate Professor, Department of Computer Science and Engineering at Graphic Era Deemed to be University, Dehradun, UK, India. He is also Co-founder and Chief Technology officer (CTO) of IntelliNexus LLC, Arkansas, USA based company. He also worked as a Senior Systems Engineer at Belkin International, Inc., Irvine, California, USA for two years. He received his Philosophy of Doctorate (Ph.D.) degree in Engineering Science and Systems specialization in Systems Engineering from University of Arkansas at Little Rock, USA with 4.0 out 4.0 GPA and M.S. degree in Systems engineering from University of Arkansas at Little Rock with 4.0 out 4.0 GPA and He received his B.Tech. degree from SRM University, Chennai including two years at University of Arkansas at Little Rock, USA as an International Exchange Student. His research interests include wireless communication networks, IoT, Vehicular ad hoc networking and network security.

Pragya Shukla is currently working as Professor in Computer Engineering Department in IET, DAVV, Indore, MP. She has 20 years of teaching experience. Her area of interest are AI, Soft Computing, Biometrics and Analysis of algorithms. She has published more than 35 research papers in reputed journals. She is guiding 8 Ph.D. students.

Ankit Temurnikar is currently working as Assistant Professor in IES College of Technology, Bhopal, Madhya Pradesh, India.

Arun Kumar Tripathi completed Ph. D. in Computer Applications with specialization in Mobile IPv6 from NIT Kurukshetra in 2018, M. Tech. in Computer Science & Engineering from Dr. A.P.J. Abdul Kalam Technical University, Lucknow (Formerly known as Gautam Buddha Technical University, Lucknow) in 2010, MCA from LNCT Bhopal affiliated to Rajiv Gandhi Proudyogiki Vishwavidyalaya, Bhopal in 2002 and B.Sc. Electronics from Dr. Hari Singh Gour Central University (Formerly known as Sagar University). At present he is appointed as Professor and Head Cyber Security and Forensic Science Division. His research interests include Computer Network, Network Security, IoT, machine Learning, Blockchain etc. He has more than fifty research publications in reputed Journals and Conferences. He reviewed more than 12 SCI-Indexed journal papers. He is a life member of various professional societies like ACEEE, IACSIT, IAENG, CSTA etc. He guided 02 M. Tech. thesis in Computer Science and Engineering and at present 01 Ph.D. thesis is on-going. He is a CISCO certified academy instructor.

Index

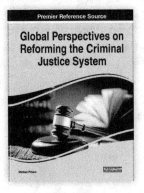

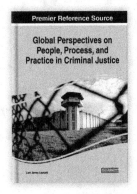

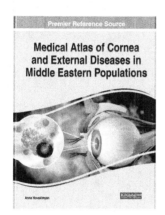
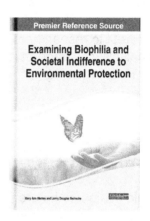

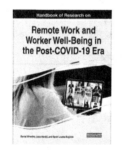

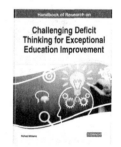

Printed in the United States
by Baker & Taylor Publisher Services